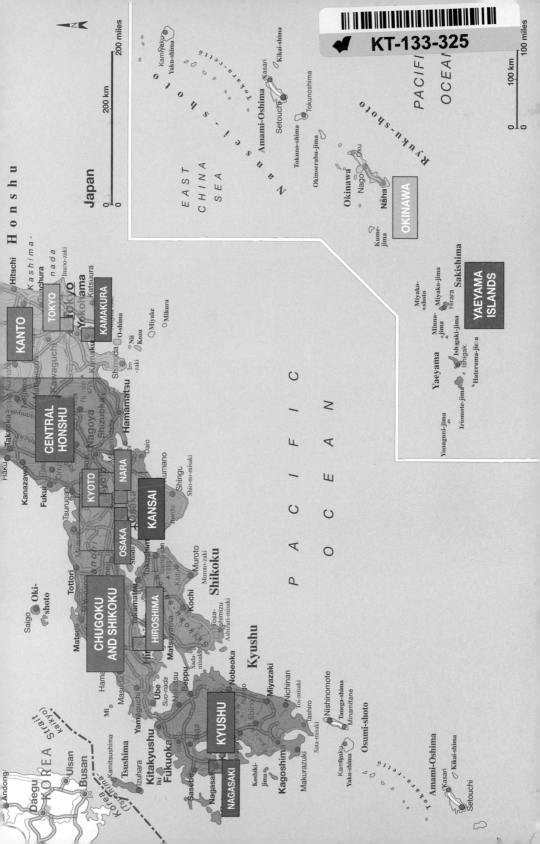

N

200 miles

200 km

100 miles

100 km

Japan

PACIFIC OCEAN

EAST CHINA SEA

Honshu

Kam'yaku Yaku-shima

Kikai-shima

Kasari
Amami-Oshima Setouchi Tokunoshima

Tokuno-shima

Okinoerabu-jima Oku

Okinawa Nago

OKINAWA

Nāha

Kume-jima

Ryukyu-shoto

Nansei-shoto

Tokara-retto

Hitachi

Kashima-nada

Kashima

Imuo-zaki

Nakaminato

Katsuura

KANTO

TOKYO

TOKYO Yokohama

KAMAKURA

Kamakura

Miyake-jima

O-shima Mikura

Nii Miyake

Kozu

Iro-zaki

Shimoda

Miyako-shoto

Miyako-jima

Minna-jima Hirara **Sakishima**

Ish-gaki-jima

Ishigak

YAEYAMA ISLANDS

Yaeyama

Ishigaki

Iriomote-jima 'Hateruma-ji 'a

Yonaguni-jima

Hakuba

Kanazawa

Fukui

CENTRAL HONSHU

Nagoya Shizuoka

Hamamatsu

Toyama

Fu_ san Fuji

12776

Tsuruga

KYOTO

KYOTO

NARA

NARA

Daio

Kumano

Shingu

Shio-no-misaki

KANSAI

OSAKA

OSAKA

Kobe

Tottori

Matsue

Saigo **Oki-shoto**

CHUGOKU AND SHIKOKU

Okayama

HIROSHIMA

Hiro hima

Shikoku

Muroto

Muroto-zaki

Kochi

Tosa-misaki

Ashizuri-misaki

PACIFIC OCEAN

Hamada

Masuda

Yamaguchi

Ube

Suo-nada

Beppu

Kyushu

Nobeoka

Miyazaki

Nichinan

Toi-misaki

Nishinomote

Tanega-shima

Minamitane

Tashiro

Osumi-shoto

Fukuoka

Kitakyushu

Saga

Saseb

Ebino

KYUSHU

Makurazuki Sata-misaki

Koshiki-jima

Kam'yaku Yaku-shima

NAGASAKI

Kagoshima

Nagasaki

Kasari Kikai-shima

Amami-Oshima

Setouchi

Tokara-retto

Andong

Daegu

KOREA Ulsan

Busan

Korea Strait (Tsushima Kaikyo)

Kamitsushima

Tsushima

Izuhara

Iki

INSIGHT  GUIDES

JAPAN

www.insightguides.com/Japan

◉ Walking Eye App

Your Insight Guide now includes a free app and eBook, dedicated to your chosen destination, all included for the same great price as before. They are available to download from the free Walking Eye container app in the App Store and Google Play. Simply download the Walking Eye container app to access the eBook and app dedicated to your purchased book. The app features an up-to-date A to Z of travel tips, information on events, activities and destination highlights, as well as hotel, restaurant and bar listings. See below for more information and how to download.

MULTIPLE DESTINATIONS AVAILABLE

Now that you've bought this book you can download the accompanying destination app and eBook for free. Inside the Walking Eye container app, you'll also find a whole range of other Insight Guides destination apps and eBooks, all available for purchase.

DEDICATED SEARCH OPTIONS

Use the different sections to browse the places of interest by category or region, or simply use the 'Around me' function to find places of interest nearby. You can then save your selected restaurants, bars and activities to your Favourites or share them with friends using email, Twitter and Facebook.

FREQUENTLY UPDATED LISTINGS

Restaurants, bars and hotels change all the time. To ensure you get the most out of your guide, the app features all of our favourites, as well as the latest openings, and is updated regularly. Simply update your app when you receive a notification to access the most current listings available.

Shopping in Oman still revolves around the traditional souks that can be found in every town in the country – most famously at Mutrah in Muscat, Salalah and Nizwa, which serve as showcases of traditional Omani craftsmanship and produce ranging from antique khanjars and Bedu jewellery to halwa, rose-water and frankincense. Muscat also boasts a number of modern malls, although these are rare elsewhere in the country.

TRAVEL TIPS & DESTINATION OVERVIEWS

The app also includes a complete A to Z of handy travel tips on everything from visa regulations to local etiquette. Plus, you'll find destination overviews on shopping, sport, the arts, local events, health, activities and more.

HOW TO DOWNLOAD THE WALKING EYE

Available on purchase of this guide only.
1. Visit our website: www.insightguides.com/walkingeye
2. Download the Walking Eye container app to your smartphone (this will give you access to both the destination app and the eBook)
3. Select the scanning module in the Walking Eye container app
4. Scan the QR code on this page – you will be asked to enter a verification word from the book as proof of purchase
5. Download your free destination app* and eBook for travel information on the go

* Other destination apps and eBooks are available for purchase separately or are free with the purchase of the Insight Guide book

Contents

THE BEST OF JAPAN: TOP ATTRACTIONS

The "Land of the Rising Sun" is a country of great contrasts between ancient and ultra-modern, and the natural and high-tech; its main attractions reflect this fascinating dichotomy.

△ **Ginkaku-ji temple and Gardens, Kyoto.** This temple is a wonderful place to see 15th-century Japanese architecture at its finest. See page 247.

▽ **Mount Fuji.** Japan's most iconic mountain dominates the skyline west of Tokyo, and is an Unesco World Heritage Site. Whether you climb it or gaze upon it from afar, it's easy to see why Fuji-san has captivated the Japanese for centuries. See page 178.

△ **Nikko.** Buried deep in forested mountains to the north of Tokyo, the outrageously lavish Tosho-gu Shrine complex in Nikko offers some of Japan's most spectacular architecture. If you just have time for one overnight trip from Tokyo, make it here. See page 181.

▽ **Hiking the Northern Alps.** Breathtaking mountain scenery and hikes to suit all levels make the Northern Alps Japan's premier hiking ground. The pretty village of Kamikochi is the perfect base from which to explore the area. See page 195.

△ **Hiroshima's Peace Memorial Park.** Built in memory of the victims of the 1945 A-bomb attack that devastated Hiroshima, the Peace Park is a moving and poignant monument to the horrors of nuclear armament. See page 306.

△ **Roppongi at night.** Raucous nightclubs, cool bars and some of the chicest restaurants in Tokyo make a night out in Roppongi a must-do. It won't be cheap, but it will be very memorable. See page 154.

△ **Naoshima Island.** With cutting-edge galleries and a host of outdoor art installations, this tranquil island in the Seto Inland Sea is a bright star in Japan's contemporary art scene. See page 305.

▽ **Yaeyama Islands, Okinawa.** With pristine beaches, prime dive spots, a refreshingly laid-back pace of life and a distinctive local culture, it's sometimes hard to believe these islands are actually part of Japan. See page 353.

△ **Ryokan.** A night at a traditional inn (ryokan) is a quintessentially Japanese experience, combining refined luxury, elegance and the ultimate in relaxation. See page 382.

▽ **Japanese cuisine.** From refined Kyoto cuisine to steaming hot bowls of cheap ramen, and so much in between, Japan is a foodie's paradise. Don't go home without having your fill. See page 115.

THE BEST OF JAPAN: EDITOR'S CHOICE

From family outings and unique attractions to historic sights and hot springs, here, at a glance, are our recommendations, plus some money-saving tips that even the locals won't always know.

Shinjuku Gyoen in spring, Tokyo.

BEST FOR FAMILIES

Kiddyland. In several districts of Tokyo, the stores are stuffed with toys and characters like *Hello Kitty* and *Pokemon*; time spent here with the kids could well lead to a temporary cash-flow problem. See page 381.
DisneySea. An addition to Tokyo Disneyland but requiring a separate ticket. The themes here are all connected to water and a full day is recommended. See page 165.
Ghibli Museum. This museum-cum- amusement park in Tokyo suburbs showcases the work of the renowned Studio Ghibli, including Miyazaki Hayao's famous anime. See page 167.
Universal Studios Japan. Hollywood special effects and fun rides, Osaka's theme park replicates its Los Angeles prototype. See page 283.
Miraikan. This museum in Odaiba has lots of hands-on activities for older kids to learn about cutting-edge robotics, space exploration and much more. See page 156.

Kiddyland, Aoyama, Tokyo.

ONLY IN JAPAN

Department terminals. A fascinating consumer concept – train platforms feeding passengers straight into department stores. Accessible station-store interfaces are found in Nihombashi, Ikebukuro and Shibuya in Tokyo.
High-tech toilets. At the other end of the spectrum to the squat toilet, many hotels, department stores and homes have *washlets*, toilets that will clean, dry and warm you, and on occasions make noises to cover any embarrassing sounds. See page 390.
Capsule hotels. Seal your door and fall into a contented sleep in these cosy, weightless cells, or sweat with claustrophobia. You either love or hate Japan's capsule hotels.
Vending machines. It's the number and range that are unique to Japan: over 5 million on the last count, dispensing everything from disposable underwear to noodles.

Japanese vending machines.

BEST PARKS AND GARDENS

Ritsurin-koen, Kagawa.

Koishikawa Botanical Garden. Although landscaped, the grounds of this fine Edo Period green haven have a natural and informal feel. The oldest garden in Tokyo. See page 149. **Shinjuku Gyoen.** Enjoy the many species of plants, trees and flowers in a Tokyo park divided into different garden styles. There is a large botanical greenhouse for chilly days. See page 160. **Daitoku-ji.** A complex of immeasurably beautiful Kyoto gardens. The most famous is Daisen-in, reminiscent of a Chinese painting. See page 248. **Ryoan-ji.** Built in 1499, this famous Kyoto dry landscape temple garden was created as both a tool for meditation and as a work of art. A truly Zen experience. See page 249. **Ritsurin-koen.** Completed in 1745, Ritsurin Park on Shikoku Island is one of the finest stroll gardens in Japan. See page 318.

Eko-in Temple and lodgings.

BEST TRADITIONAL EXPERIENCES

Visit a castle. Himeji-jo is the best of Japan's original castles. Known as Shirasagi-jo, or the White Egret Castle, its graceful lines are said to resemble the bird as it is about to take flight. See page 287. **Watch the sumo.** Centuries old and full of pomp and ceremony, an afternoon at one of the six annual 15-day grand tournaments is cracking good fun. See page 112. **Stay at a temple in Koya-san.** Many temples have spartan accommodation available for travellers, but none are as atmospheric as at this complex of temples and monasteries deep inside a mountainside forest. See page 273. **Fireworks.** Summer means firework displays. The biggest and best is Tokyo's Sumida-gawa display in late July, but there are colourful events across the country in July and August. See page 375. **Festivals.** *Matsuri* (festivals) big and small take place year-round all over the country, typified by traditional dancing, music and great street food. One of the best is the Guyo-Odori dance festival in Gujo Hachiman, Honshu. See page 192.

Nada Fighting Festival, Himeji.

BEST MODERN ARCHITECTURE

Fuji TV Building. A Tange Kenzo masterpiece, this TV studio in Tokyo's man-made island Odaiba, with its suspended dome made of reinforced tungsten, seems to resemble the inside of a television set. See page 155. **Tokyo Big Sight.** You'll probably do a double take when you see the inverted pyramids of this building in Tokyo's Odaiba district – it seems to defy gravity and common sense, but is still standing. See page 155. **Umeda Sky Building.** A striking skyscraper in Osaka's Umeda district, this soaring building is pierced by a large hole at one point in its structure. See page 279. **ACROS Centre.** Fukuoka is quite a laboratory for new architecture. ACROS, a culture centre, stands out for its ziggurat form and stepped terraces covered in hanging plants, creating the impression of a sci-fi jungle ruin. See page 330. **Tokyo Sky Tree.** Some love it, some are distinctly underwhelmed, but this landmark, which opened in 2012, can't be avoided – the world's second-tallest man-made structure towers 634 metres (2,080ft) above eastern Tokyo. See page 153.

Neon lights in Tokyo.

BEST TEMPLES AND SHRINES

Asakusa Kannon Temple (Senso-ji). Tokyo's most visited temple hosts dozens of annual events and festivals. Nakamise, the approach street, is full of craft and dry-food goods. See page 152.

Kanda Myojin Shrine. One of Tokyo's liveliest shrine compounds, especially at weekends, when weddings, rituals and festivals are held. Bright and cheerful architecture. See page 147.

Meiji Shrine. An amazing setting at the centre of a forest in the middle of Tokyo. Gravel paths lead to the shrine, an example of pure Shinto design. See page 157.

Yamadera. Tohoku's most sacred temple complex, a veritable labyrinth of steps, pathways and stone stairways across a rocky hillside. Built in the 9th century to last. See page 214.

Golden Pavilion (Kinkaku-ji). It may be a 1950s rebuild, but the gilded Kinkaku-ji is understandably still Kyoto's most iconic sight. See page 249.

Itsukushima-jinja. Fabulously located on stilts and pillars rising 16 metres (52ft) above the waters of Miyajima, the walkways and platforms of this splendid, magical shrine seem to float in space. See page 309.

Yamadera Temple complex, Tohoku.

BEST OF MODERN JAPAN

Ride the *Shinkansen*. You don't have to be a train-spotter to enjoy the super-slick shinkansen. It's extremely fast, unerringly efficient and aesthetically a joy to behold. See pages 361 and 162.

Shop for gadgets in Akihabara. Akihabara in Tokyo is known as "Electric Town" for good reason. The home electronics stores here carry the very latest gadgets and technology. See page 375.

Tokyo's urban complexes. Towering urban redevelopments like Tokyo Midtown and Roppongi Hills have redefined central Tokyo. Fashionable and sleek, this is Japan at its most contemporary. See page 154.

Explore Shinjuku. Less fashionable than Roppongi, but buzzing with energy, Shinjuku has plenty of neon, bars and shops, not to mention Tokyo's main Koreatown, main gay district and biggest red-light area. See page 159.

BEST HOT SPRINGS

Dogo Onsen. These hot springs in Shikoku are the oldest in Japan. They are mentioned in the *Manyoshu*, the ancient collection of Japanese poetry (*c.759*). See page 323.
Beppu. A very busy spa town in Kyushu with eight different hot spring areas, each with different properties. The open-air "hell ponds" of boiling mud are a crowd-puller. See page 341.
Noboribetsu. There are 11 kinds of hot spring water at this spa resort in Hokkaido, including salt (for soothing pain), iron (for relieving rheumatism) and sodium bicarbonate (to attain a smoother skin). See page 223.
Naruko. This once sacred site in Tohoku is over 1,000 years old. It is well known for its fine medicinal waters. See page 212.
Hakone. Only a couple of hours from central Tokyo, yet rich with bubbling volcanic valleys and mountain scenery, Hakone is a very popular weekend retreat for Tokyoites. See page 179.

Frank Lloyd Wright's Imperial Hotel, Central Honshu.

Hot spring baths at Dogo Onsen, Shikoku.

BEST GALLERIES AND MUSEUMS

Edo Tokyo Museum. One of the finest museums in Japan, showcasing scale replicas of historic Tokyo from the 19th century to the present day. See page 149.
Tokyo National Museum. This museum on the edge of Ueno Park houses the largest collection of Japanese art and artifacts in the world. See page 151.
Meiji Mura Museum. This magnificent 100-hectare (250-acre) site near Nagoya houses 60 original Meiji-era buildings brought from around the country. See page 190.
Nagoya City Science Museum. Entertaining hands-on exhibits abound in this museum, which also boasts the world's largest planetarium, located in a giant silver globe. See page 189.

MONEY-SAVING TIPS

Cheap to sleep: Provided you eschew top-end hotels and restaurants, and the use of taxis, Japan can be a surprisingly affordable country. Accommodation in budget inns and business hotels ranges from as little as ¥3,000 to ¥6,000.
Travel: Buying a Japan Rail Pass before you arrive in Japan can save you a huge amount of money. The JR passes are also useful for some lines into and through cities like Tokyo. Overnight buses, allowing you to save on accommodation, are cheaper than trains.
Shopping spree: Some department stores offer a 5 percent discount to foreign visitors. It's also always worth visiting local tourist offices, as many issue regional discount cards to foreign visitors that can be used at a good number of designated shops and restaurants.
Set lunch: Food can be good value with so many restaurants in competition. Look out for lunch set specials, which can be as cheap as ¥600. Fast-food joints have sets for as little as ¥350.
Cheers: Drinks at music clubs and discos are sometimes included in the ticket price, and even if not, are often cheaper than in bars. Another good option are *tachinomiya* (standing bars), where you won't be expected to buy food.
No tips: Tipping is almost non-existent in Japan.

Shoppers in Ginza.

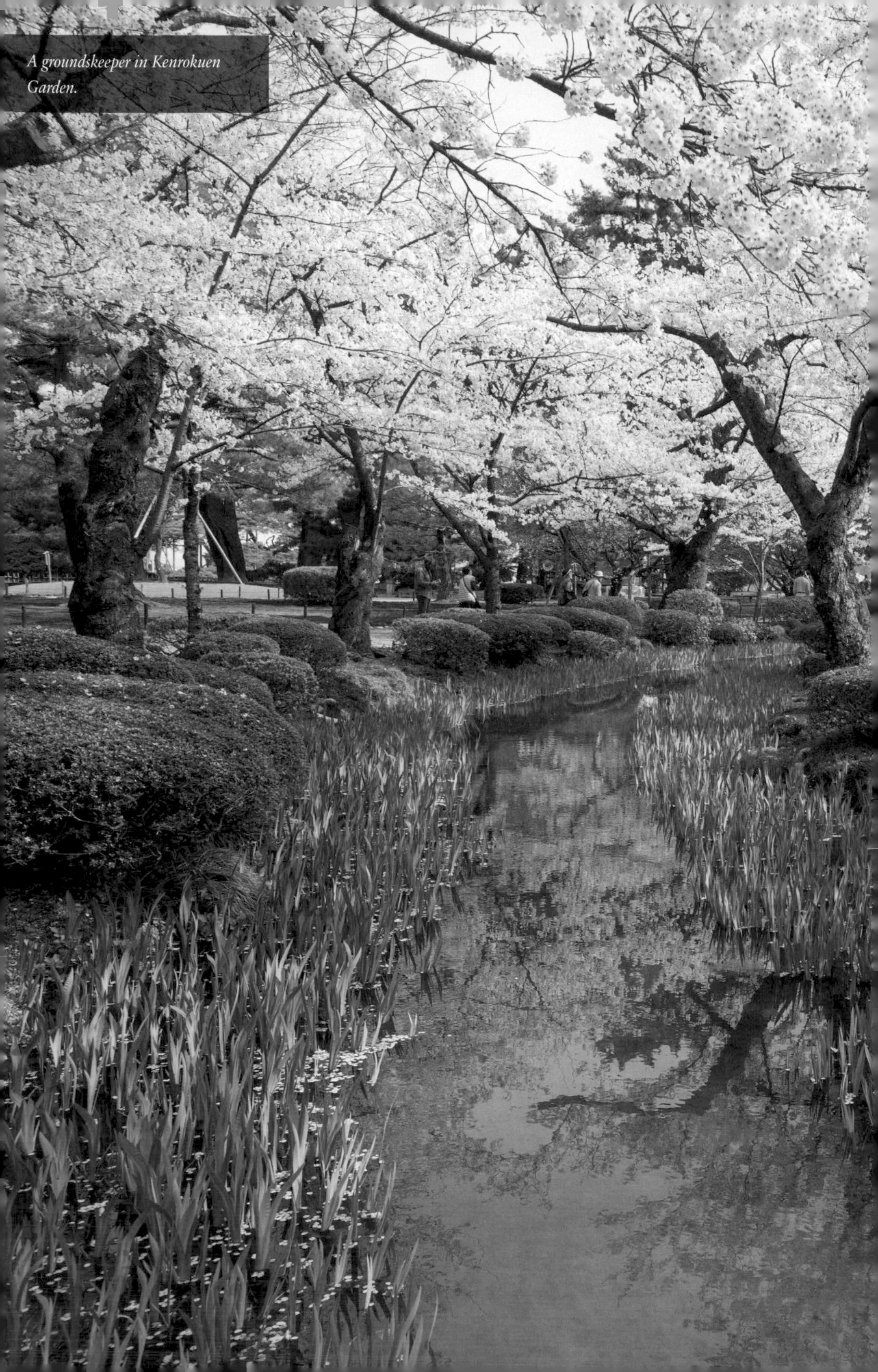

A groundskeeper in Kenrokuen Garden.

Revellers at Furukawa Festival.

Visiting the Nagoya Atsuta Shrine, Central Honshu.

A SINGULAR PLACE

From Buddhist effigies to virtual pop idols, imperial
court dancers to robot pets, bamboo forests, ski
slopes and coral reefs to mega-city fashion and
architecture: an immense cultural and geographical
diversity confronts the visitor to Japan.

Kappabashi kitchenware.

J apan is home to some of Asia's best sights, natural
landscapes, cuisine, innovative culture, not to mention
cutting-edge technologies and futuristic cities attract-
ing the world's leading architects. The Japanese are prolific,
curious travellers, but they also sense that their own country
has everything the traveller could possibly desire.

The unifying metaphor of a country defined as one family, one language, one perspective, a land of order, rituals
and rules, a xenophobic society of worker ants, conformists and whale
slaughterers, a simulacrum of Western culture, crumbles under closer
examination. If it's easy to belittle Japan's orthodoxies, it's equally easy
to praise its originality and non-conformism, the pliability that allows it
periodically to reinvent itself.

The dual stereotypes of Japan as the *Teahouse of the
August Moon*, a place of mystique and graceful manners living in an exotic costume drama, or as a people characterised as early, super-advanced adopters of
technology living in confined apartments, suffering
the indignities of crowded subways and working conditions, have their origins in the popular imagination
and the way the West, in particular, would like to think
of Japan. Although there are elements of truth in these
preconceptions, a more accurate cliché is Japan as the
land of contrast, a notion few that have lived or visited
the country would contest.

Elementary school students.

With roughly 6,800 islands, there is bound to be a
lot of diversity. It is, quite literally, possible to experience Japan's superb
powder snow on the ski slopes of Hokkaido one day, and to be testing
the transparent blue seas of Okinawa's southernmost Yaeyama Islands the
next, such is the geographical and climatic range.

Japan's vibrant cultural scene draws from the traditional arts and crafts
as much as contemporary manga, anime artists, J-Pop icons and meta-pop
fiction. The fussy aesthetics of the tea ceremony and flower arranging, the
years of formal training required to perform *noh*, *kabuki* and *bunraku*, the
rituals and ceremonies that punctuate its cultural calendar, contrast with its
laid-back bars, live music houses and vibrant youth culture and street life.

Creating an itinerary can be challenging. Will you include castles, temples and millennia-old shrines, secluded heritage villages, pottery towns, old

foreign settlements that are now cosmopolitan ports, exquisite crafts, traditional festivals, cutting-edge architecture, major art collections, hiking trails and rural hot-spring resorts, the cultural treasure houses of Kyoto and Nara, or focus on one of the world's largest concentrations of formal gardens?

Japan has rightly been called the storehouse of the world, a place where you can shop 'til you drop. Its reputation for world-class food and beverages precede it. In the spirit of trying to please every pocket, dishes can be sampled anywhere from stand-up *soba* eateries favoured by truck drivers and time-driven salaried workers, to the refinements of *kaiseki ryori*, Japan's haute cuisine.

Asian but apart from Asia, Japan may appear thoroughly to have embraced Western culture, but closer examination reveals that it has done so in a re-codified form. The glass-and-titanium panels of the multi-storey building you are gazing at may appear to be familiar, but step inside and, alongside the Starbucks and Mister Donut outlets, you are just as likely to spot a *shiatsu* clinic, rustic charcoal-grill restaurant or maid café.

Yamadera Temple complex, Tohoku.

The world's best intra-city transportation system is served not only by the bullet train, but an increasingly competitive and affordable airline network, inexpensive long-distance buses and a far-reaching ferry service, connecting visitors to Japan's intriguing small islands and their micro-cultures. Japan has never been cheap, but there has been considerable cost-cutting in recent years, reflected in more affordable deals on almost everything, from bargain-basement restaurant lunches to accommodation.

It's an extraordinary place, offering the trip of a lifetime. If Japan has a *bête noire* at all, it is the friability of the earth's crust, manifest in earthquakes, tsunamis, volcanic eruptions and landslides. In 2014, 57 people died as Ontake-san in central Japan exploded without warning. An undersea earthquake in 2015 generated tremors that were felt across the country. But the most profound disaster of recent years took place on 11 March 2011, when a magnitude-9 earthquake and resultant tsunami caused four

Utoro Port, Hokkaido.

reactors in Fukushima nuclear power plant to go critical, that both the real and metaphorical cracks in Japan were exposed. The groundswell of activism prompted by the disaster, the mistrust of government and bureaucracy that grew in the wake of the catastrophe was an encouraging sign – a harbinger, perhaps, of another new Japan.

A note on style

Wherever possible, we use Japanese terms for geographical names, appearing as suffixes to the proper name. For example, Mount Fuji is referred to as Fuji-san. Mountains may also appear with *-zan*, *-yama*, and for some active volcanoes, *-dake*. Islands are either *-shima* or *-jima*, lakes are *-ko*, and rivers are *-gawa* or *-kawa*. Shinto shrines end in *-jinja*, *-jingu* or *-gu*. Temples are Buddhist, with names ending in *-tera*, *-dera* or *-ji*. When referring to individuals, we follow the Japanese style: family name first, given name second.

Mussel picker in Matsushima.

A NATION OF ISLANDS

An archipelago formed by the meeting of tectonic plates, Japan's thousands of islands are often rugged and violent, accented by soothing hot springs.

The Japanese like to think of themselves as a small people living in a snug but confined country. Scale, of course, is relative. If you come from Russia, then Japan is, indeed, a small country. If you hail from the UK, on the other hand, Japan, twice the size of Britain, is expansive.

Japan is not the only archipelago in Asia. Like the Philippines and Indonesia, it boasts a huge number of islands – some 6,800, most of which are uninhabited. The impression of space and dimension comes from the country's length, from its northern tip on the Sea of Okhotsk – from where the Russian coast is visible on clear days – down to the subtropical islands of Okinawa, where, visibility permitting, the mountains of Taipei can be glimpsed. Buffeted by the winter ice drifts off Hokkaido and the freezing Sea of Japan on its west coast, the Pacific bathes its eastern seaboard and the East China Sea its southwestern shores.

While its inland prefectures may be relatively sheltered from the sea-born typhoons and constant threat of tsunamis that plague its coastline, geography has influenced the development of Japan in many ways. The most obvious is agriculture and fishing, with its rice fields and orchards set at a safe distance from the salt air, its coastline a series of harbours and fishing ports. It has also had an effect on architecture, evident in the pipe-stove chimneys used in private homes in Hokkaido with its bitter winters; the rurally sourced thatch traditionally used as roofing in regions like Tohoku and Hida; and in the coral, limestone and, more recently, cement used as building materials in Okinawa, whose islands stand squarely in the typhoon alley that begins its annual passage of destruction from the Philippines.

Jigoku-dani (Hell Gorge), Noboribetsu.

In Japanese mythology, the archipelago was formed from the tears of a goddess. Where each tear fell into the Pacific there arose an island to take its place. So goes the legend. But no less poetic – or dramatic – is the geological origin of this huge archipelago. The islands were born of massive crustal forces deep underground and shaped by volcanoes spitting out mountains of lava. The results seen today are impressive, with snow-capped mountain ranges and 27,000km (16,800 miles) of indented coastline.

The archipelago consists of four main islands – Kyushu, Shikoku, Honshu and Hokkaido – and about 6,800 smaller islands extending from southwest to northeast over a distance of some 3,800km (2,400 miles) off the east coast of Asia. Honshu is by far the largest and most populous of all the islands. The main islands are noted for their rugged terrain, with 70 to 80 percent of the country being extremely mountainous. Most of the mountains were uplifted over millions of years as the oceanic crust of the Pacific collided with the continental plate of Asia. The oceanic crust submerged beneath the thicker continental crust, buckling the edge of it and forcing up the mountain chains that form the backbone of the Japanese archipelago and that of the Philippines to the south.

Sign for tsunami evacuation, Tohoku.

TYPHOONS

Generally three or four typhoons hit Japan during the season, smaller ones in August building up to larger ones in September. The southern or Pacific side of Japan bears the brunt of these ferocious winds, which are quite capable of knocking down houses and wrecking ships. Fortunately for Japan, however, most typhoons have expended their energy in the Philippines or Taiwan before reaching the archipelago. While more frequent than Atlantic hurricanes or Indian Ocean cyclones, the Asian typhoons are also considerably smaller in size and strength. The Japanese don't use names for typhoons, just numbers.

Volcanoes

Other, singular peaks in Japan – including Fuji, the highest – are volcanic in origin. They were formed from molten lava that originated far below the earth's surface as the oceanic crust sank into the superheated depths of the upper mantle. The molten rock was forced up through fissures and faults, exploding onto the surface. Weather and glacial action did the rest.

One of the attractions of a visit to Japan is the possibility of seeing the milder geological forces in action. About 60 of Japan's 186 volcanoes are still active in geological terms, and occasionally they make their presence felt. Mihara on Oshima, one of the isles of Izu near Tokyo and part of Metropolitan Tokyo, exploded in 1986, forcing thousands of residents to evacuate the island. A few years later, Unzen-dake on Kyushu violently erupted and devastated hundreds of kilometres of agricultural land. Sakura-jima, also on Kyushu, regularly spews ash. As recently as 2014, 57 people died as Ontake-san in central Japan exploded without warning, which was the most fatal eruption in Japan in over 100 years. Just eight months later, Shin-dake's massive eruption made all 137 residents of tiny Kuchinoerabu-jima flee the island.

Located above the Pacific Rim of Fire, Japan sits on top of four tectonic plates on the edge of a subduction zone, making it one of the most unstable regions on earth. The caldera of Mount Aso is periodically placed off-limits to tourists because of toxic emissions; Mount Asama in central Honshu has been erupting regularly for the last 1,500 years, most recently in 2014. Even iconic Mount Fuji is an active peak.

Earthquakes and tsunamis

Earthquakes are far more frequent than volcanic eruptions, especially around the more seismologically active areas near Tokyo. On average Japan experiences about 7,500 quakes a year, though most are too small to be felt. It is an indicator, however, of how seismically active the islands are. The Japanese government currently spends billions of yen annually on earthquake detection – not that it works particularly well.

Complacency is a common problem anywhere and certainly was in Kobe, which had been declared to be outside any significant earthquake zone. Nevertheless, in 1995 a massive quake hit the city, killing more than 5,000 people and toppling high-rises. Mega-thrust earthquakes of the type that struck the coast of Miyagi Prefecture on 11 March 2011 tend to strike in pairs, with a relatively short interlude between. In 2015, tremors were felt across the country as a powerful 7.8-magnitude undersea earthquake struck south of Japan. Thankfully, no serious damage was reported.

The 3/11 tsunami revealed the dangers of locating concentrated communities along coastal areas. Local governments have been publishing hazard maps for low-lying residential coastal areas, the danger zones indicating that millions of people inhabit areas of alarming vulnerability. The ever-present threats have turned the Japanese into a stoic, resilient people, but also a rather fatalistic, even complacent one. The events of 3/11 have changed both the physical and mental landscape of Japan.

Most Japanese tend not to dwell on the morbid aspects of the islands' geological activity, preferring to enjoy its pleasures instead. *Onsen*, or hot springs, are a tangible result of the massive quantities of heat released underground. For centuries hot springs have occupied a special place in Japanese culture, until the pleasures of the *onsen* have become a national pastime.

Mountains and coastal plains

Despite the dominance of mountains in these islands, the Japanese are not a mountain people, preferring instead to squeeze onto the coastal plains or into the valleys of the interior. Consequently separated from each other by mountains, which once took days to traverse, the populated areas tended to develop independently with distinct dialects and other social peculiarities; some local dialects, such as in Tohoku or Kyushu, are completely unintelligible to other Japanese. At the same time, isolation and efficient use of land meant that agriculture and communications evolved early in the country's history.

The highest non-volcanic peaks are in the so-called Japan Alps of central Honshu. Many of the landforms in these mountain ranges were sculpted by glaciers in an ice age over 27,000 years ago. Cirques, or depressions, left where glaciers formed, are still a common sight on some higher slopes. Debris brought down by melting ice can also be seen in lower regions.

Wildlife

To the Japanese, people are a part of nature and therefore anything people have constructed is considered part of the environment. The Japanese can look upon a garden – moulded, cut, sculptured and trimmed to perfect proportions – and still see it as a perfect expression of the natural order, not something artificial.

The result of this philosophy has generally been disastrous for the wildlife and ecosystems of Japan. The crested ibis, for example, once considered to be a representative bird of Japan and common throughout the archipelago 100 years ago, is reduced today to fewer than a dozen individuals. Efforts to save the red-crowned Japanese crane (*tancho*) have met with more success, with

Japanese crane at Kushiro moor, Hokkaido.

its territory in eastern Hokkaido now secure and numbers on the rise.

Fish such as salmon and trout are no longer able to survive in Japan's polluted rivers and lakes. Brown bears have been hunted almost to extinction, and only recently have hunting laws been amended and the animal recognised as an endangered species.

Because of Japan's sheer length it is nevertheless able to host a veritable menagerie of fauna, including some, like the copper pheasant, wild boar, cormorants, kites, serow, Japanese giant salamander and horseshoe crab, that are indigenous to the archipelago. Of the other land mammals, the Japanese monkey, or macaca, is by far the most common in Japan. Originally a creature of the tropical rainforests, the macaca has adapted to the more temperate climates of these islands and can now be found throughout Kyushu, Shikoku and Honshu, although its numbers have been sharply reduced since the 1950s. During the winter months, macacas in Nagano and Hokkaido take to bathing in local hot springs.

Japan's sub-Arctic zone, centred on Hokkaido, is known for its hazel grouse, brown bears, Arctic hares, sticklebacks, foxes and humpback whales. Its temperate zone is home to mandarin ducks, sika deer, loggerhead turtles, porpoises, raccoon dogs, badgers and flying squirrels, its seas sup-

Cherry blossoms in Matsumoto.

porting fur seals and sea lions. The southern, subtropical regions support flying foxes, butterflies, crested serpent eagles, lizards, sea serpents, manta rays, redfin fusiliers, parrot fish, anemone fish, lizards and the deadly habu snake.

There are several species that face near extinction, among them the Iriomote wildcat, a mostly nocturnal creature native to Iriomote Island; the black Amami rabbit; the Japanese otter; and the short-tailed albatross.

Flora

In the far south of Japan, the islands of Okinawa have a distinctive fauna and flora. Here, the natural forests are subtropical, but many of the indigenous species of fauna have become rare or even extinct. Even so, a wealth of natural flora remains, with Japan's temperate species, like black pine, winter camellia, azaleas and plum contrasting with hibiscus, bougainvillea, giant tree ferns, luxuriant cycads, fukugi, ficus and banyan trees.

The most spectacular characteristic of these islands is the marine life. Most of the islands are surrounded by coral, home to a rich and colourful variety of warm-water fish. Yet once again the rapid growth of the tourist and leisure industry – especially that of scuba-diving – and the bleaching effects of temperature rises caused by global warming, have taken a toll. Okinawa's coral reefs, however, continue to remain some of the finest in the world. The natural coral of Amami-jima, Yonaguni-jima, Miyako-jima, Iriomote-jima and the precious blue coral of Ishigaki-jima, the largest in the world, host an extraordinary rainbow of tropical fish and marine gardens.

> *A few hundred wild bears remain, but only on Hokkaido. Most of Japan's bears are confined in amusement parks, with dozens of bears often crowded into small concrete pits.*

In Hokkaido, the greater availability of space and natural moorland vegetation has led to the growth of the cattle and dairy industries. Meat is gradually becoming a more important part of the Japanese diet, just as rice is declining in popularity. In a sense, this is symptomatic of the way Japanese culture is changing. Younger generations are gradually turning away from the fish-and-rice diet to eat more meat and bread as Japan becomes more urbanised and Western in outlook.

Climate

Extensive television and print coverage of the weather provides the Japanese with a major topic of conversation.

Japan's extremities, from its Siberian sub-Arctic zone in northern Hokkaido to the subtropical jungles of Okinawa, the Sea of Japan to the Pacific Ocean, straddle very different climatic regions.

Japan's seasons are similar to those of Europe and North America. The coldest months are December to February, with heavy snow on the Sea of Japan side of Hokkaido and Honshu, dry air on the Pacific Ocean side. Tokyo's urban growth has reduced evaporation levels, causing a drop in winter precipitation and concerns over water shortages.

Cherry blossom time

Cherry trees *(sakura)*, first blossom in Okinawa in late winter, reaching Hokkaido in mid-May. Celebrated with *hanami* parties, domestic tourism goes into overdrive. The media daily reports on the *sakura zensen* (cherry blossom front). The appeal of the blossom is its transience – it lasts at most a week.

Strong, southerly winds bring rain and the start of the *tsuyu*, rainy season. Temperatures rise and rains fall for about two months, easing around late June on the Pacific Ocean side, making way for the hot, humid summer, which lingers into September. As the warm air mass moves south, the rains return on the backs of devastating typhoons.

Natural resources

There are coalmines in Hokkaido and Kyushu, but coal production peaked in 1941 and many coalmining communities are now in serious decline. Nearly all of Japan's other raw materials, such as oil, minerals and metal ores, are imported. Timber is one resource Japan has in abundance, as most of the country's mountains are covered in natural or plantation forest. The natural cover varies from sub-Arctic conifers in Hokkaido to deciduous and evergreen temperate broad-leafed trees throughout the other three main islands. Yet despite a soaring demand for timber – used in the construction industry and for paper and disposable chopsticks – domestic production has actually fallen. The Japanese prefer to buy cheap,

imported timber from the tropical rainforests of Southeast Asia, a practice that is causing considerable concern among many environmentalists as the rainforests of Borneo and Burma, and until recently Thailand, are being reduced to barren slopes.

Fishing is another rural occupation that has declined in activity, mainly because of a decline in fish stocks as a result of overexploitation. Japanese fleets now operate in international waters far away from home, and ports that once supported fishing fleets are turning towards other endeavours. One of the most

Fishermen and their boats, Hokkaido.

WORLD HERITAGE JAPAN

A long-overdue interest in ecotourism and the environment is now firmly embedded at both the government and local levels throughout Japan. At present there are 18 accredited Unesco sites in Japan. Natural heritage sites include Shirakami-Sanchi, a highland and woodland region crossing the borders of Aomori and Akita Prefectures, valued for its Siebold's beech forest and mountains; Shiretoko, a woodland and marine peninsula in the far north of Hokkaido; Yakushima Island south of Kagoshima Prefecture, home to millennnia-old cypress trees and a warm, subtropical climate; the remote Ogasawara Islands, whose waters are a fine whale-watching venue; and the newest addition to the list, the

sacred Fuji-san, the highest mountain in Japan.

All of Japan's five main islands have national and quasi-national parks. Among the oldest are Unzen and Kirishima in Kyushu, and Ise-Shima in Mie Prefecture. In all, there are 29 designated national parks in Japan, from the remote Rishiri-Rebun-Sarobetsu National Park in Hokkaido's far northwest, the marshlands of Oze National Park in the Kanto region, the peaks and watercourses of Chichibu Tama Kai National Park near Tokyo and the Sanin Kaigan area along the Sea of Japan, with its rugged coastline and desert-like Tottori Sand Dunes, to the jungles, waterfalls and priceless coral reefs of Okinawa's subtropical Iriomote-Ishigaki National Park.

lucrative of these is tourism. As the urban Japanese become more affluent and seek recreation outside the cities, ports and harbours are becoming leisure marinas, hotels and resorts are springing up all over the countryside, and mountains are being levelled in order to make way for golf courses. Yet, to Westerners, there is a paradox with this approach to ecology. It has been one of the proud boasts of the Japanese that they live close to and in harmony with nature – a strong theme in Japanese poetry and reflected in the Japanese preoccupation with the weather.

A farmer in the Tono Valley, Tohoku.

Urban zones

By far the largest of Japan's few flat spaces is the Kanto plain, an area centred on Tokyo Bay and formed by a build-up of sediments resulting from Ice Age-induced changes in sea level. Other extensive areas of flat land occur in the Tohoku region, Hokkaido, and along the Nagoya–Osaka industrial belt.

Such is the concentration of resources in these plains that most of Japan's people, factories, farmland, housing and public facilities are all crowded onto approximately 20 percent of Japan's total land area. Thus, very little of what one might call countryside exists on the plains. Cities, towns and villages tend to merge into an indistinct urban blur that

stretches endlessly across the flat land, with fields and farms dotted in between. In general, the plains are monochromatic, congested and less than aesthetic.

The main industrial regions are the Kanto and Kansai areas, which are centred on Tokyo and Osaka respectively. The Kanto area alone produces nearly a third of Japan's entire gross domestic product. If it were an independent nation, it would produce more goods and services than the United Kingdom.

Again, it is the Kanto region and Tokyo in particular that has benefited from Japan's prosperity since World War II. Metropolitan Tokyo had a nominal population of more than 13 million in 2015, but in fact the city spreads beyond its political boundaries north, south and west to form a massive urban complex that stretches across the entire Kanto plain. The actual population of this megalopolis is estimated at nearly 38 million people.

Metropolitan Tokyo and Yokohama are the first and second cities of Japan, respectively. Third in size is Osaka, with a population of 2.7 million, followed by Nagoya with 2.3 million. These cities have experienced phenomenal growth since World War II, as Japan's urban industrialisation and rural mechanisation drew people off the farms and into the cities.

Many rural communities are now suffering from an increasingly aged population, and some have become virtual ghost towns as young people have fled the rural lifestyle. The situation is serious. A shortage of women in the countryside results in male farmers going on organised urban field trips in search of mates wanting to escape the city.

The countryside, however, lacks appeal and job opportunities, especially for the young. Farming on the typically tiny Japanese farms is inefficient and backward, made profitable only by heavy and politically motivated subsidies from the government. Unlike most other industrial nations, Japan has few natural resources and depends heavily upon manufacturing for wealth and employment. Recent years, though, have seen the advent of the so-called U-Turn, by which young and retired people are relocating to rural areas looking for an alternative lifestyle to Japan's massively crowded urban zones. Many of them are setting up co-operatives and organic farms, an encouraging tendency.

Environmental awareness

Japan has one of the strangest landscapes on earth. Managed and contained, there are few areas spared the visible effects of a human hand.

Rivers flow through tiered cement embankments, environmentally questionable dams deface once pristine valleys, and mountains, lathered with concrete casing, exist to be tunnelled through, not lived on. Sea walls and breakers give the impression of a reinforced citadel. Even when there are great swathes of woodland, closer examination reveals serried ranks of trees, an industrial monoculture. Subordination, not coexistence, appears to be the mantra.

Japan's rapid, ill-considered post-war development has had catastrophic effects. Chemical pollution from industrial, domestic and agricultural sources and growing levels of seawater toxicity remain pressing issues. Japan has lobbied against a ban on the fishing of bluefin tuna, of which it consumes roughly 80 percent of the world's catch. Japanese whaling operates under a complex set of exemptions that allow it to hunt for scientific reasons. The only country undertaking long-distance whaling in the southern sanctuary of the Antarctic, Japan primarily catches minke whales, much of the catch ending up for sale as meat. Interestingly, the vast majority of Japanese are far more interested in whale-watching than devouring the unpopular meat.

Some 67 percent of the country is tree-covered, with single-species plantations of conifers dominating. Despite the abundance of timber, Japan imports roughly 80 percent of its lumber, employing a meagre 50,000 people in the forestry sector. Reviving its forestry industry would help to restore mountain streams by providing oxygen and nutrients, which would in turn help to cleanse its embattled coastlines.

The ancient cedar trees of Yakushima are lucky to have survived. By the 1970s, 80 percent of forest trees had been destroyed, most of the wood ending up as pulp. The island's listing as a Unesco World Heritage Site in 1993 quite literally saved Yakushima from extinction.

New awareness

There is a growing awareness among citizens groups and at government levels that surviving natural beauty must be protected. The islands of Japan's Inland Sea offer hope. Petrochemical plants, oil refineries and the dumping of cyanogen and cadmium prompted one Japanese writer to comment that "the Seto Inland Sea had been turned into a sea of death". The fortunes of one island, Naoshima, home to an industrial waste-recycling plant, changed in 1992, when a small-scale art project was initiated with the idea of using art for community rejuvenation. On nearby Teshima, a former depository for toxic waste, a museum now sits among graduated rice fields, in which residents now both produce and consume their own harvests.

Cedar tree in the forest of Yakushima.

This project, and others that are planned to follow, provide an invaluable counter-model to reckless growth and industrial carnage.

As far as clean energy vehicles are concerned, Japan is at the vanguard of development, with electric cars produced by Toyota and Nissan. The country also wants to set an example for green housing with the 2020 Olympic Village – a futuristic hydrogen-powered town located in the Tokyo Bay. However, Japan's greenhouse-gas emissions hit a record high in 2014, as the country had been forced to increase its dependence on fossil fuels following the closure of all its nuclear reactors in the aftermath of Fukushima plant disaster. Amid public protests, the government has been advocating a return to nuclear energy and on 11 August 2015, the first nuclear reactor started up again.

DECISIVE DATES

Rise of civilised Japan

10000 BC
Jomon culture produces Japan's earliest known examples of pottery.

3500–2000 BC
Population begins migrating inland.

300 BC
Migrants from Korea introduce rice cultivation.

AD 300
Kofun Period begins. Political and social institutions rapidly develop. Imperial line begins.

500–600
Buddhism arrives from Korea.

Time of the warlords

710
New capital established in Nara.

794
Capital relocated to Kyoto. Rural areas neglected.

1180s
Estate holders develop military power. Warlord conflict ends Heian Period.

1185
Minamoto Yoritomo granted title of shogun, establishing base in Kamakura. The weakened imperial court stays in Kyoto.

1274
Mongols from China attempt unsuccessful invasion of Kyushu.

1333
Shogun Ashikaga Takauji returns capital to Kyoto,

further eclipsing court influence.

1467
The Age of Warring States begins. Power of feudal lords increases.

1573
Warlord Oda Nobunaga conquers Kyoto and provinces, starting process of unification.

1582
Assassinated Nobunaga replaced by Toyotomi Hideyoshi.

1590
All of Japan is under Hideyoshi's control.

1597
Hideyoshi invades Korea but dies a year later.

1600
Edo Period begins. Tokugawa Ieyasu takes control after Battle of Sekigahara.

1603
Capital moves to Edo (present-day Tokyo). Edo becomes world's largest city.

1639
National seclusion policy begins.

1707
Mount Fuji erupts.

1720
Ban on importing foreign books lifted.

1853
Commodore Matthew Perry arrives with US naval ships,

A 1796 print of a market at Nihonbashi.

forcing Japan to accept trade and diplomatic contacts.

Return of imperial rule

1868
Meiji Restoration returns emperor to power. Last shogun, Yoshinobu, retires. Name of capital changed to Tokyo (Eastern Capital).

1872
Samurai class abolished.

1877
Satsuma Rebellion crushed.

1889
New constitution promulgated.

1895
Japan wins Sino-Japanese War.

1904–6
Japan wins Russo-Japanese War.

1910
Japan annexes Korea.

1918
Economic chaos. Rice riots.

1923
Devastating Great Kanto Earthquake hits Tokyo area.

1926
Taisho emperor dies.
Beginning of Showa Period.

1931
Manchuria occupied. Japan leaves League of Nations.

1936
Officers' insurgency – an attempt by a group of young army officers to remove corrupt senior government figures – fails.

1937
Japanese military advance on China.

1941
Japan attacks Pacific and Asian targets, occupying most of East Asia and western Pacific.

1945
American bombing raids destroy many major cities and industrial centres. Two atomic bombs dropped on Hiroshima and Nagasaki in August. Japanese surrender.

1946
New constitution places sovereignty with the people, not emperor.

1951
San Francisco Peace Treaty settles all war-related issues. Japan regains pre-war industrial output.

1955
Socialist factions form Japan Socialist Party; Liberals and Democrats create the Liberal Democratic Party (LDP).

1964
The Summer Olympics are held in Tokyo.

1972
US returns Okinawa (having occupied it since the end of World War II).

1980s
Japan's economy climbs to be the world's second largest.

1989
Emperor Hirohito dies, replaced by son Akihito.

Modern times

1990
The "economic bubble" bursts.

1992
Worst post-war recession.

1993
Scandal ridden LDP members replaced by independents. Coalition government shortly replaced by another led by the Japan Socialist Party.

1995
Kobe earthquake kills over 5,000, leaving 300,000 homeless. A religious cult releases nerve gas in the Tokyo subway, killing 12.

1996
LDP return to power.

1998
Winter Olympics held in Nagano.

1999
Several die in nuclear accident at a uranium-reprocessing plant in Tokaimura.

2002
Japan co-hosts the football World Cup with South Korea.

2004
Unarmed peacekeeping mission sent to Iraq in support of US-led coalition.

2007
A 6.8-scale earthquake at the Kariwa plant in Niigata Prefecture causes fire and small amounts of radioactive leakage.

2009
LDP loses power to DPJ (Democratic Party of Japan) in landmark general election.

2010
China overtakes Japan as second-largest economy.

2011
A massive earthquake and tsunami shuts down reactors at the Fukushima power plant, causing a nuclear meltdown and release of radioactive materials.

2012
LDP triumphs in general elections and Abe Shinzo becomes Prime Minister.

2013
Tokyo wins the bid to host the 2020 Olympic Games.

2014
The government approves a major change in military policy, paving the way for military operations overseas.

2015
Japan emerges from recession although growth is slack. The first nuclear reactor begins operating again, four years after Fukushima.

The aftermath of the 2011 tsunami.

Ritual figurine dating from the late Jomon period, found in Northern Honshu.

JAPAN'S EARLY CENTURIES

Migrations of people from the mainland across now submerged land bridges evolved into a feudal system of warlords and an aesthetic of profound elegance.

Shinto mythology holds that two celestial gods, descending to earth on a "floating bridge to heaven", dipped a spear into the earth, causing drops of brine to solidify into the archipelago's first group of islands. As one of the male gods was washing his face in the fertile sea, the Sun Goddess, Amaterasu, sprung from his left eye, bathing the world in light. Japanese mythology claims its first emperor, Jimmu, was a direct descendant of the Sun Goddess. Conferring on him the title Tenno, Lord of Heaven, all emperors up to the present day have been addressed in this way.

What we can say with certainty is that the lands that are now the Japanese archipelago have been inhabited by human beings for at least 30,000 years, and maybe for as long as 100,000 to 200,000 years. The shallow seas separating Japan from the Asian mainland were incomplete when these people first came and settled on the terrain. After people arrived, however, sea levels rose and eventually covered the land bridges.

Middle Jomon earthenware bowl.

On 18 June 1877, zoologist Edward Sylvester Morse, found the remains of a shell mound as he passed through the village of Omori. Morse's discovery of the pre-Bronze Age midden signalled the beginning of archaeology as a study in Japan.

Whether or not these settlers are the ancestors of the present Japanese remains a controversy. Extensive archaeological excavations of prehistoric sites in Japan only began during the 1960s.

It is generally agreed that Japan was settled by waves of people coming from South Asia and the northern regions of the Asian continent, and that this migration very likely occurred over a long period.

Jomon Period (c. 10,000–300 BC)

The earliest millennia of Neolithic culture saw a warming in worldwide climate, reaching peak temperature levels between 8000 and 4000 BC. In Japan, this phenomenon led to rising sea levels, which cut any remaining land bridges to the Asian mainland. At the same time, the local waters produced more abundant species of fish and shellfish. New types of forest took root, sprang up and thrived. These natural developments in the environment set the stage for the Early Jomon Period. Japan's earliest pottery

– belonging to the Jomon culture – has been dated at about 10000 BC, possibly the oldest known in the world, say some experts.

The Early Jomon people were mostly coastal-living, food-gathering nomads. Dietary reliance on fish, shellfish and sea mammals gave rise to the community refuse heaps known as shell mounds, the archaeologist's primary source of information about these people. The Early Jomon people also hunted deer and wild pig. Artefacts include stone-blade tools and the earliest known cord-marked pottery (*jomon*, in fact, means cord-marked).

A Japanese dotaku (bronze bell).

Grinding stones, capped storage jars and other Middle Jomon artefacts indicate a much more intense involvement with plant cultivation.

The Late Jomon Period, dating from around 2000 BC, is marked by an increase of coastal fishing among villagers living along the Pacific shorelines of the main islands.

Yayoi Period (c.300 BC–AD 300)

Named after an archaeological site near Tokyo University, the Yayoi Period was a time of significant cultural transition. It was ushered in around 300 BC by peoples who migrated from rice-growing areas of the Asian mainland into northern Kyushu via Korea and, most likely, Okinawa.

In a brief 600 years, Japan was transformed from a land of nomadic hunting-and-gathering communities into the more sedentary pattern of settled farming villages: tightly knit, autonomous rice-farming settlements sprang up and spread so rapidly in Kyushu and western Honshu that by AD 100 settlements were found in most parts of the country, except for the northern regions of Honshu and Hokkaido.

Kofun Period (c.300–710)

The break with Yayoi culture is represented by the construction of huge tombs of earth and stone in coastal areas of Kyushu and along the shores of the Inland Sea. *Haniwa*, hollow clay human and animal figures, and models of houses decorated the perimeters of these tombs. These were made, some experts have speculated, as substitutes for the living retainers and possessions of the departed noble or leader.

Political and social institutions developed rapidly. Each of the community clusters that defined itself as a "country" or "kingdom" had a hierarchical social structure, subjected to increasing influence by a burgeoning central power based in the Yamato plain, in what is now the area of Osaka and Nara. The imperial line, or the Yamato dynasty, was probably formed from a number of powerful *uji* (family-clan communities) that had developed in the Late Yayoi Period.

Buddhism came to Japan in the 6th century from Korea. Although it is said that writing accompanied the religion, it may be that Chinese writing techniques preceded it by as much as 100 to 150 years. In any case, it was literacy that made the imported religion accessible to the nobility, also exposing them to the Chinese classics and to the writings of sages such as Confucius. Social and political change naturally followed an increase in literacy.

The power of the Soga clan was enhanced by exclusive control of the imperial treasury and granaries and by the clan's monopolistic role as sponsor for new learning brought in from the Asian mainland. The reforms they introduced were aimed primarily at strengthening the central government and reducing the power of other clans at the imperial court. The reforms were far-reaching, including changes in social structure, economic and legal systems, provincial boundaries, bureaucracy and taxes.

Nara Period (710–94)

An empress in the early 8th century again constructed a new capital, this one in the northwest of the Yamato plain and named Heijo-kyo, on the site of present-day Nara. The century that followed – the Nara Period – saw the full enforcement of the system of centralised imperial rule based on Chinese concepts (the *ritsuryo* system), as well as flourishing arts and culture.

With the enforcement of the *ritsuryo* system, the imperial government achieved tight control, with administration managed by a

The Nara-era Empress Komyo, believed to be a reincarnation of Kannon, the Goddess of Compassion, did much to alleviate the plight of the poor by creating orphanages and shelters for the sick after smallpox swept through Nara in 737.

powerful grand council. All land used for rice cultivation was claimed to be under imperial ownership, which later led to heavy taxation of farmers.

Heian Period (794–1185)

In the last decade of the 8th century, the capital was relocated yet again. As usual, the city was built on the Chinese model and was named Heian-kyo. It was the core around which the city of Kyoto developed. Its completion in 795 marked the beginning of the 400-year Heian Period.

The strength of the central government continued for several decades, but later in the 9th century the *ritsuryo* system gradually began to crumble under the bureaucratic system.

This was modified so that aristocrats and powerful temple guardians could own large estates *(shoen)*. Farmers, working imperial lands but faced with oppressive taxation, fled to these estates in large numbers. Thus the estate holders began to gain political – and military – power in the provinces.

Provincial areas were neglected by the imperial court. Banditry became widespread and local administrators were more interested in personal gain than in enforcing law and order. The result was that the lords of great estates continued to develop their own military power

using skilled warriors called samurai. Eventually they engaged in struggles amongst themselves, and the fighting ended the Heian Period dramatically and decisively.

Kamakura Period (1185–1333)

The victor of the struggles, Minamoto Yoritomo, was granted the title of shogun (military commander) rather than emperor. He set up his base at Kamakura, far from Kyoto, and established an administrative structure and military headquarters, creating ministries to take care of samurai under his control.

Painting of Japanese warlord Minamoto-no Yoritomo, who established the first Samurai shogunate in Japan in the 12th century.

He convinced the emperor to sanction officials called *shugo* (military governors) and *jito* (stewards) in each province. The former were responsible for military control of the provinces and the latter for supervising the land, as well as collecting taxes. Both posts were answerable directly to the shogun himself, and thus government by the warrior class, located at a distance from the imperial capital, was created.

The origins of the samurai warriors can be traced to the 7th century when landowners began amassing power and wealth, creating a feudal system that needed defending. Some samurai, or *bushi*, were relatives or financial dependents of lords, others hired swords. The code of honour called *bushido*, "the way of the warrior," demanded absolute fidelity to one's lord, even above family loyalty. By 1100, the feudal lords and their samurai retainers held military and political power over much of the country.

This governing system was known as *bakufu*, or shogunate. The imperial court was, in effect, shoved into a corner and ignored. The court remained alive, however, though subsequent centuries saw its impoverishment. Still, it kept an important function in ritual and as a symbol.

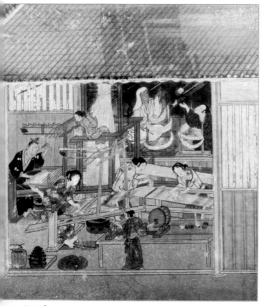

A 16th-century painting showing Japanese weavers at work.

Although the Kamakura Period was relatively brief, there were events and developments that profoundly affected the country. A revolutionary advance of agricultural techniques occurred that allowed greater production of food. Consequently, there was a significant increase in population and economic growth, with more intense settlement of the land, improved commerce and trade, the expansion of local markets, and the beginnings of a currency system. Contact with the Chinese mainland resumed on a private basis. Strong Buddhist leaders arose who preached doctrines that appealed to both the samurai and the common people.

The complexities of civil rule became top-heavy; the system of military governors and stewards started to crumble. More strain was added by the defence of the country against the two Mongol invasions in 1274 and 1281, both of which were unsuccessful due in great measure to the fortuitous occurrence of typhoons that destroyed the invading Mongol fleet.

Muromachi Period (1333–1568)

A subsequent generalissimo, Ashikaga Takauji, returned the capital to Kyoto, enhancing the power of the shogunate over the imperial court.

The name of the period, Muromachi, comes from the area of Kyoto in which a later Ashikaga shogun, Yoshimitsu, built his residence. His life represents perhaps the high point of the Ashikaga shogunate. Yoshimitsu took an active role in court politics as well as excelling in his military duties as shogun.

Overall, the Muromachi Period introduced the basic changes that would assure the

CLAN WARS

Engrossed in a dream-like lifestyle, court intrigues and romantic dalliances, the Heian nobility failed to take note of the emergence of powerful and restive military clans. Most prominent were the Genji and Heike, also known as the Minamoto and Taira.

Wishing to rid himself of the dominant Fujiwara regents, the emperor enlisted the services of the Heike, who soon became embroiled in a power struggle with the Genji, one that led to the fierce Genpei Wars (1180–85). A struggle over imperial succession led to the Heike imprisoning the emperor and putting his grandson, whose mother happened to be a Heike, on the throne. The Genji counterattack, under the command of the

cavalier young general Yoshitsune, annihilated the Heike in a decisive sea battle in 1185.

Battles took place at Mizushima, Shinohara, Yashima on Shikoku Island, and even in Uji, a town of great serenity. Shimonoseki's annual Kaikyo Festival re-enacts the scene in which the red-and-white-bannered forces of the Genji and Heike fought their final battle at Dan-no-ura in the Shimonoseki straits between Honshu and Kyushu islands. Even in remoter villages of places like Hida-Takayama in Gifu, visitors can find the descendants of communities formed from the fleeing remnants of the defeated Heike clan. The war between the two groups is the main subject of the medieval *Tales of the Heike*.

economic growth and stability of the coming Edo Period. Agricultural techniques were improved, new crops were introduced, and irrigation and commercial farming expanded. Guilds of specialised craftsmen appeared, a money economy spread and trade increased markedly. Most importantly, towns and cities arose and grew; such development was accompanied by the appearance of merchant and service classes.

A later Ashikaga shogun was assassinated in 1441, which started the decline of the shogunate; the relationship between the shogun and

> Many scholars consider the Muromachi Period (1333–1568) the apex of Japanese garden design. With the development of Zen and the growing influence of its temples, small, exquisite stone gardens were constructed as aesthetic and contemplative spaces.

the military governors of the provinces broke down. A decade of war and unrest marked the total erosion of centralised authority and a general dissolution of society. It ushered in the Age of Warring States, a century of battle that lasted from 1467 until 1568.

The almost total decentralisation of government that occurred in the Age of Warring States saw the development of what might be called a true type of feudal lord, the *daimyo*, backed up by vast armies.

Momoyama Period (1568–1600)

The short Momoyama Period is notable for the rise of Oda Nobunaga (1534–82), the first of three leaders to go about the business of unifying the country, who started by overrunning Kyoto. The other leaders were Toyotomi Hideyoshi (1536–98) and Tokugawa Ieyasu (1542–1616).

Nobunaga conquered the home provinces in a rigorous manner. He eliminated rivals and razed the temples of militant Buddhist sects around Kyoto that opposed him. Temple burning aside, he had a flair for culture.

Although he brought only about one-third of the country under his control, Nobunaga laid the foundation for the unification that would later follow. He was assassinated by a treacherous general in 1582.

Hideyoshi, Nobunaga's chief general, succeded his master. With military brilliance, statesmanship and a certain amount of brass, he proceeded vigorously with the job of unifying Japan. By 1590, all territories of the country, directly or by proxy, were essentially under his control. But the government was still decentralised in a complex network of feudal relationships. Hideyoshi's hold on the country, based on oaths of fealty, was slippery at best. Still, he effected sweeping domestic reforms. The action that perhaps had the longest-lasting social impact on Japanese history was his

A depiction of one of the battles of Kawanakajima.

"sword hunt", in which all non-samurai were forced to give up their weapons. A class system was also introduced. In some areas, rich landlords had to make a difficult choice: declare themselves to be samurai and susceptible to the demands of the warrior's life, or else remain as commoners and thus subservient to the samurai class.

Hideyoshi made two attempts to conquer Korea, in 1592 and 1597, with the aim of taking over China. His death in 1598 brought this megalomaniacal effort to an end.

The cultural achievements of these three decades were astonishing. The country was in political ferment, yet at the same time glorious textiles, ceramics and paintings were produced.

THE EDO PERIOD

The rise of the great shogunates and their samurai warlords instilled in the Japanese culture ways of thinking and behaviour that persist even today.

The political, economic, social, religious and intellectual facets of the Edo Period (1600–1868) are exceedingly complex. One often-cited general characteristic of this time is an increasingly prosperous merchant class emerging simultaneously with urban development. Edo (modern-day Tokyo) became one of the world's great cities and is thought to have had a population in excess of 1 million at the beginning of the 18th century – greater than London or Paris at the time.

The Tokugawa shogun

For many years, the shogun Hideyoshi had bemoaned his lack of a male heir. When in the twilight of his years an infant son, Hideyori, was born, Hideyoshi was ecstatic and became obsessed with founding a dynasty of warrior rulers. So he established a regency council of leading vassals and allies, foremost of whom was Tokugawa Ieyasu (1542–1616), who controlled the most territory in the realm after Hideyoshi. Members of the council swore loyalty to the infant; the boy was five at the time of Hideyoshi's death.

The death of Hideyoshi was naturally an opportunity for the ambitions of restless warlords to surface. Tokugawa Ieyasu had about half of the lords who were allied with Hideyoshi's son sign pledges to him within a year of Hideyoshi's death. In 1600, however, he was challenged by a military coalition of lords from western Japan. He won the encounter in the Battle of Sekigahara (near Kyoto) and became the islands' de facto ruler.

In 1603, Tokugawa Ieyasu was given the title of shogun by the still subservient but symbolically important emperor. He established his capital in Edo, handed his son the shogun title

Tokugawa Ieyasu (1543–1616), founder and first shogun of the Tokugawa Shogunate.

in 1605, and then retired to a life of intrigue and scheming that was aimed at consolidating the position of his family (Ieyasu himself would die in 1616).

The primary problem facing Ieyasu was how to make a viable system out of the rather strange mix of a strong, central military power and a totally decentralised administrative structure. Eventually he devised a complex system that combined feudal authority and bureaucratic administration with the Tokugawa shoguns as supreme authority from whom the various lords, or *daimyo*, received their domains and to whom they allied themselves by oath.

While the military emphasis of the domain was curtailed, each *daimyo* had considerable autonomy in the administration of his domain. The system sufficed to maintain peace and a growing prosperity for more than two centuries. Its flaws sprang from its inability to adapt well to social and political change, as would later be seen.

> Tested on criminals' corpses, the Japanese sword, or katana, was the world's most beautiful instrument of death. After the abolition of the samurai class in the late 19th century, the sword-making town of Mino-Seki shrewdly became Japan's leading cutlery producer.

Ieyasu was Napoleonic in his passion for administration, and he thought of every device possible to assure that his descendants would retain power. Wanting to keep an eye on the *daimyo*, in 1635 he established the *sankin kotai* system, which required staggered attendance in Edo for the 300 independent feudal lords. The shogunate set up a rigid class hierarchy – warriors, farmers, artisans, merchants – and adopted a school of neo-Confucianism as the theoretical basis for social and political policy.

Whether in Edo or the countryside, every individual knew exactly what his or her position in society was and how to behave accordingly. For most of the Tokugawa decades, Japan's doors were closed to the outside. Long years of isolated peace slowly replaced the warrior's importance with that of the merchant. The standards of living for all classes increased, but at times the shogunate quelled conspicuous consumption among merchants.

Growth of Edo

When Ieyasu first settled down in what would eventually become modern Tokyo, the area was little more than a collection of scattered farming and fishing villages. The little town of Edojuku, at the mouth of the Hirakawa River, contained only about 100 thatched huts in the shadow of a dilapidated castle, built in 1457 by the minor warlord Ota Dokan. A sophisticated poet and scholar, in 1485 he was betrayed and butchered at the behest of his own lord.

Ieyasu brought with him to Edo a ready-made population of considerable size. Huge numbers of peasants, merchants and *ronin* (master-less samurai) poured into the new capital of the shogun to labour in the construction of the castle, mansions, warehouses and other infrastructure required to run the giant bureaucracy. The courses of rivers were changed, canals were dug and Hibiya Inlet, which brought Tokyo Bay lapping at the base of the castle hill, was filled in.

When the major *daimyo* and their entourage were in town, the samurai portion of the city's population probably topped 500,000, maybe even outnumbering the commoners. The

Print of people walking in the Ryogoku Bridge area.

A SAMURAI'S WAY OF LIFE

The way of the samurai – *bushido* – was a serious path to follow, "a way of dying" to defend the honour of one's lord or one's own name. Often that meant *seppuku*, or ritual disembowelment. An unwritten code of behaviour and ethics, *bushido* came to the foreground during the Kamakura Period. In the Edo Period, *bushido* helped strengthen the shogunate government, by perfecting the feudal class system of samurai, farmer, artisan and merchant. The ruling samurai class was by far the most powerful. Only when the economy shifted from rice-based to monetary did the merchants take control of Edo, leaving the samurai increasingly in debt.

samurai allotted themselves over 60 percent of the city's land. Another 20 percent went to hundreds of shrines and temples, which formed a spiritually protective ring around the outer edges of the city.

By the early 1700s, an estimated 1 to 1.4 million people lived in Edo, making it by far the largest city in the world at the time. During the same period, Kyoto had a population of 400,000 and Osaka 300,000. In 1801, when Britain's navy dominated the seas, Europe's largest city, London, had fewer than a million inhabitants. Japan's population hovered around 30 million for most of the Edo era; less than 2 million belonged to the samurai families.

In general, the samurai gravitated to the hilly parts of the city, or *yamanote*, while the townspeople congregated – or were forced to do so – in the downtown lowlands, or *shitamachi*, especially along the Sumida River. More than half of Edo's residents were crammed into the 15 percent of the city comprising *shitamachi*, with a population density of about 70,000 people per square kilometre. Almost from the start, both *yamanote* and *shitamachi* began to encroach through land-fill onto Tokyo Bay. (Even today in the modern city of Tokyo, these two districts retain distinctive characteristics.)

Edo Castle

The grounds of Ieyasu's huge castle, including the defensive moat system, were extensive. The complex was not actually completed until 1640 but was razed by fire seven years later.

The shogun's capital must have been a truly impressive city, backed by Fuji-san and laced with canals. It is often forgotten nowadays that most of Edo's supplies came by sea, especially from Osaka. In fact, one of the reasons Ieyasu had chosen the area for his capital was its easy access to the sea. But the swampy shore of Tokyo Bay itself was unsuitable for building docks and wharves; instead, canals and rivers threading inland from the bay served as ports.

This is not to suggest that the five great highways from the provinces, and especially from Kyoto, converging on the city were not also important. They were, especially the famous Tokaido, or East Sea Road, along which most of the feudal lords from Osaka and Kyoto travelled to Tokyo for their periodic and mandated stays in Edo. Tokaido also formed the central artery of the city itself between Shinagawa and Nihombashi.

The dichotomy between the refined – albeit somewhat constipated – culture of upper-class *yamanote* and the robust, plebeian art and drama of lower-class *shitamachi* (which Edward Seidensticker aptly dubbed respectively as the "high city" and "low city") has been a consistent feature of life in Edo. The Edokko (Children of Edo) took delight in delight, and this appreciation of pleasure is grandly reflected in the popular culture of the time – the colour and splash of *kabuki;* the *bunraku* puppet drama;

A depiction of some of the 47 ronin taking their revenge on Kira.

THE 47 MASTERLESS SAMURAI

In 1701, the warlord Asano became angered at the taunting of a *hatamoto* (high-ranking samurai) named Kira, who had been assigned to teach him proper etiquette for receiving an imperial envoy. Asano drew his sword and wounded Kira, and so was ordered to commit ritual disembowelment, or *seppuku*. He did so. His lands were confiscated and his samurai left as *ronin*, or masterless warriors. A year later, the *ronin* took revenge by attacking Kira's mansion. Chopping off Kira's head, they took it to Asano's grave so that his spirit could finally rest. In turn, the 47 *ronin* were ordered by the shogun to commit *seppuku*, which they did together.

ukiyo-e woodblock prints depicting the world of actors, sumo stars, courtesans and geisha; the pleasure quarters, licensed and unlicensed; and the vigorous publishing world of both scholarship and trashy stories. All of these reflected the Edo pleasure in the material world and in a kind of high consumerism. The fact that men outnumbered women – two to one as late as 1721 – probably contributed to making the male population more than a bit rowdy and cantankerous. It would certainly explain the emphasis on catering to the sensual pleasures of men and in the rise of woodblock prints of a rather graphic, if not exaggerated, sexual nature.

Rise of the merchants

The establishment of the shogunate caused many economic changes. After the shogunate eliminated international trade, merchants and the increasingly powerful commercial conglomerates *(zaibatsu)* turned their attention to domestic distribution and marketing systems. The highways built by the Tokugawas, along with their standardisation of weights, measures and coinage, helped with the rise of the *zaibatsu*.

The *samurai* received their stipends in rice, but the economy was increasingly dependent

> The shogunate unsuccessfully tried banning both kabuki and prostitution. Eventually, the shogunate simply moved these debauched activities to locations that were less desirable.

upon money – not to the shogunate's liking, as the shogunate's economic foundation was based upon taxes paid in rice. The result was that the samurai borrowed from the merchants and increasingly went into debt.

Yet it was still controlled with rigid social and governmental systems. Internal pressures demanded change. Moreover, the world itself was not about to allow Japan to keep its doors closed. The industrial revolution was gaining momentum in Europe, and the Western powers were casting about for more countries into which to expand economic influence.

While others had tried rattling Japan's doors, it was the United States that yanked them open in 1853 with Commodore Matthew Perry and America's East India Squadron – the famous

"Black Ships". He reappeared the following year with additional ships to back up his gunboat diplomacy and was successful: in 1858 a treaty of friendship and trade was signed with the United States, followed shortly by treaties with other Western powers.

The turmoil and tumult of the 15 years from 1853 to 1868 have been well documented in many books. The sense of Japan afloat in a sea of hostile powers who possessed more technology and had voracious ambitions may have acted to direct domestic energies away from internal wrangling. The shogun was in a tight

Drawing of Matthew Perry arriving in Uraga, Soshu Province.

squeeze with the arrival of Perry. His consensus with the *daimyo* regarding how to respond to the Black Ships – encouraging them to strengthen and improve defences in their own domains – eventually diluted his control over the *daimyo*. At the same time, an anti-Tokugawa movement amongst lower-level *daimyo* was stewing near Osaka and Kyoto.

Rebel *daimyo* captured the then powerless emperor and declared the restoration of imperial rule. Shogunate forces sought to reverse the situation in Kyoto but were defeated. The shogun yielded to the imperial court in 1868 – the Meiji Restoration. The emperor ascended again to head of state, and his reign would last until 1912.

Mutsuhito, the Meiji emperor.

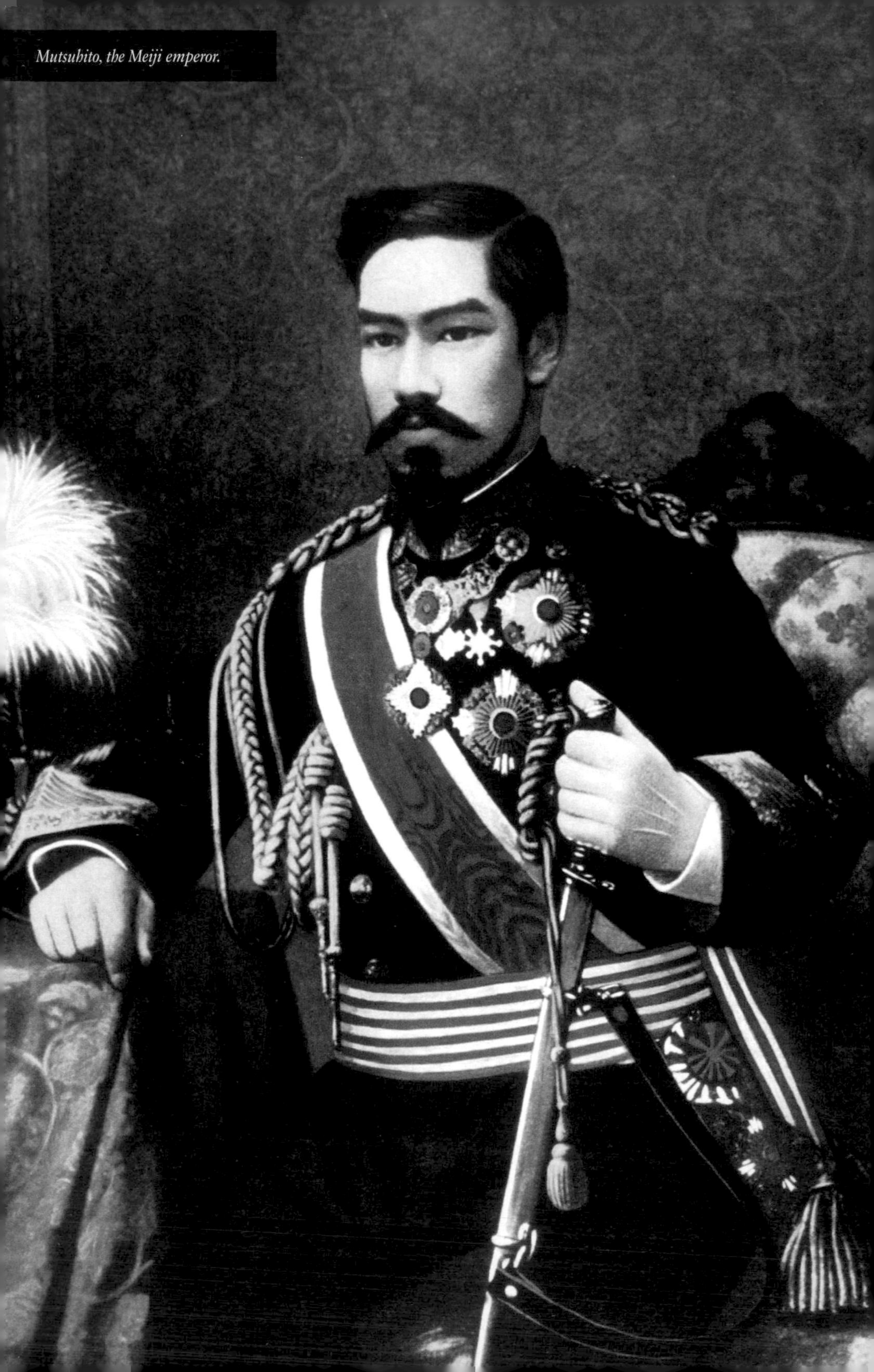

THE MODERN ERA

Once militarism was replaced by consumerism,
Japan rapidly became one of the world's
richest, safest and most advanced countries.

The Meiji Restoration of 1868, in which the ascension of the Meiji emperor as the nation's leader returned Japan to imperial rule, was a revolution of considerable proportions. Yet it was accomplished with surprisingly little bloodshed. The last shogun, Yoshinobu, in retired in statesman-like fashion and gave up Edo Castle rather than precipitate a full-scale civil war. Power was officially returned to the emperor in the autumn of 1867.

But shogunate residue remained in Edo and not all the samurai gave up easily. At the Tokugawa family temple of Kan'ei-ji, most of which is now Tokyo's Ueno Park, 2,000 diehard Tokugawa loyalists – the Shogitai – chose to make a last, hopeless stand at the bloody Battle of Ueno.

Meiji Period (1868–1912)

In 1868, an imperial edict changed the name of Edo to Tokyo, or Eastern Capital, and Emperor Meiji moved his court from the imperial capital of Kyoto to Tokyo. Because at the end of the Edo Period the office of emperor had no longer been associated with a political system, the emperor's "restoration" could be used as a convenient symbol and vehicle for choosing from a wide range of governmental structures.

In a few decades, Japan effectively restructured itself as a political entity. In retrospect, this seems astonishingly radical. Yet it did not

A Japanese print from 1870 showing the various forms of transport employed by people.

happen overnight, but rather by a series of incremental modifications to the political system.

The leaders of the Meiji-era reforms were young, highly driven men, mostly in their 20s and 30s, like the egalitarian reformer Ryoma Sakamoto, political thinker Yukichi Fukuzawa, educator Shoin Yoshida and diplomat Arinori Mori.

This was the age of slogans. Only a few years ago, "Revere the emperor, expel the barbarians," had been the most resounding cry. Now the call was for *Bunmei Kaika*, "Civilisation and Enlightenment", "Western learning, Japanese spirit" and, significantly, *Fukoku Kyohei*, "Rich country, strong army". Compulsory education, the promotion of emperor-based Shinto and

> *The new reforms included the abolition of practices like the tattooing of criminals, burning at the stake, crucifixion and torture. The mass murderess O-Den Takahashi – notorious for poisoning men – was the last person to be beheaded, in 1879.*

military service went hand in hand, laying the foundations for the nationalism and the state-sponsored indoctrination that would propel Japan towards the tragedy of World War II.

Meeting the Western powers as an equal was one of the guiding concerns of the Meiji years. This meant adopting anything Western, from railways to ballroom dancing. The pendulum first swung to extremes, from a total rejection of all native things (including an urge to abandon the Japanese language) to an emotional nationalism after the excesses of initial enthusiasm for foreign imports. But the employment of numerous for-

Portrait of Meiji, Emperor of Japan, and the imperial family in 1900.

eign advisers (upwards of 3,000) ended as soon as the Japanese sensed that they could continue perfectly well on their own.

Japan took to Western industrialisation with enthusiasm. Interestingly, reformation had begun to take place even before the Meiji era in Kagoshima, Saga and Kamaishi, where the smelting of iron ore marked the beginnings of an industrial revolution. These regions belonged to fiefs controlled by the so-called *tozama daimyo*, or "outside territorial lords", who had never seen themselves as servants of the Tokugawa shoguns.

A new cabinet, consisting of 11 departments, was established to replace an unwieldy system of court management, and local governments were

Many exhibitions were held during the Meiji era in Tokyo's Ueno Park, a showcase for new industries, technologies and gadgetry. The First National Industrial Exhibition, in 1877, attracted large crowds drawn to its displays of machinery, manufacturing, metallurgy and agriculture.

overhauled and reorganised along modern lines. New political groupings, with names like the Liberal Party and Reform Party, were formed. After a number of unsuccessful drafts over the years, a new constitution for the country was promulgated in 1889. This Meiji Constitution helped Japan become recognised as an advanced nation by the West.

Despite the creation of a parliament called the Diet, real power rested with the military, whose growing ranks were reinforced by Japan's victory in the Sino-Japanese War of 1894–5, an exercise in demonstrating the country's ability to wage modern warfare.

The clincher in making Japan a true world power, however, was winning the Russo-Japanese War of 1904–6, the first time that an Asian nation had defeated a European power. It didn't stop there. In 1910, Japan annexed Korea, ostensibly by treaty but actually under military threat, and occupied it until the end of World War II in 1945.

Emperor Meiji died in 1912. By then, Japan had consolidated its economy, defined a political system, changed its social structure and become an advanced nation.

Taisho Period (1912–26)

The short reign of Emperor Taisho saw the 20th century catch Japan in its grasp and carry it off on a strange and sometimes unpleasant odyssey.

World War I proved an enormous economic boom, and Japan seized the chance to enter Asian markets vacated by the European powers. With the defeat of Germany, some of its small Pacific territories came under Japanese control. But the inevitable deflation hit hard, and there were major rice riots in Tokyo in 1918.

The following year, politics became extremely polarised as the labour movement and leftists gained momentum. A new right, which believed in the politics of assassination rather than the ballot box, emerged from the political shadows. A series of political murders, including of prime ministers, followed over the next 15 years, helping to create the climate of violence that eventually let the military intervene in politics.

One of the founding members of the League of Nations in 1920, Japan failed to gain support from the US, Britain and Australia to have a declaration of racial equality incorporated into its charter, a bitter snub to a country that had sat with the five big nations at the Paris Peace Conference after the war.

> For a modern nation, the Shinto-orchestrated funeral of the Meiji emperor was a remarkable sight. A cortege drawn by white oxen, banner-bearers, bowmen and men bearing halberds passed through streets covered with sand to mute the sound of passing wheels.

The most transforming event of the 1920s, however, was not political but the catastrophe of 1 September 1923, the Great Kanto Earthquake, which struck at just noon, when a good percentage of the city's charcoal and gas stoves were lit: fire, not the quake itself, caused the most damage. Ninety percent of Yokohama was destroyed.

During the Taisho Period, Japan began to bubble intellectually. The growing prosperity (and the accompanying problems), the shrinking size of the world and the relative youth of Japan as a world power contributed to the "Taisho Democracy", which was actually little more than a time of good, healthy, intellectual ferment.

Showa Period (1926–89)

With the death of the Taisho emperor in 1926, Hirohito succeeded to the throne to begin the Showa Period and Japan's slide into war. Whatever the political, economic and social forces that produced the military government and the aggressive war effort, some observations can be made. The distribution of wealth was still uneven. The establishment factions included big business (the *zaibatsu*), the upper crust of government and military interests.

Political power within the country favoured establishment interests; suffrage was not universal. Non-establishment interests were weak because they had little recourse for expression, other than through imported political concepts – socialism and communism – that were distrusted and feared. A sense of territorial

insecurity, coupled with domestic economic and demographic pressures, made military hegemony seem a viable alternative, at least to the military.

Militarism's rise and fall

The pivotal point was the Manchurian Incident of 1931, in which Japanese military forces occupied Manchuria and set up the state of Manchuguo. Protest over this action by the League of Nations resulted in Japan leaving the League and following a policy of isolation.

Despite the Asia liberation rhetoric issuing from Tokyo, Japan's real aims were to secure

Photograph of a Tokyo street in the early 20th century.

OF EMPERORS AND CALENDARS

Japan has a British-style constitutional monarchy and parliament. Since the 1868 Meiji Restoration, there have been four emperors, though since World War II they have been a figurehead (coronation dates in parentheses):

Meiji (Meiji Period) 1867 (1868)–1912
Taisho (Taisho Period) 1912 (1915)–1926
Hirohito (Showa Period) 1926 (1928)–1989
Akihito (Heisei Period) 1989 (1990)–present

Japan uses two methods for indicating the year: the Western system (for example, 2016) and a system based on how long the current emperor has reigned (for example, Heisei 28).

self-sufficiency in strategic resources. Consolidating its empire in Asia would ensure this aim. The expansion of Japan's imperial hegemony was based on the European model. The European colonial powers had struck their Asian prey when they sensed a weakening or decay in the body politic of a sick state or failing kingdom. That this was done with impunity was made possible by the sense of entitlement that epitomised the West in its dealings with occupied territories.

There was little difference between the intentions of European nations and those of their Japanese colonial imitators when it came to

Inside the Peace Memorial Museum in Hiroshima.

entrapping and exploiting the peoples of Asia. The Burmese nationalist leader General Aung San couldn't have put it better when he said, "If the British sucked our blood, the Japanese ground our bones!"

Within the military itself, extremist factionalism grew, and during the 1930s several plots of one kind or another sought to win power for different groups. The most famous is the 26 February Incident of 1936, a bloody military uprising that might have been a coup d'état had it not been based on vague, romantic ideas that did not include a practical plan of how to use power. This bolstered the civilian resistance to military involvement in politics. Yet in the summer of 1937 war erupted with China, and Japanese troops

began a brutal campaign against the Chinese, which is infamous for the occupation of Nanjing and subsequent slaughter of between 150,000 and 300,000 civilians. Also known as the "Rape of Nanjing", this incident remains a controversial topic between Japan and China, South Korea and the Philippines.

Japan's colonial expansion into other parts of Asia and the Pacific was a replication of the Western powers' own search for resources, and was met with a series of economic sanctions imposed by the US, Britain and Holland. These included a crippling oil embargo, a factor which pushed Japan closer to confrontation with the Western powers. In 1940, Japan signed the Tripartite Act with Germany and Italy, thus formalising the Axis powers and promising mutual military support.

World War II

Seeking to discourage Western intervention in Japan's Asian expansion and to break the trade embargo, the Japanese military launched preemptive attacks not only on the US's Pearl Harbor in December of 1941 (as well as targets in the US-held Philippines and Guam) but against European colonial holdings throughout Asia, including Malaya, Singapore and Hong Kong. The attack had the result of formally bringing the US into World War II, with their declaration of war on Japan alongside the other Allied nations. In less than a year, Japan had gained possession of most of East and Southeast Asia and the western Pacific. Their gains were profound, but the US and Allied troops had begun to press them back through 1944, and by early 1945 Japan was on the defensive. With the European battlefronts quietened, the US concentrated on the Pacific theatre of war.

Ignoring the Geneva Convention ban, the US continued its campaign of terror bombings on civilian areas of Japanese cities. The air raids were of an unprecedented ferocity. Many of the firebombs fell on the populations of Sumida-ku and other wards to the east of Tokyo during the 102 raids that were launched between January 1945 and Japan's surrender in August. Robert McNamara, whose name would later be linked with the Vietnam War, took part in the planning of the raids, recalling later that "in a single night we burned to death 100,000 civilians… men, women, and children."

Despite Germany's defeat in May of 1945, Japanese military leaders would not yield. Japan's intransigence, combined with mounting pressure from the US scientific lobby keen to test the effects of their labour, saw the dropping, in mid-August of the same year, of atomic bombs on the cities of Hiroshima and Nagasaki.

On 15 August 1945, Emperor Hirohito spoke on the radio – the first time commoners had heard his voice – and declared an unconditional surrender. Japan lost its empire, its right to independent foreign policy, the emperor's claim to divinity, and the army. More than 6 million soldiers and civilians returned home to Japan. War-crime trials convicted several thousand Japanese; 920 of them were executed.

Although the vast majority of Japanese today readily admit to their country's culpability in the war, the view still persists among some that Japan's ultimate defeat was the result more of a failure of strategy and rationality than of a descent into inhumanity. The American campaign to capture Okinawa deftly reflected the quandary faced by many post-war Japanese, whose loathing for the savagery of American forces in the Pacific war zone and the atrocities of Hiroshima and Nagasaki was matched by a sense of betrayal and shame at the conduct of Japanese imperial forces.

A new 1946 constitution issued under the mandate of General Douglas MacArthur's occupation government guaranteed Western-style liberties, established a British-style parliamentary system, dismantled the pre-war industrial *zaibatsu* and renounced war as national policy. With the signing of the 1951 San Francisco Peace Treaty, American occupation of the country ended and Japan regained its sovereignty a year later. Okinawa, however, remained under US control until 1972.

Economic boom

Three significant characteristics help define post-war Japan in the 20th century: government-coordinated industrialisation and spectacular economic growth; the mocking of democracy by politicians; and Japan's ability to embrace transformation. With virtually every city in ruins after the US's zealous bombing campaign, young people felt a deep sense of betrayal and bitterness at having been indoctrinated into a militaristic mindset in schools and society, into an unshakable conviction in Japan's holy war. In response, they turned their backs on the past, throwing their energies into creating a culture and commerce that could be a creative and peaceful force in the world.

The decades following the war saw well-coordinated corporate and bureaucratic efforts to revive both business and the country. Protected by the American military umbrella, Japan was able to funnel maximum resources into its economy. With the urban population's explosive rise, farming's importance dropped to a fraction of the nation's gross national product, although the farmers' political power actually increased. Unusually for a developing or developed country, Japan's new national wealth was relatively evenly distributed amongst the people, leaving almost no one in an economic lower class. Unemployment remained low and industrial labour disputes and strikes were rare.

Workers at the Nissan Motor Company factory in Tokyo.

SURRENDER PREVAILED

Evidence suggests that the Japanese military ignored civilian officials' pleas to end the war. Three days after the atomic bomb on Hiroshima, the imperial army's chief of staff assured the civilian government that a foreign invasion of Japan would be turned back. Informed of the second atomic bomb on Nagasaki, he repeated his claim. Despite this, on 14 August Hirohito prepared a surrender announcement. That night, 1,000 army members attempted a coup by surrounding the Imperial Palace, executing the emperor's guard commander and searching for the emperor's surrender edict. The coup was thwarted, and Japan surrendered on 15 August.

A significant boost to Japan's remarkable economic recovery was the Korean War (1950–53), during which the country benefited from a huge procurement trade, manufacturing goods for the American military. Japan's role in the war stimulated investment in equipment and industrial plants, and increased the country's confidence in competing on the international market. By the start of the 1960s, Japan's GNP had risen to fifth place in the world and Prime Minister Hayato Ikeda introduced a plan to double incomes by 1970. His goal was achieved in just seven years.

The funeral of Emperor Hirohito in 1989.

During post-war reconstruction, government regulation had served Japan's interests well. But as Japan joined the advanced industrial economies in the 1960s and 1970s, the one-way nature of Japan's markets strained relations with others, especially the US, its largest market, and Europe. Over-regulation and chummy business–government relationships saddled consumers with ridiculously high prices. High rates of household savings created excess capital, used by business and the government for funding massive infrastructure projects. The economy accelerated with uncanny momentum, surpassing every other country except the United States. Japan became the new global paradigm for success and potency. The stock market was on a trajectory that, in the late 1980s, momentarily exceeded the New York Stock Exchange in volume and vigour. Real estate in Japan became the planet's most valuable, and banks dished out money, securing the loans with highly overvalued land. Japan's rising sun seemed, for the moment, to outshine most of the world.

Heisei Period (1989–)

Emperor Hirohito died in 1989, the longest-reigning emperor (62 years) in Japan's recorded history. His son, Akihito, took the throne and adopted the period name of *Heisei*, which means "attainment of peace". He and his family have made sustained efforts to humanise the imperial family and to deal tangentially with Japan's brutal past. But as a politically neutered figurehead, the emperor is not permitted to address politics, history or his father's place in history.

Atop the cauldron of hyper-inflated land values, Japan's "bubble economy" superheated in the late 1980s, only to begin collapsing in 1990. The stock market lost half its value in a short time, banks lost still unspeakable amounts on loans secured by deflated land values, and a blossoming Japanese self-righteousness as economic superpower took a cold shower. The country went into a recession that has continued into the new millennium.

In politics, life at the very top remained very good. For nearly four decades, one political party *has* dominated Japan – the dubiously named Liberal Democratic Party, or LDP. Institutionalised and immune to legal redress, *seiji fuhai*, or political corruption, festered unimpeded at the highest corporate and governmental levels. By the 1980s, *The Economist* opined that the ruling LDP government seemed to be "choking on its own corruption".

WHAT KIND OF ARMY?

Article 9 of the post-war constitution, set up by the US, prohibits Japan from possessing or having the potential of an external military force. However, in 2014 the government voted to lift the ban on a Japanese army fighting overseas, in the most serious shift in the country's military stance since 1945. Currently, the *Jieitai*, or Self-Defence Force (SDF), which is technically an extension of the police force, exists in place of a military. In reality the SDF is a sophisticated military entity and one of the world's strongest armies, which already concerns Japan's neighbours. The SDF's responsibility extends 1,600km (1,000 miles) from Japan's shores.

The LDP fell from grace in 1993 in an unusual backlash by voters, to be replaced by a coalition government. The LDP resuscitated itself by returning to control in 1996. By mid-1999 the party had formed a coalition with the Liberal Party and the new Komeito Party.

Disasters strike

Two events within two months in the mid-1990s eroded Japanese self-confidence and world opinion yet further. In January of 1995, an earthquake hit Kobe, an important coastal port near Osaka. Kobe had been declared a low-risk area for earthquakes. The Great Hanshin Earthquake, as it has been named, killed more than 5,000 people and left 300,000 homeless. Fires from igniting gas mains (said to be earthquake-proof) incinerated entire neighbourhoods of poorly constructed residences; elevated expressways and *shinkansen* rails toppled over like matchwood. Subway tunnels collapsed. Moreover, the local and national government response was nothing short of inept.

Two months after the Kobe earthquake, another event decimated Japanese confidence. In the heart of Tokyo, 12 people died and thousands were injured when the Tokyo subway system was flooded with sarin, a lethal nerve gas. It was in the middle of rush hour, and the prime target was Kasumigaseki Station, the subway stop for offices of the national government and parliament. The effect on the Japanese psyche was indescribable. The Japanese had long prided themselves on being perhaps the safest nation in the world, and believed that Japanese could not engage in lethal terrorism against other Japanese, but the nerve-gas attack had been seemingly random.

The sarin gas attack – and other deadly deeds uncovered by investigators – were traced to a religious cult, Aum Shinrikyo, led by a nearly blind self-proclaimed prophet.

Economic decline

The grimmest and most obvious fallout from Japan's economic decline, now well into its third decade, has been cynicism towards politicians, reflected in the humiliating losses at the polls by the LDP in the 2009 general election, resulting in the overwhelming victory of the Democratic Party of Japan (DPJ). With a succession of ineffectual

The Great Seto Bridge across the Inland Sea.

BUILDING, BUT FOR WHOM?

One of the major engines of growth in post-war Japan has been the construction industry. Following the war, most of Japan's infrastructure had to be rebuilt. Thirty years later, this development had become institutionalised to the point that it was a major political tool. Much of this money to fund lavish building projects comes from Japan's postal savings and pension funds. Public opinion has lately veered round to the belief that many of these projects are useless efforts solely for politicians' gain and glory.

Bullet-train lines have inexplicably been built to backwater towns. Two huge and quite expensive bridges between Shikoku and Honshu carry less than half the traffic that planners claimed, and tolls are more than US$50 one way. The world's longest (9.5km/6-mile) underwater tunnel, the Aqualine Expressway under Tokyo Bay, which opened in 1998, is rarely used, perhaps because of a US$40 toll and because it goes nowhere important. In the 1980s, Tokyo's former governor initiated an immense "sub-city" in Tokyo Bay at an estimated cost of US$100 billion. The city intended to sell or lease reclaimed land for huge profits, but then the economy's collapse instead put Tokyo deep in debt.

Successive recent prime ministers have come to power on the platform of structural reform. The battle over who really runs the country, though, continues.

leaders, however, the DPJ failed to staunch Japan's economic decline.

This was compounded by unprecedented levels of social destabilisation, an increase in crime, suicide and homelessness. Aware of Japan's vulnerability, American and European companies returned to Japan to buy up property and increase their market share of banking and other financial services. The success of an aggressive, highly motivated China, its enormous reserves of wealth and political clout, its ability to engage with governments in emerging economies, to access the resources and raw materials it requires to sustain

Damage caused by ships swept on land by the 2011 tsunami.

Japan's government is called a parliamentary democracy. The prime minister, of the majority party, comes from the Diet. The emperor is head of state.

its growth, flabbergasted many people, as the Japanese economy slipped and floundered into third place in world ranking, behind the United States and China. The emergence of South Korean companies like Samsung and LG Electronics and Japan's inability to compete with the design cool of makers like Apple, badly hit the country's much-vaunted electronic sector. The sense of crisis felt by once titanic companies like Sony, Sharp

and Panasonic, the engines of Japan's post-war growth, were compounded by the prospect that these giants could fall into irreversible decline. These troubling developments were exacerbated by a series of corporate scandals and setbacks, including Toyota's recall of millions of cars suspected of design faults. .

The magnitude-9 Great East Japan Earthquake of March 2011, the tsunami and radioactive meltdown it triggered, was a major setback to the immediate prospect of recovery and rebirth. The fact that the government was keenly aware of the levels of risk posed by the nuclear accident, but chose to conceal the truth from the public, served to deepen the public's distrust of a risk-averse political system, one characterised by a diffuse leadership reluctant to accept personal responsibility. As the world watched in appalled thrall the events of 11 March 2011, two things emerged: the duplicity of government, contrasted with the resilience, selflessness and stoicism of the Japanese, a people with the ability to come to terms with tragedy and the realities it dictates.

The DPJ was subsequently ejected from power as the LDP won a landslide victory in early parliamentary elections in 2012. On the appointment of his cabinet Prime Minister Abe Shinzo pledged to boost economic growth. Success came in 2013, when the weak yen resulted in export rises of over 10 percent. When the economy slipped back into recession in 2014, Abe called for snap elections to renew the mandate for his policies. Losing merely three out of 294 seats, the LDP retained its parliamentary majority.

Abe's economic policies, dubbed "Abenomics", aim to set the inflation rate at two percent, correcting excessive yen appreciation and stimulating private investment. As of 2015, there are signs of a continuing recovery from recession, although growth remains subdued. Economic malaise and structural reforms aside, the government also faces such challenges as growing tensions with China and Russia over the disputed Senkaku and Kuril islands, and reversing Japan's withdrawal from their nuclear energy programme following the Fukushima Daiichi nuclear disaster, which – as it turned out – had been largely man-made.

Two years after the triple calamity of earthquake, tsunami and nuclear meltdown, Tokyo won their bid to host the 2020 Summer Olympics, which has lifted the hopes of a sustained recovery and the stimulation of economic growth, as well as a huge psychological boost to the nation. .

Japan's royal family

The Japanese monarchy is the oldest existing hereditary monarchy in the world; its head, the emperor, is the symbol of the state.

Royal mania hit a high on 9 June 1993, when tens of thousands of well-wishers turned out for a glimpse of the royal couple, Princess Masako and Crown Prince Naruhito, the heir to Japan's 2,600-year-old Chrysanthemum Throne.

A graduate of Tokyo, Oxford and Harvard universities and fluent in several languages, Owada Masako gave up a promising diplomatic career to marry Crown Prince Naruhito. Hopes, however, that she would become a "royal diplomat" who would give a human face to the Imperial Court were quickly dashed by the notoriously protocol-ridden Imperial Household Agency, and the princess was soon seen behaving in the self-effacing tradition of female royals.

In December 2001 Masako gave birth to a girl, Princess Aiko. As the practice of crowning a female as empress was terminated under the 1889 Meiji Constitution, which now limited the throne to male descendants, there was considerable pressure on Masako to produce a male heir, even as she grew older. After the birth of her daughter, she stayed largely out of the public eye, making only rare official appearances. The Agency has not been able to muzzle the reasons for Masako's long absence from public view. Hospitalised first in December 2003 with shingles, a stress-induced viral infection, she was said to have suffered from an "adjustment disorder" in 2004.

A history of repression

Masako's problems were not the first of their kind in the modern history of the court. In 1963, after a miscarriage, Empress Michiko, then Crown Princess, went into a three-month-long retreat at the Imperial Villa. The first commoner to marry into the monarchy, she had to deal with hostility for the miscarriage from both the Agency and other royals. In a series of nervous disorders, the empress lost her voice for several months in 1993 due to "strong feelings of distress".

At a press conference on 10 May 2004, Crown Prince Naruhito made surprisingly blunt comments in defence of his wife, hinting that members of the Agency were complicit in repressing his wife's personality and gifts.

In 2006, the succession crisis was resolved after Princess Kiko, the wife of the crown prince's younger brother Akishino, gave birth to a male heir, Prince Hisahito, who is third in line to the throne after his uncle and father. The pressure on the crown prince's family continues, but in recent years, Princess Masako has made a few key public appearances, even undertaking some overseas engagements, fuelling hopes that her condition has improved.

Attempts were made by the Agency to halt the publication in 2006 of a controversial book by Australian journalist Ben Hills, *Princess Masako: Prisoner of the Chrysanthemum Throne*, which claimed that, like the

Japan's royal family: from left, Japan's Emperor Akihito, Crown Princess Masako and Empress Michiko.

empress before her, Masako's health and happiness had been sabotaged by Agency repression.

The Masako story is interesting in what it reveals about the influence of the Imperial Household Agency and the way the media in Japan works, or fails to work, with regard to the royal family. Although it was an open secret among the press that Naruhito and Masako's wedding was scheduled for June 1993, a directive from the Agency extracted a vow of silence. It was not until early that year that the story was broken – by journalist T.R. Reid of The Washington Post. The bamboo curtain has lifted a little since then, and stories have been covered by independent magazines in anonymously sourced articles, but for most Japanese publications such reporting remains off-limits.

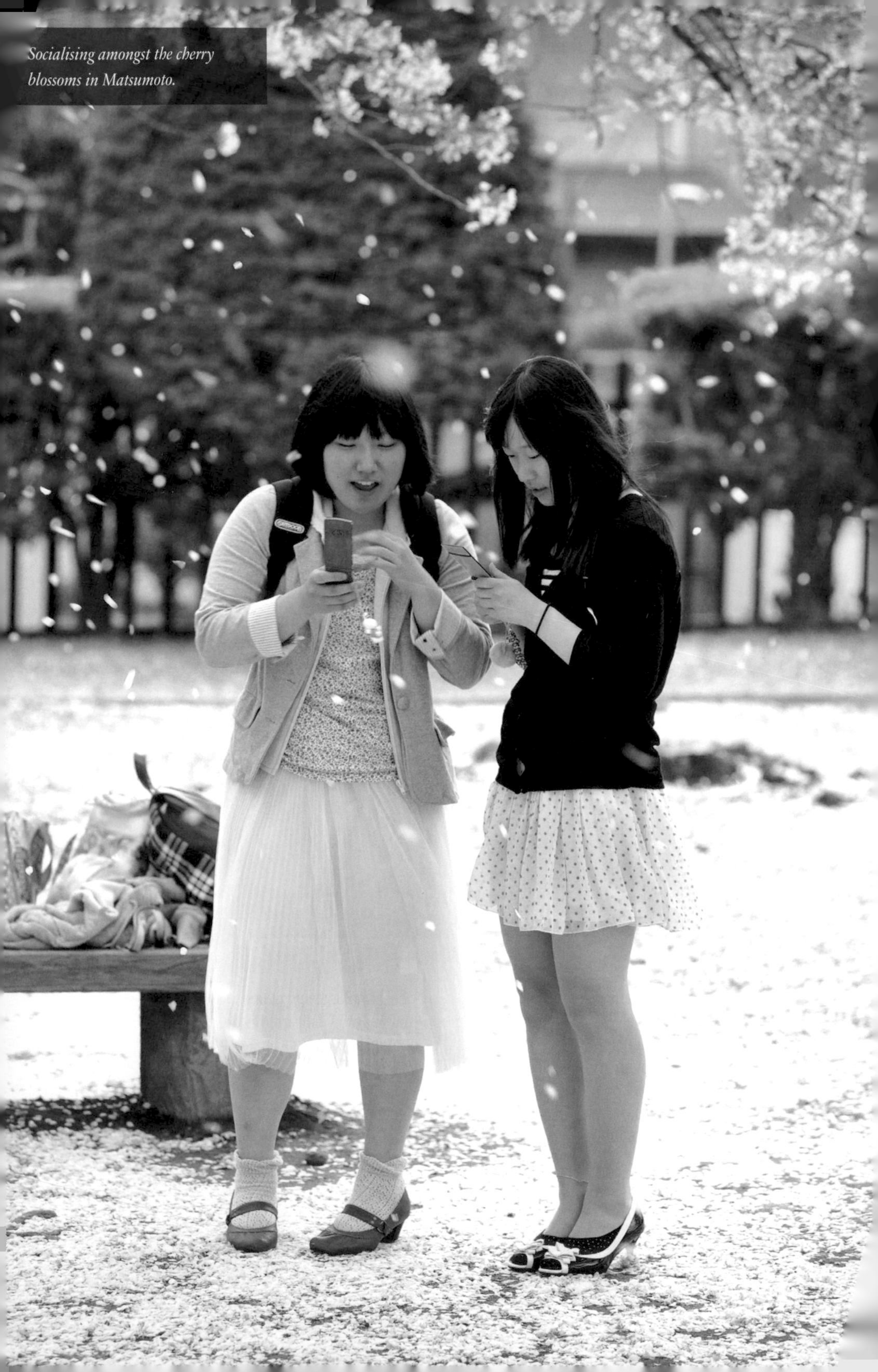

Socialising amongst the cherry blossoms in Matsumoto.

LIVING IN MODERN JAPAN

A place where social harmony is prized, Japan is beginning to embrace diversity and a more individual sense of identity.

There is an insistence on cultural stereo-types that often makes them too conveni-ently well entrenched to bother disputing. In the case of Japan they are myriad. The coun-try, we are told, is a rice culture, despite the fact that before this crop was introduced from China, wheat cultivation and hunting were the order of the day. The Japanese, we are assured, are a monolithic ethnic family, although the Japanese, representing a melting pot that takes its ingredients from as far afield as Mongolia and Polynesia, are perhaps one of the most eth-nically diverse and therefore most interesting of the Asian peoples.

Stereotypically, of whatever size or purpose, the group defines for the Japanese a person's individual purpose and function. And the group known as the Japanese – *nihon-jin*, or if especially nationalistic, *nippon-jin* – is the mother of all groups. Not exactly an irreverent comment, given that Amaterasu Omikami, or Sun Goddess, is the mythological foremother of the Japanese themselves. Television com-mentators and politicians repeatedly refer to *ware-ware Nippon-jin*, or "we Japanese" and the implicit definition of what "we Japanese" are or aren't, do or don't do, believe or don't believe. The compulsion to define identity even shows up in advertising.

Japanese origins

The Japanese sense of uniqueness extends down to a basic identity of a race and culture distinct from others. But the objective evidence strongly points to origins from the mainland.

From the 3rd century BC, waves of human migration from the Asian continent entered the Japanese archipelago, bringing along rice culti-vation (including the use of tools), metallurgy

Strolling through the streets of Tokyo.

THE AINU

The population of the Ainu people today numbers around 25,000, yet they were early inhabitants of Hokkaido and also northern Honshu. Their origins are unclear; it was once thought that they were of Caucasian heritage, but blood and skeletal research strongly suggests connections with Siberia's Uralic population. Nowadays there are few speakers of Ainu, which has much in com-mon with other northern Asian languages and also with languages of Southeast Asia and some Pacific cultures. Traditional Ainu culture was one of hunting and gathering. Bears and salmon had an especially sacred place in Ainu traditions.

and different social structures. These migrations are now considered to have brought the ancestors of today's Japanese people, the Yamato, who displaced and pushed the resident – and decidedly different – Jomon population into the northern regions or other less desirable areas of the archipelago.

Theories regarding the racial origins of the Japanese cite both the north and the south – Manchuria and Siberia, and the South China or Indochina regions – as likely possibilities. Students of the subject differ as to which origin to favour. The southern physical type is,

of course, the Malay; the northern type is the Mongolian. Today, both north and south Asia are considered equally valid as likely origins of the Japanese. Still, the precise configuration of the migrations and the cultural traits associated with areas of origin is subject to argument. (Toss in, too, other legitimate theories about migrations from Polynesia or Micronesia.)

There was substantial human immigration later – in addition to cultural and artistic influences – from the Korean Peninsula, a point vehemently denied by Japanese nationalists and racial purists despite the overwhelming archaeological and anthropological evidence. Whereas archaeology in many countries is considered the most neutral of disciplines, without political overtones of any kind, in Japan it is rife with factions and rivalries. One group of "experts" in Japan has steadfastly refuted and rejected most modern, scientific dating methods, particularly when they are used to authenticate theories proposing a Japan–Korea connection. A breakthrough of sorts in the gridlock of denial came in 2001, when Emperor Akihito, in a speech on his 68th birthday, included a statement that the mother of Emperor Kanmu came from the former Paekche Kingdom of Korea, a clear acknowledgement of blood links between the two nations and royal lineage.

It may also be possible that the Korean and Japanese languages were mutually understandable, if not identical, some 2,000 years ago and that the people on the Korean Peninsula and the Japanese archipelago may have shared a common culture.

Shopping on Takeshita Street in Harajuku, Tokyo.

THE HINOMARU

When Okinawan Shoichi Chibana, the unassuming owner of a small supermarket, set fire to the *Hinomaru*, Japan's national flag, many people in the islands applauded the act, or at least empathised with it. Used as a shield to defend the emperor at the end of the war, and then occupied by the US until 1972, Okinawans have good reason to detest the flag as a symbol of oppression. For ordinary Japanese, feelings tend to be more ambivalent.

Visitors often note the lack of national flags displayed in public in Japan. The absence of visible nationalism, the cautious approach to patriotism, has its origin in the discomfort felt by many Japanese towards the period of indoctrination and thought-control they identify with Japan's wartime experience.

The displays of fringe extremism at Yasukuni Shrine in Tokyo, where the remains of convicted war criminals are interred, are an embarrassment to many Japanese, and reflect how deeply conflicted many people feel about the flag as a symbol of nationalism. Showings of the flag coincide with singing of the national anthem, the *Kimigayo*, another area of contention, especially among schoolteachers, some of whom have refused to sing or bow towards the flag. While nobody questions their love of country, many Japanese recoil from nationalism, yet the government presses them to be more patriotic.

Unique or arrogant?

Perhaps the most substantial insulator of Japan from the outside is the modern language, which is spoken only in the islands. In fact, the grammar and syntax are considerably easier than those of most Germanic or Romance languages.

Some Japanese will retort, however, that it is undoubtedly one of the world's most difficult languages to learn. The language itself isn't, but the context of usage can be confusing and difficult for those not brought up within the Japanese culture. The increase in the number of non-Japanese speakers of the language has led to perceptions changing from an astonishment at the foreigner speaking Japanese to an expectation that anyone who stays long enough should know the language.

The undercurrent in Japanese thinking and in Japanese traditions that all things Japanese, including the race, are "special", if not unique, is undergoing some re-examination. The former conviction that outsiders were incapable of fully appreciating – much less understanding – the distinctions and nuances of *being* Japanese and of Japanese ways has altered to a genuine appreciation of non-Japanese who do.

It was not always like this. It once seemed as if, to those who stayed long enough, and listened to the conversation and media, that only Japan had earthquakes, typhoons, tasty rice, misery, hot weather, bad memories of war, trees that change colour in autumn, snowfall, and fast trains. When French ski manufacturers first tried to export skis to Japan several decades ago, the Japanese government declared the skis unsuitable for the special and unique Japanese snow. Later, in the late 1980s when American beef producers were trying to increase exports to the Japanese market, the agriculture ministry argued that only Japanese beef was suitable for the special and unique digestive systems of the Japanese people. In the 1990s, respected university researchers even claimed that the Japanese were genetically unique in their ability to appreciate to the fullest the sounds of nature like crickets and waterfalls.

These days, with many Japanese enjoying extended periods abroad, contact with foreigners living in their midst, and an economy that is nothing if not global, many of these assumptions are being questioned and the sense of a uniquely different identity undermined.

Living on eggshells

In a country where physical crowding and complex interpersonal relationships have shaped the language and social manners over the centuries, even the slightest chance of offending, disappointing or inconveniencing another person is couched in a shower of soft words, bows and grave smiles. (Or worse, giggles, a sure signal of acute embarrassment or being uncomfortable.)

The extreme urban density in which the Japanese live has been somewhat relieved by extending city boundaries, the building of more

School children bow to their tour guide at Chuson Temple, Tohoku.

spacious apartment blocks and condominiums, and the preference for smaller families. They have been able to live in close quarters because of their instinctive good manners and mutual respect. The Japanese must be the last race on earth to bow in the normal course of their daily lives, a gesture that can mean apology, gratitude, greeting or farewell, and is a reminder of the courtly practices of a former age in many other countries.

There are few places where the virtues of selflessness are so vigorously applied. Part of this consideration for others devolves from the distaste for confrontation and the idea of avoiding any cause for *meiwaku* (bother, annoyance) to other people. Language itself, embodying an elaborate system of honorifics and inclining towards the deferential, plays an important part in maintaining an extraordinary level of civility throughout these congested islands.

To some foreigners, the Japanese language is excruciatingly indirect, requiring finesse in extracting the proper message. Raised in this social and cultural context, the Japanese easily read between the lines.

Sometimes the Japanese are able to use this to their advantage. Recent prime ministers have made efforts to acknowledge the past despite the vociferous views of right-wing politicians, nationalists and university scholars. Yet the linguistic nuances, when properly translated and understood, reveal not the expected apology as it first seems to be when translated from Japanese, but rather a promise of "reflection" or "remorse concerning unfortunate events", hardly an admission of wrong action or a sincere apology. Much of this, however, is the official position. Engage individuals in discussion on these topics and very different, more informed and measured opinions will often emerge.

Samurai houses in Nagamachi.

LANGUAGE, SOCIETY, GENDER

The Japanese *keigo* (polite language) is a hold-over from the structured class system of feudal times, when politeness was reinforced with a sword. In modern times, *keigo* has been preserved as a key element in the deeply rooted Japanese tradition of deference to one's superiors and of courtesy to guests.

Proper speech is a source of pride for most Japanese, and the use of *keigo* can be an art in itself. Moreover, simply shifting the politeness level up a notch – or down – can have the effect of sarcasm or insult. The younger generation tend to favour simpler language structures.

Perplexing to outsiders are the distinctions between the talk of males and females. Consider the first-person pronoun. Men have the option of several forms, the use of each dependent upon the situation and the people involved: *watakushi, watashi, boku* or *ore,* from most polite to exceedingly casual. Women have fewer options. Modulation and tone of voice also tend to vary between the sexes. Men try to affect a deep rumble, which can approach theatrical proportions. Women often tend to inflect a high, nasalised pitch; this so-called "nightingale voice" is said to be appealing to men.

Again, many of these distinctions are blurring, a fact reflected in the grumbles of an older generation bemused at young women adopting male speech modes and young men affecting more effeminate manners.

Obligations

If apologies are linguistic puzzles, other expressions of social necessity, too, are interesting, if not curious. Strangely, the very word for "thank you" – *arigato* – literally means "You put me in a difficult position". *Oki no doku*, which is an expression of sympathy, means "poisonous feeling". And who would think of expressing regret or apology with *sumimasen*, which in strictly literal translation means "This situation or inconvenience will never end"?

Then there is that virtually untranslatable word, *giri*. To violate *giri* is simply unthinkable. *Giri* is often translated as a sense of duty and honour, but such a definition ignores the subtle communal and personal responsibilities behind *giri*. In Japan, there are unspoken responsibilities inherent by acceptance and participation within a group, whether in a friendship or with co-workers in an office, or in the sharing of communal village life. When the responsibility beckons, and the member of any group can easily recognise it without articulating it, the individual must meet and honour that responsibility while putting aside his or her work or personal desires.

> Marriage between Japanese and foreigners is hardly new, but the numbers have increased. In the past, marriage partners tended to be Westerners. Today many different nationalities form unions, impacting deeply on what is already a much more pluralistic society.

Family values

No doubt there's a proverb somewhere saying that obligation, like charity, begins at home. It's true, for example, that in Japan the eldest child (once only the male but now the female as well) is expected to care for aged parents. Likewise, it is still true that the estate, if any, of a deceased parent automatically passes to the eldest child. In fact, these mutual obligations were once inviolable. Today, however, disputes over care for the aged and for inheritance of wealth are increasingly common and often decided in favour not of the parents or children, but of the national government because of prohibitively high inheritance taxes.

Often cited as the core of Japan's traditional social stability, extended families are nowadays as far removed from the original homestead as education, job opportunities and jet planes can take them. And although nostalgia for the hometown and simpler living have taken on a trendy air in recent years, especially as affluence spreads, the urban family is increasingly defining the contours of Japanese life. On the surface, the family appears both paternal (the man is nominally the household head) and maternal (as women still control the household budget and child-rearing). More opportunities for women in business, however, along with increased affluence and broader appetites

Family day out in Matsushima.

for the good life, are slowly challenging this status quo.

A labour shortage combined with an equal opportunity employment law supposedly reinforced women's position in the workplace, but the law itself has no teeth as it does not carry penalties for companies failing to comply. The number of women in senior management positions remains deplorably low. What does continue to demand a great deal of respect in Japan is being a housewife and mother. The Global Gender Gap Index – which measures gender equality – ranked Japan 104th out of 142 countries in its 2014 survey, a deplorably low position for such a developed country.

In the Japan of pre-World War II, a young man often got married about the time his parents reminded him that he had reached the *tekireiki*, or appropriate marriageable age. His parents would take an active role in the selection of his bride, making sure she bore the markings of a good wife, wise mother and self-sacrificing daughter-in-law. They interviewed the woman's parents. Even birth records were checked (and often still are), ensuring that the woman's family tree had no bad apples or embarrassing branches. Love rarely entered the picture. Parents knew that the couple would

Visiting Dazaifu Temple, Fukuoka.

eventually become fond of each other and maybe become good friends. The wife, having severed the ties to her own family through marriage, adhered to the customs and practices of her husband's family.

Despite the hardships, the wife generally chose to stay married. To divorce meant she would have to face the censure – blame for the marital break-up was all hers – of her own family and that of the community.

The traditional wife follows a pattern that her grandmother followed in the pre-war years. Getting up earlier than her husband and children, she prepares the breakfasts and makes sure everyone gets off to work or school on time. During the day, she does

the housework, goes shopping and manages the daily household accounts. Occasionally, she takes part in activities of the neighbourhood association or of her children's school. She may also enjoy leisure activities such as learning a foreign language. At night, she and the children will eat together, since her husband comes home much later in the evening. Upon his return, she will serve him (and his relatives, if present) his dinner and sit with him while he eats.

While the above is not as common or automatic as before, it is still a marital paradigm in both cities and rural areas. Yet some husbands, like their wives, have been exposed to Western lifestyles and trends and make an effort at being liberated men in the Western sense, cultural biases aside.

> *Batsu-ichi ("one X") is a nickname for those who are divorced. When a person gets divorced, an X is put through the spouse's name in the government's family registry.*

Accelerating this process of change is the dramatic increase in the number of divorce cases since the 1990s, a reflection of the growing desire of spouses, particularly wives, to fulfil personal aspirations over those of the family. Some wives file for divorce when husbands retire from their jobs, demanding half of the husband's severance pay.

Some couples divorce before they even get started on a proper married life. It's called a Narita divorce. Modern Japanese women have usually spent more time travelling overseas than their new husbands, who may never have been outside Japan because of the emphasis on career. Their first jaunt overseas, perhaps a honeymoon, is ripe with tension and ends in disaster because the woman is more self-reliant than the man. After returning home to Narita, Tokyo's international airport, they divorce.

Changing attitudes and the greater tolerance towards later or no marriage, childless couples, divorcees, single mothers, and the sense that such groups are no longer socially defective, has come less from a bolt of progressive enlightenment than the sheer numbers, the fact that so many people now fall into one or more of these categories.

Essential education

In the 6th century, Japan adopted major elements of Chinese culture, including Chinese ideographs, Buddhism and Confucianism, not to mention a heavily bureaucratic system of government that persists today. Education was based on the meritocratic selection of talented individuals, later to be bureaucrats, who would then be taught to read and write the *Analects* of Confucius and works related to Buddhism. This Chinese system of education and civil service was absorbed within Japanese society. With the rise of the Tokugawa clan to power

model was essentially American in structure: six years of elementary school, three years of junior high school and three years of high school. The first nine years were compulsory.

> *Hikikomori, or shut-ins, people who never leave their homes, are not peculiar to Japan, but their estimated numbers are: around a million, of whom 80 percent are male. Often their only connection with the outside world is via technology.*

A tour group at Kaiyukan Aquarium, Osaka.

in 1603, the pursuit of Western knowledge was strictly limited and controlled, and the study of Buddhist works declined in favour of Confucian ethics.

During the feudal period, education was available to common people in *terakoya*. (*Tera* means temple and *koya* refers to a small room.) These one-room temple schools offered the masses instruction in the written language and certain practical subjects, such as the use of the abacus and elementary arithmetic. Texts were similar to the Chinese classics used by the samurai. Many of the teachers were monks.

Defeat in 1945 brought to Japan a total reformation of the educational system. The new

Entrance to higher education is determined by dreaded examinations, which are administered by the individual universities; for each school applied to for admission, a complete set of entrance exams must be endured. There is no universal university admissions exam.

To help them reach the goal of passing the examinations, parents budget a considerable amount of their monthly income to send children to *juku*, or private cram schools, which are a multibillion-yen business. For the most disciplined of students, every night and weekend is spent at *juku* having their brains crammed with exam-passing information. It is all learned by rote and not deduction.

There is no doubt that the Japanese are united in a consensus that education is essential for social cohesion, economic prosperity and prestige in the international arena. Unfortunately, both in the primary and university levels, form and rote usually take precedence over function and knowledge. Students are taught not analysis and discourse, but rather only the information needed to pass exams for entrance into the next level of their schooling.

Education is respected in Japan, and so are educators. In fact, the honorific for teacher – *sensei*, as in *Nakamura-sensei* – is the same as for

Uchiko Town, Shikoku

physicians. Unfortunately, the responsibility and professional pressure placed upon them is considerable, especially at the high-school level when students are preparing for their university exams. Holidays are rare for the teachers.

Even the Japanese themselves admit their educational system's shortcomings. The excessive emphasis on entrance examinations is a cause of much national concern and debate, as is the alienation of significant numbers of young people, violence in schools and bullying of pupils. The effectiveness and desirability of many of the orthodox teaching approaches are increasingly being questioned, and reforms are being considered. In the field of English, for example, several thousand

native speakers, applying more innovative, interactive methods of learning, are employed at both state and privately run schools. Universities themselves are trying to attract more foreign students, a response in part to a troubling decline in the interest shown by young people in studying abroad that has led to much hand-wringing about the lack of ambition among youth.

Generation gap

Few would contest that the majority of Japanese young people are positive, well-adjusted

> The suicide rate in Japan remains one of the highest among developed nations, although it has dropped significantly in recent years. The country has dropped to having the seventh highest rate in the world, with around 20 suicides per 100,000 people.

people with a sharper interest in and responsibility towards social issues and the need to be good global citizens than their elders. Older people, on the other hand, aided and abetted by the more established media, are apt to blame the growing insularity of Japanese youth for many of the country's troubles and its gloomy prospects.

To the young, the older generation seem soulless money-grabbers; while older people are quickly apt to label the younger generation as inward-looking, lethargic, passive and disengaged. The expression *shoshoku-danshi*, meaning herbivores or grass-eating men, is a derogative expression for flip-floppy youth, a generation that, without ambition or personal drive, are more interested in their pastimes and personal relationships than work. A more accurate picture is that, rather than aimless, they are victims of parents, cultural icons and leaders who have failed to offer them a road map for the future.

Japan's Ivy League

Japanese social institutions in general, and schools in particular, are arranged hierarchically in terms of their ability to bestow economic and social status. The university heavyweights are all in Tokyo – Keio, Waseda, but above all Tokyo University, or Todai. No institution ranks higher.

Even Oxbridge and Yale pale beside Todai, an institute that inspires both awe and fierce competition for entrance. The few who make it past its hallowed gates are virtually guaranteed a life of privilege. To prove the point, 80 percent of post-war prime ministers hail from Todai, while 90 percent of civil servants in the prestigious Finance and Home Affairs ministries call it their alma mater, and the same number in the all-important Trade and Industry Ministry.

Such orthodoxy belies Todai's radical past. In 1969, students organised a protest against the university system, barricading themselves in the lecture hall. The stand-off only ended when riot police fully armed with tear gas moved in and arrested 600 students.

Working life

If the aim of education in Japan is essentially to obtain a well-paid job with a prestigious company, the chances of reaching that goal in Japan's current economic climate have faded for many Japanese. The term *kakusa shakai*, made from the words "gap" and "society," came into vogue in the early 1990s, reflecting a growing perception that a social contract that promised to deliver on the idea of an upwardly mobile middle class had defaulted. The consequent erosion of that class after decades of meagre growth and social-policy stagnation has created disparities between the affluent and a new underclass, inequality and a troubling bifurcation in the labour market.

The collapse of the kind of lifetime employment packages the larger companies were able to provide to a relatively small percentage of the

workforce, together with the introduction of the almost universal five-day week, has changed perceptions, encouraging a view that work and leisure are not incompatible, that job-hopping can improve your prospects, and that pursuing hobbies and interests, and making room for more family and private time, are important life goals.

Driven by the need for cost saving, there has been a near doubling in the number of non-regular workers over the past two decades. As welfare systems and safety nets are largely designed to protect regular workers,

Office workers with face masks, Tohoku.

CASTE AWAY

First there were the *eta* and *hinin*, the lowest orders of the Edo Period class system. All of that was supposed to have been abolished in 1871 with the issuing of the Emancipation Edict, but discrimination is not so easily uprooted, and for many Japanese, their descendants, known as *burakumin*, have remained "impure". Outcasts were assigned the very worst jobs, working as gravediggers, tanners, executioners, butchers, and as performers in the lowest ranks of the entertainment world. No physical differences distinguish the *burakumin* today from ordinary Japanese, yet illegal lists of *burakumin*, of whom there are at least 3 million, are often bought by corporations wishing to avoid them as job applicants.

Books, film and the media have often portrayed the modern day *burakumin* as members of Japan's criminal underworld. For many outcasts this has been the only way to make a living. The great Noh playwright Zeami, however, was a member of the sensui *kawaramono*, or "riverbank people". Others made their mark in the *bunraku* puppet theatre, as garden designers, kyogen comedy performers and *taiko* drummers. Eminent novelists Mishima Yukio and Yasunari Kawabata are said to have had *buraku* roots, as did the popular *enka* singer Hibari Misora. In more recent times, the influential LDP politician, Hiromu Nonaka, made a point in his early speeches of acknowledging his *buraku* origins.

the one-third of the workforce now engaged in temporary work, often dead-end jobs that provide no health insurance coverage, social security benefits or pension programmes, are facing a bleak future as the "working poor", as the media has dubbed them.

Japan has been slow to expand its human resources, particularly in promoting the participation of women in the labour market and the hiring of more foreigners, although some firms like Uniqlo, Rakuten and Softbank have begun actively to recruit native English-speaking staff for their stores.

Characters in the America-Mura district of Osaka.

Allowing immigrant labour into the market remains a contentious issue. From the Japanese perspective, the difficulties with multi-ethnicity in European countries like Britain, France and Germany has lent legitimacy to Japan's reluctance to open its doors to unskilled foreign workers and immigration, though the number of permanent, mostly qualified, foreigners living in the country is increasing.

Sweet uniformity

The idea that you are what you wear, that "these are my clothes, ergo this is my role", is nowhere more evident than in Japan. Conformism, still a powerful force in Japanese society, lends itself naturally to uniformism. Individuality, as far as it exists – and it does – is generally of the kind that remains compatible with social rules. Even the radical urge is to be shared with others of a similar disposition.

Uniforms by their very nature unify, suggest strength in numbers – the perfect sartorial solution for a society that remains, despite all the surface experimentation, relatively rigid and tribal. Even Japanese youth, wearing clothes and accessories that highlight infinitesimal differences from the general pattern, have a way of suggesting that they are cut from the same cloth, part of a common weave.

Even the national costume, the kimono, categorises those who wear it into clearly defined groups conforming to certain unwritten rules and conventions of dress: young women are encouraged to wear

OKINAWAN LONGEVITY

Few people know how to age better than Okinawa's old folks. Sharp minds and physical vigour among those advanced in age may be a rarity in other parts of the world, but in these southern islands it's commonplace. Okinawa may have the highest proportion of centenarians in the world, with around 50 for every 100,000 people. That compares with about 10 to the same number of Americans. The authors of a best-selling book on longevity called *The Okinawa Program* (2001) discovered that elderly Okinawans have astonishingly clean arteries and low levels of cholesterol, and that heart disease and breast and prostate cancer are rare. The writers concluded that this enviable condition was attributable to the consumption of large amounts of tofu, seaweed and locally grown vegetables, regular exercise and a low-stress lifestyle.

In an effort to wean kids off burgers and cup noodles, so the young could live at least as long as their grandparents, the prefectural government launched its own health education programme. School meals now include such tried and tested local dishes as stir-fried papaya, *goya* (bitter melon) and egg, boiled pork, and rice with *wakame* (soft seaweed), in an attempt to return to their culinary roots. A case, perhaps, of the wisdom of the ages?

bright, vibrant colours that offset their youth, older women to don more muted hues that bespeak their maturity.

Shibuya, Harajuku and Shinjuku remain the centres of Tokyo's theatre of dress. Harajuku in particular is the fusion point where the assertion of Western individualism gets absorbed into oriental formalism. Here you will chance upon costumes reflecting almost every Anglo-Saxon popular culture fashion since the 1950s: from black-shirted Elvis clones, Minnie Mouse imitators, the checked shirts and chewed-up jeans of rockabilly hicks, the billowing, rainbow-coloured rags of hippie psychedelia, to post-punk and hip-hop.

While a few renegade brown and sand-coloured suits are occasionally glimpsed in commuter carriages, there isn't a great deal of colour on an average day, where black, grey and serge suits dominate among the male, white-collar class, forming an almost unbroken uniformity of taste. The only member of an institution daring enough to wear a purple suit in public is the gang or syndicate-affiliated thug, who is also, as a special concession to his outlaw status, allowed to sport ties printed with surfboards, cocktail sticks and naked women.

Oldest society in human history

In 2014, the number of centenarians in Japan reached almost 59,000. Most were women. In 1965, there were only 150 Japanese centenarians; by 1993, there were 5,000. Okawa Misao, who died in 2015 at the age of 117, was the oldest Japanese person ever. The Japanese are living longer and having fewer children, and the skewed demographics are worrying government planners. The birth rate of 1.4 children per woman is resulting in Japan becoming one of the world's oldest societies. The median age was over 46 in 2014, matched in the world only by Germany. Japan's 65-plus generation accounted for nearly 26 percent of the population in 2014, but it will reach 40 percent by 2060.

Japan as a whole has a negative population growth rate of -0.13 percent. It is expected that the number of people will shrink to under 100 million by 2050, compared to some 127 million today. Many analysts believe that the ageing population, more than anything else, is the major factor behind Japan's demise as a world economic leader as the economy shifts to support a population of which at least a quarter is in retirement.

The reasons for this low growth rate are not hard to find. Japanese women enjoy the longest life expectancy in the world, which stands at 87, for men it is 80. Furthermore, the overcrowded cities, where couples live in cramped apartments, occasionally with parents, are not conducive to large families, nor are the phenomenal costs of education and urban life.

Exploring the Sankozo Museum, Chuson Temple, Tohoku.

Of concern is the cost of providing retirement pensions and old-age benefits. In order to maintain the Japanese pension system over the coming decades it will be necessary to raise the retirement age or allow more immigration. There has already been a hike in sales tax to 8 percent to make up for the income tax shortfall. Another concern is nursing care, which will become an important problem. And as the population ages, the savings rate will drop, causing interest rates to rise and depleting the government's largest source of operating capital.

Japan may be the most over-analysed nation on earth, but the fact that issues like these are being openly debated hints also at the more vibrant civil society Japan has become.

The Giant Lantern at Senso-ji, Asakusa.

RELIGION

To the outsider, the adaptability of worship and philosophy may seem contradictory and diffused. To the Japanese, beliefs are pragmatic and without hypocrisy.

Polls asking Japanese in which religion they believe consistently yield results that total well over 100 percent – most say they are followers of both Shinto and Buddhism. The average Japanese thinks nothing of marrying at a Shinto shrine, burying loved ones in a Buddhist cemetery and boisterously celebrating Christmas. Although the devout Christian or Muslim – each with a monotheistic God demanding unswerving fidelity – might find this religious promiscuity hard to fathom, the typical Japanese sees no contradiction.

Traditionally, nearly every home was once equipped with a *kamidana*, a god-shelf with Shinto symbols, or else a *butsudan*, a Buddhist household altar containing memorials for the family's ancestors before which offerings of flowers, food, drink or incense are made daily. Most homes had both, and many still do.

The Japanese definitely seem to have a sense of religious piety and spiritual yearning, although it is very different from that in the West. The main difference seems to be that the line between the sacred and the profane is much less clearly drawn in Japan. In many ways, community life and religion are one and the same. Similarly, the distinction between good and bad, or sinful and righteous, is less clear in Japanese society. It is said that the West considers most things as black or white; in Japan, as elsewhere in Asia, there is a lot of grey.

Shinto

A basic understanding of the Japanese religious sensibility must begin with Shinto, which influences virtually every aspect of Japanese culture and society. It is hard to give any simple definition of Shinto (literally, way of the gods,

Devotees at Dazaifu Temple, Fukuoka.

or *kami*), since it is not a systematised set of beliefs. There is no dogmatic set of rules nor even any holy script. The term *shinto* was not even invented until after the introduction of Buddhism, a date traditionally given as AD 552, and then only as a way of contrasting the native beliefs with that imported faith.

In general, it can be said that Shinto shares with many other animistic beliefs the concept that all natural objects and phenomena possess a spiritual side. It is this animism – mixed with ancestor worship, a shared trait with Buddhism – that characterises Shinto. A tree, for example, was revered by the ancient Japanese as a source of food, warmth, shelter and even clothing. For that reason, when a great tree was felled to provide wood for the Buddhist temple complexes at Nara or Kyoto, it was not used for several years in order to give the spirit within time to depart safely. Mountains, forests and even the oceans were also revered.

It should be recognised that the term *kami*, although often translated as "god", is quite different from the Western concept of divinity. The classic definition, as originally understood in Japan, was made by the 18th-century scholar Moto-ori Norinaga: "Anything whatsoever which was outside the ordinary, which

possessed superior power, or which was awe-inspiring, was called *kami*."

In ancient Shinto there was also a belief in a kind of soul – *tamashii* – that lived on after death. An unrefined form of ancestor worship also existed, remnants of which can be seen in the observances of the spring and autumn equinoxes and in the Obon festivities in early autumn, which in Japan have both Shinto and Buddhist overtones.

Early Shinto had concepts of heaven and hell as well, although they were hazily conceived at best. There was no concept of sin, divine retribution or absolution for offenses committed. It was commonly thought that the dead would eventually be reborn into this world, just as spring returns after winter.

Atsuta Shrine, Nagoya.

> Prior to the arrival of Buddhism in the 6th century, Shinto lacked artistic or literary representation of beliefs and myths, and so it had no defined pantheon of deities.

There are 13 mainstream Shinto sects and numerous sub-sects in Japan today, but since World War II they have not been controlled by the government. In fact, it was only during the period from the Meiji Restoration of 1868 until the end of World War II that the state intervened in Shinto. During the Meiji Restoration, the government introduced *kokka* (national) Shinto as a political tool for controlling the people through the policy of *saisei it'chi* – the "unity of rites and politics".

LIVING FAITH

Quizzed on the degree of their religious belief, most Japanese would say they are not pious, a way, in many cases, of deflecting the Westerner from viewing them as superstitious. Visitors will notice, however, how well attended its temples and shrines are. The rites and rituals aspire almost to the level of the performing arts. Sacred *kagura* dances, in fact, *are* performances, ones that take place on covered platforms set up in front of a shrine's main hall. In this way, religion may be seen as part of Japan's cultural life.

Detached from its metaphysical character, religion in Japan became a vehicle for a practical morality, but its non-rationality and absence of an overarching

doctrinal system promoted an acceptance of things as they are and an openness to other faiths and beliefs that continues to permeate Japanese society, and to promote a polytheism that does not perceive the Buddhist temple and Shinto shrine as incompatible.

Aspects of faith are manifest. The market is carefully allocated: Shinto monopolises coming-of-age ceremonies, marriage and birth; Buddhism manages the more profitable market in death, the elaborate funerals, burial plots, posthumous names and memorial ceremonies.

Over half the population visit shrines over New Year to pray for the coming year, most often for success in examinations, luck in love and recovery from illness.

Several shrines were established by the national government for various purposes as "national" shrines, including Yasukuni-jinja in Tokyo and the impressive Meiji-jingu, to the north of Shibuya in Tokyo, whose majestic architecture reminds the traveller that Emperor Meiji, enshrined within, was considered divine.

In fact, none of the national shrines – state inventions all – has much to do with traditional beliefs found within Shinto. Dismissing them as unimportant in the modern scheme of things, however, would be a sociological, if not religious and political, mistake.

Shinto shrines

Shrines are of the Shinto religion, and their names often end in the suffixes -gu, -jinja or -jingu. Temples, on the other hand, are Buddhist and usually end with -ji, -tera or -dera. Quite often, temples and shrines are found side by side, or a temple or shrine will have an complementary adjunct on the same sacred grounds.

The thousands of Shinto shrines in Japan vary in size from tiny roadside boxes to large compounds such as the Grand Shrines at Ise and the Tosho-gu at Nikko, but nearly all share certain features.

Small shrine at the top of Kompira-san complex, Shikoku.

Yasukuni-jinja is a case in point. A large and controversial Shinto shrine just north of the Imperial Palace in central Tokyo, it is an example (and a particularly notorious one) of the national shrines set up by the government authorities before World War II. It is here that the spirits of every soldier who has died in the name of the emperor since 1853 are enshrined (including war criminals executed by the Allies after World War II). Visits here – official or not – by the prime minister and members of government, less common these days, have usually been made to appease right-wing nationalists and are vociferously denounced by neighbouring countries such as China, South Korea and Taiwan.

First, there is at least one *torii*, shaped somewhat like the Greek letter *pi*. This gateway may have evolved from a bird's perch – a certain kind of bird having been a religious symbol in many animistic cults – and it may be made of wood, stone, metal or even concrete. Like the *shimenawa* (sacred straw festoon), zigzag cuts of white paper, mounds of salt, and cleanly swept gravel, the *torii* serves to mark off areas considered sacred from those thought profane.

Often the largest building of the shrine is the inner sanctum, called the *honden*. This is the main dwelling of the deity. It is usually elevated above the other buildings and reached by a staircase. It is likely to be off-limits to visitors, but other than a mirror or, on rare occasions, an image, there is little to see inside. These objects, by the way, are the *mitama-shiro* or *go-shintai*, serving as spirit substitutes for the deity *(kami)* being worshipped. In front of the *honden* is the often quite spacious *haiden* or worship hall, used for ritual ceremonies. Usually this structure is merely a roof supported by pillars and open on all sides.

There are no elaborate rituals or prescribed procedures in worshipping at a shrine. On entering the grounds there is a stone water basin, often with ladles balanced across it. One rinses mouth and hands in preparation for approaching the deity. It is customary to toss a small offering into the cashbox at the foot of the *haiden* before sounding the shaker to attract the attention of the god. Devout worshippers also clap their hands twice, making doubly sure the god is listening. Then, a deep bow is performed and held while the prayer is offered.

During *matsuri*, or festivals, the gods are taken out for rollicking rides through the streets in *mikoshi* (portable shrines) in order

Raikyū-ji, a Buddhist temple in Takahashi.

A WESTERN FAITH

Christianity came to Japan in the person of St Francis Xavier in 1549, and was received courteously by some of the feudal lords of Kyushu, where the famous missionary docked. The fact that Xavier had sailed from Goa in India caused some initial confusion, the Japanese mistaking the faith for a new form of Buddhism.

Rightly fearing that Christian missionary activities generally represented a prelude to occupation, the shogunate took a suspicious view of the faith. The military ruler Hideyoshi ordered the execution of 26 priests and converts in 1597, initiating a period of persecution that climaxed in the death of over 37,000 Christians after the end of the Shimabara Rebellion outside Nagasaki in

1637. Henceforth, Christianity was banned and Japan's remaining Christians went underground.

Devout Catholics pay homage annually to the Nagasaki martyrs, but also to a number of Christians who were tortured and killed on the Otome Mountain Pass in the town of Tsuwano at the beginning of the Meiji Period, when there still existed much confusion over what should be done with Christians who had been secretly practising an outlawed faith for over 200 years.

With the introduction of religious suffrage, Western missionaries poured into Japan, building churches and schools, but the religion failed to make major inroads. Today there are barely 1 million Christians in Japan.

to bring the blessings of the *kamisama* to all the community. (This is one of the few times when Japanese collectively shed their social inhibitions and turn quite rowdy.)

Buddhism

The traditionally accepted date for Buddhism to have arrived in Japan is AD 552. While this may be true, it wasn't until centuries later that it ceased to be the exclusive province of aristocrats. This is somewhat ironic in view of the beliefs of the religion's founder, Sakyamuni – born a prince in eastern India (now part of

established throughout most of East Asia. It holds that every being, sentient or non-sentient, shares a basic spiritual communion and that all are eventually destined for Buddhahood. Although all beings are separate in appearance, they are one and the same in reality. Every person's present situation is determined by past deeds, Buddhists believe. This is the principle of *karma*.

Since the main *Mahayana* sutras only appeared around 100 BC, it is not known to what extent they reflect the original thoughts of the Buddha. However, by the

Ginkaku-ji Gardens, Kyoto.

Nepal) around 500 BC – who advocated a middle way between indulgence and asceticism.

The Buddha, as he came to be known (though this is a misnomer), blamed all the world's pain and discontent on desire and claimed that through right living, desire could be negated and the "self" totally done away with through entry into the blissful state of *nirvana*, or Buddhahood. Buddha's followers came to believe that one who really knows the truth lives the life of truth and thus becomes truth itself. By overcoming all the conflicts of the ego, one can attain a universal, cosmic harmony with all.

Mahayana, meaning Greater Vehicle, was the form of Buddhism that became

time it reached Japan's shores through China, Buddhism had changed tremendously from Sakyamuni's simple message, and was to undergo even more radical change when it encountered the beliefs that were held in the Japanese archipelago.

As early as the 6th century, for example, *Ryobu* Shinto began to emerge as a syncretic compromise with Buddhism. In this hybrid belief system, *kamisama* were regarded as temporary manifestations of the Buddhist deities. In time, Buddhist thought became influenced by the indigenous beliefs, deviating so far from the original that some scholars doubt whether the Japanese version really deserves to be called Buddhism.

For example, although the goal of *nirvana* is to break the cycle of reincarnation, most Japanese Buddhists seem to believe that the souls of the dead are eventually reborn. As the famed folklorist Yanagida Kunio once pointed out, if asked where people go after they die, the typical Japanese will usually answer *Gokuraku*, which translates as Paradise. Contrast this with the more orthodox Buddhist belief in death as a permanent state. In practice, however, Japanese usually return to their *furosato*, or ancestral home, for the two equinoxes as well as during the midsummer Obon, or Feast of

Byodo-in Temple in Uji, Kyoto, dedicated to the Amida.

the Dead, observances. The purpose of attending Obon is to be present when the family's ranking male ceremoniously offers food to the spirits of departed ancestors – spirits that return to earth for the occasion. From where do they return? Yanagida says most people will answer "the mountains", which hold a special place in Japanese religious lore. Certain peaks – Omine near Nara and, of course, Mount Fuji – are especially sacred.

Built of lava carried from the mother mountain, miniature Fuji replicas, known as *fujizuka*, were common in Edo, standing in as substitutes for people who, through infirmity or lack of funds, could not make the pilgrimage to the real mountain.

Combined with Buddhist notions of spirituality, the mountain became the locus of a heady mix of beliefs and doctrines during the Edo Period. The special significance of the peak to cults and quasi-religions like Shugendo, or mountain asceticism, was apparent in the length to which its followers would go to demonstrate their devotion. One celebrated mountain ascetic, Jikigyo Miroku, a man of unassailable moral rectitude by all accounts, went as far as to undertake a ritual suicide, a dedicatory fast to the death on the slopes of the mountain. Fuji's transcendent quality, the notion that it was the most proximate peak to heaven, was never questioned, even when its destructive forces were unleashed.

Amida Buddhism

There are today an estimated 56 main divisions and 170 subdivisions in Japanese

NEW CULTS

The number of new religions and cults in Japan has proliferated since the 1970s. Many of these are quite legitimate, while others, though registered as religions, have raised concerns among the authorities.

The crackdown on cults began after Aum Shinrikyo's (Aum Supreme Truth) sarin gas attack on a Tokyo subway in 1995. Headed by a nearly blind yoga instructor, Shoko Asahara, now in prison and facing execution, the group has since reinvented itself with a new image that renounces violence, calling itself Aleph. Membership is said to be growing.

There are dozens more small religious sects. Some have been publicly discredited. The scandal-ridden neo-Buddhist Ho-no-Hana, run by a guru who claimed he could divine people's past and predict their future by examining the soles of their feet, was arrested after it emerged he had swindled followers out of millions of yen.

Other organisations, like Pana Wave, a group dedicated to fighting harmful electromagnetic waves by covering trees and other natural features in white cloth, and Fukudenkai, a cult founded by a guru who taught that the gaining of positive *karma* could be furthered by praying to a mound containing the nose rings of over 7 million cows, are generally considered harmless eccentricities.

Buddhism. The single most popular sect is Jodo Shinshu, founded in the 13th century by Shinran, who preached an "easy road to salvation" by means of the *nembutsu* prayer to the Amida, a bodhisattva who made a vow aeons ago to save all who placed faith in him or her and to guide them to the Blissful Land of Purity.

About half of Japanese Buddhists belong to either Jodo Shinshu or another form of Amidaism founded by Honen (1133–1212). Jodo Shinshu offers that it is not necessary to be "good" in order to be reborn into the Western Paradise and that the laity can become Buddhas as easily as priests. Amidaism is the Buddhist form closest to core Japanese beliefs due to its concern for moral judgement and its exaltation of inclinations beyond the mere good and evil.

Zen emptiness

The impact of that particularly eclectic form of Buddhism called Zen on Japanese culture is considerable, reaching far beyond the temple and entering into interior design, gardening, ink painting, calligraphy, the tea ceremony, cuisine and even military strategies.

Two Buddhist priests in the 12th and 13th centuries – Eisai, founder of the Rinzai Zen sect, and his disciple Dogen, who established the Soto Zen sect – brought the principle of "emptiness" into Japanese Buddhism.

Soto sect followers rely almost solely on *zazen*, or sitting meditation, and seek to emulate Sakyamuni, who reached the state of enlightenment while meditating without conscious thought in such a position. In contrast, the Rinzai sect also utilises *koan* riddles, such as the famous "What is the sound of one hand clapping?" *Koan* must be tackled with something beyond logic and non-logic; the riddles' function is to stimulate (or perhaps divert) the mind into a similar state.

Zen was influenced by both Daoism and the Wang Yangming school of neo-Confucianism, which stressed the "prime conscience" and the importance of action. They would describe the "Great Ultimate" as being akin to the hub of a well: empty but the point from which all action flows. For various reasons, Zen sects proved better able than the others to satisfy the spiritual needs of the *samurai*.

Whether through *zazen* or the use of *koan* posed by the Zen master, the goal is for the disciple to be provoked, excited or irritated to the point where he or she makes a non-intellectual leap into the void and experiences reality.

Buddhist temples

Under the Tokugawa shogunate, Japanese Buddhism lost much of its vigour, leading cynics to charge that priests were good for nothing else but burying people. An exaggeration, no doubt, but crematoriums still provide a good part of the income for most temples. The main building *(hondo)*, library *(bunko)*, bell tower *(shoro)* and other buildings of a temple com-

The keisaku is a wooden stick used to stop Zen Buddhists from losing focus during meditation.

plex can be exquisite architectural creations. But the one most easily admired is the pagoda, or *to*. The form in Japan is the result of evolution from the dome-shaped *stupa* (thought to represent an upside-down rice bowl), in which the bones of the Buddha and Buddhist saints were buried in India.

Images found in temples include Nyorai (Tathagata) Buddhas, such as Sakyamuni after Enlightenment and Maitreya (Miroku) or Future Buddhas, distinguished by a pose with one leg crossed over the other. Others include the *nio*, fierce-looking images flanking gates to many temples and derived from the Hindu gods Brahma and Indra.

UNDERCURRENTS OF LIFE AND RITUAL

At the core of Japanese life is the ancient animist belief of Shinto, which informs daily life in basic ways, enriched by Buddhism introduced from India.

Buddhism and Shinto coexist, and on occasion appear to meld together. It is not uncommon to find Shinto shrines and Buddhist temples sharing the same sacred grounds, each tending to specific needs but complementing the other as a whole.

This cordial accommodation between the faiths only works in a civic society with high levels of tolerance. In the Meiji Period, with the promotion of emperor-centred Shintoism, an anti-Buddhist campaign that had as much to do with nationalism and an antipathy towards a religion perceived as being of foreign provenance was launched. This resulted in the destruction of many priceless Buddha images. During World War II, Zen Buddhists, in an effort to look patriotic, threw their support behind the militarists.

Shinto doesn't exist as doctrine, but rather as an integral undercurrent to one's daily life. Shinto is Japan's indigenous religion, but the term Shinto did not appear in any Japanese literature until the 6th century, and in fact the label came into existence only as a way to distinguish it from Buddhism, introduced from mainland Asia. Nor were there visual images of Shinto deities – *kami* – until the imagery of Buddhism established itself in the archipelago. Over the centuries, Daoism and Confucianism also influenced Shinto.

Ancient Shinto was polytheistic, maybe even pantheistic, and people believed *kami* existed not only in nature, but also in abstract ideas such as creation, growth and human judgement.

The Japanese may disclaim any strong religious beliefs, but stand in the grounds of a shrine at almost any time of the day, and you will see a steady trickle of worshippers.

Along with Mount Fuji and the bullet train, the massive torii gate that floats off the shores of Miyajima island, has become one of the most easily recognised symbols of Japan.

Kimono are rarely worn in everyday life in Japan, but shrines that host weddings, children's coming-of-age rituals and other felicitous events are good places to glimpse them.

Shinto priests perform rituals that often appear arcane, not only to foreign visitors but even to the Japanese themselves.

A LIFE OF SHINTO BLESSINGS

Traditions of Shinto (and of Buddhism, too) are the traditions of Japan itself. They pepper the daily lives of the Japanese, who perform them as routines of life when the urge or need arises.

Small votives *(ema)* are hung at shrines to seek good luck in exams or other secular rituals. Infants are brought to the shrine 30 to 100 days after birth to initiate the child as a new believer. Children dressed in kimono attend *shichi-go-san* (seven-five-three) on 15 November every year. Girls of three and seven years old and boys of five years old visit the shrine to thank the *kami* for their life so far and to pray for good health. In January, 20-year-olds return to the shrine mark their attainment of adulthood. When they are married, it is usually a Shinto ceremony (although a separate Western-style ceremony is increasingly common). Death, however, is usually a time of Buddhist ritual and family remembrance.

The final cedar torii gate in a series of three leading to Meiji Shrine in Tokyo.

Kegs of sake, a sacred drink, are often donated to Shinto shrines and then displayed in the grounds.

An unusually decorated figure at Koya-san, a vast graveyard and mausoleum located in a dense cryptomeria forest.

ART, CRAFTS AND LITERATURE

With an aesthetic that goes back scores of centuries, Japan's art and crafts of today retain the depth and layers of history, culture and outlook.

Historically Japan has drawn many of its traditional art forms from continental Asia, but sci-fi novelist and Japan watcher William Gibson has written of the country now that "cultural change is essentially techno-logically driven". Sourcing the past in everything from painting, computer graphics, manga and an extraordinary craft legacy, rather than aban-doning it, yokes the authority of the traditional with the innovative new. Traditional Japanese dramas, among the oldest still to be performed in the world, remain spectacles of unparalleled beauty and power, but so do the new work of its installation, pop and video artists, not to mention avant-garde flower arrangers. The international success of conceptual art figures like Kusama Yoyoi, the overseas exposure provided for art col-lective Chim Pom, and the success of individuals like 3D artist Miyanaga Aiko, hint at a restless and creative exploration of ideas and forms that have their roots in centuries of creativity.

The earliest preserved distinctly Japanese art-works are those of the late Yayoi Period (300 BC–AD 300). These were small, tubular clay figurines called *haniwa*, some of which were set up like fences around imperial mausolea. Whatever their purpose may have been – substitutes for people buried alive in the tombs or magical instruments to ward off evil spirits or bandits – their imme-diate interest lies in their simplicity and charm. Although many of them are only cylinders, some of the *haniwa* (and there are hundreds) are fig-ures of men and women, horses, monkeys and birds. Most are very simple, with only a few details of decoration – perhaps a sword or a necklace. They have large hollow spaces for the mouth and eyes, which prevented them from cracking when being fired and which adds not only to their charm, but to their mystery, too.

Haniwa figurine (terracotta funerary art).

Aesthetic impulses

The *haniwa* figures are also important for another reason. We find in them – at the very beginning of the culture – many of the salient characteris-tics of almost all Japanese art. The *haniwa* are, so to speak, decorative. They are very much in this world, regardless of how much they may evoke the next. They are narratory – we want to create stories for them; as still in time as they are, we imagine a time before and after their mouths opened. And with their soft modelling and indolent lines they are recognisably human. These figures are not gods or angels: they smile, they shout, they gaze. In fact, there is little that is abstract about them. This is an "art of the real", which does not elimi-nate the fantastic or even the artificial.

The *haniwa* possess a beauty that seems almost uncannily to come from a natural aesthetic impulse. They occur during a lull in Japanese absorption of outside influences at a time when the culture was developing its own native hues.

Recognising the conventions

The viewer needs only a few moments to get used to looking at Japanese art. He or she will soon recognise the conventions – the raised roofs to reveal scenes (no perspective here), the hooks for noses and slits for eyes, the seemingly abstract patterns that resolve themselves into a

A sculpture of a future Buddha (maitreya), at Koryu-ji, Kyoto.

few variations on plants and birds and insects.

Just look a little closer and the clothes and faces will soon take on individual qualities. There is no reason, either, to fear that cliché, "open space". There is and isn't any great metaphysical principle at work here – the idea is simple enough: like European Symbolist poetry of a millennium later, the Japanese knew that art evokes, it does not depict.

Nara and Kamakura sculpture

There are some superb examples of sculpture that date from before the Nara Period, such as the Miroku at Koryu-ji, in Kyoto. This is a delicately carved wooden statue of the Buddha of the Future.

In the Nara Period (646–794), with Japan's full-scale welcome of things Chinese, the native response to the real is fused with its spiritual aspirations without ever abandoning the former. Work is done in wood, clay, bronze, or by using the curious technique of hollow lacquer.

There are some fine early pieces to be seen in the Yakushi-ji, in Nara, but visits must especially be made to the Kofuku-ji and the Todai-ji to see the numerous sculptures of the Buddha, of guardian deities and of monks.

It was also during this time that the 16-metre (52ft) high bronze Daibutsu (Great Buddha) in Nara was created. It was originally gilded bronze and incised with designs that can now only barely be discerned on some of the lotus petals upon which the figure sits.

The Nara Period ended with the move of the capital to Kyoto. With that – the beginning of the Heian Period (794–1185) – Japanese sculpture declined as other arts ascended and did not revive until the Kamakura Period several centuries later.

While Nara Period sculpture was both human and ideal, that of the Kamakura Period (1185–1333) was primarily human, passionate, personal and emotional. For example, the Kamakura Period produced more portraits of monks and demons than of aloof gods. Many of these can be seen in Todai-ji and Kofuku-ji in Nara. The Kamakura Period also produced its Daibutsu, which, though somewhat smaller than that in Nara, is equally affecting. Now sitting uncovered in the Kamakura hills, its impressiveness has been enhanced by time.

Painting

In the Heian Period, life itself became an art, and works of art became its decorative attendant. Kyoto's Byodo-in may have been meant as a model of the next world, but it only showed that life in this one was already exquisite. Japanese painting had long existed, particularly in the form of long, rolled and hand-held scrolls, but it had not flowered into great sophistication. These paintings, known as *Yamato-e*, might depict the changing seasons, famous beauty spots or illustrate well-known stories.

The best *Yamato-e* were of the latter type and depicted popular legends, warrior tales, or works of great literature such as the *Ise Monogatari* and *Genji Monogatari*, or *Tale of Genji*. The popular legends might include a satirical look at pompous officials turned into battling frogs and rabbits, or a man who can't stop farting. Post-Heian warrior tales drew on the many heroic or sentimental tales collected in the *Heike Monogatari* and other stories. The scrolls are easy to follow and with their delicacy of line reveals the Japanese gift of design.

In the Kamakura Period, war and religion came together. This was the great period of Zen art, when *suiboku* (water-ink, or painting with black *sumi* ink) comes to the fore. One of the world's masterpieces of *suiboku-ga* can be seen in the National Museum in Tokyo: Sesshu's *Winter Landscape*. Owing to the sense of composition and the moods he evokes, Sesshu seems at times to be a contemporary artist. In fact, he died in 1506 at age 86.

In addition to calligraphy, *suiboku-ga* includes portraiture and landscape. An example of the principle "the line is the man himself" in portraiture is the stark portrait of the priest Ikkyu, in the National Museum in Tokyo (Tokyo Kokuritsu Hakubutsukan).

In *suiboku* landscape paintings, the emphasis is again on the real and on the visually pleasurable (Japanese landscape is rarely as profoundly mystical as that of China), and quite often also on the grotesque, the curious and the purely fantastic.

The Momoyama Period (late 16th century) is Japan's age of baroque. Filled with gold and silver, with very bright, flat colours (no shading or outlining), and embellished with lush scenes painted on screens and walls, it is one of the high points of Japan's decorative genius.

This is not to imply that monochrome was abandoned during the Momoyama Period. Far from it: there was a great deal of superb *sumi-e* (ink picture) screens and paintings done at this time. The overwhelming impression of Momoyama Period art, however, is of brilliance and gold, as one can see in the Jodan-no-ma and other ceremonial halls in Nijo Castle in Kyoto, with its painted walls and gilded ceilings, or at nearby Nishi Hongan-ji, to the south of Nijo Castle, in the expansive *taimensho* (audience hall) and *Konoma* (stork room).

Floating world

The Edo Period (1603–1868) is the great age of popular art, even though much great decorative art was also being made for the aristocracy or the military classes, especially by Koetsu, Sotatsu and Korin. The last's gorgeous *Irises* – all violet and gold – is an excellent example of the art of the period and can be seen at the Nezu Institute of Fine Arts in Tokyo.

In the rigid society of the Edo Period, the artisan was the third of the four social classes, one step above the merchant, who was at the bottom (in theory, but increasingly at the top in practice). This was the age of the unknown craftsman, whose tools, hands and skills were part of a tradition and who learned techniques as an apprentice.

The art most associated with Edo Tokyo is *ukiyo-e* (literally, pictures of the floating world). Once again, the sublunary, fleshy human existence was a key element. Although woodblock

Lacquerware from Nagano.

The link between tattooing and woodblock printing during the Edo period was strong. As woodblock printing acquired more colour and complexity, tattoo motifs and pigments grew more ambitious and subtle. Look up ukiyo-e artists Utagawa, Yoshitoshi and Kunichika for stunning tattoo images.

printing had been used to reproduce sutras, for example, the technique first began to be used in a more popular vein in the early 18th century. At first, the prints were either monochromatic or hand-coloured with an orange-red. In time, two colours were used, then four, and so on.

Notable artists included Hiroshige Ando, Utamaro Kitagawa and Hokusai. Although the names of hundreds of *ukiyo-e* artists are known, it should be remembered that the production of these prints was a cooperative effort between many highly skilled people.

Early *ukiyo-e*, especially those by the first great master, Moronobu, are usually portraits of prostitutes from the Yoshiwara district of Old Edo or else illustrations for books. With polychrome printing in *ukiyo-e*, a number of "genres" became established. There were, for example, portraits of female beauties, often courtesans (*bijin ga*),

Bizen-yaki: a type of Japanese pottery from Okayama.

kabuki actors in famous roles, the ever-present scenes of renowned places, and of plant and animal life. Suffice to say that *ukiyo-e* is one of the world's great graphic art forms, and in more ways than one. For example, the charmingly named *shunga* (literally, spring pictures) represent pornographic art of stupendous imagination, and comprised a large part of every *ukiyo-e* artist's *oeuvre*. Ironically, *shunga* is only occasionally exhibited in Japan (too pornographic, even though it is considerably tamer than what is found in some magazines).

The Japanese have never considered *ukiyo-e* to be "art". It was a publishing form and not art until foreigners started collecting it. Only in the past few decades have Japanese collectors

begun to realise the value of *ukiyo-e*. Yet the influence on Western artists has been considerable, especially amongst the Impressionists of the late 19th century. French engraver Félix Bracquemond fuelled the increasing interest in Japanese art – *Japonisme* – when he started distributing copies of Hokusai's sketches. Soon Manet, Zola, Whistler, Degas and Monet were all collecting *ukiyo-e* and adopting *ukiyo-e* motifs and themes in their own works.

Lacquerware

Japanese lacquer (*urushi*) is the sap of a certain tree (*Rhus verniciflua*) that has been refined and which may have pigment added. It has been used as a decorative coating on wood, leather and cloth for 1,500 years, but the earliest-known examples of lacquer in Japan – red-and-black-lacquered earthenware pots – date back 4,000 years. Lacquerware (*nurimono*) is a community craft – no one person can do all of the 50 steps involved in the plain coating on a wooden bowl. Decoration may involve another 30. The most common Japanese examples of lacquerware are food bowls and serving trays – tableware known as *shikki*.

Ceramics

Japan is a treasure house of ceramic techniques, a craft that has long attracted many students from abroad. There are famous and numerous wares (*yaki*), the names of which have a certain amount of currency in antiques and crafts circles throughout the world. In general, pottery in Japan is stoneware or porcelain, that is, high-fired wares.

Earthenware and low-fired pottery are found in small quantities, usually in the form of humble utensils, in *Raku-yaki* – a rustic style produced by hand and without the use of a potter's wheel – and in some of the enamelled wares of Kyoto and Satsuma, in southern Kyushu.

Located along the San-in coast, the great historical town of Hagi is a veritable time slip. The warren of old lanes that form a protective cobweb around the grounds of its ruined castle are full of craft shops and kilns busy with potter's wheels. Good pieces of the milky, translucent glazes of *Hagi-yaki* (Hagi ceramicware), ranked second only to *Raku-yaki* as utensils in the tea ceremony, are collectors' items. Quality *Hagi-yaki* improves with age, as the tea penetrates its porous surfaces, darkening them and adding a rich lustre.

Other major ceramic towns of note that lend their names to the pottery they produce can be found in Mashiko in Tochigi Prefecture and Imbe, near Okayama City, the home of Bizen-ware. There are a number of An unglazed ware, of which the most famous is Bizen, which is made from hard clay and has a bronze-like texture after firing. Traditional glazes are mainly iron (ash glazes), though feldspathic glazes are sometimes used.

A fine concentration of pottery towns exists in Kyushu's Saga Prefecture, famed for Karatsu and Arita-ware as well as fine Imari porcelain. Porcelains are decorated with underglaze cobalt and overglaze enamels. The decorated porcelains produced by numerous kilns in the Arita

> Okinawan bingata, a cotton and linen fabric, is soaked in natural pigments and vegetable dyes taken from wild plants. Covered in dazzling subtropical bird, flower, fan and shell motifs, quality bingata can take a craftsman between two and three weeks to complete.

area of northern Kyushu, shipped from the port of Imari from the 17th to the 19th century, are still avidly sought by antiques collectors, as is the Kutani porcelain of the Kanazawa area. The Kyushu Ceramic Museum in Arita (Kyushu Toji Bunkakan) is a good starting point for exploring the Saga region in more depth.

Textiles

This craft includes weaving and dyeing, as well as braiding *(kumihimo)* and quilting *(sashiko)*. Japan is a vast storehouse of textile techniques, one that Western craftspeople have yet to tap.

Of course, silks are the most famous and highly refined of Japanese textiles. The brocades used in *noh* drama costumes and in the apparel of the aristocracy and high clergy of bygone ages are among the highest achievements of textile art anywhere, as are the more humble but lyrical 16th-century *tsujigahana* "tie-dyed" silks.

Though little worn these days, the formal kimono, with its sumptuous silk and brocade designs, remains the national costume. In recent years, young people and modern designers have adapted the kimono so that it can be worn in a more casual way over Western clothes.

Japanese folk textiles are a world unto themselves. Cotton, hemp and ramie are the most common fibres, but the bark fibres of the *shina* tree, *kuzu* (kudzu), paper mulberry, plantain (in

Okinawa) and other fibres were used in remote mountain areas.

Indigo is the predominant colour, and the *ikat* technique (known as *kasuri*) is the most popular for work clothes, quilt covers and the like.

Modern literature

Japan has never been short of good writers. In over 1,000 years of literature, from *Genji Monogatari (The Tale of Genji)*, the world's first full-length novel, playwrights and novelists have recorded the Japanese experience and the mutations of the human condition.

Designing textiles for kimonos in Kyoto.

MINGEI REVIVAL

Sensing a decline in Japanese folk crafts with the advent of the machine age, philosopher and art critic Yanagi Soetsu (1889–1961) set about reviving the production of simple, utilitarian but aesthetically beautiful objects, in a movement dubbed Mingei, or "ordinary people's art". Yanagi set up the Mingeikan (Japanese Folk Craft Museum; www.mingeikan.or.jp) in Tokyo in 1936. It celebrates the legacy of such renowned craftsmen as the textile designer Kiesuke Seizawa, the potters Kawai Kanjiro and Hamada Shoju, and the English ceramicist Bernard Leach. Thanks to Yanagi, and those who have followed, the movement today is alive and well.

The publication of Natsume Soseki's novel *Kokoro* (1914), concerned with the conflict between the old and a newly emerging Japan, arguably marks the beginning of modern Japanese literature. The immediate post-war period, with its more liberal values, saw an extraordinary efflorescence of literary works.

Jiro Osaragi's *The Journey* examines the upheavals of the American Occupation of Japan, while Nagai Kafu, that great chronicler of Tokyo life, consistently rejected the contemporary in works of plangent nostalgia such as *Geisha in Rivalry* and *A Strange Tale from East of*

A bookstore in Tokyo.

the River. The doubtful role of Western culture in Japanese life surfaces in the popular nihilism of Osamu Dazai's *The Setting Sun* and *No Longer Human*.

An astonishing number of Nobel-quality writers are associated with the period from the 1950s to early 1970s. The great Junichiro Tanizaki, author of modern classics like *The Makioka Sisters* and *Diary of a Mad Old Man*, never won a Nobel (although he was nominated), but two other contemporary writers, Yasunari Kawabata and Kenzaburo Oe, did. Yukio Mishima was nominated for works like *The Golden Pavilion* and *Forbidden Colours*, whose controversial topics, such as homosexuality, reflected the sensational life of the author himself.

Shusaku Endo wrote novels that are philosophical but strongly narrative. *Scandal* is a tale about muddled identities set in the Tokyo of the 1980s.

For a blistering look at modern Japan, its drug addicts, dropouts and dispossessed, Murakami Ryu's *Almost Transparent Blue* is hard to beat. Haruki Murakami is the best-known author outside of Japan for his wondrously offbeat stories, such as *Kafka on the Shore* and *1Q84*, and has been a long-time favourite to win a Nobel.

Social issues are the stuff of a new wave of writers, many of them women. Miyuki Miyabe's *All She Was Worth* and *Shadow Family* are good examples of the Japanese social novel. The works of prize-winning novelist Kirino Natsuo, like all the titles mentioned here, have been translated into English. *Out*, a story of women working the night shift in a food-packing company, is darkly feminist, right down to the murder and dismembering of an ingrate husband.

HAIKU

In sharp contrast to the lavish indulgence enjoyed by the townspeople of Edo during the Genroku Period (1688–1704), the great haiku poet Matsuo Basho lived in a modest wattle hut on the east bank of the Sumida River. Here he changed his name from Tosei to Basho, in tribute to a banana plantain palm *(basho)* that his disciples planted in the garden beside his hut. According to his own account, he identified with the ragged, easily torn but enduring fronds of the plant. The tree, which the poet loved to sit beneath, appears in an early haiku:

*Storm-torn banana tree
All night I listen to rain
In a basin*

Basho is rightly revered as a master of the form, but there are many other great haiku writers. Masaoka Shiki (1867–1902) was a major figure in the development of modern haiku, and Santoka Taneda (1882–1940), a mendicant Zen priest, was a highly original poet of the "new haiku movement".

There were also *haijin* (women haiku poets), foremost among them, perhaps, the Buddhist nun Chiyo-ni (1703–75). The strikingly observed details of her work are clear in this dramatic example:

*How frightening
Her rouged fingers
Against white chrysanthemums*

Manga: the disposable art

Hard-copy manga may be declining, but the image-powered entertainment, combining narrative, humour, stylised violence and sexuality, has made a natural transition to computer tablets and mobile phones.

The term 'manga' covers magazine and newspaper cartoons, comic strips, comic books and digitalised formats. Like all cultural forms it has its historical antecedents. Comic drawings and caricatures have been found in the 7th-century temple complex of Horyu-ji in Ikaruga; in Toshodai-ji, an 8th-century Buddhist temple in Nara; and in the ancient scroll drawing called Choju Jinbutsu Giga, in which creatures satirise the aristocracy and clergy of the time.

The master woodblock artist Hokusai is credited with coining the expression 'manga' to describe a form of adult storybook popular in the Edo Period (1600–1868). The popularity of newspapers and magazines during the Taisho Period (1912–26) saw the dissemination of cartoons by popular illustrators such as Okamoto Ippei. Artist, Osamu Tezuka, is credited as the "father of manga". Tezuka brought film techniques like panning, close-ups and jump cuts to manga, but is also credited with creating the unique look of Japanese manga, its characters un-Japanese in appearance. From the early Astro Boy, Tezuka went on to explore more complex themes in Black Jack, about a brilliant, unlicensed surgeon, and Adorufu ni Tsugu (Tell Adolf), which examined anti-Semitism.

More recent works, like Dragon Ball by Toriyama Akira, Naruto by Kishimoto Masashi or Oda Eiichiro's One Piece, all of whose total circulation runs into several hundred million copies, have been adapted into anime TV series and/or internationally marketable anime films. Ongoing One Piece is reportedly the best-selling manga of all time.

An all-pervasive form

It's almost impossible in Japan to avoid the manga-influenced cute and cartoonish, manifest in advertising, company and city mascots, stuffed animals and cos-play events, where young people dress up as their favourite characters. British architect Richard Rogers commented, "Tokyo's coming more and more to resemble an adult KiddyLand."

Manga appeals to all age groups and sexes. The late prime minister, Hashimoto Ryutaro, is said to have enjoyed quiet evenings at home with his wife reading manga. Though the appeal is broad, categories exist. Shonen (young boys') magazines often feature noble crusades or quests to win the heart of a seemingly unobtainable girl, while shojo (young girls') comics take a look at human relationships, often blurring gender lines. The Shonen-ai (boy's love) genre are popular with women who enjoy explicit images of gay couples. The much commented-upon hentai (pervert) magazines, featuring violent sex and horror, represent only a small part of the market.

Today's manga includes a range of subjects from flower arranging to 'how-to' approaches to social rela-

Kyoto Manga Museum.

tions, to abridged versions of classics like The Tale of Genji. Manga is often used to explain and simplify complex subjects like international finance. A special genre known as benkyo-manga, or "study comics", is aimed at students. Needless to say, manga is a massive, multi-billion yen business, and successful illustrators have achieved the celebrity status of TV talents and pop idoru (idols).

Because the manga style is so pervasive, it has influenced advertising, graphic and book design, and the appearance of the internet. Manga magazines, in fact, are decreasing in sales as the stories are effortlessly downloaded onto the more convenient handset of a mobile phone. As Donald Richie has said in his book The Image Factory, "Eyes that were once glued to the page are now pasted to the palm of the hand."

THE PERFORMING ARTS

Most of Japan's traditional performing arts look and sound otherworldly, if not sacred, to outsiders. Yet some were designed to entertain commoners.

For many of the traditional Japanese performing arts, the distinction between dance and drama is tenuous. Most traditional Japanese drama forms today developed out of some form of dance, and all, accordingly, employ musical accompaniment. Several of the forms also involve vocal disciplines to some extent, but not enough to qualify as opera.

There are five major traditional performing-art forms in Japan: *bugaku*, *noh*, *kyogen*, *bunraku* and *kabuki*. Only *bugaku*, *noh* and *kyogen* could be called classical – all are tightly contained and formal entertainments performed originally for the aristocracy. Both *bunraku* and *kabuki* are traditional stage arts but derived from the vigorous common-folk culture of the Edo Period. Another form, *kagura*, needs to be mentioned as well. Although it falls within what could be called folk drama, there is no single form of *kagura*. Rather, these offertory dance-drama-story-religious performances, held on festival days before the deity, all differ greatly throughout the country, involving anything from religious mystery to heroic epics, to bawdy buffoonery and symbolic sexual enactments – or a combination of all these elements.

Bugaku

What the ancient indigenous dance and drama forms in Japan were is not known. There certainly must have been such expression before the cultural imports from the Asian mainland. During the 7th and 8th centuries, mainland culture from both Korea and China dominated the life of the archipelago's imperial court.

In AD 702, the court established a court music bureau to record, preserve and perform the continental music forms *(gagaku)* and dance *(bugaku)*. Influences included not only

Bugaku, a traditional Japanese dance.

dance from China and Korea, but also from India and Southeast Asia. These dances are so highly stylised and abstract that there is little or no sense of story or dramatic event. The choreography is rigid and is usually symmetrical, since the dances are most often performed by two pairs of dancers.

The *bugaku* stage is a raised platform erected outdoors, independent of other structures and ascended by steps at the front and back. The performance area is carpeted with green silk, the stairs are lacquered black, the surrounding railings and posts are in cinnabar lacquer. Given that the *bugaku* repertoire has been preserved for almost 15 centuries, it is amazing to consider that about 60 different dances are known and performed today. These dances are categorised into "right" and "left", as was the custom in China. Left dances are slow, flowing and graceful, while right dances are relatively more humourous and spirited. *Bugaku* is classified into four categories: ceremonial, military, "running" (a more spirited genre) and children's dances.

Masks are often part of a *bugaku* dance. Those used for the dances still performed (and many of those preserved in temples and other repositories associated with dances no longer performed) closely resemble some of the masks employed in religious performances in Bhutan.

The Imperial Household Agency (keeper and administrator of the imperial family) maintains a *bugaku* section for the preservation and performance, at certain times of the year, of this ancient form. Additionally, some shrines and temples have kept up *bugaku* performances as part of festivals and other yearly observances.

Noh and kyogen

What is called *noh* drama today dates from the early part of the 15th century. As an art form, its high degree of stylisation, monotonous-sounding vocal declamation (*utai*, a cross between chanting and dramatic narrative), and lack of overt action, makes it a distinctly acquired taste.

Such terms as classic dignity, grace and symbolism are used to describe the *noh* drama. It is said to have been developed from a dance-drama form called *sarugaku*. Little is known about *sarugaku*. There is evidence that it belonged to the same category as *kagura* – a calling-down into physical manifestation and

an offering to a deity or deities. Also, it seems there were wandering troupes who performed *sarugaku*. Considered part of the *noh* repertoire, the sprightly dance *sanbaso* is performed by tradition as part of the rituals to invoke a felicitous beginning, such as for the upcoming new year or for a new company.

Whatever its origins, *noh* was perfected by Kan'ami Kiyotsugu (1333–84) and his son, Zeami Motokiyo, who were playwrights, actors and aesthetic theorists of the highest level. Together they created about one-third of the 240 *noh* plays known today.

A Japanese harp player in Kyoto.

THOUSAND-YEAR-OLD MUSIC

There are solo or small-ensemble musical forms, particularly those featuring the harp-like *koto*, *shakuhachi* bamboo flute, *shamisen* and the numerous *taiko* (drum) and *minyon* (folk singing) troupes. But the most authentic (if not typical) form of Japanese music performed apart from drama or dance is *gagaku* (literally translated as "elegant music"). It is a kind of orchestral music developed in the 9th century and little changed since.

Quite unlike the popular entertainments described elsewhere, *gagaku* was strictly court music, almost never performed in public before World War II, and only occasionally now.

It employs esoteric instruments resembling – sometimes identical to – those used in India and China long before high-tech instruments such as the *koto* or the *sitar* were developed. These include drums, nose-flutes and bowed, single-stringed droners. Together with a slow, "courtly" tempo, *gagaku* is ideal for (and to most Japanese ears, synonymous with) funeral music. In fact, probably the first and only time the Japanese public has heard it in recent times was during the elaborate televised funeral of Emperor Showa (Hirohito) in 1989. Devotees to the form find tremendous excitement in *gagaku's* extended, soulful sounds and unrelieved tensions.

Buddhism had a profound influence on the content and dramatic structure of *noh*. The veil of "illusion" that we perceive as everyday "reality" is, in a sense, pierced momentarily by *noh* to expose something more basic, something that subsumes the senses.

Masks, highly stylised sets and props (when such things do appear), a tightly controlled style of movement, a voice style that projects and declaims but does not entice, and musical accompaniment – *hayashi* – of a few types of drum and a piercing fife mean that this form of play relies mostly on imagery and symbolism for its dramatic impact. In contrast to this sparse and uncluttered form of drama, the textiles used for *noh* costumes are the diametric opposite. The world's most opulent and gorgeous gold and silver and polychrome brocades are what the *noh* actor wears on stage. And *noh* masks are an art form in themselves.

As with Greek drama, the heavy and sober *noh* is performed in tandem with the light farces of *kyogen* (literally *crazy words*), itself thought to reflect more directly the *sarugaku* antecedents it shares with *noh*. Although the dramatic methods have something in common with *noh*, *kyogen* does not use masks and is more direct and active. Traditionally it is performed during intermissions of a *noh* performance, but today it is often performed by itself. These farces are both part of and independent of *noh* – lighthearted, concerned with nonsense, and simple.

Bunraku

Japan's glorious puppet drama is a combination of three elements, which, about 400 years ago, fused into a composite: *shamisen* music, puppetry techniques and a form of narrative or epic-chanting called *joruri*. The result is *bunraku*, the puppet drama that is considered to be an equal with live-stage theatre performance. Although *bunraku* developed and matured in the two centuries after its creation, the origin of the puppetry techniques used is still shrouded in mystery. There are folk-puppet dramas scattered throughout Japan, but the centre of *bunraku* puppet drama is in Osaka.

The *shamisen* (a banjo-like instrument) entered Japan from the kingdom of the Ryukyus (now known as Okinawa) sometime in the 16th century and was adapted and spread throughout the country very quickly. Although the instrument only has three strings, music produced by the *shamisen* has great versatility and, in particular, lends itself well to dramatic emphasis.

Bunraku puppets *(ningyo)* are manipulated directly by hand and are quite large – it takes three men to handle one of the major puppets in a play. The skills involved in manipulation of *bunraku* puppets are considerable. The narrative style derives from classic epics of heroism chanted to the accompaniment of a *biwa*, a form of lute that made its way to Japan from central Asia at an early date. Although there may be more than one *shamisen* to give musical density to the accompaniment, there is only one chanter.

Performance at the Prefectural Noh Theater.

He uses different tones of voice to distinguish male from female characters, young from old, good from bad. Accent and intonation convey nuances of feeling and indicate shifts of scene.

While *bunraku* and *kabuki* share many traits and have some plays in common, *bunraku* is the older of the two and it was *kabuki* that adopted elements of the puppet drama. The important point is that both *bunraku* and *kabuki* are popular theatre. *Bunraku* was for townspeople and intended as popular entertainment, much like Shakespeare's plays were in his day.

Kabuki

Plays for *kabuki* are still being written. Not many, granted, but the genre is alive, and like *bunraku* it is not "classical". *Kabuki* is the equivalent of cabaret spectacular, soap opera, morality play, religious pageant and tear-jerker. It is music and dance and story and colour and pathos and farce, everything any theatre-goer could want.

The highly stylised language of *kabuki*, the poses and posturing and eye-crossing for dramatic emphasis, the swashbuckling and acrobatics and flashy exits, instant costume changes and magic transformations – all are part of the fun.

Kabuki originated in the early years of the 17th century with a troupe of women who performed on the river bank at Kyoto what seems

A puppet play (bunraku).

There are some 240 plays in the kabuki repertoire of jidai-mono, or historical events and episodes, and sewa-mono, which deals with the lives of townspeople.

to have been a kind of dance (based on a dance performed at Buddhist festivals) and perhaps comic skits as well. Whether there was anything untoward in this performance probably will never be known, but the shogunal authorities seemed to think there was, and so in 1629 they banned women from appearing on stage. Male performers took their place, and to this day all *kabuki* performers are men; the discipline of

the actor who takes female parts (*onnagata*) is particularly rigorous.

The female troupes were supplanted in short order by itinerant troupes of young men, who also got into trouble with the authorities. These groups were disbanded and the permanent theatre companies then developed in Kyoto, Osaka and Edo (now Tokyo) after the middle of the 17th century. *Kabuki* soon became the Edo Period's most popular entertainment.

The production of a *kabuki* play involves strict conventions governing gestures and other movements, colours, props, costumes, wigs and make-up. Even the types of textiles used for costumes are determined. (But there are places in a play left for spontaneous ad-libs.) The audience directs much attention to the performer or performers. The story is secondary and it will be well-known anyway. *Kabuki* devotees want to see favourite stars in familiar roles. Indeed, *kabuki* has been actor-centred since its beginning.

The training of a *kabuki* actor starts at about the age of three, when children are left by their actor parents backstage. The children internalise the atmosphere and the music's rhythms. With this kind of training, *kabuki* naturally becomes part of one's core early on in life. This facilitates the years of rigorous apprenticeship and training that every *kabuki* actor must undergo.

The *kabuki* stage has a number of unique features. The most striking is the walkway that extends from the stage to the doors at the rear of the theatre at stage level. Actors enter and exit through this stage extension (*hanamichi*, meaning flower path), and it is sometimes used as a venue of action. Another feature is the curtain, decorated in vertical stripes of black, green and orange, opened from stage right to left. The *kabuki* theatre also featured a revolving stage long before the concept arose in Europe.

Dramatic pause

Neither noh and *kabuki* show a clear-cut distinction between dance forms and stage movements. Still, *kabuki*'s grandiloquent gestures are a far cry from the austere containment of *noh*. The *kabuki* technique called *mie* illustrates the formalised beauty of performance. A *mie* occurs at certain climactic moments when the starring actor, projecting dramatic energy at top output, freezes into a statuesque pose with rigid stare and eyes crossed to emphasise a dramatic peak of intense emotional power. Glorious overkill, indeed.

The new J-culture

Modern Japanese drama dates from the emergence of *Shin-geki*, experimental, Western-style drama spearheaded by directors like Kaoru Osanai and Hogetsu Shimamura in the early 20th century. The first performance of Ibsen's contentious *A Doll's House* in 1910, with Matsui Sumako as Nora, electrified audiences.

The post-war period witnessed an extraordinary flowering in new theatre and performance. Young playwrights and directors, attuned to political polemic, placed their audiences in open areas, tents, and street venues, collapsing conventional ideas about space.

The performing arts in contemporary Japan are alive and well. The internationally acclaimed director Ninagawa Yukio is known for his innovative productions of classic Japanese theatre and Shakespeare (he has staged eight different versions of *Hamlet*, the most recent in 2015), while theatre of the absurd figurehead Tanino Kurou is active on the international stage.

Music has always been a dynamic sector of the entertainment industry. Audiences for Enka, a soulful, vernacular form of song, with the emphasis on lament, have declined, but filling its place has been a surge in roots music. *Minyo* (folk music) from the Tohoku region, led by *shamisen* players the Yoshida Brothers, and drum troupes like Kodo from Sado Island, have toured abroad, but the biggest roots phenomena has been the resurgence of Okinawan music.

The haunting sound of the *sanshin*, a three-stringed instrument similar to the Japanese *shamisen*, defines, along with its unique vocal delivery, the sound of these remote islands. According to Okinawan music specialist John Potter, "the *sanshin* predates the Japanese *shamisen* and evolved from the larger Chinese *sanxian*".

While *shima-uta* (island song) remains the core of Okinawan music, the form has undergone exciting new developments. There have been several fruitful collaborations with overseas musicians. *Sanshin* player Yasukatsu Oshima has collaborated with US pianist Geoffrey Keezer, the singer Tomoko Uehara recorded with Irish fiddler Nollaig Casey, while Kina Shoukichi and his band Champloose, key figures in the creation of contemporary Okinawan music, made an album with legendary blues guitarist Ry Cooder.

Japan's most successful and exportable musical entertainment form, however, has been J-Pop. With its origins in British sixties pop, the genre is big business. To many observers, J-Pop suggests transience, but there are several performers, like Hamasaki Ayumi and Amuro Namie, and bands like SMAP, all well into their late thirties, who continue to be popular, packing out concerts and selling millions of songs. An interesting outgrowth of the movement has been its mirror image in Korea, K-Pop, a brand that is enormously popular among Japanese youth.

Kabuki performed in Oshika.

SHOCK DANCE

Performances may be announced at the last minute, venues moved from theatres to car parks, audiences exposed to sensory shocks. Welcome to *butoh*, Japan's most radical underground dance form. Stripped of the formalism of traditional Japanese dance, *butoh's* intensity, the nerve points and emotions it explores in almost total silence, the vision of semi-naked dancers smeared in white body paint, are definitely not for mainstream Japanese audiences. *Butoh's* rejection of Western dance influences, its avowed aim to return to more elemental Japanese emotions, and its incorporation of taboo subjects have ensured it remains radical.

THE CINEMA OF JAPAN

Japanese cinema has always refused to embrace the values of Hollywood. In doing so, it has produced some of the world's most aesthetic and powerful films.

The Japanese cinema has been pronounced dead so many times over the past few years – perhaps most often by Japanese critics and filmmakers – that its stubborn survival, if not full resurrection, comes as a relief. Just when it seemed that Japanese audiences had of films detailing their country's history, along came *Mononoke Hime (Princess Mononoke)* from Miyazaki Hayao, which smashed the previous all-time box-office record. What was so heartening about the success of the Miyazaki film was that Japanese were indeed interested to see an epic historical fantasy about Japanese history, set in an ancient time filled with gods and demons. *Mononoke Hime* is a cartoon, or more accurately, anime (see page 95), which has always been taken more seriously in Japan than in the West.

Japanese style

Dramatically, the classic three-act structure of Hollywood holds little place in Japanese cinema. Character and mood, rather than plot, are what propel many of its best films. Stories often trail off without a "proper" ending, storylines (especially in *jidai-geki*, or historical dramas) can be convoluted and confusing, even to the most ardent devotees, and most move at a slow pace.

In a typical Japanese movie, dynamic action stands in contrast to long, sustained scenes of inactive dialogue, or just silence. Directors not only take the time to smell the roses but to plant them, nurture them, and then watch them grow, quietly. Landscape and atmosphere also play key roles in Japanese cinema, perhaps tied into the other major religion of the country, the pantheistic Shinto. Floating mists, drops of water slowly falling into a stream, the soft, sad sound of cherry blossoms falling on an April day – all are familiar to Japanese audiences. Of course, it must also be

Poster for the film 'Yojimbo' (1961), starring Toshiro Mifune.

OZU'S CAMERA EYE

Yasujiro Ozu (1903–63) was, arguably, Japan's greatest film director. The originality and technical skills of works like *Floating Weeds, But...* and *Record of a Tenement Gentleman* are still admired by film buffs and students. Ozu's work is a good example of Japanese cinema's ability to define a style and approach through limitation. In Ozu's case this took the form of the lingering single, long shot. An aesthetic objectivity results from this restricted view. Ozu's best-known classic is *Tokyo Story (Tokyo Monogatari)*, a wonderful work of directorial understatement routinely voted one of the best films of all time by bodies such as the British Film Institute.

said that such mass-market genres as *kaiju* (giant monster) and contemporary *yakuza* (gangster) movies are often just as breathlessly mounted as the latest Hollywood action flick.

There's also considerably more space in Japanese cinema for morally dubious protagonists since, in both the Shinto and Buddhist traditions, life is a balance between forces of good and evil, with both necessary to maintain life as we know it. Thus, a cold-blooded killer like the *ronin* (master-less *samurai*) Ogami Ito, who roams Japan with his tiny son Daigoro, dispatching others by decapitation and disembowelment in the

A scene from 'Tokyo Story' (1953).

GODZILLA

To the Japanese people, Godzilla isn't some huge, lumbering, atomic-born giant lizard. He's their huge, lumbering, atomic-born giant lizard. With the 31 movies since his debut in 1954's *Gojira* (a combination of the Japanese words for "gorilla" and "whale", anglicised to Godzilla for its US release two years later), this monster who towers above Tokyo smashing everything in his path is one of the most famous icons of post-war Japan. Naturally, despite (or more probably because of) its special effects and far-fetched plot, the first of the many Godzilla movies became a huge hit, not only in Japan but throughout Southeast Asia, the US and Europe.

popular *Sword of Vengeance* series of films, would baffle most Western audiences. Is he a good guy or a bad guy? The answer is both. The dirty, amoral bodyguard in Kurosawa Akira's *Yojimbo* and *Sanjuro* would also fit this bill quite beautifully. He was the prototype for Clint Eastwood's man with no name in Sergio Leone's operatic spaghetti Westerns *A Fistful of Dollars* (a remake of *Yojimbo*) and *The Good, the Bad and the Ugly*.

But what really makes Japanese film special isn't so much the bloodshed and ultra-violence, but rather the profound humanism and compassion ranging through its entire history. Look no further than Kurosawa's *Ikiru* and *Ran*, Ozu's *Tokyo Story*, Kinoshita Keisuke's *Twenty-Four Eyes* or Mizoguchi's *The Life of Oharu*.

Filmmaking stars

The great, golden age of Japanese film, which lasted from the post-war 1950s until the late 1960s when the burgeoning availability of television laid it to waste, is certainly gone. The three major studios still surviving – Toho, Shochiku and Toei – barely crank out enough domestic films in a year to fill a couple of the multiplexes that are suddenly springing up. But it's not over yet.

The death of Kurosawa Akira in 1998 was a particular blow. "Sensei", as he became known, almost single-handedly put Japanese film on the international map with *Rashômon*, which won top prize at the 1951 Venice Film Festival. His rising and falling fortunes over the next half-century were emblematic of the Japanese industry itself. Endlessly frustrated by unreceptive Japanese studios and aborted projects, Kurosawa attempted suicide after a box-office failure in 1970. Yet he would go on to make five more films, at least two of which – *Kagemusha* and, particularly, *Ran* – would be counted among his greatest works. However, Kurosawa repeatedly had to look outside Japan to Francis Ford Coppola, George Lucas, Steven Spielberg and Serge Silberman for support.

Imamura Shohei, one of Japan's acclaimed filmmakers, who died in 2006, brought a gritty realism to Japanese cinema, preferring to make films portraying people from the lower classes. He won the Palme d'Or at the Cannes Film Festival for *The Ballad of Narayama* (in 1982) and *The Eel* (in 1997).

Japanese film suffered a shocking and unexpected blow by the still inexplicable 1997 suicide scandal of Itami Juzo. (A tabloid newspaper was about to reveal a supposed relationship between the filmmaker and a younger woman.) Itami was responsible for smart and funny dissections of contemporary life, all of them starring his wife, Miyamoto Nobuko: *The Funeral*, *Tampopo* and the societal exposés of the *Taxing Woman* films.

Another shock to the system was the 1996 death of actor Atsumi Kiyoshi, Japan's beloved Tora-san. Over a span of nearly 30 years and 47 films, this itinerant amulet seller was to Japan what Chaplin's Little Tramp was to the world during the Silent Era, only more so. Within the restrictive, often suffocating bounds of Japanese society, Tora-san's gypsy-like existence had strong appeal to the millions of businessmen, and his endlessly disappointing romances held women in thrall.

Bright lights, new generation

Although filmmaking styles have been altered for scaled-down financial resources and changing audience tastes, there's much to recommend in Japan's current generation of filmmakers. Suo Masayuki's delightful *Shall We Dance?* (1996) was the highest-grossing foreign-language film ever to play in US movie theatres at the time. The anarchic, dark, violent and often funny ruminations by Takeshi "Beat" Kitano – a tremendously successful and popular comedian, actor, game-show host, raconteur and moviemaker – have won international acclaim, particularly the alternately tender and cataclysmic *Hana-Bi (Fireworks)*, and *Zatoichi*, which won the Silver Lion award at Venice in 2003, as well as *Outrage*, which competed for the 2010 Palme d'Or in Cannes.

Nationalistic dramas

Japan's economic downturn of the 1990s produced even greater box-office revenues. Much of this is due to to foreign films such as *Titanic*, but domestic product was also on the rise.

Elsewhere there was scrutiny and criticism from the Japanese and international media with another film, *Unmei no Toki (Pride)*, a big-budget, nationalistic biopic from director Ito Shunya that sympathetically portrayed Japan's wartime prime minister, General Tojo Hideki. A storm of controversy erupted around the region upon the film's release. Asians were incensed that the man generally considered to be the prime instigator of Japanese Asian aggression – and the person responsible for what has become known as the Rape of Nanjing – was depicted in the film to be

Hung along Kyuome Kaido, the main street of Ome, a town west of Tokyo, are many old hand-painted movie signboards called kanban. From Nakahira Ko's 1956 Crazed Fruit to scenes from chanbara (samurai action films), the street is a boulevard of nostalgia.

battling for Asian interests against Western imperialism. *Pride* was made for a huge (by Japanese standards) US$11 million and starred the highly respected actor Tsugawa Masahiko as Tojo.

The 1997 film 'Hana-bi' (released as 'Fireworks' in the US) was written by and starred Takeshi Kitano.

Japanese films about World War II have always veered wildly between the powerfully pacifistic (Ichikawa Kon's harsh *Fires on the Plain* and the stunningly emotional *The Burmese Harp*, also directed by Ichikawa) and jingoistic flag-waving. Often, war films try to have it both ways, especially in recent war movies in which popular teen idols, male and female, are cast in primary roles and then killed off tragically.

Hollywood's Japan

The claim that the Japanese enjoy nothing more than seeing themselves through the eyes of the outside world is corroborated by a glut of well-received Hollywood-made movies with Japanese locations and subjects. Hollywood had been fascinated with Japan as a setting for its dramas even before the 1958 John Wayne hit *The Barbarian and the Geisha*, or the 007 thriller *You Only Live Twice*, but the years round the turn of the millennium witnessed a Japan boom that seems unstoppable.

Memorable films include Ridley Scott's *Black Rain* (1989), filmed in Osaka, where a thriving criminal underworld provided theme and visual substance, and Paul Schrader's *Mishima (1985)*, which looked at the troubled but intriguing life of literary giant and right-wing imperialist Yukio Mishima.

'*Mogari no Mori*' ('*The Mourning Forest*') won the Grand Prix at the 2007 Cannes Film Festival.

Quentin Tarantino's 2003 *Kill Bill Volume 1* and its sequel *Kill Bill Volume 2* were homages to the Japanese *yakuza* film; Tom Cruise's portrayal of a transplanted American Civil War veteran in *The Last Samurai* was a smash hit in Japan; Sophia Coppola's Oscar-winning comedy *Lost in Translation*, which nevertheless received some criticism for its dated view of the Japanese, was filmed almost entirely in a Tokyo hotel and picked up an Oscar in 2003. The 2005 film version of Arthur Golden's novel *Memoirs of a Geisha* became a hit in Japan, where it was released under the title of its main character, *Sayuri*. Clint Eastwood's look at warfare from the American and Japanese perspective in *Flags of Our Fathers* and *Letters from Iwo*

Jima (2006) are more sophisticated examples of how Japan continues to inspire Hollywood.

Contemporary film

The silver lining for Japan's silver screen after the erosion of the studio system has been more freedom for independent directors. Although many independent production companies have become mainstream now, their works are among the best being made today. Early film successes were Ichikawa Jun's *Tokyo Lullaby* and Iwai Shunji's 1996 *Swallowtail*, a story about mindless materialism in a fictional urban setting called Yen City.

Addressing other shortcomings of contemporary existence are a number of thoughtful films by Kiyoshi Kurosawa, including the future-set *Barren Illusion*, the 2000 film *Charisma* and the later *Tokyo Sonata*, which addresses the dilemmas faced by an unemployed salaryman. His *Journey to the Shore*, a story about love and death, won the Un Certain Regard Award for Best Director at the 2015 Cannes Film Festival.

Another serious take on society's shortcomings is Koreeda Hirokazu's drama about children switched at birth, *Like Father, Like Son*, which won the Jury Prize in Cannes in 2013.

Kawase Naomi's *Morning Forest* won the prestigious Grand Prix at Cannes in 2007, her second nomination for the award. *Still the Water* and *Our Little Sister* both competed for the Palme d'Or at the Cannes Film Festival in 2014 and 2015 respectively.

Other films with serious themes and excellent casts are *Bad Company* (2001), the sombre *I Just Didn't Do It* (2006), *All Around Us* (2008) and Yamada Yoji's *About Her Brother* (2010). Yojiro Takita's life-affirming *Departures*, which took the prize for best foreign film at the Oscars in 2009, is set in a funeral parlour in Yamagata Prefecture. Narushima Izuru's award-winning *Rebirth* (2011), Ishii Yuya's *The Great Passage* (2013) about a dictionary editor, and Yamazaki Takashi's war drama *The Eternal Zero* (2013), depicting Kamikaze pilots, are some of the best films produced in recent years.

Japanese directors are not renowned overseas for their comedies, but there are some exemplary films, like Uchida Kenji's *A Stranger of Mine* (2005), Naito Takasugu's *The Dark Harbour* (2009), and Yoshida Daihachi's *The Kirishima Thing* (2012). Writer-director Ogigami Naoko's 2010 feature *Toilet*, a light but delightful comedy about values and bonding in an insecure world, was made entirely in English.

Anime

The Japanese have been in the anime business for a long time. Cartoonists like Kitayama Seitaro and Terauchi Junichi experimented with animated motion pictures as early as 1913.

Terauchi's first silhouette animation, *Kujira (The Whale)*, was made in 1927, a year before Walt Disney released his first Mickey Mouse cartoon. Highly influenced by manga (see page 83) – the thick comic books read by young and old in Japan – the link to anime is logical: the comic-book manga is a series of storyboards, a model used to great effect in anime. The structural similarities are natural as the majority of animated films in Japan are adapted from bestselling comic books.

As for the more adult fare… well, here's where presentational differences are quite clear. Ultra-violence, raw sexuality and nudity, visionary and often apocalyptic views of the future, and extreme graphic style are the hallmarks of this genre, with most efforts falling into the science-fiction category. The better examples of these are truly stunning and original, such as Otomo Katsuhiro's 1989 classic *Akira* and, more recently, Oshii Mamoru's *The Ghost in the Shell*. Oshii went on to make the 2001 experimental anime *Avalon*, and to direct the 2008 feature *The Sky Crawlers*. One of the most commercially successful projects, tying in anime with the toy market and computer software, has been the 1998 *Pocket Monsters (Pokemon)* series, a huge hit overseas.

Miyazaki Hayao and Studio Ghibli

But there's an alternative to the endless parade of animated juggernauts, cuddly toys and bare breasts – and his name is Miyazaki Hayao. Miyazaki heads the famed Studio Ghibli, which has been responsible for what many would consider to be the finest anime to emerge from Japan. Miyazaki got his start in TV anime, directing a popular multi-part version of Heidi before moving into features with *The Castle of Cagliostro*, based on a popular James Bondian character known as Lupin the Third. Since then, his films as director have included such fanciful, haunting and often humorous fantasy efforts as *Nausicaa of the Valley of the Wind*, *Laputa – The Castle in the Sky*, *Porco Rosso*, *My Neighbour Totoro*, *Kiki's Delivery Service* and the gigantic box-office hit *Mononoke Hime*, or *Princess Mononoke*.

Shinto strongly informs *Princess Mononoke* – a complex story that is essentially about the inevitable clash between humans and the deities of nature – and the remarkable *Heise Tanuki Gassen Pompoko* (supervised by Miyazaki but directed by Ghibli's Takahata Isao), which is about raccoons fighting the destruction of their forest home in what would later become the Tokyo suburb of Tama. Miyazaki's *Sen to Chihiro no Kamikakushi (Spirited Away)* received an Oscar for best animated feature in 2003. Miyazaki has since made *Ponyo*, a 2009 animated feature about a little girl who is half fish but wants to become human, and *The Wind Rises*,

'Spirited Away' is one of Studio Ghibli's best known anime films.

an award-winning drama about the designer of Mitsubishi fighter aircrafts. Released in 2013, it was the director's last film before his retirement.

There are other fine examples of ambitious anime directors who defy the supercharged sci-fi traditions, including Hosada Mamoru, the acclaimed director of the 2006 *The Girl Who Leapt Through Time*, *Summer Wars* (2009), *Wolf Children* (2012) and *The Boy and the Beast* (2015).

The genre has exercised an enormous influence on movie-making itself, a tendency corroborated by film auteur Donald Richie, who wrote, "The majority of new films are now constructed like manga since this is the only narrative form that most young people know."

Thatched houses in Central Honshu.

地酒 おみやげ　山峡の家

ARCHITECTURE

With its post-and-beam construction, Japanese architecture allows flexible use of interior space and dissolves the rigid boundary between indoors and outdoors.

What kind of house would one build in Japan if one knew it might be blown apart in a natural disaster? Besides typhoons and earthquakes, Japan also has severe rains, which often cause flooding and landslides. How would one make a palace or temple or hall, a farmhouse or a gate to survive such destructive forces? These questions had to be faced by the designers of buildings in Japan's remote past and are still faced today.

The fact that Japan has the world's oldest wooden buildings (Horyu-ji, built about AD 607) and the world's largest wooden structure (at Todai-ji, some 50 metres/165ft high and said to have been rebuilt at only two-thirds its original size) suggests that the architectural system adopted by the Japanese was at least partially successful in creating structures that last. The devastation of the 1995 Kobe earthquake suggests otherwise. Indeed, rather than wind, earth or water, it is fire that is the greatest destroyer of buildings in Japan, although few buildings could have withstood the type of tsunami the world witnessed on 11 March 2011 along the devastated Tohoku coastline.

Nonetheless, Japanese architecture has influenced architectural design throughout the world. Its concepts of fluidity, modularity, making the most of limited space, and use of light and shadow have a great power and appeal, both aesthetically and as solutions to architectural problems in contemporary times.

Whatever factors determined how buildings were constructed in Japan – survival, tradition, aesthetics – some common characteristics can be found that define the tradition of Japanese architecture.

The oldest Japanese dwellings are the pit houses of the Neolithic Jomon culture, but the

The roof and gables of the Atsuta Shrine in Nagoya.

oldest structures to which the term "architecture" might be applied are the Grand Shrines of Ise (see page 275). First completed in the 5th century, the shrines have been ritually rebuilt 60 times – every 20 years. Each rebuilding takes years to accomplish, starting with the cutting of special cypress trees deep in the mountains, and involves special carpentry techniques as well as time-honoured rituals.

Early influences

The introduction of Buddhism to Japan in AD 552 brought with it a whole raft of cultural and technical features, not least of which was the continental style of architecture. It is said that Korean builders came over to Japan and either built or supervised the building of the Horyu-ji (AD 607). The foundations of the vast temple that was the prototype of Horyu-ji can be seen in Kyongju, South Korea.

In the 7th century, at the capital in Nara, Chinese architectural influence became quite obvious, not only in the structures themselves, but in the adoption of the north–south grid plan of the streets, based on the layout of the Chinese capital. At this time, secular and sacred architecture were essentially the same, and palaces were often rededicated as temples. Both displayed red-lacquered columns and green roofs with pronounced upswinging curves in the eaves. Roofs were tiled.

From the Heian Period to the Edo Period

The mutability of residence and temple held true in the subsequent Heian Period as well, as evidenced by the villa of the nobleman Fujiwara no Yorimichi (990–1074), which became the Phoenix Hall of Byodo-in, in Uji near Kyoto. The graceful *shinden-zukuri* style of this structure, utilised for the residences of Heian court nobles, is characterised by rectangular structures

The Horyu-ji complex, Nara.

FORTIFIED ARCHITECTURE

Feudal-era castle towns were highly schematised. Revolving around the central fortress were merchant and shopkeepers' quarters. The temple district was positioned in the southeast, close to the elegant villas and attached gardens of the samurai. In small rural cities like Hikone, Inuyama and Matsue, this architectural paradigm remains largely intact. A shift in castle design took place in 1579, when the warrior Oda Nobunaga chose a low hill with commanding views of the surrounding plains to build his towering, many-tiered *donjon*. Of the 12 original Japanese fortresses still in existence, and the countless replicas that have sprung up in the last century, most follow this template.

To make wooden structures more durable, castles were built on top of colossal, cut boulders. Each level was reinforced with plaster and clay to defend it against fire and artillery. Overhanging gables lend elegant curves to the design, colourful pendants were hung from the eaves, and symbolic dolphin statues were placed on the roof to act as talismans against fire.

Few Edo Period castles were destroyed in battle. Instead it took a more enlightened age to dismantle Japan's martial architecture. The new Meiji government, coming to power in 1868, demolished all but a handful of its citadels. Others were pulled down by local patriots, who saw them as symbols of feudalism.

in symmetrical arrangement and linked by long corridors. The layout of Kyoto's Old Imperial Palace is similar, though it is a replica of this style.

When the imperial court at Kyoto lost the reins of power to the military government of the shogunate, located far to the west in Kamakura, the open and vulnerable *shinden* style was supplanted by a type of residential building more easily defended. This warrior style *(bukke-zukuri)* placed a number of rooms under one roof or a series of conjoined roofs and was surrounded by a defensive device such as a fence, wall or moat, with guard towers and gates. Tiled roofs gave way to either shingled or thatched roofs. This period also saw the importation of Chinese Song-dynasty architectural styles for temples, particularly the so-called Zen style, which is characterised by shingled roofs, pillars set on carved stone plinths, and the "hidden roof" system developed in Japan, among other features.

In the subsequent Muromachi Period, which saw the purest expression of feudal government and its break-up into the Age of Warring States (15th century), Zen Buddhist influence transformed the warrior style into the *shoin* style. This at first was little more than the addition of a small reading or waiting room *(shoin)*, with a deep sill that could be used as a desk, and decorative, built-in shelves to hold books or other objects. This room also displayed an alcove, the *toko-noma*, in which treasured objects could be effectively displayed. This *shoin* room eventually exerted its influence over the entire structure. Both the Golden Pavilion and the Silver Pavilion of Kyoto are examples of this style.

At the end of the Age of Warring States, firearms became common in warfare, and in response to this, massive castles were built. Few original structures remain today. Himeji Castle, with white walls and soaring roof, is the finest example.

Political change brought the country into the Edo Period, and architecture saw a melding of the *shoin* style and teahouse concepts to produce the *sukiya* style, the grandest example of which is the Katsura Imperial Villa in Kyoto. This residential architecture displays an overall lightness of members, a simplified roof and restrained, subtle ornamentation.

A box with a hat

The favoured material of building construction is wood. Walls, foundations of castles, the podia of some structures, and a few novel experiments saw stone in limited use, usually without mortar. Yet, undoubtedly because it was plentiful, wood remained the material of preference, particularly the wood of conifers. This is reflected in the reforestation laws of the shogunate and various feudal lords. The disappearance of certain types of large tree due to lumbering is reflected in certain historical changes in temple and shrine buildings.

This preference for wood is directly related to the fact that the basic structural system in Japanese architecture is post and beam. The structure is basically a box upon which a hat – the roof – rests. This system allows great freedom in the

Himeji Castle, Okayama.

design of the roof, and the Japanese seemed to prefer large ones, sometimes exceeding half the total height of a structure. Roofs also became elaborate, with generous eaves, and often very heavy.

Straight lines dominate Japanese architecture, seemingly a natural result of using wood and the post-and-beam system. There are few curves and no arches. Post-and-beam boxes can also be combined and strung together in many ways to create fine aesthetic effects. The Katsura Imperial Villa in Kyoto represents the height of such architecture. Since posts or columns bear the weight of the roof, walls could be – and were – thin and non-supporting. This lightness was developed to the point that walls often ceased to be walls and became more like movable partitions instead.

This is the origin of fluidity or modularity, perhaps the single most noteworthy aspect of Japanese buildings. Interior spaces were partitioned so that rooms could become more versatile, to be combined or contracted. The former was accomplished through the use of sliding and removable door panels. A room could be divided by decorative standing screens, especially ones with gold backgrounds to act as a reflective surface and bring light into gloomy castle or palace interiors. Corridor width was the necessary width for two people with serving trays to pass one another.

In effect, this means that the indoor–outdoor fluidity is mainly visual and for circulation of air, not for movement of people.

In rural areas the veranda, when open, becomes a meeting place, to sit and talk with a neighbour.

Traditional materials

The materials used in traditional Japanese room interiors are few and limited, reflecting an ambivalence between interior and exterior, or perhaps a pleasure in harmonising rather than sharply demarking interior and exterior.

A house in Uchiko, Shikoku.

Inside is outside

The distinction between wall and door often disappears. This applies to outside walls – the "boundary" between interior and exterior – as well. External walls are often nothing more than a series of sliding wooden panels that can be easily removed, thus eliminating the solid border between inside and outside, a feature very much welcomed in Japan's humid summer. The veranda thus becomes a transitional space, connecting interior with exterior.

Since the floors of traditional Japanese buildings are generally raised, house floor and ground surface are not contiguous (except in the case of the packed-earth *doma*, the work and implement storage area of a farmhouse).

Sliding door panels are either translucent *shoji* or the heavier, opaque *fusuma* paper screens, or of wood. Floors are of thick, resilient straw mats surfaced with woven reed (*tatami* mats), or of plain wood.

Supportive wooden posts remain exposed, and ceilings are generally of wood or of woven materials of various kinds. With the exception of lacquered surfaces, wood remains unpainted.

Because of the generous eaves of Japanese buildings, interiors tend to be dark and often enough may be gloomy. The use of translucent paper *shoji* screens to diffuse soft light helps, but the soft, natural colours of the room materials generally absorb rather than reflect light. The colours, lighting and textures of traditional

Japanese rooms influenced the qualities of all objects to be used in them, including clothing.

Design principles

The artistic unity or harmony of a building extends to its properties as well. Master carpenters, who were both the architects and the builders of traditional buildings, developed aesthetic proportions that applied to all elements of a single structure, as well as to individual buildings in a complex. There are special and sophisticated carpenter's measures that apply this system of aesthetic proportion to construction.

A Japanese ceramic bowl and a kimono look very different when seen in a traditional Japanese room rather than a room with plaster walls and glass windows.

Development is still taking its toll on Japan's architectural legacy, though an awakening preservation ethic is beginning to take root among citizen groups with an affection for older structures and a sense of the importance of visible history.

The Edo-Tokyo Open-Air Architectural Mus-

Nishida-ke garden, Kanazawa, Ishikawa.

Teahouses show an awesome skill in building. Their lack of surface ornament, as seen in the rustic simplicity of unpainted wood, is itself a design statement, the signature of the skilled artisan.

Historically, Japanese architecture shows a dialectic between imported and adapted continental styles (mainly from China, but some also from the Korean Peninsula) and native Japanese styles.

Preservation ethic

In Japan, natural disasters, an erosive climate and a weak preservation ethic militate against architectural heritage. As Japan architecture scholar Mira Locher has written, "Buildings were understood to be part of the changing environment rather than permanent fixtures".

eum in Musashi-Koganei is a collection of buildings and structures that have been saved from the wrecker's ball and collected inside a sympathetic setting in Koganei Park.

Exhibits include the former homes of the Mitsui family, the important Meiji Period economist Korekiyo Takahashi, a Taisho-era bungalow from the garden suburb of Denenchofu, and a home designed in 1925 by the modernist architect Sutemi Horiguchi. Visitors can enter these homes and explore the rooms. Supplementing private residences are a photo studio, soy sauce and cosmetic shop, dry food store, and a number of intriguing urban features of the city, such as a fire observation tower, and even a Meiji-era police box that once stood at the entrance to Mansei Bridge.

The museum is a fitting introduction to the historical architecture of the capital and to the design aspirations of two very different ages.

Into the future

From the humble capsule hotel, a uniquely Japanese design that was not only based on space shuttle accommodation for astronauts but also the humble rental container, city architecture today is more ambitious. New structures like Tokyo Midtown, Design Sight 21_21, the Iceberg Tokyo Building, Keyaki Omotesando

21_21 Design Sight, a design museum in Tokyo.

Building, Tokyo Sky Tree (the highest structure in the country, completed in 2012), Toranomon Hills, and Abeno Harukas in Osaka (the tallest skyscraper in Japan, opened in 2014), are the results of this experimentation. The modern anti-earthquake technology that provides shock absorbers and floating plates for cutting edge

> To see authentic, steep thatch-roofed, A-framed farmhouses (gassho-zukuri), visit the villages of Shirakawa-go. The villages were made a Unesco World Heritage Site in 1995.

projects like these and for the more utilitarian new office blocks and upmarket condominiums is only available to the very affluent, however.

For the modernist, this is clearly a good time to be an architect in Japan. The country has the highest number of professional architects per capita in the world. After periods of hubris, showmanship and unlimited budgets, serious designers are in the ascendancy. Many of today's building projects are stand-out structures, designs of almost transcendental beauty and managed semantics in the midst of unconsidered construction sprawls. No ordinary structures, these are experiments by a distinguished group of designers to promote discourse on architecture.

A prime example is the De Beers Ginza Building, where the undulating facade appears to be experiencing a dramatic mutation, not unlike the self-regenerating surfaces of Shinjuku buildings in William Gibson's science fiction novel *Idoru*, or the folding structures in the film *Inception*.

AND THE WINNERS ARE...

They call it "architecture's Nobel": the annual Pritzker Prize was established in 1979. Since then, Japanese architects have been recipients no less than six times.

The first Japanese laureate, in 1987, was Tange Kenzo. Tange's famous aphorism, "Learning happens in corridors," marks his highly original, empirical approach to architecture. Fumihiko Maki won the prize in 1993. His designs include the National Museum of Art in Kyoto, the Tokyo Metropolitan Gymnasium, and the iconic Tower 4 at the World Trade Center in New York. The 1995 winner Ando Tadao's body of work includes galleries, churches, shopping centres, museums, auditoriums and private homes. His preferred material is pre-cast

concrete, his style spare and minimalist, combining Japanese aesthetics and modernism.

The work of Sejima Kazuyo and Nishizawa Ryue, recipients of the prize in 2010, is characterised by a sense of weightlessness and spatial ambiguity, seen in their designs for private homes, art venues and public buildings. The 2013 laureate was Ito Toyo, whose Sendai Mediatheque emerged almost unscathed from the 2011 earthquake. Ban Shigeru, who experiments with building materials such as cardboard tubes, garnered the prize in 2014. Today, Japan is experiencing a period of phenomenal creativity in architecture. Over the coming years there will probably be more award contenders.

City surfaces

Building materials are a response to environment, climate and design preference. The connection, even in the artefact of a Japanese city, is essentially one of nature to structure.

From the thin sliver of titanium that coats the soaring Global Tower in Beppu, through the Umeda Sky Building in Osaka, with its vaulting walls and great cavities of open, aerial space, to the honeycombed glass panels of the superb Prada building in Tokyo, Japan is a dreamscape for the experimental architect.

What characterises many of these new creations more than anything else is their surfacing. The "bubble" years of the 1980s were distinguished by a shift from industrial expansion to a post-industrial, information-oriented society with software elements dominating over hardware ones. In the shift towards an information-based economy, buildings have become sounding boards, global-age transmitters. One can almost see on the surfaces of these buildings the alternating currents of the economy.

This flexible system of choreographed space, layers of artificial skin and surface, is achieved with hi-tech materials which, at their most successful, create illusions of depth and space. This tendency is visible in the new surfaces and the floating contraptions surrounding the core of the building, in the use of lighter, non-durable, hi-tech industrial materials such as liquid crystal glass, polycarbon, Teflon, perforated metal and stainless-steel sheets.

The merits of insubstantiality, of surface units that can be replaced at will, are highly visible in the works of architects Fumihiko Maki, Ando Tadao and Ito Toyo.

Writing on the wall

In acquiring the added function of advertising props, Japanese urban centres have been transformed into surfaces of running commercial text and scroll. In cities like Tokyo and Osaka, where pedestrians for the most part see one side of a building – the one overlooking the street – views are flattened into two-dimensional planes. Urban geographer Paul Waley has observed that "space in the Japanese city is conceived only in the context of the immediate visual field. This gives it an episodic quality." If each panel is visualised as an episode,

it is one in a narrative that is set on constant replay, or rewrite.

Where a former age delighted more in the texture and tone of walls and other urban exteriors, in contemporary, space-depleted urban Japan, utility dominates the use of walls and other surfaces. The result is panels hung with a forest of signage. Commercial advertising inscribes the city in a deliberate, expressive manner. The textual quality of Japanese cities, from their daylight advertising to night-time electrographics, permits urban spaces to be scanned and read: the city as streaming text. Like the city itself, this commercial script can only

Detail of the Prada Building in Tokyo.

be digested piecemeal, in lines of haiku length or even just a few syllables.

Signage in Japanese cities has developed to such an extent that, in some instances, entire buildings may be obscured by hanging objects and structures. Increasingly these are liquid constructions, facade-scale TV screens so carefully aligned and affixed that they appear as a seamless part of the building itself. These screens create, in what was hitherto an unassuming visual void, "a gate and a field within whose false depth a new, antithetical dimension of space and time opens up", as Vladimir Krstic has expressed it.

Are such liquid dreams the shape of things to come? For some, these seductive LCD screens may indeed be the writing on the wall.

THE ART OF LANDSCAPING

Compact, organised and introspective: words stereotypically used to describe the Japanese might just as well be applied to their gardens.

In Japan, gardening as a conscious art form can be traced to its introduction from China and Korea in the 6th and 7th centuries. The balance between nature and man-made beauty, with water and mountain as prototypical images, are the principles that form the basis for the traditional Japanese garden. Artfully blended with ponds, banks of irises and moss-covered rocks, carefully contrived Japanese gardens are objects of quiet contemplation.

"In order to comprehend the beauty of a Japanese garden," the 19th-century writer Lafcadio Hearn wrote, "it is necessary to understand – or at least learn to understand – the beauty of stones." This is especially true of the *karesansui* (dry-landscape) garden. Zen Buddhism's quest for "inner truth", its rejection of superficiality and attachment embodied in the over-ornate styles of the day, gave birth to medieval temple gardens of a minimalist beauty.

The stroll garden, by contrast, was used to entertain and impress and creates an illusion of a long journey. As visitors strolled along carefully planned paths, around every twist and turn a new vista would appear. Famous scenes were recreated without the visitor having to undertake the arduous journey to the original sights. Among the views represented were miniaturised scenes from Kyoto, such as the hillsides of Arashiyama. The idea of confined space, combined with the Zen idea of discovering limitless dimensions in the infinitely small, saw the creation of the *kansho-niwa*, or "contemplation garden": gardens created as both tools for meditation and works of art. Carefully framed to resemble a scroll, they are intended to be appreciated like a painting that changes with the seasons.

There is constant work to be done in the Japanese garden. When monks and gardeners are not raking sand and gravel, they are raking leaves.

Visitors pause on the small stone bridge over the pond that is part of the outer garden of the iconic Ryoan-ji stone garden.

The water lily is a common motif in Japanese gardens. Along with the sacred lotus, it is at its best in summer.

The creation of bamboo fences in Japan is an art in itself, with dozens of differing styles and wood types.

THE RIVERBANK PEOPLE

Although routinely ascribed to the prominent designers of the day, or to professional rock-setting priests, many Kyoto gardens were likely to have been built by sensui kawaramono, the much despised riverbank underclass. The "*mono*" of the designation stands for "thing", clearly stigmatising this pariah class as non-humans. A combination of Buddhist and Shinto taboos against the killing of animals and other sordid forms of work – slaughtering and skinning of animals, execution of criminals, burial of the dead – placed these people well beyond the sphere of a rigidly hierarchical class system with the nobility and clergy at the apex, descending to farmers, artisans and merchants. The trade of stripping and tanning hides required large quantities of water, forcing the kawaramono to build their abodes along the banks of the waterways. The kawaramono services became indispensable as they acquired greater skills in planting trees and in the placing of rocks: they were able to surpass their masters in the art of gardening. Ironically, it may be that some of Kyoto's "purest" gardens were created by the hands of men regarded as impure to the point of being inhuman.

A solitary stone in Ryoan-ji, one of the most photographed gardens in the world. The ancient clay wall at the rear has been designated a national cultural treasure.

Raikyu-ji Temple garden in Bitchu-Takahashi is a wonderfully curvaceous work, with its lines created from azalea bushes and sand, replicating waves, water and currents.

Japanese gardens provide the opportunity to display Buddhist, and occasionally Shinto-style statuary.

SPORT AND LEISURE

The most popular sports are sumo, baseball and football – one indigenous to the archipelago, the other two introduced from abroad. All are passionately followed.

A lthough baseball has long been the athletic obsession of Japan, sumo (pronounced "s'mo") remains the "official" national sport. This is fitting, partly because of its history, which dates back as far as the 3rd century, and also for its hoary, quasi-religious ritualism – but mostly because, in Japan, it's a more exciting sport.

While baseball and sumo are the two perennial spectator sports in Japan, professional football, introduced in the 1990s under the "J-League" banner, has proved its staying power in competing for the title of Japan's favourite sport.

Participant sports are few within Tokyo. It's just too expensive. Golf, the world knows, is fantastically popular in Japan, but only the well heeled can afford to play a proper round; the rest stand in cubicles at driving ranges and hit balls towards distant nets. Skiing is a fashionable sport and Japan has the mountains. The heyday of its popularity saw crowds and blaring loudspeakers everywhere, even on the slopes, making skiing here less than satisfying. The economic slowdown means more space for those who can still afford it. Taking up some of the slack have been large numbers of Australian visitors drawn to Hokkaido's fine powder snow. The Taiwanese, Chinese and Koreans have also been descending on Japan's slopes in recent years.

Now that the country is gearing up to host the 2020 Olympic and Paralympic Games – which will be held in Tokyo from 24 July to 9 August and from 25 August to 6 September respectively – it hopes to attract a ever-growing number of sports fans. Several of the 1964 Summer Olympics venues will be reused for the 2020 Games, 11 new ones are to be built,

High school baseball practice in Sapporo.

and the National Stadium will receive a total revamp. The location of most sites is planned within 8km (5 miles) of the Olympic Village in Tokyo Bay.

Baseball

Less popular than it used to be, baseball can still draw huge crowds, although there is only one club in Japan – the Yomiuri-owned, Tokyo-based Giants – who are able to turn a profit from the game.

A national sport that sustains its year-round interest, baseball was introduced in the early 1870s by university professors from the United States. Its popularity quickly spread and soon became the country's number one school sport. *Yakyu*, as baseball is technically called in Japanese (although *basuboru* is more common), rivals sumo in both its popularity and declining audience numbers. The first professional baseball team was established in 1934, and today the two-league professional baseball system is a commercial business, drawing millions of spectators to stadiums.

Millions more watch on national television, and train commuters devour the pages of Japan's daily national sports newspapers, from April to October, for details of the previous night's baseball league action. The final of the All-Japan High School Baseball Championship is held at Koshien Stadium near Osaka in the summer, but even the play-offs attract keen audiences and are televised.

There are two major leagues in Japanese professional baseball. For top teams, the advertising and promotional value for the parent company (department stores, media giants and food processing companies) is considerable. The winners of each league pennant meet in Japan's version of the World Series, the best-of-seven Japan Series beginning the third week of October.

> If you ever wondered how sumo wrestlers bulk up, look no further than chankonabe, a staple stew consisting of meat, fish, udon noodles, vegetables, broth and tofu. The Ryogoku district of Tokyo has several chankonabe restaurants open to the public.

The Japanese rule allowing *gaijin* players in its professional leagues is one of the most interesting aspects of the system. Each Japanese team can list three foreign players on its 60-man roster, which includes the "major league" team and one farm team. There are critics, but most feel the situation is fine, since the colourful American players, with their occasional outbursts, make the Japanese game that much more interesting; the limit does, nonetheless, allow baseball in Japan to keep its identity as Japanese.

The rules of Japanese baseball are generally the same as for the US. There are, however, several peculiarities, such as the reversal of the ball-strike count in Japan making a full count 2-3, rather than 3-2.

Teams have their own supporters' sections, with trumpets, drums and tambourines, headed by cheerleaders paid by the team. The resulting din shatters the eardrums.

Sumo

Some people say sumo is the national sport, some say it's the national spirit. Sumo wrestlers, or *rikishi*, would probably say it's a long, hard grind to fleeting glory.

Sumo is a fascinating phenomenon because it involves so many different things: physical strength, centuries-old ritual, a complicated

Sumo tournament in Nagoya pavilion.

code of behaviour, religious overtones, a daunting hierarchy system and feudalistic training regimes.

The *rikishi* wrestle on a raised square of mud and sand, the *dohyo*. A circle within the square, the *tawara*, is made of rice-straw bales. The wrestler's goal is to force his opponent to touch the surface of the *dohyo* with some part of his body (other than the feet), or to set foot out of the ring. This happens very fast. The average sumo bout lasts no longer than six seconds.

Appearances to the contrary, *rikishi* are not slabs of flab. They are immensely strong, rigorously trained athletes, with solid muscle often loosely covered in fat. The biggest *rikishi* in history (a Hawaiian named Salevaa Atisa-noe, retired and now a Japanese citizen, and whose sumo name was Konishiki) reached 253kg (557lbs) before slimming down a bit for his wedding. Most grand champions, however, have weighed between 110kg and 150kg (220–330lbs).

There are no weight divisions. During a tournament, the smallest will fight the largest. The waist is wrapped in sumo's only garment, a belt called the *mawashi*. The most dignified (and probably dullest) winning technique – called *yorikiri* – requires a two-handed grip on the *mawashi*, which allows the winner to lift and push his opponent out.

The sport was tainted by a series of scandals in 2011, connecting players and managers to gambling rings and even organised crime. Allegations of game-fixing were raised, the collective impact doing much to harm the sport's image and reduce audience attendance, although this image is now recovering.

Six two-week tournaments are held each year. Three of these are in Tokyo's Kokugikan, in the Ryogoku area in the eastern part of the city, in January, May and September. There is

Japanese football fans at the Asian Cup.

FOREIGN INVASIONS

It's no small irony that Japan's national sport, one replete with native Shinto-inspired rituals, should currently be dominated by foreigners. There has long been a sprinkling of Hawaiian and Fijian players, but recent years have seen the rise of Mongolian wrestlers into the very top ranks of sumo. Strong evidence suggests that the sport originated in Mongolia, and the reigning champion is Mongolian. But what of Russian players, and even a European or two, making it to the semi-finals? Could it be that, like everything else Japanese, sumo is about to be embraced by the West not merely as a spectator sport, but a participant one?

a tournament in Osaka in March at the Osaka Furitsu Taiku Kaikan; the Aichi-ken Taiku-kan in Nagoya hosts the event in July, and Fukuoka's annual sumo tournament takes place at the Fukuoka Kokusai Centre in November.

Football

Like mountain climbing, football came to Japan via the enthusiasm of an Englishman, one Lieutenant Commander Douglas, a navy man who organised the first game here in 1873.

The turning point in Japanese football came much later though, with the establishment of the J-League in 1993, a costly undertaking that provided its national team with the players, just a few years later, to compete in the 2002 World

Cup, which Japan co-hosted with Korea; Japan reached the last 16 for the first time in its football history. State-of-the-art stadiums, like those in Yokohama and Saitama, were built in readiness for the event.

> Popular with retired Japanese of both genders, gateball is ubiquitous. Similar to croquet, played with a wooden mallet and three gates, the team game is ideal for land-pinched Japan. Grass being rare, the game is usually played on compacted earth.

Oddly, Tokyo was excluded from the J-League when it was first founded, an omission that has since been rectified with the creation of the first-rate FC Tokyo and Tokyo Verdy 1969 clubs. These teams play at the Ajinomoto Stadium in Chofu City, just to the west of Tokyo. The National Stadium was located right in the middle of the capital, but has since been demolished, to be replaced by a larger-capacity venue that will host both the 2019 Rugby World Cup and the 2020 Summer Olympic Games (including athletics, rugby and some football finals, as well as the opening and closing ceremonies).

The J-League currently has 18 teams. A crop of cups, contests and tournaments, including the Yamazaki Nabisco Cup, the Jomo Cup and December's Emperor's Cup, have helped sustain the popularity of the game. Matches are played between March and October, with a summer break.

Standards are rising in the game, with several Japanese players now among the ranks of the major European squads. The ruling that Japanese clubs can employ up to four foreign players has helped both to kindle interest in the game and to raise the quality of play. The Nadeshiko Japan team won the Women's World Cup in 2011, sparking massive media interest in female football players.

Japanese football fans have created their own counter-entertainment to the matches, with colourful pennants, painted faces, team-inspired costumes, and a barrage of drums and other musical instruments that provide a continuous soundtrack to the games and the well-synchronised, good-natured frenzy of the supporters. Thankfully, hooliganism is still a foreign concept.

Other leisure activities

Leisure activities soared after companies adopted the five-day week in the 1980s. It's a serious business, and the Japanese manage to give the impression that leisure is hard work.

Originating in Nagoya, *pachinko*, a cross between pinball and the one-arm bandit, is a multimillion-yen business, and the parlours are everywhere. *Pachinko* has had to deal with a negative image. Notorious tax dodgers, many of the owners are second- or third-generation Koreans, whose donations to North Korea were a mainstay of that regime's economy. Recent

A pachinko parlour.

years have seen the industry clean up, and the newer parlours offer coffee shops and smoke-free areas.

Melding technology and music, karaoke was always bound to be huge. Karaoke bars are still popular, but the karaoke box, rented by friends, is ever better as it provides privacy and a full menu of drinks and snacks.

Cycling clubs are popular in Japan, even in cities like Tokyo and Osaka. Country routes are the best options, though, for touring. Cycling terminals are located all over the country, catering to bicyclists with inexpensive accommodation.

Fishing remains largely the domain of men. The number of fishing publications and websites is staggering. With so many mountains, Japan is perfect for hiking, offering peaks up to 3,000 metres (10,000ft), or day hikes that start outside local railway stations. Mountains usually have huts providing very basic accommodation and meals for climbers. Others have cabins where hikers can spend the night; bring your own food. One twist on the theme of hiking includes ice-climbing, the scaling of frozen waterfalls in winter.

Surrounded by sea and with so many rivers and lakes, Japan is a great destination for wind-surfing, jet-skiing and yachting, and renting equipment is easy. Decades ago, off-duty American servicemen took their surfboards down to Kamogawa on the Boso Peninsula in Chiba and, unwittingly, began the country's surf boom. White-water rafting, kayaking and canoeing are common in the spring and summer months, with regions like Hakuba in Nagano Prefecture, Niseko in Hokkaido and Hakuba in Nagano providing ideal stretches of river. In Okinawa, ocean and river kayaking among the mangrove forests is an option for ecotourists.

Interest in ecotourism has led to the growth of accommodation run by conservationists for people interested in flora and fauna. The number of birdwatchers in Japan is very high. The Wild Bird Society was founded in 1935, and today has more than 80 chapters nationwide. The opportunities for whale- and dolphin-watching have also increased. One of the best places to observe mammals in the spring months is the Ogasawara Islands. Ogata in Kochi Prefecture is a good option between April and October, while humpback whales appear off the shores of the Kerama Islands from the middle of January to the end of March.

Health has become synonymous with leisure, resort clinics and health centres now common features of most cities. Health and beauty treatments are often available at hot springs, where massage, mud baths, aromatherapy and facials are available.

With over 2,000 hot springs in Japan, the competition to attract visitors is intense. There is nothing quite like soaking in an outdoor bath in the winter, watching the steam rise and snowflakes fall into the steaming hot waters.

Diving in Okinawa.

DIVING IN JAPAN

Many Japanese beaches and waters have been ruined by industrial pollution or commercial overuse. Beyond the main urban centres, however, the clear, emerald-green waters off the coast of Sado Island's west coast are well regarded by divers.

Most divers make for Okinawa. The translucent sea and dazzling coral lent the chain its original name, the Ryukyu Islands, which means "circle of jewels" in Chinese. Mainland Okinawa is a fine place to start, but the further south you go, the clearer the waters and the better the coral. Miyako-jima is flat, a fact that has saved its crystalline waters from the chemical run-offs from farms located on hillier islands. Ranking high among the Okinawa's ecological wonders is the immensely important Shiraho Reef on Ishigaki Island, the world's largest expanse of blue coral.

Thankfully, the effects of global warming have yet to leach out the colours from Okinawa's milk-bush coral, home to large shoals of white-spotted parrot fish. Diving in this undersea world of honeycombed coral, caves, hollows and fish like rainbow runners and red fin fusilier is like swimming through a dense, aquatic forest.

At the other extreme, Abashiri Lake in the far north of Hokkaido offers the chance of ice-diving during the winter, where you plunge beneath frozen water to see the coral – only recommended for the hardy.

The martial arts

Martial arts masters are revered for their extreme physical fitness, rigorous mental training and discipline. Two categories exist: ones using weapons, and ones that are open-handed.

A general term for various types of fighting arts that originated in the Orient, most martial arts practised today came from China, Japan and Korea.

Two major martial arts evolved in Japan: the *bujutsu*, or ancient martial arts, and the *budo*, or new martial ways. Both are based on spiritual concepts embodied in Zen Buddhism. Most of the martial arts end in the suffix *-do*, usually translated as "way" or "path". Thus, kendo is the way of the sword. *Do* is also the root of *budo* and of *dojo* – the place where one studies and practises a martial art.

Japanese forms

The original form of *judo*, called *jujutsu*, was developed in the Edo Period (1603–1868). It was made up of different systems of fighting and defence, primarily without weapons, against either an armed or bare-handed opponent on the battlefield. The best-known *judo* hall in Japan is the Kodokan in Tokyo, where one can observe judoists practising in early evenings.

Karate, meaning "empty hand" in Japanese, is a form of unarmed combat in which a person kicks or strikes with the hands, elbows, knees or feet. In Japan, *karate* developed around the 1600s on the island of Okinawa. A Japanese clan had conquered the island and passed a strict law banning the ownership of weapons. As a result, the Okinawans – racially and culturally different from the Japanese – developed many of the unarmed techniques of modern *karate*.

Aikido is a system of pure self-defence derived from the traditional weaponless fighting techniques of *jujutsu* and its use of immobilising holds and twisting throws, whereby an attacker's own momentum and strength are made to work against him. Since *aikido* is primarily a self-defence system and does not require great physical strength, it has attracted many women and elderly practitioners.

Kendo ("the way of the sword") is Japanese fencing based on the techniques of the samurai's two-handed sword. *Kendo* is a relatively recent term that implies spiritual discipline as well as fencing technique. It is taught to most upper-level schoolchildren. (At the end of World War II, the US occupation authorities banned *kendo* as a militaristic practice, but it returned to Japanese schools in 1957.)

Another martial art form that developed in Japan is *ninjutsu* ("the art of stealing in", or espionage). People who practise *ninjutsu* are called *ninja*. Mountain mystics developed *ninjutsu* in the late 1200s. At that time, *ninja* were masters in all forms of armed and unarmed combat, assassination and the skilful use of disguises, bombs and poisons. Although the rulers of Japan banned *ninjutsu* in the 1600s, the *ninja* practised it secretly and preserved its techniques.

Children learning judo.

Today, *ninjutsu* is taught as a martial art with a non-violent philosophy.

One of the most sublime of martial arts is *kyudo*, the "way of the bow". Zen archery originated with the samurai class, but is now taught at Japanese schools and performed at special events like the famous women's annual archery performance and competition at the Sanjusangendo temple in Kyoto during the New Year holiday. A famous women's *kyudo* competition takes place at the Sanjusangendo temple in Kyoto during the New Year holiday. *Yabusame*, or horseback archery, is another Zen discipline dating back to the Kamakura Period, in which an archer shoots an arrow at a wooden target. One of the best-known performances takes place at the Tsurugaoka Hachiman Shrine in Kamakura.

RIKISHI: LIFE ON THE BOTTOM AND ON TOP

Not only is the *rikishi*'s training one of harsh days and a long apprenticeship, but competition at the top is without weight classes or handicaps.

In sumo, life is best at the top. Only when a *rikishi*, or wrestler, makes it to the top ranks of *ozeki* or *yoko-zuna* (grand champion, the highest rank and rarely achieved) does life become easy. Those in the lower ranks become the *ozeki*'s or *yokozuna*'s servants and valets, doing nearly everything from running errands to scrubbing backs.

In most *beya* – the so-called stables in which wrestlers live a communal lifestyle with other *rikishi* – the day typically begins at 6am with practice, not breakfast. Harsh and tedious exercises work to develop the wrestlers' flexibility and strength, followed by repetitive practice matches amongst the *beya*'s wrestlers (the only time they wrestle one another, as wrestlers of the same *beya* don't compete during actual tournaments). Practice ends around noon, when the wrestlers bathe. Then the high-ranked wrestlers sit down to the day's first meal, served by the lower-ranked wrestlers. The food staple of the stable is *chankonabe*, a high-calorie, nutritious stew of chicken, fish, *miso* or beef, to mention just a few of the possibilities. Side dishes of fried chicken, steak and bowls of rice – and even salads – fill out the meal.

Financially, *rikishi* can be divided into two groups: those who earn a salary and those who don't. Lower-ranked wrestlers receive no salary, although they earn a small tournament bonus (and food and lodging are provided). When a wrestler reaches the *juryo* level, he becomes a *sekitori*, or ranked wrestler, and so worthy of a salary of at least US$8,000 a month. An *ozeki* receives about $25,000 monthly, and a *yokozuna* $30,000. The winner of one of the six annual tournaments receives $100,000.

Few people know that the sumo practice tournament at Tokyo's Kokugikan arena in the district of Ryogoku, is open to the public.

Colourful nobori (sumo banners), with wrestlers' names on show, add to the spectacle of the wrestling events.

Squatting in readiness for a practice session. Because of the weight and ritual poses, sumo wrestlers' knees have to be especially strong.

1972 champion Hasegawa Tatsutoshi is honoured with a portrait that hangs in the lobby at Ryugoku Station, where the Kokugikan National Stadium is located.

AN ANCIENT SHINTO SPORT

Sumo has been around for at least 2,000 years. Japanese mythology relates an episode in which the destiny of the Japanese islands was once determined by the outcome of a sumo match between two gods. The victorious god started the Yamato imperial line.

While wrestling has always existed in nearly every culture, the origins of sumo as we know it were founded on Shinto rituals. Shrines were the venue for matches dedicated to the gods of good harvests. In the Nara and Heian periods sumo was a spectator sport for the imperial court, while during the militaristic Kamakura Period sumo was part of a warrior's training. Professional sumo arose during the 1700s and was quite similar to the sumo practised in today's matches.

Shinto rituals punctuate sumo. The stomping before a match *(shiko)* drives evil spirits from the ring (not to mention loosening the muscles) before a match. Salt is tossed into the ring for purification, as Shinto beliefs say that salt drives out evil spirits. Nearly 40kg (90lbs) of salt is thrown out in one tournament day.

Two wrestlers who appear to be slapping each other are actually following one of the many combat techniques that trainees have to acquire.

The sumo pit, which is a sacred site made of earth and encircled by Shinto ropes, is kept immaculately clean.

The oiled hair of this sumo wrestler will be shaped into the form of an icho, or gingko leaf, before he participates in a bout.

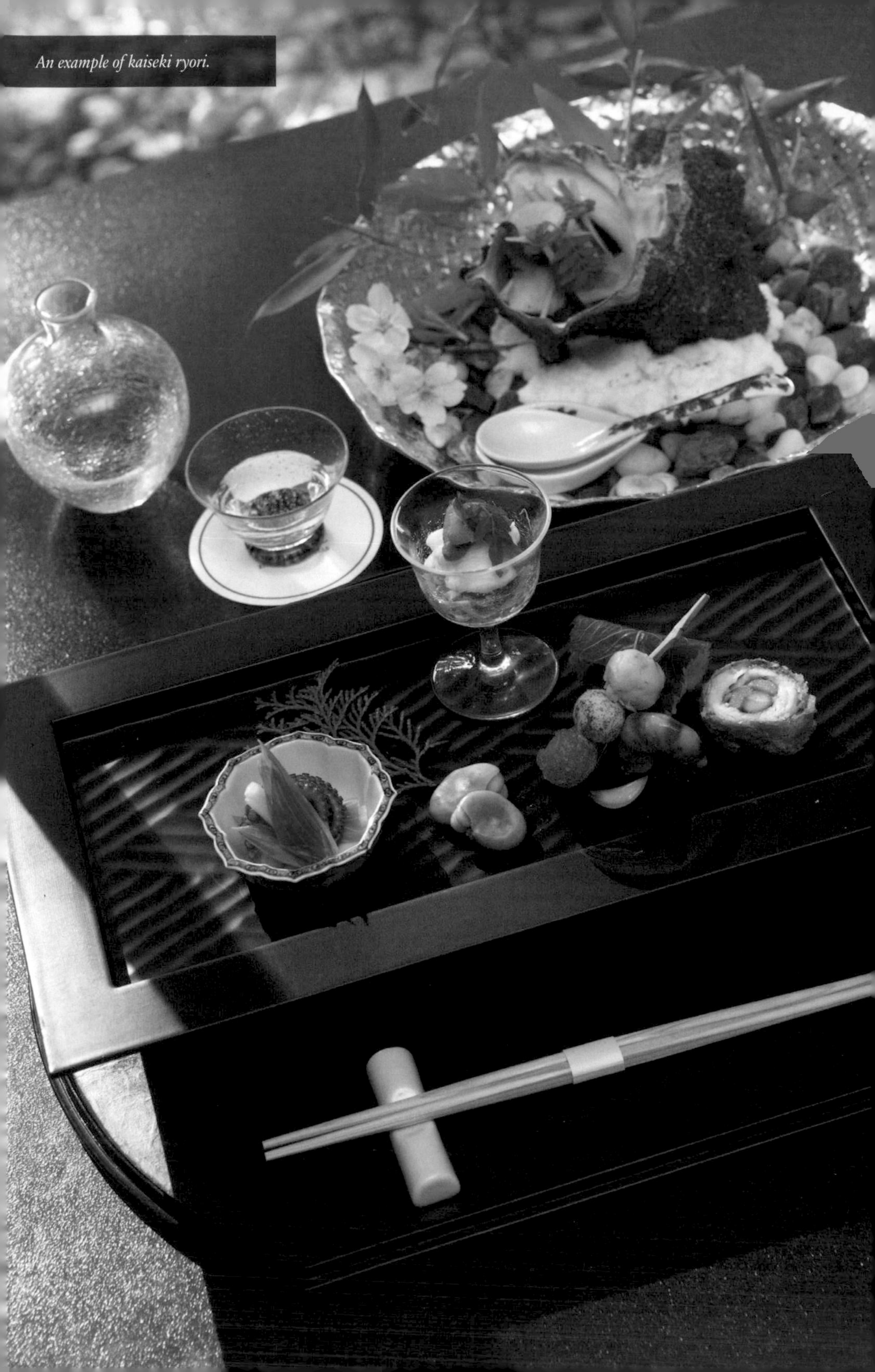

An example of kaiseki ryori.

FOOD AND DRINK

The Japanese islands are home to what is probably the world's most eclectic, diverse, detailed, healthy and aesthetically appealing cuisine.

One of the myths about modern Japanese food is that it is healthy. In its original, purest form, when people ate brown rice, grilled fish, tofu and fresh mountain vegetables, it was everything a dietician would endorse. The food the Japanese typically eat today, on the other hand, contains an inordinate amount of salt, sugar and less healthy white rice, post-war additions to an otherwise healthy cuisine, which is now held responsible for the above-average incidence of stomach cancer in Japan and the alarming rise, especially among the young, of diabetes. Many people live on a diet of processed and ready-made food. Japan is the world's biggest importer of beef. Vegetarians are not well provided for in Japan, with few restaurants catering to their needs. Fortunately, this doesn't mean that healthy food, corresponding to earlier Japanese tastes, is no longer popular or easily available.

Japan is a country of regional cuisines and, too, of seasonal cuisines. In fact, sampling local dishes is a fundamental purpose of travelling for many Japanese, whether it be a local *ekiben* box-lunch bought at the train station or an exquisite dinner at a remote *ryokan*. It would be foolish to even attempt a survey of the multitudinous regional and local cuisines. Even the Japanese don't try to know them all. To sample them all would be a worthy life's goal.

In the cities, there are almost too many places from which to choose. Two types of establishment that particularly deserve attention for their pure Japanese atmosphere are the *izaka-ya*, or pub, often with a string of red lanterns above its door, and the *taishu-sakaba*, a much larger tavern-like eatery that may also sport red lanterns. These red lanterns (*akachochin*)

Restaurants in Dotonbori, Osaka.

signify a traditional Japanese place for eating and drinking. Specialities include fried fish, shellfish, broiled dishes, tofu (bean curd) dishes, *yakitori* (skewered and broiled meat), fried rice balls and simple sashimi.

Kaiseki ryori

At least one meal in Tokyo should be *kaiseki ryori*, a centuries-old form of Japanese cuisine served at restaurants or in *ryokan* in several elegant courses. (Be warned that authentic *kaiseki ryori* is very expensive.)

Fastidiously prepared, *kaiseki ryori* is so aesthetically pleasing that it's virtually an art form in Japan. The ingredients must be as fresh as the dawn.

The taste of *kaiseki ryori* relies on the inherent taste of the food itself, not on spices or similar additions. Rather than create distinctive flavours for their dishes, Japanese chefs seek above all to retain the natural flavours.

Noodles

Japanese noodles are of three main types: *soba*, *udon* and *somen*. Made of buckwheat, *soba* noodles are thin and brownish, with a hearty consistency. *Udon* noodles, made of wheat, are usually off-white and thick to very thick. *Somen* noodles, also made of wheat, are

Mentaiko (marinated roe of pollock) for sale in Fukuoka.

as thin as vermicelli. *Udon* is usually eaten in hot dishes, while *soba* and *somen* may be eaten hot or cold, depending upon season.

Another type of noodle called *hiyamugi* (iced noodles) is eaten only cold. *Hiyamugi* is made of the same ingredients as *udon* but much thinner.

The most common type is *soba*, particularly delicious if not overburdened with non-buckwheat flour extender. *Soba* is usually served with wasabi (green horseradish), thinly sliced spring onions (scallions), a dip made of *mirin* (sweet sake), and *katsuobushi* (shaved flakes of dried bonito fish). *Soba* noodles in this form, when served chilled on a *zaru*, a type of bamboo tray, are called *zarusoba* and make a

delicious summer meal. A rich source of vitamins B1 and C, *soba* is extremely nutritious, the more so the higher the buckwheat content in proportion to *sobako* (wheat flour).

Somen is another hot-weather favourite. Noted for its delicate flavour and adaptability to many garnishes, it can be served *gomoku*-(five-flavour) style with strips of omelette, chicken and vegetables; *gomadare*-style, with aubergine (eggplant), fish and *shiso* (beefsteak plant or Japanese basil); with fruit and hard-boiled swallow's eggs; or *hiyashi*-style: cold, with nothing but soy sauce containing sesame oil. As a light, refreshing treat on a hot summer day, *somen* is hard to beat.

One of Japan's great cold-weather favourites is *udon* served in a hot, soy-based broth with an egg, spring onions and other vegetables. Unlike *soba* and *somen*, *udon* is not placed in a dip before being eaten. A real body-warmer, this noodle is prized for its excellent texture.

Although essentially Chinese, so-called *ramen* noodles are eaten so obsessively in Japan that to omit mentioning them would be remiss. *Ramen* is served very hot in soy-flavoured broth with savoury ingredients, most typically strips of bamboo shoot and slices of spring onion and roast pork. Instant *ramen* is a mainstay of the home.

If short on time, try a *tachiguisoba-ya*, "stand-and-eat *soba*". Train stations always have them, and a stand will sometimes be found on the platform. Prices are very reasonable, usually ranging from ¥200 or so for *kakesoba* (basic *soba* in broth) to somewhat higher for *tendama* (*soba* with raw egg and mixed ingredients fried together, tempura-style). Priced in between are tempura *soba*, *kitsune* (with fried *tofu*), *tanuki* (with tempura drippings), *tsukimi* (with raw egg), *wakame* (with kelp) and countless others.

Sushi and sashimi

Taste and visual pleasure converge in sushi and sashimi, both prepared with uncooked seafood. A good sushi shop, or *sushi-ya*, can be both expensive and confounding if one doesn't know what to ask for. Try, instead, a *kaiten sushi-ya*, where small dishes of sushi pass by on a conveyor belt along the counter. It lacks a certain elegance, but in a *kaiten sushi-ya* the uninitiated can study the sushi offerings at leisure and sample it for less cost. Then later, armed with new-found expertise, visit a proper *sushi-ya*.

Good sushi requires that the ingredients should be of high quality, that the rice be properly vinegared and steamed and that the topping should be as fresh as possible. (Thawed-out frozen fish just doesn't cut it.) Those who prefer raw fish and seafood without rice should order sashimi, served in a tray or on a plate with attention to the appearance. Often small bowls of sauce will be offered for dipping the sashimi.

Nabemono

If hotpot dishes are your favourite, Japan is the place to be in autumn and winter. Every part of Japan, without exception, has its own distinctive *nabe-ryori* (pot dishes).

Nabemono are typically winter dishes and include *ishikari-nabe* (Hokkaido Prefecture), containing salmon, onions, Chinese cabbage, tofu, *konnyaku* (a jelly made of root starch) and *shungiku* (spring chrysanthemum); *hoto* (Yamanashi), with handmade *udon*, *daikon* (white radish), *ninjin* (carrot), *gobo* (burdock), squash, onions, Chinese cabbage and chicken; and

The art of making noodles.

THE OKINAWA EFFECT

Japanese of all ages, with an eye to a more healthy diet, are turning their eyes south to the islands of Okinawa, or to one of the many Okinawan restaurants that have sprung up in recent years in cities throughout Japan.

Traditional cuisine can be summed up in the Okinawan concept of *nuchi gusui*, the healing power of food. The expression recalls the words of Dr Tokashiki Tsuka, a physician to the king of the Ryukyus, who wrote in his 1832 *Textbook of Herbal Medicine*, "If we nourish the spirit through food and drink, illness will cure itself."

Low in calorific density, rich in protein, fibre, flavanoids and other health-promoting properties, Okinawan cooking tends toward the stronger, spicier flavours found

in Chinese cooking styles. Black sugar and *koregusu*, a condiment made from red peppers marinated in *awamori* (Okinawan firewater), are used in Okinawan cooking. A degree of self-discipline is required to follow the Okinawan way. The expression *hara hachi bu* is often invoked in Okinawa, meaning something like "leave a little bit of room in your stomach after a meal".

Many private houses in Okinawa have kitchen gardens, where the owners grow their own vegetables and cultivate dragon fruit, bananas, passion fruit, mango, papaya and custard apple. A visit to an Okinawan food market is a reminder that these islands sit in the sun-drenched subtropics.

chiri-nabe (Yamaguchi), containing *fugu* (blow-fish) meat, Chinese cabbage, mushrooms, tofu and starch noodles.

Bento

Like most modern countries, Japan is increasingly a land of fast food. The traditional Japanese box-lunch, *bento*, or, more respectfully, *obento*, has become a form of fast food in itself, with both convenience stores and *bento-ya* offering wide selections to take out. A *bento* box, flat and shallow, is used with small dividers to separate rice, pickles and whatever else

A platter of sushi.

EAT AND DRINK LIKE A LOCAL

At a traditional Japanese pub or *izaka-ya*, try the likes of *saba* (mackerel) or *nijimasu* (rainbow trout). Eat them *shioyaki*-style (salt broiled), accompanied by a good, cold Japanese beer or a very dry sake.

Izaka-ya, essentially drinking places, serve a wide variety of Japanese snack foods but not complete meals, whereas *koryori-ya*, being essentially eateries, serve light Japanese meals. Both types of establishment serve beer and sake, often *shochu* (a vodka-like spirit), and sometimes whisky. Both *izaka-ya* and *koryori-ya* often feature popular regional foods, invariably served with rice. Eating at one is a very Japanese experience.

might be inside. *Bento* is eaten at work, school, picnics and parties.

Just about anything can be used in *bento*, including Western imports such as spaghetti, sausage and hamburger. Schoolchildren take *bento* to school for lunch.

A special type of *bento* that has become an art in itself, not to mention a pursuit for the connoisseur, is the *ekiben* (from *eki*, for train station, and *bento*). Japan is a nation of obsessed train travellers.

Trains often make stops of just long enough duration to permit passengers to get off briefly and buy some of their favourite *meisanbutsu* (local specialities), especially the ubiquitous *ekiben*, to be eaten aboard the train.

Tsukemono

A Japanese meal always comes with *tsukemono*, or distinctive Japanese-style pickles. Pickles probably owe their origins to the practice of preserving foods in anticipation of famines. During the Edo Period pickles came into their own, and the *tsukemono-ya* (pickle shop) emerged as a new type of business. Ingredients used in Japanese pickles vary somewhat with the seasons. Common ingredients are Chinese cabbage, bamboo, turnips, *kyuri* (Japanese cucumber), hackberry, *daikon*, ginger root, *nasu* (Japanese aubergine), *udo* (a type of asparagus), *gobo* and many others.

Tsukemono add colour to a meal and offer a wide range of appealing textures, from crunch to squish, that might be missing from the main dishes. Pickles can serve to clear the palate for new tastes – such as in sushi, in which a bite of pickled ginger root rids the mouth of the aftertaste of an oily fish such as *aji* (mackerel) and prepares it for the delicate taste of *ebi* (prawn).

Seasonal food

Freshness equates with seasonality. Spring is the season for fresh fish and mountain vegetables and supplements like lotus root, butterbur, milk vetch and chrysanthemum leaves. Typical garnishes would be a sprig of prickly ash leaves, rice with chopped spring herbs. *Ayu* (sweetfish) is a great summer delicacy, along with horse mackerel and tuna. Chilled wheat noodles and cold tofu with grated ginger are served in this humid time. One-pot dishes like *yudofu*, tofu heated in hot water and served with soy sauce and citrus juice, are popular in the autumn. Saury pike are eaten and small snacks made of chestnuts and persimmon. This is also the crab and oyster season. *Teriyaki* dishes are popular in winter, especially chicken preparations grilled with sweet soy sauce. Yellowtail is a great favourite, along with carp and sardines.

Alfresco

The Japanese like to eat alfresco. Even in the cooler months, some eateries will keep their chairs outside, hanging a transparent plastic curtain between terrace and pavement, or setting a stove among the tables. *Yatai* are outdoor eateries resembling tents. Cosy and intimate, customers usually sit and order from a counter. Some *oden* (fish cake stew) stalls provide miniature tables and chairs for customers.

> *Fugu (blowfish, puffer or globefish), is the deadliest delicacy in Japan. It's prepared only by licensed chefs, as the liver and ovaries contain a poison with no known antidote. However, the taste of the finely cut sashimi slivers is superb.*

Fukuoka in northern Kyushu is famous for its highly varied *yatai*. Besides local dishes like *tonkotsu ramen* (Chinese noodles in a white, garlic-laced soup made from a pork-bone stock), *tempura* and pieces of skewered chicken broiled over a charcoal fire, sophisticated Fukuoka *yatai* serve up salted bream, yellowtail and even steak dishes, Hakata's food stalls going out of their way to create an ambience not unlike that of an intimate restaurant.

Snacking

The Japanese are inveterate snackers. Rice crackers called *sembei* are eaten with tea but also between meals. *Onigiri* rice balls are a mainstay as a snack for busy people. *Yakitori* (grilled chicken and vegetable skewers) goes well with cold beer; *oden*, fish cakes and vegetables simmered in a broth, are a light meal; while *okonomiyaki*, sometimes called "Japanese pizza", consists of bean sprouts, cabbage, carrot, boneless pieces of chicken breast, shrimp, shredded red ginger, dried bonito flakes,

seaweed flakes and Japanese mountain yam and assorted garnishes added to a flour and baking-powder base.

Foreign influences

Western food is routinely eaten, though it is often changed to satisfy the native palate. This means that spaghetti may have a topping of seaweed or *natto (fermented soy bean)*, that steak is served with rice and that Western breakfasts are accompanied by a small salad.

Curry dishes have been a big favourite of the Japanese ever since curry powder was imported

A street vendor offering snacks.

THE EELS OF SUMMER

Travellers will encounter many unusual dishes in Japan. Some fit in a category that Japanese commonly refer to as *stamina ryori*, or dishes intended to raise energy levels and "staying" power. Japan and especially Tokyo can be pretty enervating, so "stamina restaurants" (and drinks) are a common phenomenon. A popular summer dish is *unagi*, or broiled eel served on rice. It's said to help one withstand the hot and humid days of the Japanese summer – *doyo no iri*. Usually served with a sweetish *tare* sauce, *unagi* is rich in vitamins E and A, and it exceeds pork and beef in protein content yet contains fewer calories.

in the 19th-century by the British community living in Kobe. English-style curry, less fiery than its Indian counterpart and without the food taboos that might exclude meats like beef, quickly established itself into the Japanese range of adapted tastes. To the despair of Indians living in Japan, the Japanese version is served with sticky rice and *fukujinzuke*, seven different thinly sliced vegetables pickled in sweetened soy sauce and salt. *Kare-udon* (curry-*udon*) is *udon* served in a thick, mildly spicy gravy.

Imported fruits such as loquat, fig, banana, papaya and mango have been enthusiastically

Wagashi - Japanese confectionery.

absorbed onto the Japanese table. Some fruits have been adapted in creative ways, like the ubiquitous strawberry, which was imported by the Dutch in the 17th century. Strawberry and cream sandwiches may not always be to the taste of foreigners, however.

Japanese confections

The Japanese had long enjoyed Chinese confections, but in the years between 1500 and 1640, the arrival of Europeans saw the advent of various types of sweet confectionery and cakes.

Desserts are usually limited to fresh fruit or *anmitsu*, a mixture of *agar* jelly cubes, *azuki* bean paste and boiled peas, served with tinned fruit like peach. Ice cream, *shiratama*

dango (sweet rice-flour balls) and a sweet black syrup called *mitsu* are often added.

Japanese confectionery, known as *wagashi*, is usually served with *matcha*, powdered green tea, or just after a meal. The main ingredient is *an*, a paste made from sugar and *azuki* beans, sweet potato and other ingredients. The two main types are *namagashi* (raw), a fresh sweet made from rice-flour doughs, and *higashi*, a hard, dry form made from sweetened powder. The more interesting and often decorative *namagashi* are seasonal in their ingredients and motifs. A puree made from boiled beans is combined with *kanten* (agar-agar) to make the popular *yokan*, a kind of jelly.

Minding your manners

Although non-Japanese are not expected to know the rules, following them wherever possible creates a good impression. When you enter a Japanese restaurant the staff will greet you with a hearty *Irrashaimase!* (welcome). It is not necessary to respond, except with a smile. *Oshibori*, hot towels, are given out in many places. Use them to wash hands, but not the face.

Japanese food is eaten with chopsticks. You should never pass food from one set of utensils to another. With the exception of hot *nabe* dishes, when tucking into a communal dish, reverse the chopsticks so that the clean ends are used. Never place them sticking upwards in rice, which reminds people of the offering of rice made to the dead at funerals. Fingers can be used when eating sushi at a counter, but not at the table, where chopsticks are the norm. Slurping noodles is thought to improve their taste. Drinking the broth directly from the bowl is normal.

Unless you are required to buy a ticket for a dish at a vending machine, payment is usually made after the meal. There is no system of tipping. Generally, the Japanese frown upon eating in the street or in the subway, though you do see more people breaking this unwritten rule these days.

When drinking alcohol, never pour your own drink. The custom is to allow the host to pour first, then you reciprocate. You should raise the glass a little to receive the drink. After filling other people's glasses, it is acceptable, especially with beer, to pour for yourself.

Spirits in bottles

Whoever wrote the line, "If Venice is built on water, Tokyo is built on alcohol," was spot on. Drinking, in fact, is a national pastime.

Although Sapporo beer is probably Japan's largest liquid export these days, the quintessential Japanese drink remains sake.

A staple as much of Shinto ceremonies as of the rituals of the modern Japanese table, the quality of sake depends largely on the rice and water used in its fermentation. There are over 500 local sake breweries throughout Japan, and those in Niigata Prefecture are reckoned to be the best.

Sake is graded as *tokkyu* (special), *ikkyu* (first grade) and *nikyu* (second grade). Connoisseurs generally ignore these categories, established largely for tax purposes, in favour of the high-grade *junmaishu* (sake unmixed with added alcohol or sugar) and the very superior *ginjo-zukuri*, the purest sake on the market, a complex brew bulging with the kind of fragrance and fruity undertones associated with top French clarets. Serious drinkers tend to favour dry sake *(karakuchi)* over the sweet variety *(amakuchi)*.

Besides the classic clear sake, there is a variety, called *nigori-zake*, in which the rice solids have been left to sit in a thick sediment at the bottom of the bottle, resulting in a milky colour when shaken. A relative newcomer on the drinks scene, effervescent sake makes a lively end to a drinking session, or a light coda to a meal.

Unlike wine, sake does not age well and is best drunk within six months of bottling. Premium sake is at its best cold. Cheaper brands are often drunk hot during the winter.

A stronger tipple is *shochu*, a distilled spirit made from grain or potato. *Shochu* is often drunk with a soft drink or fruit juice, but straight, high-quality *shochu* has become *de rigueur* among young people. It can also be drunk *oyu-wari* (with a little hot water), which is a great way to warm up in cold weather.

Other spirits

Okinawa has its own firewater, a spirit known as *awamori*. Made exclusively from Thai rather than Japanese rice, it is a reminder that these islands once enjoyed a thriving trade with Southeast Asia. Some *awamori* makers play music while the alcohol is fermenting in the belief it enhances the process. The Onna distillery in Okinawa places jars of *awamori* under the sea for a day, producing what they believe to be a more rounded, mellow Shinkai (Deep Sea) brand.

Ocha, Japanese tea, with variations, is a year-round drink. Japanese tea means green tea of various qualities. Tea is graded into the coarse and very cheap *bancha*, the better-quality leaves of *sencha* and, at the top, *gyokuro*, a fine brew made from the most tender bud leaves of the

Bottles of sake.

more mature bushes. *Mugicha* is a summer drink of chilled buckwheat tea. *Hoji-cha* is a roasted tea made from *bancha*. *Genmai-cha* is mixed with grains of roasted rice, giving it a rustic, nutty flavor.

Matcha, the thick, high-caffeine powdered green tea drunk in the tea ceremony, was originally intended to keep Zen monks from falling asleep during long hours of meditation. Bowls of *matcha au lait*, powdered green tea with hot or cold milk, have become a fixture with people who appreciate the tea ceremony or the abbreviated version of the powdered green tea that is often served in Japanese garden teahouses, but don't have the time or the requisite setting for the elaborate steps in the ritual.

JAPANESE FOOD

In his book *A Potter in Japan*, ceramicist Bernard Leach wrote, "There is a saying that the Chinese eat with their stomachs and the Japanese eat with their eyes".

A presentational, almost ritual cuisine, Japanese cooking demands that dishes should be contemplated, then consumed. According to this system of thinking, the satisfaction is as much aesthetic as gustatory.

Colours are important, a good example being *san-shoku*, a *soba* dish containing three types of buckwheat noodles: brown, white and green. Another popular three-colour combination consists of purple, green and white pickles. Asymmetrical arrangements of food on the plate are preferable, so that round fish or dumplings will be served on a long, narrow dish.

Great lengths are gone to in order to create aesthetic appeal. One popular rice cake, known as "the beautiful bay of Tango", is a pink-and-yellow confection resembling the form of a chestnut burr and named after a scenic spot that appears in the 8th-century poetry collection, the *Manyoshu*.

In spring, Japanese sweets, *wagashi*, may have a cherry blossom crest marked on them; in autumn a seasonally apposite chrysanthemum design. Tableware is also often visually matched with the season, especially in more expensive restaurants. Glass dishes and green bamboo vessels are associated with summer; stoneware and rough ceramic pots, along with wooden plates decorated with maple leaves, with autumn and winter. Fresh leaves may appear on dishes as a seasonal reminder. Visual appeal, of course, is not enough: the dishes must be beautiful, but good enough to eat.

Soba, sometimes called buckwheat noodles, is a staple of working Japanese, and restaurants, of both the sitting and standing variety, are ubiquitous.

The batter for tempura, a dish adapted from a Portuguese preparation, is used not only for fish, but a wide spectrum of vegetables and even leaves.

Osaka is known as one of the best cities in Japan to eat. Osakans, as this boldly advertised restaurant in the popular Dotonbori district shows, are not a shy or retiring people.

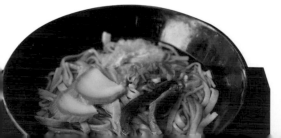

Mochi rice-based sweets, like this green tea flavoured offering, are popular gifts.

EMPIRE OF PLASTIC

The practice of making life-like *sanpuru* (food samples) appears to have begun in the early years of the Meiji Restoration with the arrival of anatomical models made of hardened wax, which were used as teaching aids in the newly built schools of Western medicine. A businessman from Nara hit upon the idea of creating food models to promote restaurant menus. As visual aids models proved indispensable in demonstrating scale. The only problem was the models were apt to melt during Japan's humid summer months, so the material eventually changed to glazed plastic.

By the mid-70s the unsung creators of this highly original, uniquely Japanese genre had refined their products to such a degree that foreigners could discover in the finest examples a new pop art form. While they are certainly the most functional of sculptures, the best examples are mesmerising in their veracity. Viewed on an empty stomach they can seem like works of towering genius.

Handmade noodles are considered the best, though restaurants serving them may charge a little extra.

Like a lot of contemporary Japanese food, o-bento, or packed lunches, are heavy on salt, but wonderfully convenient and often tasty.

In fish and meat-eating Japan, seijin-ryori, or temple food, is the closest the country gets to an authentic traditional vegetarian cuisine.

Visual overload in the Dotonbori district of Osaka.

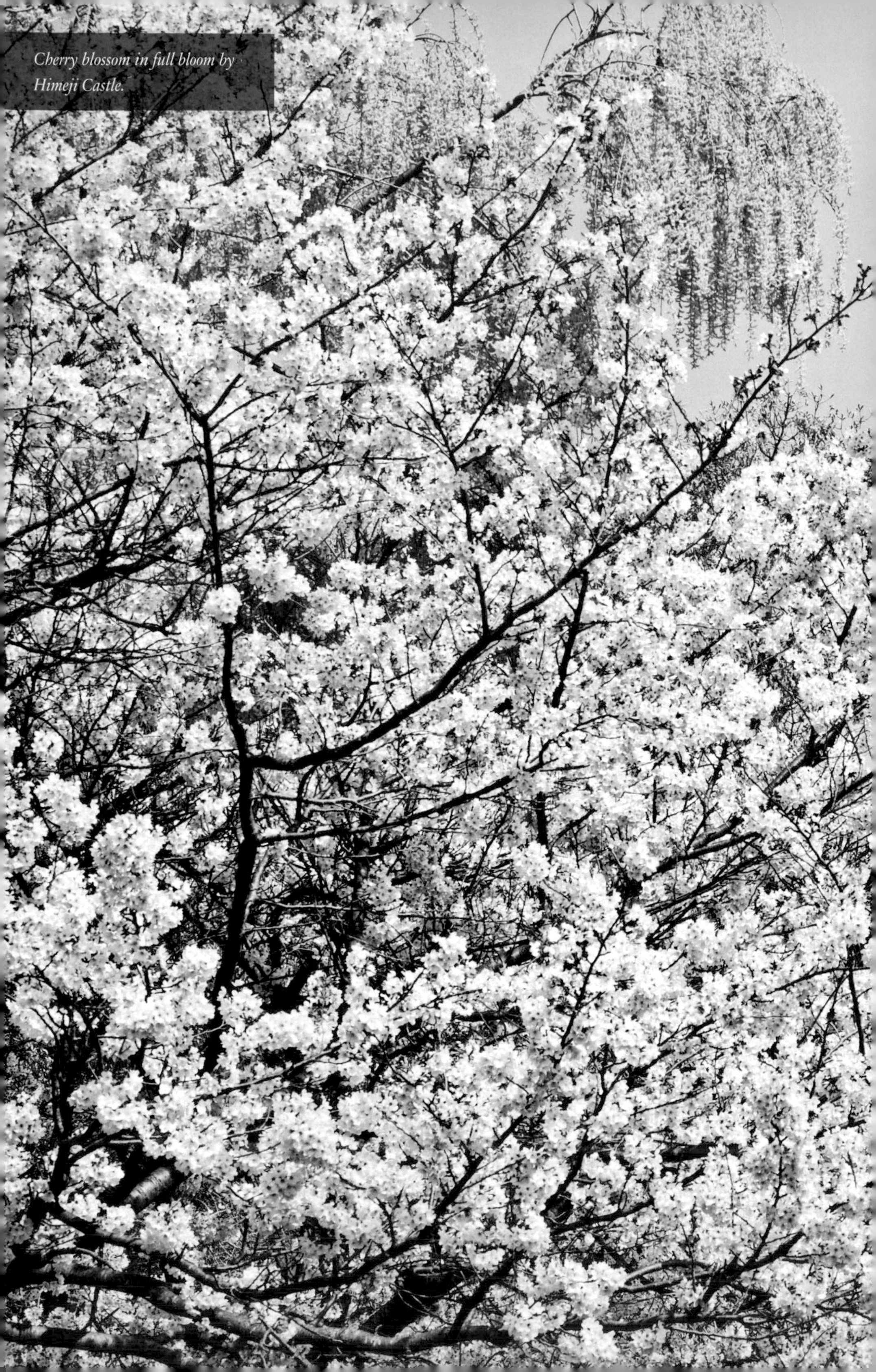

Cherry blossom in full bloom by Himeji Castle.

*Enjoying Japanese powder at
Sapporoteine Ski Area, Mount Teine.*

INTRODUCTION

A detailed guide to the entire country, with principal
sites clearly cross-referenced by number to the maps.

A kara-mon in Nikko.

Spread like cultured pearls in the western Pacific, the islands of the Japanese archipelago lie off the coast of China, Russia and Korea. Strung out for over 2,800km (1,700 miles) and covering 380,000 sq km (147,000 sq miles), the 6,800 or so islands are home to 127 million residents – twice the population of Italy, yet almost the same land area.

Nearly a third of Japan's population – over 42 million – lives in the Kanto region, on the main island of Honshu, where we begin with the nation's capital, Tokyo. Separate sections then cover areas around Tokyo, including Nikko and its lavish Tosho-gu Shrine complex to the north, Yokohama and the ancient capital of Kamakura to the south, and the iconic snow-capped Mount Fuji. Moving westwards, the Central Honshu section covers the commercial city of Nagoya, the breathtaking Northern Alps and areas along the northern coast of central Honshu.

Next is the largely rural Tohoku region in northern Honshu. Although its east coast was devastated by the 2011 earthquake and tsunami, Tohoku's inland attractions have remained untouched. The sedate Tono Valley and mountainside Yamadera temple complex are a couple of the highlights. After Tohoku comes the northernmost island of Hokkaido, known for its harsh winters and stunning natural scenery, seen at its best in Daisetsuzan National Park.

Beppu Hot Springs, Kyushu.

We then move to the Kansai region, several hundred kilometres west of Tokyo, where many of Japan's most noteworthy sites are clustered. The focus here is on ancient Kyoto, the nation's capital city for over 1,000 years: a fabulous collection of temples, sanctuaries, geisha and Zen gardens. Nearby is the beauty of Nara – the country's cultural and artistic cradle. Also in Kansai is Osaka, Japan's second city, a lively business and nightlife centre.

Heading south, the next stops are Honshu's Chugoku region and the slow-paced islands of Shikoku and Kyushu. Chugoku's most famous sight is the city of Hiroshima, while Shikoku is home to the 88 temples of the centuries-old Shikoku pilgrimage route. Kyushu's warm climate, hot springs and active volcanoes give it a feel quite distinct from the rest of Japan.

Lastly, our attention turns to the Okinawa Islands. Stretching southwest from below Kyushu, they offer a unique culture and the best beaches and diving in Japan.

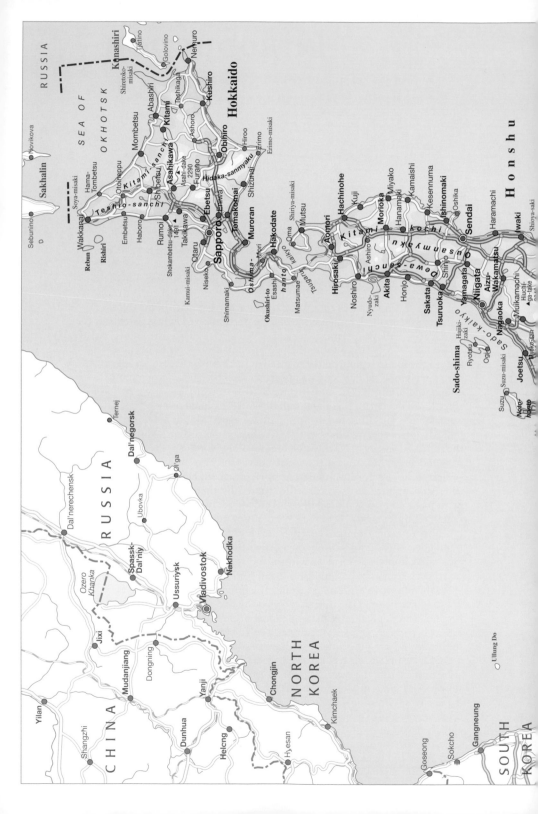

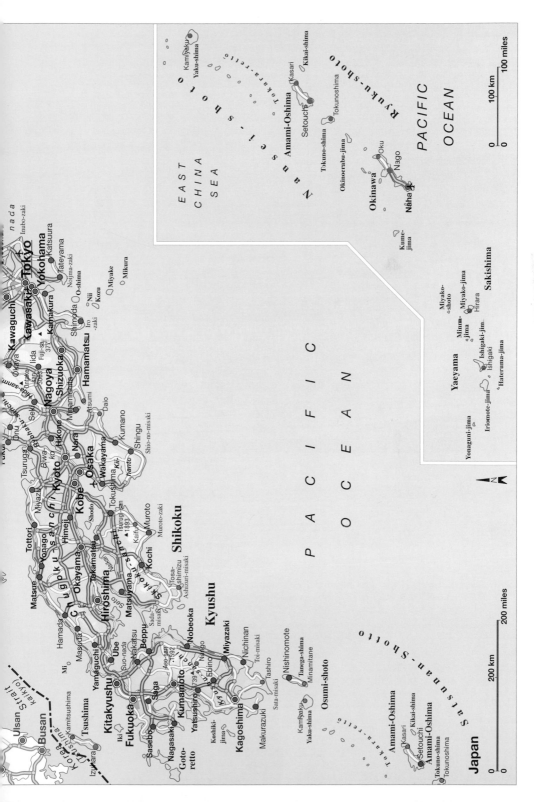

PACIFIC OCEAN

100 miles
100 km

Nansei-shoto

Ryuku-shoto

Kamiyaku
Yaku-shima

Tokara-retto

Kasari
Amami-Oshima
Setouchi
Kikai-shima
Tokuno-shima
Tokunoshima

Okinoerabu-jima
Oku
Nago
Okinawa
Naha

Kume-jima

EAST CHINA SEA

Miyako-shoto
Miyako-jima
Hirara
Sakishima

Minami-jima
Ishigaki-jim
Ishigaki
Yaeyama
Iriomote-jima
Hateruma-jima

Yonaguni-jima

N

nada
Inubo-zaki
Katsuura
TOKYO
Kawaguchi
Tateyama
Kawasaki
Yokohama
Kamakura
Nojima-zaki
O-shima
Miyake
Mikura
Shimoda
Iro-zaki
Nii
Kozu

PACIFIC OCEAN

Fuji-san
3776
Iida
Seki
Nagoya
Shizuoka
Hamamatsu
Minamata
Atsumi
Daio
Kumano
Shingu
Shio-no-misaki

Tsuruga
Biwa
Ko
Nara
Kyoto
Hikone
Kobe
Osaka
Wakayama
Kii
hanto

Tottori
Yonago
Miyazu
Himeji
Shodo
Shikoku
Tsurugi-san
1893
Muroto
Muroto-zaki

Matsue
Izumo-san-chi
Okayama
Takamatsu
Kochi
Tosa-shimizu
Tosa-wan
Ashizuri-misaki

Hamada
Masuda
Hiroshima
Seto
Matsuyama-sanchi
Kaifu

Suo-nada
Ube
Yamaguchi
Kitakyushu
Fukuoka
Saga
Kumamoto
Aso-san
1592
Ebino
Kirishima
Nakatsu
Beppu
Nobeoka
Miyazaki
Nichinan
Toi-misaki
Tashiro

Kyushu

Nishinomote
Tanega-shima
Minamitane
Osumi-shoto

Kamiyaku
Yaku-shima
Tokara-retto
Kasari
Setouchi
Amami-Oshima
Kikai-shima
Tokuno-shima
Tokunoshima

Satsunan-Shoto

Ulsan
Busan
Korea Strait
(Tsushima-kaikyo)
Kamitsushima
Izuhara
Tsushima
Iki
Goto-retto
Nagasaki
Sasebo
Koshiki-jima
Makurazaki
Kagoshima
Sata-misaki

Japan

200 miles
200 km

Souvenir stalls at the Senso-ji temple in Asakusa, Tokyo.

KANTO PLAIN AND CHUBU

The central part of Honshu is Japan's heartland: the vibrant metropolis of Tokyo spreads out on the Kanto plain, while beyond the capital lie other historic cities and the beauty of the Japan Alps.

Tsurugaoka Hachiman-Gu temple, Kamakura.

Descriptions of the Kanto region can be misleading. It is Japan's largest alluvial plain, but it is certainly not an area of wide-open spaces. None of the flat land extends far enough to offer a level, unbroken horizon. Most of Japan's longest rivers – the Tone, Naka, Ara, Tama and Sagami – pass through Kanto and empty into the Pacific, but few would call these concrete-lined conduits, managed and contained into near-obscurity, rivers at all.

Virtually nothing of interest about the region is recorded until Minamoto Yoritomo, the first Kamakura shogun, endowed Tokyo's Asakusa-jinja with 36 hectares (90 acres) of arable land around 1180. Later, in 1456, a village called Edo (Estuary Gate) was recorded when the first Edo castle was built by a small-time daimyo on the site of today's Imperial Palace. In 1600, a shipwrecked Englishman became the first foreign guest at Edo, tutoring Tokugawa Ieyasu. Three years later, Ieyasu started the 250-year reign of the Tokugawa dynasty. Then, after centuries of growth, Edo got a name change – to Tokyo – when it became the country's capital with the Meiji Restoration of 1868.

Hakuba Ski Resort, Nagano.

Today, with nearly 38 million people living in the Greater Tokyo area, Ieyasu's city is the heartbeat of Kanto. It offers visitors everything from the busy neon-drenched streets of Shinjuku and contemporary cool of Roppongi and Omotesando, to more traditional (though just as vibrant) neighbourhoods such as Asakusa.

The areas surrounding Tokyo have plenty of their own charms. To the west are Mount Fuji (or Fuji-san) and Hakone, offering beautiful scenery and relaxing hot springs, and to the north is Nikko and its magnificent Tosho-gu shrine complex. South is the Western-influenced city of Yokohama, which came to life with foreign trade after the Meiji Restoration, and the temple-laden ancient capital of Kamakura.

In the area known as Chubu, or Central Honshu, beyond Kanto, Japan is both highly industrial, as in Nagoya to the southwest, and rural, as in the delightful Noto Peninsula and elsewhere along the Sea of Japan (East Sea) coast. Here are also the historical city of Kanazawa, the mountainous resort city of Nagano, and the remoteness and drumming thunder of the island of Sado.

Crowds at Shibuya Crossing, Tokyo.

TOKYO

One of the most captivating cities in the world, the Tokyo metropolitan area and its nearly 38 million people exist in the former capital of the shoguns – and in an earthquake zone.

Japan has always been a country of villages. If Tokyo is Japan's biggest village – and it is by far, at over 620 sq km (240 sq miles) and over 12 million people in central Tokyo alone – then one can easily reduce Tokyo itself into a gathering of smaller villages anchored around major railway stations. Indeed, these stations are helpful for understanding Tokyo's layout, which doesn't have a central urban core.

Most of Tokyo's smaller "villages" lie on a circular rail line called Yamanote-sen, or Yamanote Line. There are 29 stations on the Yamanote and it takes about an hour to make the complete loop, actually an oval in shape. Whether on the Yamanote or one of the numerous other train and subway lines criss-crossing the city, most of Tokyo is accessible by one station or another, by one train or subway line, or many.

Roughly, Tokyoites consider the areas of Ginza, Hibiya, Marunouchi, Nihom-bashi and Yurakucho to encompass the very centre of the city – it's here that you will find some of the city's more expensive hotels, as well as Tokyo Station, the Imperial Palace and its vast grounds, and some of the most upmarket shopping and dining options in town. Moving northeast from here, but still in the larger central area, are the Akihabara

Enjoying the sunshine in Ueno Park.

and Kanda areas, and further on from them come Ueno and Asakusa, the point at which the centre becomes the "northeast" or "east end" (depending on who you ask) and Tokyo begins to reveal a more down-to-earth, traditionally working-class side – a part of town the Japanese call shitamachi (literally low city). Following the Sumida River south from Asakusa comes Ryogoku, on the Sumida's east bank, a part of Tokyo's shitamachi known for its sumo connections. After Ryogoku the Sumida passes Nihom-bashi

Main Attractions
Imperial Palace
Ginza
Akihabara
Korakuen
Ryogoku and Kiyosumi
Asakusa
Roppongi
Shibuya
Meiji-jingu
Shinjuku

FACT

Tokyo was the world's largest city, with over 1 million people living within its borders, in the 17th century. Following World War II, the population was around 3 million. By 1970 it had reached 9 million, while the 2012 census recorded 13.22 million – a population density of 6,038 people per square kilometre.

The Imperial Palace.

to its west and then begins to bend southwest, skirting the Tsukiji and Tsukishima districts before reaching the modern Odaiba and opening out into Tokyo Bay.

Heading west from the Imperial Palace grounds, Tokyo shows its modern sides – both brash and cultured. Here, Shinjuku is the epitome of a modern, thriving Asian city, mixing neon lights and skyscrapers with crowded, energetic streets. Shinjuku is home to the Tokyo Metropolitan Government, as well as the city's biggest red-light district, numerous department stores, Japan's best-known gay district, a Korea town, and so much more. Just a few stations away on the Yamanote Line, Shibuya and Harajuku are colourful and youthful, while, also in the west, Omotesando and Roppongi represent cool, contemporary Tokyo like nowhere esle – here it's all sleek design, great restaurants and cool cafés, hip boutiques and fashion houses.

It is something of a travel writing cliché to describe a city through its contrasts, or to mention how traditional elements of a city sit beside modern. But in Tokyo's case, that's what really does define the city. Walk 10 minutes from the Imperial Palace, for example, and you'll be surrounded by high-end European fashion houses and expensive department stores in Ginza. After a visit to Meiji-jingu and its sprawling park land, you are just a few minutes' walk from the teen fashion and cosplay stores (where fans can buy the outfits of their favourite manga characters) that cram the packed Takeshita street in Harajuku. Here glistening skyscrapers really do tower over centuries-old shrines, and as jumbled and chaotic as it can be for the senses, the city wouldn't feel right any other way. There really is nowhere else on earth quite like Tokyo. Today, the city is looking forward to the future and for ways to speed up progress as it gears up to host the 2020 Olympic Games.

Central Tokyo

Imperial Palace

In the centre of Tokyo is the **Imperial Palace**, or **Kokyo** ❶ (http://sankan.

kunaicho.go.jp), a functioning palace where the emperor and his family reside. Much of the grounds – including the palace itself – are closed to the public and secluded behind massive stone walls, old trees and Edo Period moats. Exceptions are the Emperor's birthday, 23 December (9.30–11.20am) and 2 January (9.30am–2.10pm), when the imperial family gives a public appearance and waves to the crowds from a balcony in the palace.

Most of the 110-hectare (270-acre) palace complex is forested or given over to private gardens and small ponds. The Showa emperor (Hirohito), who reigned from 1926 until 1989, was a skilled biologist, and much of the inner garden area is a nature preserve.

Kokyo Gaien ❷, the palace's outer garden to the southeast, is an expansive area of green and impeccably sculpted pine trees planted in 1889. A large, gravel-covered area leads to the famous postcard scene of **Niju-bashi** ❸, a distinctive bridge across an inner moat and one of the most widely recognised landmarks

in Japan. Tourists come here by the busload for a group portrait in front of the bridge (bashi) and moat. Niju-bashi is both elegant and a functional entrance – the main gate – into the palace grounds. If you visit on 23 December or 2 January, this is where you enter. Behind is **Fushimi-yagura**, a lookout turret of the original Edo castle. Parts of the outer grounds were unpleasant places in 1945 immediately after the Emperor Hirohito announced Japan's surrender on the radio. Numerous loyal soldiers, refusing to admit defeat or surrender to the Allies, disembowelled themselves outside the palace.

Visitors are also permitted in the **Kokyo Higashi Gyoen** ❹ (tel: 03-3213-1111; http://sankan.kunaicho.go.jp; tours usually on weekdays at 10am and 1.30pm), the East Imperial Garden of the palace, which can be entered through Ote-mon, Hirakawa-mon and Kitahanebashi-mon, three of the eight gates (mon) into the palace grounds. Inside are remains of the defences of Edo-jo, the shogunate's castle (jo), and the foundations of the castle's donjon,

The Yasukuni shrine in Chiyoda is dedicated to those who died fighting on behalf of the Emperor of Japan.

FROM EDO CASTLE TO IMPERIAL PALACE

The original Edo Castle, built by the Tokugawa shoguns, was an epic construction project of its time. It was built of granite and basaltic rocks quarried in the Izu Peninsula, 100km (60 miles) south. Several thousand boats made the two-week round trip. Offloaded near Kanda to the north, the stones were dragged on sleds by oxen and men provided by the shogun's warlords. In all, the castle took 40 years to build. That work, however, was soon lost: less than two decades after completion in 1636, much of the castle was reduced to ashes in a fire.

Of the original 21 defensive guard towers, or yagura, three still stand, including the Fushimi-yagura near Niju-bashi. Unfortunately, nothing substantial remains of the old Edo Castle itself, except for the three turrets and the donjon foundations, not to mention the moats and gates.

The Meiji emperor chose the shogunal castle site to be the new imperial residence in 1868 and moved there from Kyoto a year later, the city that until then had been the imperial capital for more than a millennium. The new Imperial Palace was completed in 1889 of exquisitely designed wood, but, like Edo Castle before it, it wasn't to last: in 1945 the Meiji palace was destroyed in Allied bombing raids. The current palace, still home to the imperial family, is a post-war construction.

FACT

In 1921, Prime Minister Hara Takashi was assassinated by a railway worker at Tokyo Station, and in 1930, also at Tokyo Station, an assassination attempt was made on Prime Minister Osachi Hamaguchi. He was wounded in the attack, and though he struggled on to win the 1931 election, he died a year later.

the primary lookout tower of the shogun's residence.

At the northern part of the old castle grounds in **Kitanomaru-koen** is the **Kokuritsu Kindai Bijutsu-kan ⑤** (National Museum of Modern Art; www.momat.go.jp; Tue–Sun 10am–5, Fri until 8pm). The modern building displays fine examples of Japan's contemporary artists, many of whom studied in Europe in the 20th century, in well-presented galleries. In the northern corner of Kitanomaru-koen is the octagonal martial-arts hall known as the **Nippon Budokan**. Built to host Olympic judo events in 1964, its gold topknot a gesture to the hairstyles of sumo wrestlers, the building is also used as a rock-concert venue.

Yasukuni shrine

West from Kitanomaru-koen, Yasukuni Avenue (dori) leads to **Yasukuni-jinja ⑥**. What is said to be Japan's largest *torii* – eight storeys high, made of high-tension steel plates and weighing 100 tons – boldly announces the shrine. Its entrance nipping the northern tip of the Imperial Palace grounds, this Shinto shrine is Japan's most controversial. Proponents say it honours those who died for Japan and the emperor; opponents say it glorifies Japanese aggression and honours convicted war criminals. Pinched between the two extremes are politicians, who must decide whether or not to attend annual ceremonies at the shrine. When a prime minister does visit, governments throughout Asia respond in loud disapproval. When a prime minister doesn't, Japan's vocal and politically influential rightists do likewise.

The souls of more than 2.5 million Japanese soldiers killed between 1868 (the shrine was founded in 1869) and World War II are enshrined at Yasukuni (literally peaceful country; www.yasukuni.or.jp; daily 6am–6pm, May–Aug until 7pm, Nov–Feb until 5pm; free). In the shrine's archives, the names, dates and places of death for each soldier are recorded. The **Yushukan** (War Memorial Museum; daily 9am–4.30pm, unitl 9pm during Mitama Festival), part of Yasukuni-jinja, includes among its 100,000 pieces samurai armour and a rocket-propelled kamikaze winged bomb.

Marunouchi and Tokyo Station's southwest side

Directly east from the Imperial Palace and Kokyo Gaien is the **Marunouchi district ⑦**, once an inlet of Tokyo Bay. Atop this landfill of Marunouchi – meaning "inside the wall" of the Edo castle fortifications – an exclusive residential area for Tokugawa samurai lords was created in the early 17th century. Known as Daimyo Koji, or the Little Lanes of the Great Lords, Marunouchi served not only as a buffer between the shogun's castle and the outside world of commoners but also permitted the shogun to keep an eye on his provincial warlords, whom he required to live in Edo on a

Part of the Tokyo Station building.

rotating basis. Today it is filled with corporate headquarters and government offices.

A wide boulevard slices through these corporate buildings from the grounds of the Imperial Palace to **Tokyo-eki** ❽ (Tokyo Station). While not Japan's busiest station – Shinjuku holds that honour – Tokyo Station is nonetheless sizeable, with 10 raised island platforms serving 20 tracks side by side, including the terminus for the *shinkansen* or bullet train. Beneath the main station are additional platforms for more trains and JR lines. The Marunouchi side of the station is fronted by the original station, built in 1914 of red brick in a European style. Air raids in 1945 damaged the station, taking off the top floors; renovations, finished in 1947, left it somewhat lower. An extensive renovation completed in 2012 restored the Marunouchi side to its former grandeur. Inside the concourse is the **Tokyo Station Gallery** (Tue–Sun 10am–6pm, Fri until 8pm), which puts on exhibitions mostly comprised of 20th-century Japanese artists.

The red-brick facade of the station is surrounded by a grove of modern skyscrapers. The reconstructed and extended **Marunouchi Building** (Maru Biru, as it is commonly called), one of Tokyo's mini-city complexes, immediately catches the eye. Its gourmet food basement and four shopping levels attract large numbers of Japanese tourists from the countryside. The views of the palace grounds from the dozen or so restaurants on its 35th and 36th floors are especially good, as are the restaurants themselves. Maru Biru is the most visible example of the trendy makeover Marunouchi has recently been undergoing. Another is just south at the **Mitsubishi Ichigo-kan Museum** (Tue–Sun 10am–6pm, Fri until 8pm), opened in 2010 in a Josiah Conder-designed redbrick building dating from the 1890s. The museum exhibits an eclectic mix of art, with past exhibitions having included French Impressionists and Japanese paper stencils.

Two blocks south of the Marunouchi Building, on the ground floor of the Shin-Tokyo Building, is the

The Sumida River.

BRiDGES WORTH CROSSING

How grateful I feel/As I step crisply over/The frost on the bridge – Matsuo Basho. When Shin Ohashi, or New Great Bridge, was completed in the capital of Edo in 1693, the great poet Matsuo Basho was sufficiently elated to compose the above haiku. Like many Edo Period writers and artists, Basho was a great admirer of the new bridges that were springing up across the capital.

Tokyo's Sumida River provides the setting for what is, perhaps, one of the most interesting concentrations of bridges in Japan. Each bridge has its own identity, and, if the woodblock prints and gazetteers of the time are to be believed, major bridges provided common, unlicensed space for all manner of activities, from full-moon viewing, freak shows and archery (read "prostitution") tents, to the shackling and public display of criminals.

The painted girders and bolts of the older bridges that have survived earthquakes, intense volumes of traffic and the hellfire of war, are reassuringly durable presences amidst the accelerated confusion of today's city. Sakurabashi, the last bridge of note, is an example of how such structures can have a benevolent effect on the environment. In 1985, river-facing Sumida and Taito wards constructed the bridge exclusively for the use of pedestrians.

Tourist Information Centre (daily 9am–5pm; tel: 03-3201-3331). If you are expecting to travel around Japan, visit this centre for extensive information on everything from walking tours through Tokyo to lodging in Okinawa. The staff speak English. Adjacent is the **Tokyo International Forum** ❾ (www.t-i-forum.co.jp), an echoing complex of concert and exhibition halls that is worth visiting just to check out Rafael Vinoly's sweeping steel and glass design, created to give the impression of a sailboat. On the first and third Sundays of each month the Forum is also the site of a great antiques market. South again are elevated train tracks extending from **Yurakucho-eki** ❿ (Yurakucho Station), constructed in 1910; the *shinkansen* and Yamanote-sen trains snake along the overhead tracks. Beside the station is a giant BIC Camera home electronics store selling everything from the latest camera gear to massage chairs. An elevated expressway over Harumi-dori defines the boundary between Ginza and Yurakucho. Towering on the opposite side of the expressway is the tall, curving exterior of the Han-kyu department store, anchored at the ground by a musical clock and a hard-to-miss (or ignore) police box.

Even further southwards, along Hibiya-dori, is the towering **Imperial Hotel** ⓫ (Teikoku Hoteru). The first Imperial Hotel opened in 1890. Its modest structure was later replaced by a wonderful Frank Lloyd Wright design; the day after it opened to the public in 1923, the Great Kanto Earthquake hit Tokyo. The hotel was one of the few buildings to escape destruction. The Wright building was replaced by the current structure in 1970. Across from the Imperial Hotel, **Hibiya-koen** ⓬ (Hibiya Park) was Japan's first European-style plaza, opened in 1903. It quickly became a popular venue for rallies and demonstrations against rises in rice prices during the early 1900s. Nowadays, especially at weekends, it's a popular venue for all sorts of happier events – from annual fun runs to train festivals.

Nihom-bashi

Extending from the **Yaesu** central exit of Tokyo Station is Yaesu-dori, which intersects the major arteries of Chuo-dori and Showa-dori, running south to nearby Ginza and north to Ueno. On the corner of Yaesu and Chuo-dori, the **Bridgestone Museum of Art** (www.bridgestone-museum.gr.jp; closed for renovation since 2015, will reopen after several years) houses an important collection of European paintings. Highlighting the Impressionists and later artists like Picasso and Van Gogh, it also includes the work of Meiji-era Japanese painters. Moving north from here, Chuo-dori crosses Nihom-bashi-gawa over **Nihom-bashi** ⓭ (Nihon Bridge). The ugly elevated Shuto Expressway directly above was erected for the 1964 Tokyo Olympics. Both the concrete-lined river and expressway serve to diminish the significance of the original 1603 arched wooden bridge, which was the centre

The interior of the Marunouchi Building.

of Edo Period Tokyo and the zero point for the five main roads leading out of Edo to the rest of Japan. The present stone bridge dates from 1911, and one can only look at the ornate dragons that decorate some of its pillars and wonder how impressive the bridge would have looked prior to the arrival of the eyesore above it. Just one block southwest of the bridge is the altogether more pleasant **Tako no Hakubutsukan** (Kite Museum; www.tako.gr.jp; Mon–Sat 11am–5pm). Over 2,000 kites cover the walls and ceiling of this cramped museum, many displaying Japanese motifs: manga characters, images from famous woodblock prints, armour-bearing warriors and depictions of Mount Fuji. Also in Nihom-bashi are the original branches of the Takashimaya (www.takashimaya.co.jp) and Mitsukoshi department stores, both stately affairs.

Ginza

Moving southwards on Chuo-dori from the Bridgestone Museum leads to Ginza, probably the most famous part of Tokyo. Ginza derives its name from *gin*, or silver. Japan once used three different coinage systems, each based upon silver, gold and copper. Tokugawa Ieyasu decided to simplify the system to only silver, and in 1612 he relocated the official mint from the countryside to Ginza. Two centuries later, the mint was once again shifted, to Nihom-bashi, but the name of Ginza stayed.

Ever since then, Ginza has always been associated in some way or another with money, or rather an excess of it. During the super-heated bubble economy of the late 1980s, for example, land in Ginza became the most expensive real estate in the world. Today, the boutiques and department stores that make Ginza Tokyo's most renowned shopping area are some of the priciest going, stocking the most recognisable high-end fashion brands. Likewise, the hostess clubs here, which boomed in the 1980s, are where seriously well-heeled businessmen can still drop hundreds of thousands of yen in a night on champagne and flirting.

TIP

If you are strolling in the Ginza area and fancy a quick snack, head beneath the elevated train tracks leading south from Yurakucho Station. Here you will find many affordable stands and shops offering *yakitori* (grilled chicken and vegetable skewers) to accompany a glass or two of cold beer.

The day's catch at Tsukiji Fish Market.

Not that Ginza is always prohibitively expensive these days. Many of the better restaurants in the area (and it has some of Tokyo's best; see page 364) are no more expensive than in Omotesando or Roppongi, and you will find places to suit all budgets. Even the shopping has become cheaper in recent years – rubbing shoulders with the likes of Cartier and Luis Vuitton are affordable and extremely popular stores such as Gap, Uniqlo, Muji and H&M.

To get your bearings in Ginza head to the Mitsukoshi department store that anchors **Ginza 4-chome** ⑭, where Chuo-dori intersects Harumi-dori, the second main avenue. (Most Tokyo districts are subdivided into *chome*; Ginza has eight.) This intersection, **Ginza Crossing**, is the central point of Ginza. Head in any direction from here, on Chuo-dori, Harumi-dori or the many backstreets that shoot off the main avenues, and you will find the three things that define Ginza: places to eat, places to drink and even more places to shop.

High-end designer stores in Ginza.

Along Harumi-dori

Harumi-dori extends from Hibiya-koen back down through Ginza 4-chome and Tsukiji and across the Sumida-gawa, Tokyo's barely accessible river (*gawa* or *kawa*). Down Harumi-dori, just past Showa-dori is the site of the **Kabuki-za** ⑮ (Kabuki Theatre; www.kabuki-za.co.jp), founded in 1889. The theatre reopened in 2013 after extensive restoration, and now it boasts an English translation captioning system. *Kabuki* performances are staged twice-daily (usually 11am and 4.30pm). Single act tickets are recommended for those who just want to get a general feel of *kabuki*. Although these are available only on the day of the performance and one person can buy just a single ticket, you will almost certainly have to queue as they remain very popular with tourists.

Closer towards the Sumida-gawa is **Tsukiji** ⑯ and its wholesale fish market (*chuo oroshiuri ichiba*), where merchants arrive long before dawn to select the best of the day's fresh catch. Other produce is also auctioned here and there is a storage refrigerator large

enough to chill ten days' food supply for the entire city. *Tsukiji* means, simply, built land. As with Marunouchi, another landfill area near the Imperial Palace, the newly created land provided space for samurai estates, although of lower ranking than Marunouchi. In the mid-1800s, a part of Tsukiji was set aside for foreigners and a hotel was constructed, which later burned to the ground. If you can get up before sunrise, the early morning tuna auctions here are almost as theatrical as *kabuki*, and are certainly more energetic. Registration for the auctions starts at 5am and is limited to 120 people on a first-come, first-served basis. Even if you can't get into an auction, other parts of the massive market are open to the public (details at www.tsukiji-market.or.jp), and the sushi restaurants that open from breakfast through lunch outside the market have some of the best fresh sushi going, and at reasonable prices.

Kanda

If there is a book, however old and in whatever language, that seems unattainable, it can be found in **Kanda** ⑰, especially around Jimbocho Station. There are stores here specialising in art books, second-hand books, comic books – in English, French, German and Russian. The bookshops have been in Kanda since the 1880s, nearly as long as the nearby universities. Many of the early book printers established their shops in Kanda, followed later by several of the most famous publishers in Japan.

A short walk north past Ochanomizu Station and across the Kanda River are two important shrines. **Kanda Myojin**, a vividly coloured and decorated shrine dedicated to the rebel general Taira no Masakado, is a lively venue for Shinto-style weddings, rituals, cultural performances and one of the city's main festivals, the Kanda Matsuri. Continue up the slope to **Yushima Tenjin**, the city's foremost shrine of learning, a place much frequented by students supplicating the shrine's tutelary spirit for favourable exam results. The grounds of the shrine are a popular spot for plumblossom viewing in mid-February.

Central Tokyo in summer.

THE HEAT ISLAND

Tokyo is developing some climatic features that give new meaning to the expression "concrete jungle".

Parakeets and hemp palm trees, normally associated with tropical zones, are now commonplace in a city where the number of humid "tropical nights" (called *nettaiya*), defined by temperatures that fail to drop below 25°C (77°F), are increasing every year. Tokyo's tropical temperatures, averaging 2–3° higher than surrounding areas, are no longer confined to the summer either, inching into late-spring and early-autumn days.

More rooftop greenery, the use of moisture-retaining building materials, experiments in creating grass car parks and water-retaining road materials are underway, but before any progress is made, expect more sultry tropical nights and days.

There are intricately constructed models of villages and a life-size reconstruction of Nihom-bashi, the Edo Period bridge. It has always been one of the finest museums in Japan, well planned and meticulously thought out. It still stays on top of museum trends – it reopened in 2015 after a revamp with several new interactive exhibits and two floors completely overhauled to cover the history of the 21st century.

Several other notable sights are located within this area, east of the Sumida River. Directly south along Kiyosumi Avenue, a few blocks in from the river, the intimate human scale of the exhibits and reconstructed buildings at the **Fukagawa Edo Museum** (daily 9.30am–4.30pm, closed second and fourth Mon each month) is appealing after the massive Tokyo-Edo Museum. Opposite the museum, the **Kiyosumi Teien** (daily 9am–4.30pm) is a distinctive and very spacious Edo Period garden replete with a central pond set with miniature islands. The garden is especially worth a visit in November to take in the autumnal colours, and in June, when its small iris garden comes into bloom. South again from here, towards Kiba Station, is the **Museum of Contemporary Art** (www.mot-art-museum.jp; Tue–Sun 10am–6pm), a cavernous concrete building set beside pleasant parkland, which displays a mixture of works by contemporary Japanese and overseas artists.

Northern and eastern Tokyo

Around Ueno

North of Tokyo Station and Akihabara, exactly eight minutes on the Yamanote train, is **Ueno-eki** ㉓ (Ueno Station). It was once the commoners' part of town, in what was called *shitamachi* (literally the "low city"). Nowadays there's an aspect of urban life around Ueno not typically noticeable in Japan – the hundreds of homeless men and women who live in Ueno-koen.

Running parallel with elevated rail tracks leading south from Ueno Station is the bustling **Ameya Yokocho**

Sumo practise tournament at the Kokugikan arena.

(or Ameyoko; www.ameyoko.net; store times vary, but typically daily 10am–7pm) street market, which, like Akihabara's electrical stores, has its roots in post-war black-market trading. Although some people go a bit far in calling this one of Asia's great bazaars, the long, narrow street is undoubtedly one of the liveliest markets in Japan; the stalls and vocal traders here deal in everything from fresh fish and vegetables to Chinese medicines and cheap fashions.

West of the station, **Ueno-koen** (Ueno Park) is Tokyo's most distinctly park-like park: sprawling grounds with trees, flocks of scrounging pigeons, monuments and statues, homeless Japanese, a zoo, a big pond with lilies and waterfowl, and national museums. It's not quite as tidy and pristine as one might expect in Japan.

In the spring, Ueno-koen is cherished amongst Japanese for its blossoming cherry trees. The idea of blossom-viewing – *hanami*, a tradition extending back centuries – seems aesthetically appealing; in fact, it is often a drunken and crowded party with few serene moments.

The **Tosho-gu 24**, a shrine adjacent to a five-storey pagoda, was established in 1627 (the present buildings date from a 1651 renovation) by a warlord on his own estate to honour the first Tokugawa shogun, Tokugawa Ieyasu. The path to Tosho-gu (literally, Illuminator of the East) is lined with dozens of large, symbolic stone or copper free-standing lanterns, all donated by warlords from throughout the land to cultivate a little merit with the shogun. Although not as embellished as it was in the Edo Period, the main shrine building is still a magnificent, ornate building. The outer hall features murals painted by the famous Edo artist Kano Tanyu. Also interesting is the Chinese-style Kara-mon, a gate decorated with dragons that are meant to be ascending to and descending from heaven. It's said that the dragons

slither over to the park's pond, Shinobazu-no-ike, under the cover of night to drink the water.

Shinobazu-no-ike (Shinobazu Pond) was once an inlet and is now a pond *(ike)* dense with lotus plants. A small peninsula juts into the pond with a Buddhist temple to Benten – goddess of mercy – perched on the end. A promenade follows the pond's 2km (1.2-mile) circumference. The **Shitamachi Fuzoku Shiryokan** **25** (Shitamachi Museum; Tue–Sun 9.30am–4.30pm), near the pond at the park's south entrance, is a hands-on exhibit of Edo commoners' daily life in the *shitamachi*, as this part of Edo Tokyo was known.

The **Kokuritsu Seiyo Bijutsukan** **26** (National Museum of Western Art; www.nmwa.go.jp; Tue–Sun 9.30am–5.30pm, Fri until 8pm) has a collection of nearly 1,000 pieces, ranging from the Renaissance to the contemporary and including Gauguin, Rubens and Jackson Pollock, not to mention several sculptures by Rodin and a sizeable collection of 19th-century French art. The **Tokyo Kokuritsu**

Map on page 136

TIP

In late autumn and winter, the paths around Shinobazu Pond provide an earthy setting in which to sample *oden* (fishcakes, fried tofu and vegetables cooked in broth). Served from carts with seating around hot cauldrons, these warming snacks are best washed down with a glass of beer or sake.

Girls posing as maids for a game launch in the Akihabara district of the city.

Minamiaoyama, Akasaka, Roppongi, Nishiazabu and Hiroo. The area is peppered with embassies and high-priced expatriate (and company-subsidised) housing – US$10,000 a month rent is not unusual – and liberally spiced with trendy shops, cafés, bars and restaurants.

Up on a hill, **Roppongi** ㉛ is the heart of the area's social life and nightlife. Its main avenues are bright and loud, but don't confuse the activity here with the sex trade of Shinjuku's Kabukicho. A few of the bars and nightclubs aside, Roppongi is mainly a place for upscale food and drinks.

East of Roppongi along the road towards the Imperial Palace, the **Ark Hills** complex of offices, apartments and stores is the work of Mori Taikichiro. Riding the real-estate boom of the 1970s and 1980s, he advocated urban redevelopment and replaced some of the claustrophobic neighbourhoods of Tokyo with modern complexes. At his death in 1993, he owned more than 80 buildings in central Tokyo and was considered the world's richest private citizen.

Pressing west along Roppongi-dori from the main crossing, the gigantic **Roppongi Hills** ㉜ is another Mori Corporation project, one of the most publicised in Japan. Towering and brash, the 16-hectare (40-acre) site, with its restaurants, nine-screen Toho cinema, public amphitheatre, apartments, Grand Hyatt hotel, and over 200 shops and interconnecting walkways, is undeniably impressive. A first-rate modern gallery, the **Mori Art Museum** (www.mori.art.museum; Wed–Mon 10am–10pm, Tue 10am–5pm), located on the 52nd and 53rd floors, holds temporary exhibitions. Superb views of the city can be had from the observation deck (Tokyo City View; www.roppongihills.com; daily 10am–11pm, Fri–Sat until 1am), adjacent to the gallery. There is also an open-air rooftop terrace on the 54th floor, which offers visitors views from 238 metres (780 ft) above the ground (Sky Deck; daily 11am–8pm).

Check the horizon to the south, towards the area known as Shiba: the red-and-white **Tokyo Tower** ㉝ (www. tokyotower.co.jp; daily 9am–11pm) juts

*Driving through
Roppongi Hills.*

skywards, looking industrial and out of place. Finished in 1958, its primary purpose was to broadcast television signals. Subsequent lyrical allusions to the Eiffel Tower or urban elegance were fabrications of creative writing. It's a less than graceful projection into the skyline – 333 metres (1,093ft) high – but views from the observation deck at 250 metres (820ft) are excellent.

Competing with Roppongi Hills, in fact right across the road from it, is the newer **Tokyo Midtown** ❸ complex, built by the Mitsui Fudosan real-estate development company. Midtown's 248-metre (813ft) main tower is the most visible of its five buildings, which between them are home to 73,000 sq metres (785,000 sq ft) of restaurants and shops. Of special note are Midtown's art venues: first, the **Suntory Museum of Art** (www.suntory. com/sma; Wed–Mon 10am–6pm, Fri–Sat until 8pm) and its exhibitions of traditional Japanese artworks; second, Tadao Ando and Issey Miyake's **21_21 Design Sight** (www.2121designsight.jp; Wed–Mon 11am–8pm), a slick gallery and workshop focusing on modern art and design.

Adding to Roppongi's art credentials is the magnificent **National Arts Center** ❸ (www.nact.jp; Wed–Mon 10am–6pm, Fri until 8pm), open in 2007. With 14,000 sq metres (150,000 sq ft) of exhibition space, but no permanent exhibits of its own, the centre has a constantly changing line-up of modern and traditional art on display.

Tokyo Bayside

Tokyo-wan (Tokyo Bay) has shrunk over the centuries due to extensive landfill. The shoguns did it for the housing of their samurai, while politicians have done it in the past decades for glory and political favour. **Odaiba Island** is extremely popular with young people who flock to shopping and amusement treats like **Decks Tokyo Beach** (www.odaiba-decks.com); **Joyopolis**, a virtual-reality amusement park (http://tokyo-joypolis.

com); **Palette Town** (www.palette-town. com), a leisure centre that includes a giant wheel; and **Venus Fort**, a bizarre indoor shopping street with over 160 shops under an artificial sky that changes from sunny, to grey, to violet and stormy depending on the time of day and whims of its programmers.

The island has become an experimental zone for architects. One of the most outstanding designs is the highly visible **Fuji TV Building** ❸, a Kenzo Tange design, whose titanium-clad surfaces are connected by "sky corridors" and girders. The blue arch of the **Telecom Centre** is another chunk of postmodernism, but one that pales against the extraordinary **Tokyo Big Sight** ❸ (www.bigsight. jp), a convention centre and exhibition hall consisting of four inverted pyramids standing on a narrow base, which seems to defy gravity.

A curious addition to the island's futuristic structures is the **Oedo Onsen Monogatari** ❸ (www.ooedo onsen.jp; daily 11am–9am next day, last entry 7am), a traditional hot-spring bath designed along theme-park lines,

Inside Tokyo Midtown.

JAPAN'S TRAINS

The *shinkansen*, which means "new trunk line", is a technological symbol of Japan to the world, but it's not the only train plying the islands.

Other countries have trains that are as fast as Japan's *shinkansen*. Others have trains with equally high levels of comfort, or that are arguably as aesthetically pleasing. But nobody puts all that into a single, unerringly efficient package quite like the Japanese. When it comes to fast trains, the Japanese simply do it better, and have been doing it longer – since 1959, when construction of the Tokaido *shinkansen*, or bullet train, began. Five years later, service on the Tokaido Line began between Tokyo and Osaka with 60 trains daily. Today, more than 150 million passengers a year use the Tokaido *shinkansen*. As for speed, several regularly scheduled trains operate at 300kmh (185mph), while currently in development is a Maglev train that registered top speeds of 603kmh (375mph) in testing in 2015, a world speed record for a manned train. By 2027, it should link Tokyo and Nagoya.

The Japanese live by the train and play by the train, literally and figuratively. The highest real-estate values are found near the railway or subway station in any city, and entire mini-cities sprout near most stations. A train will take you nearly anywhere in the islands – to the remotest cape or valley.

For the Japanese, train travel is a life experience in itself in which the journey can be just as much fun as the destination. Take a train from Tokyo to a weekend getaway like Hakone, and the carriages can take on the atmosphere of a social club – everyone eating special bento and having a drink or two. It is even possible to charter a special train with *tatami*-mat carriages and go nowhere in particular, just party in locomotive style.

Sleek, speedy and smooth, the shinkansen is the ultimate high-speed train. It takes years of experience before a driver can ever think about joining the elite shinkansen ranks.

Not all trains are high-speed. Japan is very fond of its slow-moving historic lines too, like the 100-year-old Enoshima Electric Railway that serves the Kamakura area.

Japan Rail trains and private rail lines crisscross Japan's four main islands, affording access to all but the remotest of areas.

The Tokkaido shinkansen has an average delay of just 36 seconds, inclusive of natural disasters and other uncontrollable causes.

A PRIMER OF AMAZING FACTS

According to Japan Railways (JR), on any given day there are 8,600 people – drivers, train staff, controllers and maintenance engineers – involved in operating the Tokaido *shinkansen* line between Tokyo and Osaka. Each day the route's Series N700 trains, launched in 2007, or state-of-the art Series N700A, launched in 2013, make more than 400 regular runs along the 515km (320-mile) stretch of track between Japan's two biggest cities, each 16-car train carrying up to 1,323 passengers.

Each 16-car N700 weighs in at 715 tonnes, its motors generating 17 megawatts to move it through the 66 tunnels that the *shinkansen* uses between Tokyo and Osaka. The longest of these is 8km (5 miles), the shortest a mere 30 metres (100ft) long.

When the *shinkansen* is travelling at 270kph (170mph; not its top speed, but the limit imposed on the route), it will take almost 5km (3 miles) to come to a complete stop. Thanks to a system that allows the train to tilt up to one degree on bends, the N700 can maintain that 270kph (170 mph) even as it corners.

Inside the carriages, to cater to business travellers, the N700 comes with a power outlet for each pair of seats and free wireless LAN. It's a comfortable ride too, with spacious, reclinable seats, and a smoke-free environment (not always a given in Japan), as well as concession carts regularly going up and down the aisles.

Shinkansen and express trains have concession trolleys selling food and drinks, while the stations they stop at offer ekiben, a version of the bento box made with local ingredients and packaging.

Outside of rush hour, the painful grimaces of crushed commuters are replaced with vacant stares and heads buried in books or mobile phones.

White gloves are common on people working in public places. Conductors and drivers always wear them, as do the people who help squeeze passengers on to the worst rush-hour trains.

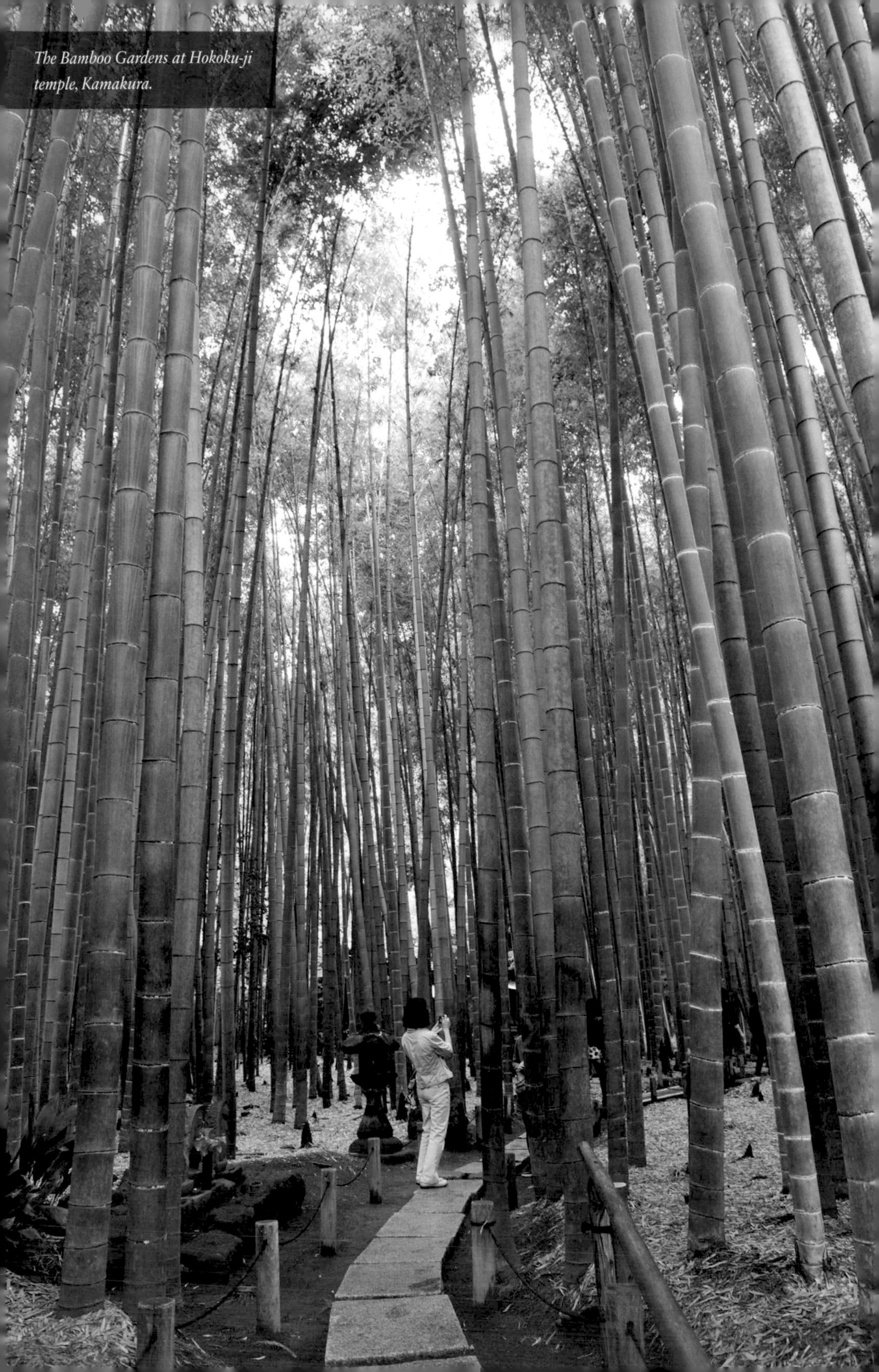

The Bamboo Gardens at Hokoku-ji temple, Kamakura.

AROUND TOKYO

Trains make day trips from Tokyo easy. To the east is Disneyland; to the south are Yokohama, Kamakura and the Izu Peninsula; west, Mount Takao; and to the north, the historical sights of Kawagoe and Nikko.

Tokyo has enough to keep visitors captivated for weeks, but anyone spending more than a few days in the capital should really make an effort to get out and explore the incredible array of attractions that surround it. What's there? Well, to the south of Tokyo is the city of Yokohama, richly influenced by an influx of foreigners in the latter half of the 19th century, and beyond it are the ancient temples and shrines of the one-time capital Kamakura. West is the iconic Mount Fuji and in its shadow the restful hot springs of Hakone, while to the immediate east of Tokyo is the cute allure of Tokyo Disneyland and DisneySea. Arguably the most rewarding side trip, however, is to the north, to the lavish Tosho-gu shrine complex built by the Tokugawa shoguns. And those are just the starters.

East of Tokyo

Disneyland and Chiba

Besides Narita Airport, what brings most visitors east to Chiba Prefecture today is **Tokyo Disneyland ❶** (www.tokyodisneyresort.co.jp; daily, usually from 8–9am until 10pm). Located on 874 hectares (2,160 acres) of reclaimed land in Urayasu, a city just across the Edo River from Tokyo, it is only a 15-minute train ride from Tokyo Station on the JR Keiyo Line to Maihama

Station. All the attractions of the US and Hong Kong sister sites are here at Japan's own take on the Magic Kingdom.

Adjacent is a newer, contingent complex, the very popular **DisneySea** (www.tokyodisneyresort.co.jp; daily, usually from 8–9am until 10pm), which offers attractions designed along aquatic themes and legends. You may want to spend a whole day at each park, or you may want to avoid the crowds and cloying cuteness like the plague (see page 381). Directly and indirectly, Tokyo

Main Attractions

Yokohama
Kamakura
Enoshima
Mount Takao
Izu Peninsula
Mount Fuji
Hakone
Kawagoe

Hakone hot springs.

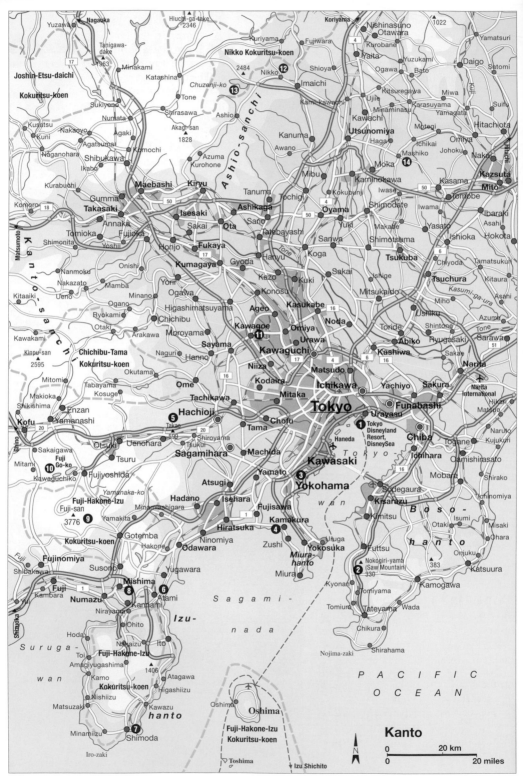

Kanto

0 — 20 km
0 — 20 miles

Disneyland is responsible for somewhere in the region of 100,000 jobs – its total economic impact on a par with Japan's camera industry.

Fans of anime have flocked to **Ghibli Museum** (www.ghibli-museum. jp; Wed–Mon 10am–6pm; online booking recommended) in Mitaka, in the west of Tokyo metropolis, since its opening in 2001. This museum-cum-amusement park showcases the work of the renowned Studio Ghibli, who are behind the finest anime that has emerged from Japan in recent years, including Miyazaki Hayao's *Princess Mononoke* and *Spirited Away*.

Around Narita

Most people are in a hurry to leave Narita Airport (officially known as the New Tokyo International Airport), which is a shame as the area has much to offer. First and foremost is Shinsho-ji, usually referred to simply as **Narita-san** (www.naritasan.or.jp). A 15-minute walk from JR Narita or Keisei stations, this temple, said to date back to AD 940, is one of the most important in the entire Kanto region, drawing 12 million visitors a year, worshippers and sightseers alike, especially during the first three days of the New Year. It is the headquarters of the Shingon sect of esoteric Buddhism. The three-storey pagoda in front of the Great Main Hall is the original 18th-century building and is richly decorated with golden dragons' heads. A large garden with rivers and ornamental ponds is adjacent to the temple. Narita-san is also well known for its drive-in chapel at the side of the complex that welcomes drivers – and their vehicles – to be blessed by a priest and, for a fee (blessings everywhere always come with a charge), to be adorned with lucky amulets to protect against accidents.

For a digest of Japanese social history, the **Kokuritsu Rekishi Minzoku Hakubutsukan** (National Museum of Japanese History; www.rekihaku.ac.jp; Tue–Sun, Mar–Sept 9.30am–5pm,

Oct–Feb 9.30am–4.30pm), in the former castle town of **Sakura**, is a short hop from the airport on the Keisei and JR Sobu lines. The comprehensive museum is set within the extensive landscaped grounds.

Nokogiri-yama ❷ (Saw Mountain) is located along the southwestern coastal region of Chiba's Boso Peninsula. It was known for its Boshu-seki stone from the 14th to the 18th centuries. The sites of the quarries left jagged edges resembling a saw, hence its name. The foot of Nokogiri-yama is a short walk from Hamakanaya Station on the JR Uchibo Line.

A cable car (www.mt-nokogiri.co.jp; daily 9am–5pm, mid-Nov–mid-Feb until 4pm, summer until 6pm) takes visitors halfway up the mountain, a number of steep flights of steps from there on providing enough physical effort to give the sensation of being a pilgrim, at least for the day. The top of the mountain affords a fine panorama of Tokyo Bay and Mount Fuji. On exceptionally clear days, faraway Suruga Bay in Shizuoka Prefecture can also be glimpsed. The holy mountain

TIP

With queues of up to one hour for some of the popular attractions, Disneyland can be a tiring place. If possible, avoid weekends and the school summer holidays (July–Aug), and aim to arrive as close to opening time as possible to secure a FastPass, which lets you skip the queues on certain rides.

Disney character Mickey Mouse poses with a visitor at Tokyo Disneyland.

TIP

Descend a long flight of steps from Nokogiri-yama and visit Japan's largest figure of the Buddha, the impressive Yakushi Nyorai. The distance from the base to the tip of the giant lotus bud that stands behind the statue's head measures an astonishing 31 metres (100ft).

The Minato Mirai 21 development in Yokohama.

has quite an illustrious history, with enough sights to please everyone, including a 33-metre (110ft) Kannon, Goddess of Mercy, carved into the rock face near the top of the mountain, and a cluster of 1,553 stone statues of *rakan* (disciples of the Buddha).

South of Tokyo

Yokohama

The very sound of **Yokohama** ❸ is somehow exotic. And although the city today is both an integral part of the Greater Tokyo area and a major urban centre in its own right, Yokohama has a distinctive personality and even a mystique, much of it stemming from its vital role as one of the greatest international seaports of the Far East.

When Commodore Matthew Perry and his armada of "black ships" arrived in 1853, Yokohama was just a poor fishing village next to a smelly swamp. Under the terms of a treaty negotiated in 1858 by the first US envoy to Japan, Townsend Harris, the port of Kanagawa, located on the Tokaido (the East Sea Road between Edo Tokyo and

Kyoto), was to be opened to foreign settlement. But given its proximity to the important Tokaido, the shogunate reconsidered and instead built an artificial island on the mudflats of Yokohama for the foreigners.

That attempt to segregate the "red-haired barbarians" proved fortuitous for all concerned, since Yokohama's superb natural harbour helped international trade to flourish. The wild early days of the predominantly male community centred around such recreational facilities as Dirty Village, the incomparable Gankiro Teahouse and the local racetrack. Periodic attacks by sword-wielding, xenophobic samurai added to the lively atmosphere.

Eventually, foreign garrisons were brought in and the merchants could live in a more sedate environment. Honcho-dori became the centre of commercial activities, and the street is still lined with banks and office buildings. With a population of 3.7 million, Yokohama is second in size only to Tokyo.

Happily, however, many of those places worthy of exploring are concentrated in a relatively small area and can

be covered for the most part by foot. Another aspect that makes Yokohama – only a 30-minute train ride from Tokyo – alluring is that its broad, relatively uncrowded streets (except on weekends) and laid-back atmosphere provide a perfect antidote to Tokyo's claustrophobia and frantic pace.

Central Yokohama

Start a walking tour of central Yokohama at **Sakuragicho-eki** (Sakuragicho Station), which is the terminus for the Toyoko Line originating at Tokyo's Shibuya Station. Sakuragicho was also the last stop on Japan's first railway, which began service to Shimbashi in Tokyo in 1872. Central Yokohama is now dominated by the massive **Minato Mirai 21** (mm21) shopping and leisure complex, between Sakuragicho Station and the ocean. Trumpeted as the last great Japanese mega-complex to be constructed before the millennium (and after the economic meltdown in the 1990s), its 190 sq km (75 sq miles) are dominated by the 73-storey **Landmark Tower**, one of Japan's

tallest buildings at 296 metres (970ft), with one of the highest observatory decks in Japan – Sky Garden on the 69th floor (www.yokohama-landmark. jp; daily 10am–9pm, Sat and summer until 10pm). Other buildings of note are the Yokohama Grand InterContinental Hotel, strikingly designed to resemble a sail, and the **Yokohama Port Museum** (www.nippon-maru. or.jp; Tue–Sun 10am–5pm). The *Nippon Maru*, a traditional sailing ship anchored nearby, is the museum's most impressive feature. The **Yokohama Museum of Art** (http://yokohama.art.museum; Fri–Wed 10am–6pm) has an excellent collection of 19th- and 20th-century paintings and modernist sculptures.

Southeast side

On the southeast side of the Oka-gawa, a stream that separates Yokohama from Sakuragicho Station, is an area of old government buildings, banks and the like. Further on is a tree-lined street with red-brick pavements: Bashamichi-dori (Street of Horse Carriages). Here is the **Kanagawa Prefectural Museum**

TIP

Yokohama and Kamakura are easily accessible from Tokyo Station on the same train, the Yokosuka Line. Other lines run from Shinjuku and Shibuya stations. Yokohama is exactly 30 minutes from Tokyo, Kamakura just one hour.

Sketch of Matthew Perry and his staff arriving at an imperial tent during the 1854 negotiations.

PERRY'S ARRIVAL

More than two centuries of isolation evaporated in 1853 when Matthew Perry, a US naval officer, sailed four ships into Uraga, near Yokosuka. His sole mission was to force Japan into trade and diplomacy with the US, which then became an equal with Britain, France and Russia in East Asia.

He refused demands to leave and insisted that he be received. Mindful of China's recent defeat in the Opium Wars, the Japanese agreed to stall for time while improving their defences. In 1854 Perry reappeared in Tokyo Bay with nine ships to conclude a first treaty, which included a US consul in Japan and trade rights. Other countries then demanded treaties, which the shogun realised he could not refuse. This weakness helped hasten the collapse of the shogunate system.

The Yokohama Marine Tower.

A street in Yokohama's Chinatown.

of Cultural History (http://ch.kanagawa-museum.jp; Tue–Sun 9.30am–5pm). The building, dating from 1904, was formerly the head office of a bank. As one of the best surviving examples of the city's old commercial architecture, it has been designated a so-called Important Cultural Property by the national government. North of here, **Shinko Pier** is a man-made island jutting out into Yokohama Bay. For Japanese, the old "Akarenga" red-brick warehouses here, which now serve as a shopping mall, are a big attraction. Near them, the **Yokohama Cosmo World** amusement park (http://cosmoworld.jp; Fri–Wed 11am–at least 9pm, Sat–Sun and summer until 10pm) has plenty of fun attractions, including roller coasters, arcade games and a 112-metre (367ft) high Ferris wheel that affords great views of the city and bay.

In the same neighbourhood are the stately Yokohama Banker's Club and on the right, four blocks down, the lovely red-brick Yokohama Port Opening Memorial Hall, which miraculously survived the Great Kanto Earthquake of 1923 and the bombings

of World War II. Also in the area are numerous offices for the prefectural government. This district is sometimes called the Bund and its oldest buildings have a distinctly European look, something shared with buildings along the Bund in Shanghai, built about the same time.

The **Yokohama Archives of History** (www.kaikou.city.yokohama.jp; Tue–Sun 9.30am–5pm), on the site of the former British consulate, houses a museum with various exhibits about Yokohama's fascinating history and a reading room with related audio-visual materials. Across the boulevard is the **Silk Centre**, with a delightful museum (www.silkmuseum.or.jp; Tue–Sun 9am–4.30pm) on the history of that alluring fabric; at one time, Yokohama owed its prosperity primarily to silk, in which the local Indian community was intimately involved.

Yamashita-koen (Yamashita Park) is well worth a visit for the people-watching. On a clear summer night, a rock band is liable to be wailing away on a temporary stage several hundred metres offshore. The former passenger liner and hospital ship *Hikawa Maru* is permanently moored here and can be visited (Tue–Sun 10am–5pm). Further down the same road are the somewhat garish 106-metre (348ft) **Marine Tower** and the **Doll Museum** (www.doll-museum.jp; Tue–Sun 9.30am–5pm), with its collection of 3,500 dolls from Japan and overseas.

The aquarium at **Yokohama Hakkeijima Sea Paradise** (daily, but times vary, see www.seaparadise.co.jp) is very popular. Aquariums abound in Japan, and this is one of the finest in the country. Also at Sea Paradise is a 1.2km (0.75-mile) long roller coaster and the Blue Fall – a 107-metre (350ft), 125kph (80mph) chair-drop that claims to be one of the highest in the world.

Chinatown

No visit to Yokohama would be complete without a meal in **Chukagai**, Yokohama's Chinatown. This dozen

or so blocks is the largest Chinatown in Japan and is nearly as old as the port. The area within its five old gates accounts for 90 percent of the former foreign settlement. Chinatown also takes pride in the historical role it had in providing staunch support to Sun Yat-sen when he was here in exile trying to rally support for revolution on the Chinese mainland.

On days when a baseball game is on at nearby Yokohama Stadium, the area is visited by more than 200,000 people, the majority intent on dining at one of the approximately 150 local restaurants. Most also sneak in at least a peak at the exotic shops selling imported Chinese sweets and sundries from elsewhere in Asia. There are also many herbal medicine and teashops.

Back in the old days, the waterfront Bund often stood in contrast to the **Bluff**, or **Yamate Heights**, where the leading foreign merchants lived in palatial homes. Nanmon-dori in Chinatown was the central street that ran through the international settlement and connected the two. It became a local tradition – known as Zondag, from the Dutch word for Sunday – that on every Sunday the flags of the many nations represented there were flown and brass bands marched down the road. There is a foreign cemetery (*gaijin bochi*) where around 4,200 foreigners from 40 countries are buried. The adjacent **Yamate Museum** (Tue–Sun 11am–4pm), with quaint displays on the life of early foreign residents, sits near where one of Japan's earliest breweries was located.

Motomachi, a popular shopping street just below the Bluff and several hundred metres inland from Yamashita-koen, means "original town". This is somewhat of a misnomer because the area was developed long after Yokohama itself was established. Still, Motomachi, adjacent as it was to the foreign district (now Chinatown), has played an important role in the city's history by serving the needs of foreign vessels and their crews visiting the port. Motomachi's legacy of "foreignness" led to its revival in the 1960s and 1970s. However, the focus of fashion in Yokohama has shifted to Isezakicho, south of Kannai Station, and to the big

TIP

At weekends during the summer (and at festival times in April and mid-September), Kamakura is elbow to elbow with people. Unless crowds bring you joy, you will have little fun trying to shop and sightsee.

The Enoshima Electric Railway (Enoden).

FACT

Zen and Nichiren forms of Buddhism reflect the removal of boundaries between Buddhism and Shinto, with Shinto the realm of daily life and Buddhism of the afterlife. Zen Buddhism's emphasis on austerity and simplicity harmonised well with the outlook of the Japanese samurai class.

A souvenir shop in Kamakura.

department stores around Yokohama Station. A short bus ride south of the Yamate will bring you to the contiguous Negishi district and the **Sankeien Garden** (www.sankeien.or.jp; daily 9am–5pm). This classic Japanese garden was built by a prosperous silk merchant in 1906 and incorporates into its spacious grounds and lakeside area several teahouses, a three-storey pagoda and the restored Rinshunkaku, a villa built by the shogun Tokugawa Yoshinobu.

Kamakura

Cradled in a spectacular natural amphitheatre, **Kamakura** ❹ is bordered on three sides by wooded mountains and on the fourth by the blue Pacific. From 1192, when Minamoto Yoritomo made it the headquarters of the first shogunate, until 1333, when imperial forces breached its seven "impregnable" passes and annihilated the defenders, Kamakura was the de facto political and cultural capital of Japan. During those years, the military administration based here built impressive temples and commissioned notable works of art, a great deal of them

Zen-influenced. Despite the endemic violence of Japan's middle ages, most survived and can be viewed today.

It is a pity that the majority of visitors spend only a day or two in Kamakura, since it is best appreciated leisurely with visits to famous historical sites – there are 65 Buddhist temples and 19 Shinto shrines – interspersed with walks through the quiet surrounding hills. Kamakura is only an hour from Tokyo Station and 30 minutes from Yokohama on the JR Yokosuka Line. For that reason, much of it resembles an open-air madhouse at weekends, a time when it is highly recommended for the traveller to be elsewhere.

Visitors customarily begin their sightseeing from **Kamakura-eki** Ⓐ (Kamakura Station). In addition to the main rail line, there is a private electric-trolley line, the delightful Enoden (Enoshima Dentetsu; www.enoden. co.jp). The Enoden, which began operations in 1902, plies a meandering route with some wonderful views between Kamakura and Fujisawa, with 13 stops in between. For about half its 10km (6-mile) length, the carriages run along the ocean. When the trains are not crowded, the conductors allow surfers to bring their boards aboard. Unfortunately the charming old carriages have been replaced with modern ones, but if time permits, take the Enoden the entire length.

Great Buddha

Hop off the Enoden at Hase, the station closest to the **Daibutsu** Ⓑ (Great Buddha). A road leads to the statue. In the hills to the left and along the way are **Goryo-jinja** (next to the Enoden tracks), which holds a unique festival every 18 September with humorous characters sporting macabre masks; **Hase-dera** (www.hasedera.jp; daily, Mar–Sept 8am–5pm, Oct–Feb 8am–4.30pm), a temple with a 9-metre (30ft), 11-headed Hase Kannon statue, along with thousands of small *jiso* statues decked out in colourful bibs and bonnets and dedicated to lost

babies (mostly due to abortion); and **Kosoku-ji** (daily sunrise–sunset), a temple known for its collection associated with the priest Nichiren. On a knoll to the right of the approach to the Buddha is the 1,200-year-old **Amanawa Shinmei shrine** (daily sunrise–sunset; free). Dedicated to the Sun Goddess, Amaterasu Omikami, the shrine offers majestic views.

Even first-time visitors to Japan have no doubt seen photos of Daibutsu, the Great Buddha. But if not, there's little chance of missing the colossus. At 11 metres (40ft) in height – not counting the pedestal – and weighing 93 tonnes, this representation of the compassionate Amida is unlikely to get lost in crowds posing for pictures below. The features of the statue were purposely designed out of proportion when it was cast in 1252 so that they look right when one is standing 4–5 metres (15ft) in front of it. For a fee, you can crawl around inside the statue. Astonishingly, the Great Buddha has survived the onslaughts of earthquakes, typhoons and tsunamis, like the one in 1495 that ripped away the wooden building that once enclosed it.

On the east side of Kamakura Station is **Wakamiya-oji C**, a broad boulevard that begins at the beach and heads inland under three massive *torii* archways to the Tsurugaoka Hachiman-gu. Parallel to Wakamiya-oji is **Kamachi-dori**, Kamakura's modest answer to Ginza and with little elbow room at weekends. The area abounds with all kinds of trendy shops and eating places, and many of the Japanese-style restaurants here and elsewhere in the city have incorporated Zen principles of cooking.

Along Kamachi-dori and especially on some of the side alleys, craft shops encourage serious browsing. Kamakura is most famous for *Kamakura-bori* (lacquerware), which originated in the area in the 13th century for the production of utensils used in religious ceremonies. Unlike the traditional Chinese lacquerware from which it drew its inspiration, the first step in *Kamakura-bori* is to carve the design and then apply the lacquer. Like fine wine, *Kamakura-bori* improves with age, taking on richer and subtler hues and lustres.

Nichiren temples

The area due east of Kamakura Station, on the other side of Wakamiya-oji, is largely the province of temples of the Nichiren sect. Although most foreigners have heard of Zen, few know much about Nichiren (1222–82) and his teachings, despite the fact that the iconoclast priest founded the only true Japanese Buddhist sect. Nichiren was an imposing personality who in his lifetime was nearly executed, exiled twice, and set upon by mobs on more than one occasion, and who continues to generate feelings of both respect and disdain centuries after his death. Nichiren's importance in political (as opposed to religious) history lies in his prediction of the Mongol invasion as divine punishment for the failure of the authorities to accept

The Great Buddha in Kamakura.

his arguments. The irascible Nichiren seems to have been quite put out that the Mongols did not actually conquer the country.

The temples of **Myohon-ji** , **Hongaku-ji**, **Chosho-ji** (all free and always open), **Myoho-ji** (daily 9.30am–4.30pm) and **Ankokuron-ji** (Tue–Sun 9.30am–5pm) are all Nichiren temples and are worth a visit. The Myohon-ji, for example, although only 10 minutes from the station, seems a world apart.

Tsurugaoka Hachiman-gu

At the top end of Wakamiya-oji, the approach into **Tsurugaoka Hachiman-gu** (www.hachimangu.or.jp; daily, Apr–Sept 5am–8.30pm, Oct–Mar 6am–8.30pm; free) crosses a steep, red, half-moon bridge that separates the Gempei Ponds. The name Gempei refers to the Minamoto (Genji) and Taira (Heike) clans, which fought to the end in the samurai power struggle known as the Gempei War. The three islands on the right – the Genji side – signify the Chinese character for birth, symbolising the victory of Yoritomo and his followers, while the four in the Heike Pond stand for the death of the rival Taira. Yoritomo's indomitable wife, Masako, who ironically was of Taira blood, apparently built the pond to rub in her husband's victory over the ill-fated heirs of Taira.

Behind the Heike Pond is the **Museum of Modern Art, Kamakura** (www.moma.pref.kanagawa.jp; Tue–Sun 9.30am–5pm), and a little past the Genji Pond is the modern and disaster-proof **Kokuhokan** (National Treasure Hall; Tue–Sun 9am–4pm). Each month the Kokuhokan teasingly changes the limited displays of the 2,000 treasures from the temples of Kamakura. Still, whatever is being shown at any given moment should be stimulating for those interested in Buddhist art.

Continuing up towards the main shrine, cross a 25-metre (80ft) dirt track, along which every 16 September mounted archers gallop and unloosen their arrows at targets in the ancient samurai ritual of *yabusame*. Next is an open area below the steps to the *hongu*, or shrine hall. Here is the red stage upon which Shizuka, Yoshitsune's paramour, danced defiantly at the order of his vengeful half-brother Yoritomo, head of the Minamoto clan, using the occasion to sing the praises of her lover. The pregnant girl's courage sent Yoritomo into a furious and vengeful rage, and although he spared her life, he later executed her son.

Tsurugaoka Hachiman-gu's prominence on the top of Stork Mountain and the shrine's dedication to Hachiman, the god of war and tutelary deity of the Minamoto, made it the central point of reference for the numerous offices of the military government situated below. Actually, the shrine was founded way back in 1063 by one of Yoritomo's ancestors. Yoritomo's very unpretentious tomb is to be found off to the right of the shrine near a hill. It is an austere grave befitting a samurai, unlike the monstrous mausoleums for the Tokugawa shoguns at Nikko, which look as if they were built for

Tsurugaoka Hachiman-gu.

mafioso dons. Before exploring the hills north of the Tsurugaoka Hachiman-gu, **Hokuku-ji Temple** (daily 9am–4pm), a 10-minute walk, offers a closer retreat. Follow the road that runs east of the main entrance to the Hachiman-gu until you see signs on the right, pointing you across the river to the temple. Hokoku-ji's main draw is its tranquil bamboo forest, where visitors can repair to a tea pavilion for a bowl of thick, green *matcha*, the brew used in the tea ceremony.

Temples around Kamakura

Two isolated temples of great interest and few crowds are the **Kakuon-ji** (guided tours only, between 10am and 3pm; call 0467-22-1195, in Japanese, to arrange), back in the hills behind Yoritomo's tomb, and the **Zuisen-ji** (www.kamakura-zuisenji.or.jp; daily 9am–5pm, Oct–Mar until 4.30pm), considerably to the east. The former was founded in 1296. Its Buddha Hall, dating to 1354, houses a beautiful Yakushi Nyorai flanked by guardians representing the sun and moon, as well as a shrine to the Black Jizo, whose indelible colour results from its constantly being scorched by the flames of hell in its efforts to save souls. Zuisen-ji has a Zen rock-and-water garden designed by its founder, the monk Muso Kokushi.

Another spot to visit that is not so far off the beaten track, but which is nevertheless largely missed by the tourist packs, is so-called **Harakiri Cave**, a 20-minute walk to the northeast of Kamakura Station past the shallow, meandering Nameri-gawa. In 1333, in what was then a temple called Tosho-ji, the last Kamakura regent, who had been scorned for his patronage of dog fights, died by his own hand while surrounded by more than 800 of his cornered followers.

North of Tsurugaoka Hachiman-gu is **Kencho-ji** ❶ (www.kenchoji.com; daily 8.30am–4.30pm), established in 1253 and perhaps Kamakura's most significant Zen temple. Before fires in

the 1300s and 1400s razed the temple, Kencho-ji had 49 sub-temples. To the right of the main gate, San-mon, is the temple's bell *(bonsho)*, cast in 1255 and inscribed by the temple's first abbot, a priest from China. The large juniper trees beyond the main gate are said to have been planted by the Chinese priest.

To the north is the station at **Kita Kamakura** (North Kamakura), the first stop beyond Kamakura. East of the station is **Engaku-ji** ❷ (www.engakuji. or.jp; daily, Mar–Nov 8am–4.30pm, Dec–Feb 8am–4pm), which dates from the late 13th century and was intended for the souls of those killed during the unsuccessful Mongol invasion the previous year. After the main gate and on the right are steps to a 2.5-metre (8ft) high bell cast in 1301, the largest temple bell in Kamakura. The bell's sound, it is said, guides souls that have been spared by the king of hell back to earth and the living. Engaku-ji's Butsu-den dates from 1964 and has been rebuilt many times over the centuries after fires and earthquakes.

Not far from Engaku-ji and on the main road across the tracks between

Throngs of tourists visit the popular island of Enoshima during Golden Week.

FACT

Not only are there appropriate clothes and tools for every activity in Japan, but there are definite times when sports can, and cannot, be undertaken. The first of September is the end of summer and thus the end of ocean swimming, even if summer's heat still lingers into October.

Beautiful scenery at Hachijojima Island.

Kita Kamakura and central Kamakura is **Tokei-ji**  (www.tokeiji.com; daily, Mar–Oct 8.30am–5pm, Nov–Feb 8.30am–4pm), which can be seen from Engaku-ji's bell tower. Begun in the 1280s as a nunnery, Tokei-ji became noted as a refuge for abused wives. Women who found sanctuary here worked as lay helpers for three years, during which time they were safe from husbands. At the end of the three years, the women were released from marriage.

Enoshima

The wooded islet of **Enoshima**  (Bay Island) has many attractions in any weather and is easily reached either from Shinjuku in Tokyo on the private Odayku Line (a pleasant 75-minute ride), or from Kamakura on the quaint and rattling Enoden electric railway. As always, avoid weekends and holidays.

The island, about 2km (1.2 miles) in circumference, is a wooded hill surrounded by rocky beaches and cliffs. But these days it hardly deserves the name of island: the 600-metre (2,000ft) long Benten Bridge, which connects Enoshima to the bright lights of the resort town of Katase, has gradually turned into a major causeway. The usually crowded beaches of Shichirigahama and Miami stretch far to the east and west. Still, access on foot or by car is simple, and there is plenty of parking space at the foot of the hill. Just beyond where the causeway meets the island is the yacht harbour, constructed for the Summer Olympics in 1964.

The ascent of the hill begins at the end of Benten Bridge along a narrow street crammed with restaurants and souvenir shops. This narrow street leads up to the start of a series of covered escalators, which make the upward progress simple. First stop is the charming **Enoshima-jinja** (http://enoshimajinja.or.jp; daily 8.30am–5pm), built in 1182 and dedicated to Benten, the goddess of fortune. Her naked statue used to reside in a cave on the far side, but fears for her safety led to a place in the shrine itself. On top, in the **Samuel Cocking Garden** (http://enoshima-seacandle.jp; daily 9am–8pm)

IZU SHICHITO

Time permitting, overnight or several-day trips can be made from Tokyo to the ruggedly beautiful **Izu Shichito** (Izu Seven Islands; though there are actually nine), a group of mostly volcanic islands accessible only by boat or air. **Oshima** is the largest and closest. It is also the most touristy, albeit not yet overly so, with good deep-sea fishing, snorkelling, surfing, hot springs and an active volcano, Mount Mihara. Each of the seven main islands has something different to recommend it, **Niijima** is popular with young people during the summer, and has curious saltwater hot-spring pools at the edge of the sea. **Toshima** is the smallest, with a warm microclimate that supports camellia flowers; **Shikinejima** is a tranquil islet known for its hot springs; **Kozushima** is said to be the finest island for fishing; **Mikurajima** is the most unspoilt. Until 2013 visitors to **Miyakejima** had to wear gas masks to protect against the toxic gas produced by Mount Oyana, which erupted in 2000. The furthest-flung and most exotic of the islands is **Hachijojima**, 45 minutes by plane from Haneda. It is known for its semi-tropical flora and fruits, and locals produce an exquisite silk fabric known as *ki-hachijo*. For details, visit the Izu Islands Tourist Association website: www.tokyo-islands.com.

are tropical plants, greenhouses, miniature trains, and restaurants and patios providing views of the ocean. An observation tower, the **Sea Candle** (same times as the garden), 59 metres (190ft) high and accessible by lift, gives more exposed views.

The more spiritually minded might like to visit the famous **Ryuko-ji**, a temple near the station that features a fine pagoda, albeit no older than the 20th century. The temple is dedicated to Nichiren, founder of the only genuinely Japanese sect of Buddhism. It was here that Nichiren was allegedly saved from execution by a timely stroke of lightning that hit the uplifted blade of the executioner's sword.

West of Tokyo

Mount Takao

If you have a hankering to do some nature hiking within the boundaries of Greater Tokyo, the 599-metre (1,965ft) **Mount Takao ❺**, easily accessed on the Keio Line from Shinjuku Station, is the obvious choice. Seven trails wind up the mountain, three of them from just outside the Takao-san-guchi railway station. No. 1 trail is the most popular route up, though some visitors prefer to take the cable car or chairlift, which cuts almost 400 metres (1,300ft) off the climb, and then walk down via trail No. 6, a forest walk that includes a stream and freezing-cold waterfall popular with religious ascetics. The ascent takes you through the gloriously vivid colours of **Yakuo-in**, a temple founded in the 8th century. Mount Takao is something of a pilgrimage spot for botanists, its slopes and trails covered in nearly 500 types of wild as well as cultivated plants and flowers. Serving the vast number of Tokyoites that head to Takao (almost 2.5 million annually), especially at weekends, are a plethora of food and souvenirs stalls dotted between the upper cable-car station and the summit.

Izu Peninsula

Extending into the Pacific between Sagami and Sugura bays is **Izu-hanto** (Izu Peninsula), 60km (40 miles) long and 30km (20 miles) wide, and where countless bays, beaches and *onsen* (hot springs) meld with a very inviting climate to give Izu its reputation as a resort for all seasons. Seafood is excellent here, too. Trains run only along the eastern coast, however.

Eastern Izu begins at **Atami ❻**, a hot spring dating back more than 1,000 years. During the Edo Period, the shogun had its waters brought to the Edo palace so he could enjoy a relaxing bath. Today, Atami is still known for its *ryokan* and hot springs. Access from Tokyo is easy via the *shinkansen*, as well as on regular (and cheaper) trains. The **MOA Museum of Art** (www.moaart.or.jp; Fri–Wed 9.30am–4.30pm), located above the train station, has a fine collection of *ukiyo-e* (woodblock prints), ceramics and lacquer works, many of which have been designated as National Treasures and Important Cultural Properties by the national government.

TIP

It may have been humiliating for Japan at the time, but nowadays Perry's arrival is a tourist attraction. In the middle of May, Shimoda celebrates the Kurofune Matsuri (Black Ship Festival) in commemoration of Perry's landing with ceremonies, brass band parades, and, of course, spectacular fireworks.

Mount Fuji viewed from Lake Motosu.

Those travellers who have read James Clavell's *Shogun* may recognise **Ito**, south of Atami on the eastern coast of Izu-hanto, as the temporary abode of the shipwrecked Englishman who ingratiated himself into Japanese affairs. Today it is a popular hot-spring resort, punctuated by the Kawana resort complex in the south part of the city. The **Ikeda Museum of 20th-Century Art** (Thu–Tue 9am–5pm) offers some 600 paintings and sculptures by Matisse, Picasso, Chagall, Dalí and other masters. South is another hot-spring outpost, **Atagawa**, noted for **Atagawa Banana-Wanien** (Atagawa Tropical and Alligator Garden; daily 8.30am–5pm).

Shimoda ❼ is a somewhat sleepy resort city at the southern terminus of the railway line. A fine view of **Iro-misaki** (Cape Iro) to the south can be had from the top of **Nesugata-yama**, three minutes by cable car from Shimoda Station. The view includes volcanically active Oshima, an island to the east and part of Metropolitan Tokyo.

The first US consul general to Japan, Townsend Harris, was based here, arriving in 1856. This was the first permanent foreign consulate in Japan, chosen by the shogun in part for its remoteness and thus its distance from centres of power. A monument in **Shimoda-koen** (Shimoda Park) commemorates the occasion. The friendship treaty between Japan and the US was signed at **Ryosen-ji** in 1854.

Central Izu is the cultural heart of the peninsula. The **Taisha-jinja** in **Mishima** ❽ (www.mishimataisha.or.jp; daily 8.30am–5pm; free) is revered as Izu's first shrine; its treasure hall keeps documents of the first Kamakura shogun as well as swords and other artefacts. The Egawa house in **Nirayama** is the oldest private dwelling in Japan. **Shuzen-ji**, along the Katsura-gawa, sprang up around a temple founded by the monk Kobo Daishi; this quiet hot-spring town became a favourite hideaway for Japan's great literary talents such as Natsume Soseki, Nobel Prize-winner Kawabata Yasunari, and Kido Okamoto.

Mount Fuji and Hakone

The region around **Fuji-san** ❾ (Mount Fuji but never Mount Fuji-san) has been the inspiration for the works of many of Japan's most celebrated writers, poets and artists. Japan's most celebrated woodblock print artist, Katsuhika Hokusai (1760–1849), in particular, dedicated much of his work to capturing the iconic peak. It would be hard to find a mountain more highly praised for its beauty than Fuji-san or a lake more often photographed than Hakone's Ashi-no-ko. The mountain also boasts Unesco World Heritage status, granted in 2013. Most of the region is designated a "national park", but due to Japan's rather weak laws protecting and restricting commercial exploitation of such assets, one can often consider a national park to be a "nature" amusement park.

Sweeping up from the Pacific to form a nearly perfect symmetrical cone 3,776 metres (12,388ft) above sea level,

Hikers on Mount Takao.

the elegantly shaped Fuji-san watches over Japan. Fuji's last eruption, in 1707, covered Edo Period Tokyo, some 100km (60 miles) away, with ash. Like many natural monuments held to be sacred and imbued with a living spirit, Fuji-san was off-limits to women for many centuries. It was not until 1867, when an Englishwoman boldly scaled the mountain, that there is any record of a woman climbing the peak. Today, half of the estimated 400,000 annual hikers are women.

Although climbers are known to set out to challenge the mountain throughout the year, the "official" climbing season for Fuji-san begins on 1 July and ends on 31 August. The mountain huts and services found along the trails to Fuji's peak are open only then. Expect thick crowds and a distinctly commercial atmosphere, not only around the facilities but along the entire trail to the top.

For those who wish to see the rising sun from Fuji's peak, start in the afternoon, stay overnight (forget sleeping – it's noisy) at one of the cabins near the top, and make the remaining climb while the sky is still dark. The other option is to climb through the night. The trails are well travelled and hard to miss.

Fuji Go-ko ❿ (Fuji Five Lakes) skirts the northern base of Fuji-san as a year-round resort, probably more than most visitors seeking Japan's sacred mountain would expect or want. From east to west, the lakes are Yamanaka, Kawaguchi, Sai, Shoji and Motosu. (A -ko added to the end of these names signifies "lake".)

Yamanaka-ko, which is the largest in the group, and the picturesque Kawaguchi-ko are the most frequented of the five, but some of the best spots are hidden near the smaller and more secluded Motosu-ko, Shoji-ko and Sai-ko. Some recommended visits include the Narusawa Ice Cave and Fugaku Wind Cave, both formed by the volcanic activities of one of Fuji's early eruptions.

Hakone is set against the backdrop of Fuji-san and has long been a popular place for rest and recreation. Hakone's 16 hot springs, including Tenzan (http://tenzan.jp), Hakone Kamon (www.hakone-kamon.jp), Hakone Yuryo (www.hakoneyuryo.jp), Yunosato Okada (www.yunosato-y.jp), Kappa Tengoku (www.kappa1059.co.jp) and Rakuyujurin Shizenkan are nestled in a shallow ravine where the Hayakawa and Sukumo rivers flow together. The inns here have natural mineral baths, but bathing is just part of Hakone's appeal.

North of Tokyo

Kawagoe

Kawagoe ⓫, a former castle town of dark wood, plaster and tile godowns (called *kura*), and ageing temples, prospered as a supplier of goods to Edo during the Tokugawa Period, hence its sobriquet "Little Edo".

It's a 15-minute walk north along Chuo-dori from Kawagoe Station to reach the historical core of the town. **Ichiban-gai** is Kawagoe's most famous

Lake Ashi, Hakone, with a view to Mount Fuji.

street and the one with the largest concentration of *kura*.

The first main site reached on Chuo-dori is the **Yamazaki Art Museum** (www.mazak-art.com; Tue–Fri 10am–5.30pm, Sat–Sun 10am–5pm), which houses the Meiji-era paintings of Gaho Hashimoto and, unusually, includes a cup of green tea and traditional sweet in the admission fee.

One block up from the Yamazaki Art Museum, down a lane to the right is the **Toki no Kane**, a wooden tower that has become the most photographed image of Kawagoe. The current structure was built after a fire broke out in 1893. Two blocks up across the street, the narrow lane on the left is **Kashi-ya Yokocho** (Confectioners' Row). Souvenirs and trinkets have been added to shops selling old-fashioned sweets and purple, sweet-potato ice cream. Several small atmospheric temples can be found just off of Kashi-ya Yokocho, and there is also the **Kurazukuri Shiryokan** (Tue–Sun 9am–5pm), a small museum housed in an 1850s tobacconist's that looks at *kura* and local history.

Heading several hundred metres east, little remains of Kawagoe Castle, but the exquisite **Honmaru-goten Palace** (Tue–Sun 9am–5pm), with its beautifully painted screens and archaeological artefacts, more than makes up for that. A 10-minute walk south takes you to **Kita-in**, an important Buddhist temple-museum with a traditional Japanese garden. Kita-in's main crowd-puller is the **Gohyaku Rakan** stones, 540 statues (although, oddly, *gohyaku* means 500) depicting disciples of the Buddha in different, highly realistic, sometimes humorous poses and expressions.

Nikko

After learning that the main attraction at Nikko, a temple called Tosho-gu, comprises 42 structures and that 29 of these are embellished with some sort of carving – 5,147 in all, according to a six-year-long survey concluded in 1991 – more than a few travellers begin to realise that they've allotted too little time for Nikko.

The small city of **Nikko** ⑫, just under two hours north of Tokyo's Ueno Station on the Tobu Line, is of little interest in itself, serving merely as a commercial anchor to the splendours that decorate the nearby hillsides and plateau across the river to the west from the main railway stations.

How this region – once a several-day trek from the shogunate's capital in Edo (present-day Tokyo) – was chosen as the site of Tokugawa Ieyasu's mausoleum is a story in itself. True, Nikko forms a sort of crown at the northern perimeter of the great Kanto Plain, of which Edo was the centre. However, Ieyasu was from Kansai, not Kanto, and he had established his capital in Kanto primarily to distance himself from the imperial forces in Kansai's Kyoto, forces he had vanquished to seize power in the first place.

Still, Ieyasu's grandson Iemitsu (1604–51) set in motion the process that turned this once out-of-the-way region into Tokugawa territory

Kawagoe Bell Tower.

about 20 years after Ieyasu's death. In fact, Iemitsu himself and his successor Ietsuna – and the Tokugawa shoguns and princes for the next 250 years – made at least three annual pilgrimages to the site to pay tribute to the founder of the dynasty that kept Japan and its people isolated from the outside world.

Through the gates

Ironically, however, given the Tokugawa aversion to things from outside Japan, many of the 5,000-odd carvings at **Tosho-gu** (www.toshogu.jp; daily, Apr–Oct 8am–5pm, Nov–Mar 8am–4pm) depict things foreign. The facade of the main shrine, for example, features carvings of three Chinese men, said to represent important figures of that country who, having turned down their chances to be kings or emperors, became folk heroes.

Most ironic of all is the famous, not to say fabulous, **Yomei-mon** (under restoration until 2019), the gate beyond which only the highest-ranking samurai could pass into the inner sanctum of the shrine, and then only after laying aside their swords. This gate is a masterpiece. Technically, it is a 12-column, two-storey structure with hip-gable ends on right and left, and with cusped gables on four sides. This description, while accurate, is somewhat misleading, however. Even though its *keyaki*-wood columns are painted white to make it appear larger, the gate is quite small. Nearly every surface of the gate is adorned with delicate carvings of every sort – children at play, clouds, tree peonies, pines, bamboo, Japanese apricots, phoenixes, pheasants, cranes, wild ducks and other waterfowl, turtles, elephants, rabbits, a couple of furry tigers, Chinese lions and the traditional symbols of regal power, dragons.

A large, white dragon (one of 92 in and around the shrine) is the main feature of the central beam in front of the second storey of this fanciful structure, and two drawings of dragons appear on the ceiling of the porticoes. The drawing nearer the entrance is known as *nobori-ryu* or ascending dragon, while the other is *kudari-ryu* or descending dragon.

QUOTE

Explaining Shinto's lack of ethical codes: "It is because the Japanese were truly moral in their practice that they require no theory of morals."

Moto-ori Norinaga
(1730–1801)

Yomei-mon, Nikko.

What lies beyond this gate? Another gate, of course: **Kara-mon** (Chinese Gate), also a National Treasure. It is smaller than the Yomei-mon (at about 3 by 2 metres, or 10 by 6.5ft, overall) and is also laden with carvings – dragons (ascending and descending, and lounging around), apricots, bamboo, tree peonies and more.

The ceiling has a carved figure of a fairy playing a harp, while on the ridge of the front gable is a bronze figure of a *tsutsuga*, which like quite a few other carvings and castings in the shrine precincts is not quite a real animal, but rather one created from hearsay and ancient myth and mixed with a healthy imagination.

To help get your bearings, the Kara-mon is the last barrier to pass through before reaching the entrance to the *haiden* (oratory) and the *honden* (main hall), which is the place most visitors remember as they are requested to remove shoes. An official guidebook describes *haiden* and *honden* as the "chief edifices of the shrine". Chief they are, but interesting they are not – at least not to the casual visitor who, not knowing what to look for, tends to shuffle along with the crowd and then returns to the shoe lockers without a pause.

Unfortunately, many of the key elements inside are partially or entirely hidden from the view achieved by this method. Confused (and no doubt somewhat bored) after their shuffle through the "chief edifices", most visitors exit, re-don their shoes and spend the next 10 minutes or so looking for the famous **Nemuri-neko**, or carving of the Sleeping Cat. Some never find it at all and make their way back down the hillside feeling somewhat cheated. To make sure this doesn't happen to you, do not follow the logical path back towards the Yomei-mon. Instead, turn left (right if facing the *haiden/ honden* complex) until you are back on the terrace between Yomei-mon and Kara-mon. Next, advance straight ahead (paying the small fee charged at a makeshift entrance to the Oku no In, or Inner Precincts) and into the open-sided, red-lacquered corridor that skirts the foot of the steep hillside, atop which is the actual Tokugawa tomb. Nemuri-neko, a painted relief carving, is over the gateway.

This small grey cat, well-enough executed and rather cute but otherwise unremarkable, is said to symbolise tranquillity. The fact that it is asleep is taken to mean that all "harmful mice" have been sent packing and the shrine is therefore safe. The carved sparrows behind the dozing cat presumably aren't a threat.

Shogunate tomb

While here, climb the 200-odd stone steps to the top of the hill and the Tokugawa tomb, called **Hoto**, wherein it is said are the remains of Tokugawa Ieyasu. Some spectacular views of rooftops and the surrounding terrain are had from here. On the way past Tosho-gu, through the Yomei-mon to the main entrance and beyond, be sure to stop by the **Yakushido**, one of the few places in these sacred Shinto surroundings with a Buddhist

Kara-mon.

atmosphere. It's off to the right. Here, too, remove shoes. The attraction of this building (it is not exactly a Buddhist temple) is the huge *naku-ryu*, or crying dragon, drawing on the ceiling. It seems that when people stood under the original – drawn in India ink by Kano Yasunobu (1613–85) – and clapped their hands as in prayer, the dragon was heard to utter a long, agonised groan. What this was meant to signify is not recorded and perhaps we will never know, because in 1961 a fire destroyed the building – and the original drawing along with it. You can hear the current dragon cry today, if you pay for a brief tour of the temple that ends with one of the priests banging two wood blocks together under the dragon's head.

Among the other sights to take note of as one leaves the shrine are the sutra library, which boasts nearly 7,000 volumes of the Buddhist sutras in a large, revolving bookcase that was invented by the Chinese. Its other treasures include numerous stone, bronze and iron lanterns presented by the *daimyo* paying their respects to the shogunate and a pair of stone *tobikoe no shishi* (leaping lions) as the main pillars of the stone balustrade.

The bronze candelabrum, bronze lantern and large revolving lantern were presented by the government of the Netherlands to Japan in 1636. The revolving lantern in front of the drum tower is adorned with the three-leaf crests of the Tokugawa clan, but they are placed upside down, perhaps, as an official guidebook to the sutra library explains, "by mistake".

Here, also, are the sacred storehouses on the sides of the middle court. The upper one shows two elephants carved in relief, as well as the *mikoshi-gura* (sacred palanquin house), the repository for the sacred portable shrines used in the annual festival, and the *kagura-den* (sacred dance stage). The flower basket in the gilded panel at the right corner was probably inspired by a basket used by early Dutch traders;

it is the only carving in the precincts that shows Western artistic influences.

Beyond the 40-metre (130ft) high, five-storey pagoda, its first storey decorated with the 12 signs of the Chinese zodiac, and just before reaching the 9-metre (30ft) tall **Omote-mon** (Front Gate), with its large images of the two deva kings, there is what may be the most famous carvings of all – not just in Nikko, but in all the world. Just under the eaves of the royal stables building, which is the only unlacquered structure in the shrine precincts, are the **Three Monkeys**: hear no evil, speak no evil, see no evil. Small carvings they are, despite their fame, but so are all 5,000-plus carvings at Tosho-gu.

Just a short stroll down the broad avenue leading from the Thousand Steps (there are only 10) entrance to Tosho-gu is the **Tosho-gu Homotsu-kan** (Tosho-gu Treasure House; daily, Apr–Oct 8am–5pm, Nov–Mar 8am–4pm), a small museum housing various ancient articles, including carvings, from Tosho-gu and other places around Nikko. During peak

A carving of the Three Monkeys in Nikko.

TIP

As a side trip from Nikko, one option is the quirky Edo Wonderland Nikko (www.edowonderland.net), a theme park where the extensive grounds look like a movie set of the old Edo days. You can catch a "real" ninja show, a mock trial in a magistrate's court, and see many other attractions. It is great entertainment and an enjoyable way to learn about the old days of pre-Meiji Japan.

Chuzenji-ko.

tourist seasons, a number of kiosks will set up in the small adjoining park, Koyoen, to sell beverages and food, lending a commercial flair to the area.

Continue west along the wide avenue for a few minutes to reach **Futarasan-jinja** (www.futarasan.jp; Apr–Oct 8am–5pm, Nov–Mar 8am–4pm), on the right side and away from Tosho-gu. Futarasan-jinja enshrines the three primary Shinto deities: Okuninushi no Mikoto, his consort Tagorihime no Mikoto, and their son Ajisuki-takahikone no Mikoto. All three are revered for having helped to create and then make prosperous the Japanese islands.

Within the grounds is a large bronze lantern called **Bake-doro** (Goblin Lantern), which is said to have once taken on the shape of a goblin so frightening that a samurai attacked it one night, leaving "sword scratches" that are still visible to this day.

Beyond Tosho-gu

Further afield but still within the general area of Tosho-gu are several other places of interest. One is the Futarasan-affiliated **Hon-gu**, established in 767 by the priest Shodo and one of the oldest shrines in Nikko. The present buildings date back only to the end of the 17th century, when the shrine was rebuilt after being destroyed by fire. Just behind it is **Shihonryu-ji**, also founded by Shodo. In fact, it is not a Shinto shrine but rather a Buddhist temple. It also was destroyed by fire and the present three-storey pagoda was erected in its place at the end of the 17th century. The pagoda and the image of the thousand-hand Kannon inside are the temple's main attractions.

Then there is **Rinno-ji** (http://rinnoji.or.jp; daily Apr–Oct 8am–5pm, Nov–Mar 8am–4pm), a temple of the Tendai sect of Buddhism. Its significant claim is the fact that General Ulysses S. Grant, the 18th president of the United States and a hero of the American Civil War, stayed here during his eight-day trip to Japan and Nikko in 1879. It was one of Grant's few trips outside of North America. Actually, the temple has more than Grant-slept-here going for it. In its spirit hall are the tablets of its long line of abbots, all drawn from the imperial family. In another building, built in 1648 and still the largest in Nikko, are three quite amazing Buddhist statues, all measuring 8 metres (26ft) in height and worked in gilded wood.

Nikko's forests

The lush forests of Nikko are filled with ancient trees. The majority are *sugi*, or Japanese cedar. When veiled in mist, one might think they have stood here since the beginning of time, or at the very least are part of a primeval virgin forest. They don't go back quite that far, but they are nevertheless very old, especially those trees in the Tosho-gu precincts proper and along the many kilometres of avenues and roads within and leading to Nikko. These cedars were planted as seedlings, one by one, from year to year, under the direction of a man named Matsudaira Masatsuna (1576–1648).

Matsudaira, so the story goes, was the *daimyo* of Kawagoe and one of the two persons honoured by edict of the shogun to supervise the construction of Tosho-gu. The extent of the man's personal wealth is not recorded nor how much of it was spent, in addition to the budget he was given by the Tokugawa shogun, in planting these trees.

However, it can be assumed that he wasn't very well off to begin with. When his turn to present a grand offering to the shrine came – all the *daimyo* were obliged to do this – Matsudaira was broke. What could he do as an offering, he wondered. Around 1631, several years before the shrine itself was finished, he began to transplant cedar seedlings – plentiful in the surrounding mountains (which he owned) – into strategic positions around the shrine grounds and along the seemingly endless roads. It took him 20 years and an estimated 25,000 seedlings. Today, these trees are what in part define Nikko and its surroundings for travellers. The beneficence continues. The trees and the banks along the avenues are protected as Natural Treasures and Places of Historical Importance under Japanese law.

Thanks to the numbers of visitors who flock to Nikko and the region's fine scenery, the area abounds with other diversions. Unfortunately, getting around without a vehicle is a problem. If money permits, rent a car (not cheap). If time permits, take a taxi or a bus (this will take longer) up the famed I-Ro-Ha switchback road to **Chuzenji-ko** ⓭, a large and quite picturesque lake due west of Nikko. From there, savour the altitude of 1,270 metres (4,170ft), clear air and lakeside scenery. A sightseeing boat leaves the pier, just across the road from the bus stop, for a one-hour tour of the lake. Its heavily wooded shores are lined with hotels, inns, campsites and other tourist wonders. Five minutes' walk in the opposite direction is the observatory of the 100-metre (320ft) high **Kegon Falls** (Kegon no Taki); a lift descends right to the bottom of the gorge (daily 8am–5pm), where a platform allows views of the thundering falls.

Mashiko

Synonymous with a rustic, earthenware ceramic, the village of **Mashiko** ⓮, just 30km (20 miles) southeast of Nikko, is a living pottery village, with some 300 working kilns scattered among the surrounding paddy fields. Although Mashiko has been a craft village for over a millennium, its name was made in the 1930s when renowned potter Hamada Shoji built a kiln here, later to be joined by English ceramicist Bernard Leach. **Hamada's house and kiln**, located in the **Togei Messe** complex (www.mashiko-sankokan. net; Tue–Sun 9.30am–5pm), have been lovingly restored. Tourist information booths located in Utsunomiya Station (50 minutes from Tokyo Station by *shinkansen*), from where buses make the hour-long trip to Mashiko, provide leaflets and maps in English. A lively village with dozens of ceramic shops and stalls, Mashiko stages regular pottery fairs and festivals.

Wares for sale at the pottery market in Mashiko.

View of the Japan Alps in the morning.

CENTRAL HONSHU

Central Honshu offers a large modern city – Nagoya – a rugged coastline along the Sea of Japan (East Sea) and historic castles, but above all it is the stupendous mountain scenery of the Japan Alps that draws visitors here.

entral Honshu has an air of mystery about it. Yes, it has a big city in the shape of the industrial Nagoya, but elsewhere it oozes history and tradition. In places, it feels like it is still living parts of its past. All over the region, traditional crafts thrive – *kutani* ware in Kanazawa and Hida lacquerware in Takayama perhaps the two best known. Just outside Nagoya, in Gifu and Inuyama, they still practise a 1,300-year-old form of fishing, while in the charming town of Gujo Hachiman the main draw is a 400-year-old dance festival. In Shirakawa-go many villagers still live in traditional thatched houses that haven't changed for generations. And while tourism has no doubt played a part in keeping these traditions thriving, you get the feeling they would still be here even if the tour buses hadn't started to pull up.

Central Honshu is blessed with rich nature too. The breathtaking peaks around Kamikochi are considered Japan's best hiking grounds for good reason, while Sado-jima off the northern coast of Niigata is beautifully rugged and wild. Visit the island in winter and you will soon understand why being exiled here – as so many were – was once considered a punishment. Better still, visit other parts of Niigata and Nagano in winter for fantastic skiing and snowboarding opportunities,

or retreat to one of the region's hot spring resorts.

Nagoya and around Nagoya

Although known in Japan for its food – its flat, white *kishimen* noodles, its moriguchi-zuke pickles, its confection called *uiro*, its deep-fried *tebasaki* chicken wings, and all manner of dishes that use the local *miso* paste – **Nagoya ❶** is better recognised as a centre of industry, producing construction materials and automobiles,

Main Attractions
Nagoya
Inuyama
Gujo Hachiman
Takayama
Shirakawa-go
Kamikochi
Kiso Valley
Kanazawa
Sado-jima

Crowds at Nagoya Station.

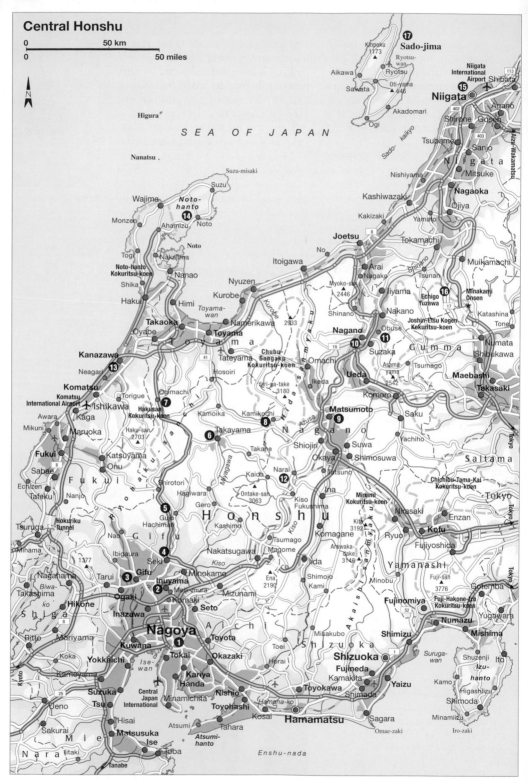

Central Honshu

0   50 km

0   50 miles

N

SEA OF JAPAN

Higura

Nanatsu .

Sado-jima ⑰

Kinpoku 1173

Aikawa

Sawata

Oti-yama 646

Ryotsu-wan

Ryotsu

Akadomari

Ogi

Sado-kaikyo

Niigata International Airport

Shibata

113

⑮ **Niigata**

Agano

Shirone   Gosen

402

Tsubame

Sanjo

403

Niigata

Mitsuke

Nishiyama

Nagaoka

Kashiwazaki

Ojiya

Kakizaki

Yamato

Muikamachi

Suzu-misaki

Suzu

Wajima

Noto-hanto ⑭ Noto

Monzen

Ahamizu

Noto

Togi   Nakajima

Nanao

Shika

Noto-hanto Kokuritsu-koen

Hakui   Himi

Toyama-wan

Takaoka

Oyabe

Toyama

Namerikawa

Kurobe

Nyuzen

Itoigawa

No

Joetsu

Arai

Nagako

Myoko-san 2446

Iiyama

Shinano

Tokamachi

Tsunan

8

Echigo Yuzawa   ⑯

Minakami Onsen

Katashina

Tone

Joetsu

Mizu-Wakamatsu

Gumma

2933

Hida-sanmyaku

Kuroke

Nakano   Obuse

⑪

Nagano

⑩

Suzaka

Ueda

Komoro

Saku

Yachiho

Asama-yama 2542

Tsumago

Maebashi

Shibukawa

Numata

Takasaki

Toyama

Tateyama   Sangaku

Chubu Sangaku Kokuritsu-koen

Hosoiri

Yari-ga-take 3180

41

Kamoika

⑦

Ogimachi

Hakusan Kokuritsu-koen

Kanazawa

⑬

Neagari

Komatsu

Komatsu International Airport

Awara

Mikuni

Fukui

Sabae

Echizen

Tafeku

Ishikawa

Kaga

Onu

Katsuyama

Haku-san 2703

Hakusan

Shirotori

Hagiwara

Gero

Takayama ⑥

Kamikochi

⑧

Nagano

Matsumoto ⑨

Shiojiri

Suwa

Okaya   Shimosuwa

Tatsuno

Ina

Komagane

Saitama

Chichibu-Tama-Kai Kokuritsu-koen

Nirasaki

Enzan

Kofu

Ryuo

Fujiyoshida

Takane

Narai ⑫

Ontake-san 3063

Kaida

Kiso Fukushima

Kiso

Minami Kokuritsu-koen

Kita 3192

Arakawa-dake 3146

Akaishi-sanmyaku

Yamanashi

Fuji-san 3776

Honshu

Gujo

⑤

Hachiman

Nao

Kashimo

Tsumago

Magome

Gifu

Nakatsugawa

Iida

Shimojo

Kami

Minobu

Fujinomiya

52

Fuji-Hakone-Izu Kokuritsu-koen

Gotemba

Yugawara

Ibigaura

1377

Tarui

Seki

Gifu ③

Inuyama ②

Meiji-mura

Minokamo

Mizunami

Ena 2190

Shimoji

Misakubo

Shizuoka

Shimizu

Fujinomiya

Numazu

Mishima

Shuzenji

Ito

Izu-hanto

Nagahama

Biwa-ko

Takashima

Hikone

Shiga

Ritto

Moriyama

Koka

Yokkaichi

Kameyama

25

Ueno

Sakurai

Mie

Iitaki

Matsusaka

Ise

Toba

Ogaki

Inazawa

Kuwana

Tokai

Seto

Nagoya ①

Toyota

Aichi

Okazaki

Komaki

Kariya   **Handa**

Nishio

Minamichita

Central Japan International

Toyohashi

Atsumi

Tahara

Atsumi-hanto

Kosai

Toei

Horai

Toyokawa

Shimada

Kamakita

Yaizu

Kamo

Minamiizu

Shimoda

Suruga-wan

Iro-zaki

Sagara

Omae-zaki

Enshu-nada

Hamamatsu

Hamana-ko

Shizuoka

Fujieda

1

Hisai

Tsu

Suzuka

Minamichita

Ise-wan

Kaniyama

Mihama

Tsuruga

Hokuriku Tunnel

Nanjo

Kyoto

Tokyo

Tokyo

8

Shiga

Tsunan

Nagako

with just a few sights for the traveller. Nagoya is located almost precisely in the centre of Japan along the old Tokaido highway and is a major transport hub to and from other cities, including Tokyo and Osaka. It is Japan's fourth-largest city, with 2.2 million people.

Nagoya was originally planned by the shogun Tokugawa Ieyasu to be a castle town. He built **Nagoya-jo** (Nagoya Castle; www.nagoyajo.city. nagoya.jp; daily 9am–4.30pm) in 1612 for his ninth son, Yoshinao, but the town didn't really develop into a powerful presence. Much later, Nagoya had to be redesigned and reconstructed after suffering extensive air-raid damage in 1945. The castle, rebuilt in 1959 and now functioning as a cultural and historical museum, is considered Nagoya's primary attraction. The museum displays treasures of the Tokugawa family.

Nagoya's **Atsuta-jingu** (temple precincts always open and free; museum daily 9am–4.30pm, closed last Wed of the month and the following day) is second only to the Ise-jingu, in Mie Prefecture, in its importance to the emperor of Japan and Shintoism. One of the imperial family's three sacred treasures, the Kusanagi sword (*kusanagi no tsurugi*) is kept here. (The other two sacred treasures, the jewel and mirror, are kept at the Imperial Palace in Tokyo and at Ise, respectively.) All three treasures are said to have been given to the imperial family by the Sun Goddess Amaterasu Omikami. None are viewable by the public. Hundreds of ancient trees thrive amidst ancient artefacts, including the 600-year-old Nijugocho-bashi, a bridge made of 25 blocks of stone. The shrine's main festival is in June, though other events also take place throughout the year. More centrally located than Atsuta (which is south of the city centre) is the **Osu Kannon** temple. Originally located in Gifu, Tokugawa Ieyasu moved it to Nagoya in 1612, and although all the

buildings are modern reconstructions, it's still an imposing sight – especially striking is the giant red paper lantern hanging before its main hall. Every 18th of the month, the grounds are used for a lively flea market.

There are museums all over Nagoya, ranging from the treasure-laden **Tokugawa Art Museum** (www. tokugawa-art-museum.jp; Tue–Sun 10am–5pm), displaying heirlooms of the Owari-Tokugawa family, and **Aichi Bijutsukan** (Fine Arts Museum; www. aac.pref.aichi.jp; Tue–Sun 10am–6pm, Fri until 8pm), which features work from the 19th century to the present, to the state-of-the-art **Nagoya City Science Museum** (www.ncsm.city. nagoya.jp; daily 9.30am–5pm), which has plenty of entertaining hands-on exhibits for both children and adults to enjoy, and boasts the world's largest planetarium located in a giant silver globe. Another enjoyable and popular venue for a family visit is the **Port of Nagoya Public Aquarium** (www.nagoyaaqua.com; usually Tue–Sun 9.30am–5.30pm, summer until 8pm, winter until 5pm).

Inuyama Castle.

A devotee at the Atsuta shrine in Nagoya.

Celebrating part of Nagoya's more recent history is the **Toyota Commemorative Museum of Industry and Technology** (www.tcmit.org; Tue–Sun 9.30am–5pm). Situated in cavernous red-brick buildings that once housed Toyota's looms (Toyota was a textile giant long before it branched out into cars), the museum gives insights into Japan's *monozukuri* (art of making things) culture and provides plenty of fun, hands-on activities aimed at kids. Alternatively, the **SCMAGLEV and Railway Park** (http://museum.jr-central.co.jp; daily 10am–5.30pm), operated by Central Japan Railway Company, celebrates Japan's fast-train developments. Here, visitors can enter a life-size reproduction of a driver's cabin on the SeriesN700 *shinkansen*, learn how the superconducting Maglev works or ride train-driving simulators.

Outside Nagoya

Some 25km (15.5 miles) north of Nagoya is **Inuyama ❷**, site of Japan's oldest castle, built in the mid-1400s (http://inuyama-castle.jp; daily 9am–5pm). Standing in its original state above the Kiso-gawa, it has been owned by the same family since the 1600s. A little east of the castle is the exquisite **Uraku-en** (daily 9am–5pm, Dec–Feb until 4pm), a lush garden replete with several traditional teahouses, one of which, Joan, is considered to be one the country's top three historic teahouses. Near Inuyama is **Meiji-mura** (Meiji Village; www.meijimura.com; Mar–Oct daily 9.30am–5pm, Nov daily 9.30am–4pm, Dec–Feb Tue–Sun 10am–4pm), with 67 Meiji-era structures collected from around Japan and reassembled here. Of special note is the entrance hall and lobby of Frank Lloyd Wright's original Imperial Hotel, built in Tokyo and moved here when the latest hotel was built. Every March, one of Japan's strangest festivals (Hounen Matsuri) occurs not far from Inuyama, at a little shrine – **Tagata-jingu** – dedicated to phalluses (www.tagatajinja.com). A huge and anatomically correct phallus is carried through the streets, and crowds of people try to touch it, hoping to enhance their fertility. Equally traditional are the *ukai* (cormorant fishing) displays that take place on Inuyama's Kiso River from June to mid-October.

Further north of Nagoya, **Gifu ❸** has a modern clothing industry. But for Japanese tourists, Gifu is undoubtedly better known for its 1,300-year history of cormorant fishing *(ukai)* on the three rivers – the Kiso, Ibi and Nagara – that cut through the city. Today, *ukai* is distinctly a tourist attraction, with the collared birds doing their thing at night, illuminated by small fires suspended in iron baskets from the front of the boats (the displays take place most evenings from mid-May to mid-October; tickets can be bought at the tourist office in Gifu Station, www.gifucvb.or.jp). Gifu's highly respected craftsmen add another touch of tradition to the city, especially its lantern and umbrella makers.

Gifu's castle (**Gifu-jo**; times vary, but daily at least 9.30am–4.30pm; charge) commands an impressive view from the top of Kinka-zan (Golden Flower

Meiji-mura, near Inuyama, contains the interior lobby of Frank Lloyd Wright's Imperial Hotel, transported from Tokyo.

Mountain). It was built about seven centuries ago, has suffered numerous razings, and was last rebuilt in 1956. A three-minute gondola ride to the foot of the mountain arrives at Gifu-koen (Gifu Park) and the unspectacular **Museum of History** and the more interesting **Nawa Insect Museum** (www.nawakon.jp; Fri–Tue 10am–5pm, Feb also closed Tue). The latter, though small, contains various bugs, butterflies and spiders – some of which are uncomfortably large – from around the world. In all, its collection includes 300,000 specimens. Not far from here is **Shoho-ji temple** (daily 9am–5pm), an otherwise small and fairly run-down affair that has one spectacular saving grace – a giant gilded Buddha, 13.7 metres (45ft) high, that's well worth the admission fee to the main hall that it fills.

Finally, no summary of the Nagoya region would be complete without mention of **Seki** ❹, a sword-forging village a bit east of Gifu and the site of the Battle of Sekigahara, waged in the early 17th century between the forces of Tokugawa Ieyasu and Toyotomi Hideyori. The battle was a significant turning point in Japanese history and a catalyst for a complete shift in the archipelago's power structure. Although Tokugawa was outnumbered nearly two to one, his warriors slaughtered more than a third of the enemy troops to put Tokugawa on the shogun's throne, which he and his descendants held for the next 250-odd years. Today, only an unassuming stone marks the spot of Tokugawa's heroic triumph.

Gujo Hachiman

Writer and long-distance walker Alan Booth (who moved to Japan in 1970) was quick to sense something special when he wrote about **Gujo Hachiman** ❺ in his classic travelogue *Looking for the Lost*: "What I was in fact approaching was a town of a kind I'd dreamed of finding when I'd first arrived in Japan almost 20 years before, a town so extraordinary that, when I went out to stroll around it that evening, I almost forgot to limp."

Gujo sits at the confluence of the very clean and beautiful Nagara and

Cormorant fishing on Nagara River.

Yoshino rivers, their *ayu-* (sweetfish) rich waters popular with fishermen. The town sits in a mountain valley that long ago was a way station on an important trade route that led to the Sea of Japan (East Sea). An imposing fortress once stood here. Built as a symbol of the town's former importance, the current castle (**Gujo Hachiman-jo**; times vary, but at least daily 9am–4.30pm), dating from 1934, replaced the original. It's a stiff walk to the pinnacle, but the views from the top are commanding. This is the best place to appreciate the shape of the town, which, as all the local travel information will tell you, resembles a fish.

Hashimoto-cho, an old merchant area, remains the commercial heart of the town. Look behind the modern facades here and you will discover buildings which, in some cases, have stood here for centuries. The physical fabric of the town is as appealing as the setting, consisting of dark, stained-wood homes and shops, white plastered buildings, wooden bridges, steep walls constructed from boulders, and narrow stone-paved lanes. Museums, galleries

The Sanmachi Suji area, Takayama.

and attractive shops selling local products like Tsumugi textiles can be found along these lanes.

Gujo Hachiman is known for its festivals, in particular the **Gujo-Odori** dance festival that runs from mid-July to early September, climaxing in the middle with a frenetic four-day main festival in August. The 400-year-old event features thousands of dancers clad in colourful *yukata* (light kimonos), performing carefully choreographed movements accompanied by an almost hypnotic chant-like singing. During the festival, the local tourist office gives daily free **dance lessons** (at 11am, 1pm, 2pm and 3pm) to visitors, which are well worth trying. While you are at the tourist office, pick up one of their self-guided walking tour maps (also available online on www.gujohachiman.com) – following one of these for half a day is by far the best way to explore the town.

Interior mountains

Takayama to the coast

High in the mountains is **Takayama** ❻, luring travellers with *onsen* (hot

springs), hikes, tennis courts and other activities. Originally established in the 1500s as a castle town for the Kanamori family, Takayama retains an old charm nurtured by its *ryokan* (traditional inns), sake breweries and craft shops. One of its highlights, **Takayama-jinya** (Administrative House; daily 8.45am–5pm) dates from the early 1600s, although the current buildings are early 19th-century reconstructions. Among its displays is a torture chamber.

In the centre of Takayama, just east of the Miyagawa River, which runs through the town, is the **Sanmachi Suji** area, with three streets lined by museums, traditional shops, sake breweries and countless spots to eat. In the summer months it can be yet another tourist madhouse, but is well worth exploring nonetheless to soak up the old-Edo atmosphere given off by the area's old, wood buildings.

Museums abound in Takayama, but the not-to-miss museum is **Hida no Sato** (Hida Folk Village; www. hidanosato-tpo.jp; daily 8.30am–5pm), an open-air assembly of traditional houses that were collected from around the Takayama region and reassembled here. Artisans demonstrate regional folk crafts, and you can also try your hand here at making your own *sashiko* quilting and straw crafts. The **Kusakabe Mingeikan** (Folk Craft Museum; daily, Mar–Oct 9am–4.30pm, Nov–Feb until 4pm, Dec–Feb closed Tue) is another one worth checking out if you are interested in crafts. This former warehouse – designated as a National Treasure – displays wonderful examples of local Hida woodcarving *(ichii itobori)* and lacquerware work *(Hida-nuri)*.

Takayama is especially famous within Japan for two festivals: one in mid-April called *Sanno matsuri* (festival) with a procession of *yatai* (floats), and the Hachiman matsuri in October. If you aren't in Takayama for one of the festivals, you can get a good feel for them at the **Takayama Matsuri Yatai Kaikan** (daily, Mar–Nov 8.30am–5pm, Dec–Feb 9am–4.30pm), which displays some of the festivals' floats.

A thatched house in Shirakawa.

EAVES DROP

The name for Shirakawa-go's unique style of farmhouses, known as *gassho-zukuri*, or "praying hands," comes from the sharp "A" shape of their wooden frames, resembling the hands of monks pressed together in prayer. The thatched houses have been cleverly designed to withstand deep snowdrifts in the winter months.

Gently soaring structures, the roofs alone can reach an astonishing height of 9 metres (30ft). Constructed without nails, the wooden beams, tightly secured with rope, are a tribute to the traditional skills of Japanese carpenters. The smoke from *irori* open-hearth fires rises through the buildings, blackening rope and wood with soot, but also preserving them and killing off termites and thatch bugs in the process.

With the development of sericulture in the late 1800s, the large upper floors under the eaves were used to raise silkworms. Up to 30 people could inhabit one house, parents and their immediate family sleeping in a private room, servants and unmarried sons sharing an entire floor or two.

As privacy was virtually impossible in such circumstances, couples would retreat to the nearest wood or glade for snatched moments of intimacy, a practice that manifested itself nine months after the end of winter, with a noticeable rise in the birth rate.

Shirakawa-go and Gokayama

A safe haven for the defeated Taira clan, the regions of Shirakawa-go and Gokayama were once so secluded that during the later Edo Period Lord Maeda secretly produced gunpowder here. Until a road was constructed in 1925, villages here, set among thickly forested mountain valleys, were virtually inaccessible. Not so these days, especially after the area's designation in 1995 as a Unesco World Heritage Site, a mixed blessing guaranteeing the preservation of the region's unique architectural heritage, while inviting a blight of tourism on its fragile eco-structure. The beauty of the valleys and their distinctive A-frame thatched houses – *gassho-zukuri* – somehow manages to transcend the crowds.

The largest collection of steeply angled *gassho-zukuri* houses are concentrated in the village of **Ogimachi** ❼, easily accessed these days by buses from Takayama or Kanazawa. Hike up to an observation spot 10 minutes north of the main bus terminal for sweeping views of the valley and houses. **Wada-ke** (daily 9am–5pm),

the first notable structure walking back in the direction of the main village, is one of several *gassho-zukuri* serving as museums. This one is a former family residence, once occupied by the Wada family, replete with household items and an impressive lacquerware collection.

A little south, **Myozen-ji Temple Museum** (daily, Apr–Nov 8.30am–5pm, Dec–Mar 9am–4pm) is a large building even by local standards. The great beams of its five storeys, once used by monks and priests as living quarters, are blackened from smoke from the first-floor open hearth used for cooking and to provide warmth. An adjacent thatched temple and bell tower add to the mood.

Although it has a rather contrived feel, the **Gassho-zukuri Folklore Park** (Shirakawa-go Minkaen; Mar–Nov daily 8.40am–5pm, Dec–Feb Fri–Wed 9am–4pm), a showcase collection of farmhouses relocated here after a dam on the nearby Sho-kawa threatened their existence, is well worth seeing. The open-air museum has 25 farmhouses and puts on

Hiking amongst spectacular scenery in Kamikochi.

demonstrations of weaving, carving and other handicrafts. Despite its World Heritage designation, Ogimachi, like all the villages here, is a working farming community. To get a sense of life here, an overnight stay in one of the *gassho-zukuri*, many now serving as guesthouses, is highly recommended.

Some 10km (6 miles) from Ogimachi, the hamlet of **Suganuma** consists of just 14 houses, 10 of which are *gassho zukuri*. Despite its diminutive scale, it has two interesting museums, the **Gokayama Minzoku-kan** and the **Ensho-no-Yakata** (both daily 9am–4pm), the first displaying household items from daily life, the second highlighting the clandestine production of gunpowder.

Another 8km (5 miles) north, **Ainokura** is another gem of rural architecture and life. Though requiring a 30-minute uphill hike from the village of Shimonashi, the village attracts a good number of visitors. The **Ainokura Minzoku-kan** (daily 8.30am–5pm) has interesting displays of local crafts, including handmade toys and washi paper, but it's the spectacular location of the village and endless meandering hiking trails leading from it across densely forested mountains that visitors come for.

Kamikochi

In his novel The House of Nire, Kita Morio writes, "In the already fading light the linked peaks of the Alps were solid and harsh, all ranged there in the early dusk like a huge folding screen." One of the most ravishing panels of that folding screen, snow-dusted or gilded with sunlight according to the season, is Mount Hotaka and the high valley of **Kamikochi** ❽ at its feet.

The valley is a part of the **Chubu-Sangaku National Park** in the region of Nagano Prefecture known as Azumi. You know you have reached the area of Kamikochi when you begin to see cameo images of mountain peaks reflected in the ponds of the Azusa River Basin.

The unsettling paradox of visiting a rural area crowded out with nature-lovers can be avoided by visiting Kamikochi on a summer weekday, in

Matsumoto Castle.

The waki-honjin at Tsumago used to be the main inn of the post town.

Narai-juku, Nagano.

early October, or in the spring shortly after the opening of the mountain road, which is unusable from 15 November to 22 April.

Most walkers set off from the bus terminal in the village, crossing the fast currents of the Azusa River by way of Kappa Bridge. The origin of this strange name (in Japanese folklore, *kappa* are malignant water sprites known in their worst tantrums of violence to tear a victim's bowels out through the anus) can only be guessed at.

After negotiating the bridge, trekkers usually pay brief homage at the Weston Memorial, which has a plaque dedicated to the Englishman who pioneered mountain climbing here at the turn of the 20th century. Trekkers then strike out on anything between a half-day excursion and a full two-day-three-night circuit of a region many seasoned walkers regard as home to some of the finest hiking trails in Japan. For more information, the tourist offices in Takayama and Matsumoto can be a real help.

Matsumoto ❾ is popular in summer with Japanese heading off into the mountains on bikes and on foot. In the 14th century it was the castle town of the Ogasawara clan. **Matsumoto-jo** (daily 8.30am–5pm) is an excellent example of a Japanese castle with its original *donjon*, dating from late 1590s. Three turrets and six floors are punctuated with fine historical displays and a nice view of the city and the Japan Alps from the top. South of the castle is the modern **Matsumoto City Museum of Art** (http://matsumoto-artmuse.jp; Tue–Sun 9am–5pm), home to many artworks by sculptor Kusama Yayoi, recognised the world over for her flamboyant polka dots.

Venue of the 1998 Winter Olympics, **Nagano ❿** is a moderately sized city of nearly 400,000 people and was established in the Kamakura Period as a temple town. That temple, Zenko-ji, dates from the 7th century and was the site for Ikko Sanzon, the first Buddha image in Japan. Northeast of Nagano, in **Obuse ⓫**, is the **Hokusai-kan** (Hokusai Museum; daily 9–5pm; charge), with a decent collection of Hokusai's *ukiyo-e*, or woodblock prints.

Kiso Valley

Taking the Chuo Line southwest of Matsumoto, you soon enter the Kiso Valley region between the Northern and Central Alps. The valley once formed part of the Nakasendo, one of the five key highways linking Edo with central Honshu. Despite vigorously promoted tourism, the region still manages to convey a sense of pre-industrial Japan.

The most affluent of the 11 post towns along the valley, **Narai ⓬** and its 1km (0.6-mile) long main street boast some of the best-preserved wooden buildings in the valley. Look out for the exquisite lattice-work called *renji-goshi*, as fine as filigree. **Nakamura-tei** (daily, Apr–Nov 9am–5pm, Dec–Mar until 4pm), a former comb merchant's shop, is now a museum where you can pick up a pamphlet on local architecture. Unlike the other post towns along the valley, this one permits traffic to pass along its main street. Depending on your point of view, this spoils the town or confirms that it is a living, working community rather than a historical showcase.

Time permitting, a half-day stopover in **Kiso Fukushima**, a sleepy, far less touristy post town south of Narai, provides a nice respite from the crowds. Inns line the Narai-gawa River. **Sumiyoshi-jinja**, an ancient shrine on a slope above the town, has an unusual sand and gravel garden designed by the modern landscape master Mirei Shigemori.

Following the Chuo Line south, **Tsumago** is a beautiful, well-appointed town whose carefully preserved buildings bespeak the efforts of the local community to restore and save their heritage. All high-tension wires and TV aerials have been banished from the scene, improving it no doubt, but giving the impression of a carefully managed open-air museum. It is still a beauty and well worth an overnight stay, if only to see the superb **Waki Honjin Okuya** (daily 9am–5pm), a folk museum located inside a spacious villa

and former inn. The museum provides an excellent introduction to the town, with a large display of local products and daily items, as well as a fascinating photo display on the town before and after its restoration. Another, but smaller, local history museum sits next door. Ask at the **tourist information office** (www.tumago.jp; daily 8.30am–5pm) about a useful local service that arranges to have your luggage sent forward for you to your next accommodation in Magome, freeing you to follow the lovely 8km (5-mile) hiking trail between the two towns.

Where Tsumago is tucked into the valley, **Magome** clings to the side of a hill offering terrific views of nearby Mount Ena. The town suffered a series of fires, the worst in 1895, so it is not as old as the other towns, but its stone paths, wood and plaster buildings, many now serving as shops and inns, have a weathered quality that makes them feel older. Shimazaki Toson, a Meiji Period author, is the town's pride and joy. The **Toson Kinenkan** (daily, Apr–Oct 8.30am–4.45pm, Nov–Mar until 4.15pm), a museum housed

The teahouse in the grounds of Kenroku-en Garden, Kanazawa.

An installation at the 21st Century Museum of Contemporary Art.

Creating lacquerware in Wajima, Ishikawa.

in a former inn, traces the writer's life through displays of original works and personal effects.

Hokuriku and the Sea of Japan (East Sea) coast

Sea of Japan (East Sea) coast

On the coast of the Sea of Japan (East Sea), **Kanazawa** ⑬ came under the rule of the Maeda clan in the 16th century, a stewardship that lasted nearly three centuries and which supported a vigorous artistic effort. Lacking military or industrial targets, Kanazawa was spared bombing during World War II. Today, samurai houses in the Nagamachi area still line twisting streets, and the Higashi-no-Kuruwa area still has geisha working its old tearooms. But that isn't the main reason Kanazawa is firmly planted on Japan's domestic tourist trail. The crowds come for **Kenroku-en** (Kenroku Garden; daily, Mar–mid-Oct 7am–6pm, mid-Oct–Feb 8am–5pm). Considered one of Japan's top gardens, it has its heritage in an ancient Chinese garden from the Song dynasty.

Be warned, however, that being feverishly crowded, the garden is not for the contemplative.

A more peaceful, and much smaller, garden is **Gyokusen-en** (usually daily 10.30am–4pm). Designed by Korean Kim Yeocheol in the early 17th century, it combines a main pond in the shape of the Chinese character for water *(mizu)*, with two waterfalls, moss-covered rocks and several hundred varieties of plants to create a tranquil environment far removed from the nearby Kenroku-en. The garden's teahouse is an especially nice place for a break.

Gardens aside, Kanazawa is known for an overglaze-painted porcelain called *kutani-yaki*. You can see vibrant examples of that and other crafts at the **Ishikawa Prefectural Museum of Art** (www.ishibi.pref.ishikawa.jp; daily 9.30am–6pm), just to the west of Kenroku-en. An even better museum is the 21st **Century Museum of Contemporary Art** (www.kanazawa21.jp; Tue–Sun 10am–6pm, Fri–Sat until 8pm), to the south of Kanazawa Park. The sleek circular building focuses only on art post-1980, both overseas and

MINAKAMI

Minakami Onsen, in the north of Gunma Prefecture and bordering Niigata, calls itself a "four-season outdoor adventure resort" for good reason. In winter, the area is all about skiing, its nine ski fields (www.snowjapan.com) especially popular at weekends with Tokyoites. The rest of the year, Minakami is geared to hikers and adrenalin junkies, with rafting, bungee jumping, paragliding, canyoning and other activities available. For something a little more restful, year-round the area's 100 or so *onsen* (hot-spring baths) also make for the perfect place to unwind. If you are feeling really brave, head to the mixed-gender baths at Takaragawa Onsen (www.takaragawa.com; they also have gender-separated baths). Minakami is two hours from Tokyo, first by *shinkansen* to Jomo-Kogen, then by bus.

Japanese, and besides some very cool permanent installations it also puts on an ever-changing line-up of temporary exhibitions. Rounding out Kanazawa's main attractions is its castle, in **Kanazawa Castle Park** (daily, Mar–mid-Oct 7am–6pm, mid-Oct–Feb 8am–5pm). It's mostly a reconstruction, but worth checking out anyway.

From Kanazawa consider an excursion out onto **Noto-hanto** ⓮ (Noto Peninsula), which jabs out into the Sea of Japan (East Sea) like a crooked finger. The sedate eastern coast, encircling a bay, is moderately developed for tourism. The western coast, sculpted by the vigorous winds and currents of the Sea of Japan (East Sea), is rocky and rustic. Noto's main town, **Wajima**, is noted for Wajima-nuri, a type of lacquerware, which you can learn more about at the **Wajima Shiki Kaikan** (Wajima Lacquerware Museum; www.wajimanuri.or.jp; daily 8.30am–5pm). Wajima is also known for its morning market (*asa-ichi*), which can take on a tourist-focused mood at times but is still interesting to visit.

Niigata and around

Moving north along the coast, there are few highlights until Niigata Prefecture. Although the city of **Niigata** ⓯ itself isn't the most exciting of places, it has enough affordable hotels and restaurants, not to mention transport links, to make for a good stepping stone before exploring the rest of the prefecture or before setting off north or east into Tohoku (see page 207). Being snow country, Niigata Prefecture is, not surprisingly, known for its skiing. It was here, inland in the Joetsu region of southern Niigata, that Austrian Major Theodore von Lerch first introduced skiing to Japan in 1911. The most popular ski area in Niigata today, **Echigo Yuzawa** ⓰, is also the most easily accessible from Tokyo – just 77 minutes on the *shinkansen* from Tokyo Station. The town has plenty of hotels and *ryokan*, most of which have their own hot springs, and

is within a short bus ride from several good ski fields, including the modern and English-speaker-friendly **GALA Yuzawa** (season mid-Dec–early May; www.galaresort.jp).

Sado-jima

Two hours from Niigata by ferry, **Sado-jima** ⓱ was first an island of exile in the 13th century and later, during the Edo Period, a prison colony. Japan's fifth-largest island at 1,900 sq km (850 sq miles), Sado is mountainous and probably most famous for the Kodo drummers, from a village near **Ogi**. In August is the Earth Celebration, three days of world music – from Africa to Japan to Europe – and dance. Workshops are also offered, but if you are planning to go, transport and accommodation must be arranged well in advance. The island is associated in many Japanese minds with old, salt-encrusted temples, the clear bathing waters of its west coast, the old goldmine of **Sado Kinzan** (www.sado-kinzan.com; daily, Apr–Oct 8am–5.30pm, Nov–Mar 8.30am–5pm), and okesa, Sado's haunting music of exile.

Women relaxing at a hot spring in Yuzawa, Niigata.

Minakami Onsen.

Path through ancient cedar forest to the Yamadera Temple complex.

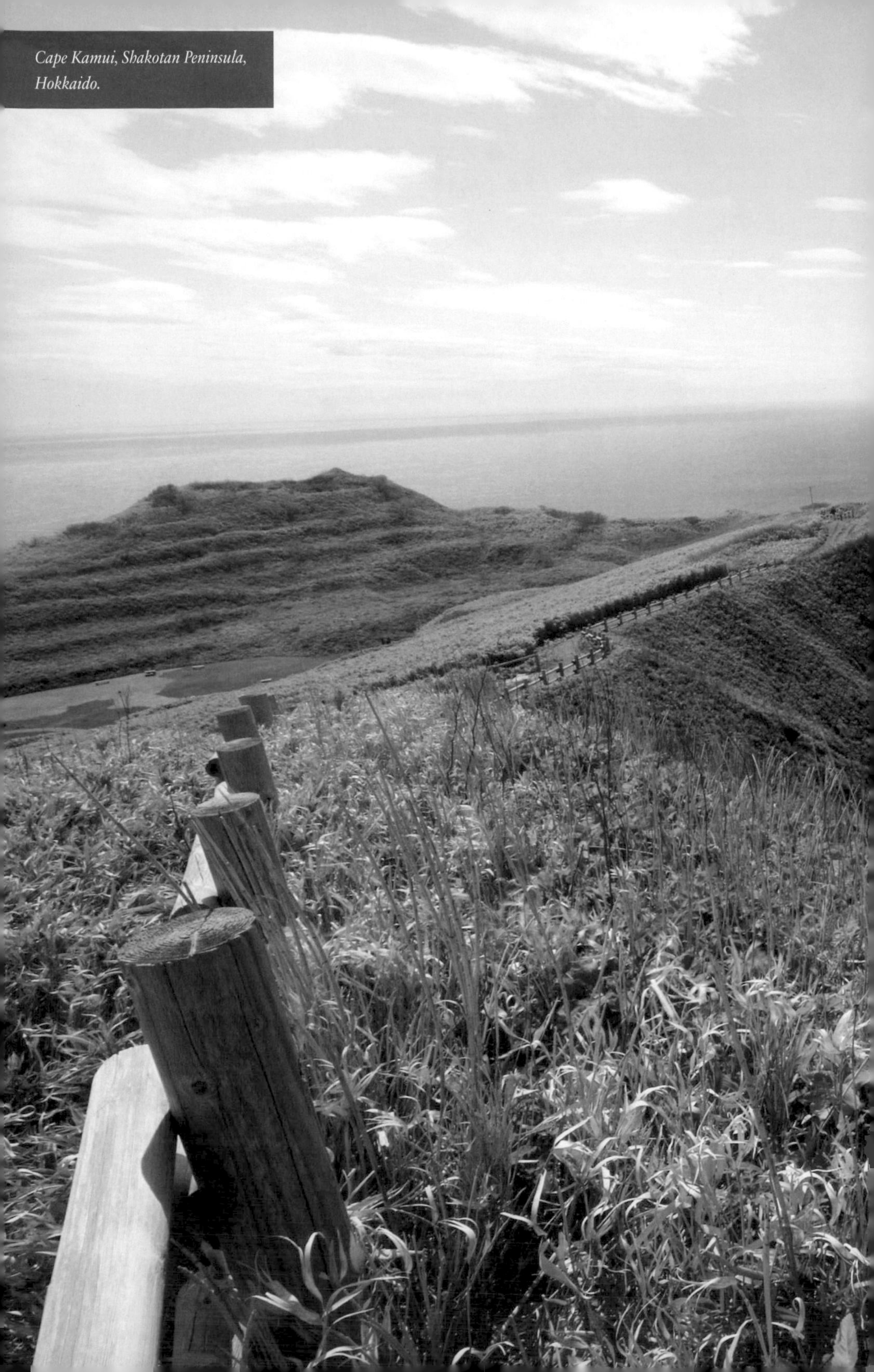

Cape Kamui, Shakotan Peninsula, Hokkaido.

THE NORTH

Most Japanese regard the northern extents
of Tohoku and Hokkaido as the ends of the
earth, however close they are.

Chuson Temple.

"I might as well be going to the ends of the earth." That's
how Basho, Japan's great 17th-century haiku poet, put it
on the eve of his departure into the north in 1689. Back
then, when Basho decided to prowl the backcountry, the
roads were narrow and minimal, or non-existent. Today,
Sendai, Tohoku's predominant city and north of Tokyo along
the Pacific coast, is only two hours from Tokyo via shinkansen. From Sendai, you are then within striking distance
of the Tono Valley – the epitome of rural Japan – the World
Heritage shrines of Hiraizumi, the atmospheric mountainside temple complex of Yamadera, and many other intriguing sites.

Even the large island of Hokkaido, forcibly settled during the Meiji
Restoration in the late 19th century, is but nine hours from Tokyo by
train or two hours by plane. It's a relatively short
trip to be transported to a remarkably different
world – to ski the perfect powder snow of Niseko
or explore the breathtaking natural surrounds of
the Shiretoko Peninsula.

The north has always been perceived as remote
and strange, existing outside the normal sphere
of Japanese life, much like Alaska feels removed
from the rest of the US. This is more down to
psychology than distance – there is a seemingly
limitless amount of open space and nature
untouched by people.

The people of the north bear some responsibility, too. Tohoku was originally settled by itinerant
warlords and soldiers who constructed castle fortresses to keep out potentially unfriendly neigh-

Native Ainu carvings on sale.

bours, mostly from the south. These castle towns developed into insular
communities with their own unique lifestyle, crafts, cottage industries
and dialects.

Since the earthquake, tsunami and Fukushima nuclear disaster in
March 2011 (see page 217), overseas perception of Tohoku is of a place
that has been entirely devastated. Certainly, the level of destruction and
loss along much of the east coast was beyond comprehension, and the
rebuilding there will continue for decades. Yet much of Tohoku is as
accessible, inviting and mysterious as it ever was.

The Matsushima Coastline.

TOHOKU

Its dialect is as thick as the winter snows that blow in over the Sea of Japan (East Sea) from Siberia. Tohoku's hold on northern Honshu makes it seem another world to Japan's urban majority.

Perhaps as a way of explaining and coping with the difficult realities of weather and topography, the northern portion of Honshu, known as Tohoku, remains filled with myths – clever foxes who turn into beautiful women and lure unsuspecting men to their doom, green-headed river creatures who snatch small children venturing too close to the water, and devils and ghosts in great abundance.

By Japanese standards, the Tohoku region is sparsely populated, with 9 million people in an area just under 67,000 sq km (26,000 sq miles). This northern part of Honshu comprises six prefectures: Aomori, Akita, Iwate, Miyagi, Yamagata and Fukushima – of these, it was Iwate, Fukushima and Miyagi on the east coast that bore the brunt of the damage from the March 2011 earthquake and tsunami (see page 217).

Its climate is comparable to New England in the United States, with the possible exception of the month of August, when certain parts of southern Tohoku slyly pretend they are on the equator. (In fact, the city of Yamagata held the record for the highest recorded temperature in Japan, 40.8°C or 104°F, from 1933 until it was topped, by 0.1°C, by Tajimi in Gifu Prefecture in 2007, and then by 0.2°C by Shimanto in Kochi Prefecture in 2013.)

Long known for its natural beauty, rugged mountains, sometimes incomprehensible dialects, innumerable hot springs and harsh winters, especially on the Sea of Japan (East Sea) side, which gets the brunt of Siberian storms, Tohoku was once known as Michinoku (literally, interior or narrow road). The name was not as benign as it seems, for it implied a place rather uncivilised and lacking in culture. In the old days, a barrier wall was constructed at Shirakawa, in southern Fukushima, to separate the civilised

Map on page 208

Main Attractions
Sendai
Matsushima
Aizu-Wakamatsu
Yamadera temple complex
Zao Onsen
Tono
Aomori
Towada-Hachimantai National Park

Large lanterns at the Aomori Nebuta Festival in August.

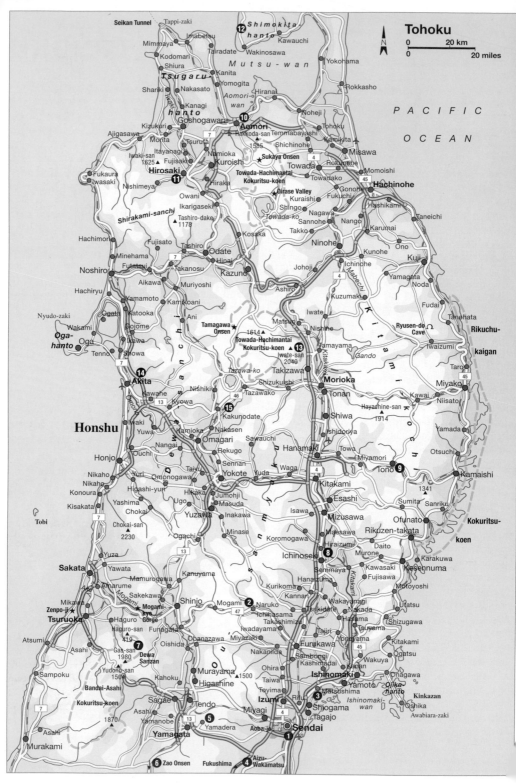

Tohoku

world of the south from the barbarians in the north. Although the name was eventually changed to the innocent *tohoku* (literally, northeast), the region's image of cultural immaturity lingers for many urban Japanese to the south.

There is a certain irony in this, since it is generally agreed that Tohoku is perhaps the last bastion of traditional Japanese culture. To a large degree, the region has escaped the rapid modernisation that the rest of Japan has undergone since the end of World War II. In the north it is still possible to discover farms growing rice by methods used hundreds of years ago, tiny fishing villages nestled into cliffs overlooking unspoilt sea coasts, isolated hot-spring inns, and a people whose open friendliness is unstinting even as their dialect remains an exclusive mystery. No longer unknown, Tohoku is a place of spectacular beauty and a must-see for adventurous visitors.

Sendai

The largest city in Tohoku and on the eastern coast, **Sendai ❶** was originally called Sentaijo after the Thousand Buddha Statue Temple that once graced the top of Aoba-yama, the wooded hilltop park. The name was changed to Sendai, or Thousand Generations, by the Date clan during their reign over the area, possibly in the mistaken belief that they would reign supreme for that long.

Sendai is today a cosmopolitan city of a little over 1 million people, the capital of Miyagi Prefecture, and the pre-eminent city of the entire Tohoku region. Sendai is the logical jumping-off point for exploring the rest of Tohoku. It is known as the Green City and the City of Trees, and visitors arriving on the *shinkansen* from treeless urban points south will understand why. From **Sendai-eki** (Sendai Station) the main boulevards running east and west are all tree-lined.

Those wide, European-style avenues are a pleasure to stroll along. The entire downtown area is small enough

to cover in an hour or so of leisurely walking, if you feel so inclined. In one of Sendai's tallest buildings, the **SS-30 Building** with its 30 floors, one can relax in numerous top-floor restaurants that offer an excellent view of mountains to the north and west, the Pacific Ocean to the east and the city below. Close to the Sendai Station is **AER**, an even taller building with a free observation deck on the 31st floor (www.sendai-aer.jp; daily 10.30am–8pm; free)..A 10-minute walk west up Aoba-dori from Sendai Station is **Ichiban-cho**, Sendai's main shopping arcade. Parts of it are covered in skylights and all of it is vehicle-free. Evenings suggest a walk a little further to Kokobuncho-dori, Sendai's main after-hours strip, where there are the usual (and seemingly endless) Japanese-style bars, nightclubs, discos, karaoke boxes and other entertainment.

Just beneath the surface, the traditional ways of Tohoku remain in Sendai. The visitor can still watch artisans and craftsmen making knives, *tatami* flooring and the famed *kayaki tansu*, or chests, in the traditional shops

The statue of Date Masamune.

Leafy Jyozenji Street in Sendai.

Wooden kokeshi dolls.

Naruko onsen, Miyagi.

but the walls of Aoba-jo remain. In addition, a small museum, souvenir shop, shrine and statue of the great Masamune himself now occupy the grounds. Looking northwards and down from the castle grounds, one can see the Hirose-gawa river, unpolluted and thus unusual in Japan. Edible trout still swim downstream.

Zuihoden (www.zuihoden.com; daily, Feb–Nov 9am–4.30pm, Dec–Jan 9am–4pm), the burial site of Date Masamune, sits atop Kyogamine-yama. There are several cemeteries along the way up, as well as a beautiful Rinzai Zen temple, **Zuiho-ji**. Above the temple are steps leading to the mausoleum at the very top, and nearby are the tombs of samurai who committed ritual suicide when Masamune died. There is also an exhibition room displaying pictures taken when the mausoleum was opened during restoration, necessitated by bomb attacks near the end of World War II.

Osaki Hachiman-jinja (www.oosaki-hachiman.or.jp; daily sunrise–sunset) was originally built in 1100 and later moved to its present location by Date

tucked into the shadows of much larger and more modern architecture.

Sendai didn't come into its own until Date Masamune, the great one-eyed warlord of the north, moved to his newly constructed castle on Aoba-yama. Both **Aoba-jo** (Aoba Castle; also known as Sendai-jo; daily 9am–5pm, Nov–Mar until 4pm) and the Date family collapsed during the Meiji era,

Masamune. Dedicated to the god of war or of archery, this shrine is one of Japan's national treasures. Walk up the 100 or so steps to the top – reportedly the count is never the same twice. Follow the stone-paved path lined with enormous cedar trees to the shrine, picturesquely set back in a small forest. It is done in Momoyama style with gold, black lacquer and bright colours.

There are several more modern attractions worth a look, especially in **Aobayama-koen** (Green Hill Park), including **Sendai-shi Hakubutsu-kan** (Sendai City Museum; Tue–Sun 9am–4.45pm) and a prefectural fine-art museum. The municipal museum is interesting architecturally, with an extensive and permanent exhibition of the area's history. There is also a children's section where everything on display can be touched. The prefectural fine-art museum has a sculpture wing with an outdoor sculpture garden. The **Sendai Mediatheque** (www.smt.jp), housed in an award-winning modern building, plays host to numerous cultural events and runs

the "center for remembering 3.11", a project enabling all citizens to document restoration in the aftermath of the 2011 earthquake.

If you have the time and energy, consider the **Tohoku University Botanical Garden** (21 Mar–30 Nov Tue–Sun 9am–5pm, entry until 4pm), a place to cool off on a hot summer afternoon as well as to observe owls, bats and the region's flora and fauna. The observatory here is a relatively good place for star- and planet-viewing if you don't mind waiting in line. Finally, there's Kotsu-koen, a "traffic park" for children complete with roads, red lights, busy intersections and train tracks. Kids can cruise around in pedal-powered cars and get a taste for what real life is like on Japan's claustrophobic roads.

On the northern outskirts of Sendai, near Kitayama Station and a delightful place for a mountain stroll, are two Zen temples, **Rinno-ji** (daily 8am–5pm) and **Shifuku-ji**. Both date from the 15th century and were destroyed then rebuilt many times over the years. They offer beautiful Zen-inspired

Statue of Basho at the Yamadera temple complex.

THE POETRY OF BASHO

Matsuo Basho, the pseudonym of Matsuo Munefusa (born 1644), is considered to be the greatest of Japan's haiku poets. Basho took the 17-syllable haiku form and enriched it with descriptive simplicity and contrast. Frequently used to describe Basho's poetry is *sabi* – the love of the old, faded and unobtrusive. In 1679 Basho wrote his first verse:

On a withered branch
A crow has alighted:
Nightfall in autumn.

A samurai for a local feudal lord, Basho moved to the capital city of Edo (now Tokyo) after his lord's death. In 1684, Basho made the first of many journeys through the islands to Tohoku, and written of in *Oku no Hosomichi (The Narrow Road to the Deep North)*, considered by many to be one of the most beautiful works in Japanese literature.

HOKKAIDO

The northern island of Hokkaido holds a special place in the Japanese imagination, conjuring up romantic images of misty mountains and wild lands where anything is possible.

Hokkaido has been part of the Japanese nation only since it was settled in the 19th century as an example of Meiji Restoration development. Nowadays, Hokkaido is to many Japanese as Alaska is to Americans: the northern extremity with a romantic sense of frontier, where summers are short and winters exceedingly cold, and where the people are just a little bit different for living there in the first place. Japan's northern island is where the temples and castles of the southern islands give way to mountains, forests and farms. You will find the residents here more direct and friendlier than their southern counterparts and, due to the Meiji-era Westernisation, quite sophisticated.

Hokkaido is also home to Japan's last indigenous people, the Ainu (see page 55), who are of Caucasian ancestry and with no genetic connection to today's Japanese. With a population of only 25,000, the Ainu are nowadays a phantom culture with a nearly forgotten language. Although most noticeable dressed up in traditional costume, posing for tourist photos, most Ainu live normal Japanese lives undistinguishable from any other Japanese.

Hokkaido has the feeling of remoteness, but this is mostly psychological. The Tokyo–Sapporo air corridor is one of the busiest in the world, and rail lines running through the Seikan

Tunnel also connect Honshu to southern Hokkaido – a journey that will get faster from March 2016 when trains on a new *shinkansen* route start service. Hokkaido offers the standard over-developed and tacky tourist traps and loudspeaker-enhanced "scenic" places so common throughout Japan. But Hokkaido can also be high adventure in the rustic north, with some of Japan's most undeveloped areas. Its climate parallels Quebec and Finland, and in winter icebergs scrape its shores. In summer, hills and fields are

Main Attractions

Sapporo
Otaru
Niseko
Shikotsu-Toya National Park
Hakodate
Furano
Akan National Park
Shiretoko Peninsula
Abashiri

Dog sledge race, Wakkanai.

Gion, central Kyoto.

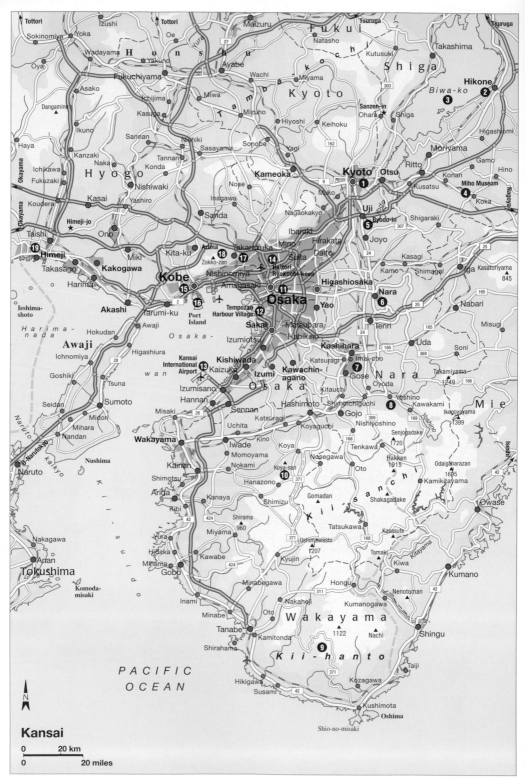

Kansai

0   20 km

0   20 miles

THE KANSAI REGION

In contrast with Kanto to the north, Kansai vibrates with entrepreneurial intensity and historical importance.

Statue at Fushimi Inari Taisha, Kyoto.

The old Tokaido (Eastern Sea Road) that connected the ancient capital at Kyoto with the seat of the feudal shogunate at Kamakura (and later, with Edo Tokyo) has all but disappeared. But it was along that much-travelled highway, at a point where it passed through the Hakone hills, that the Kamakura *bakufu* (military government, or shogunate) set up a heavily armed outpost in the 13th century to stifle threats by the western warlords and imperial loyalists. It is from this post that the regions to the west got their name: Kansai, or Western Barrier.

In the Kamakura days, virtually all lands west and south of those barriers – including the Nagoya and Gifu regions (covered in the Central Honshu chapter) – were considered to be in Kansai. Since the Edo era, the definition has come to cover only the Kyoto, Nara, Osaka and Kobe areas.

Although much of Kansai is still rural, as we will see in the Southern Kansai chapter, declaring that one is from Kansai doesn't evoke a backwater image. Kyoto, Japan's capital for more than 1,000 years prior to Tokyo, is still the sophisticated heart of cultural Japan. Within day-trip distance of Kyoto's historic temples and shrines are the even more ancient temples of Japan's first capital, Nara, while the Kansai region also offers incredible natural beauty in places such as Lake Biwa and the hot springs of Arashiyama.

Todai-ji temple complex, Nara.

Osaka, only 40km (25 miles) from Kyoto, is quite different from Kyoto. An energetic, street-smart city, it is also the base for Japan's well-known electronics manufacturers, Panasonic Corporation (formerly called Matsushita Electric) and Sharp Corporation, and is a leader – together with Nagoya in Chubu – in the development of robotic production techniques. Tokyo may be Japan at its most modern, but the great commercial and industrial complexes of Osaka (and Kobe) are the centres of Japan's international commerce.

Put all its parts together and the Kansai region probably offers more diversity to the first-time visitor than does that megalopolis 500km (300 miles) to the north, Tokyo.

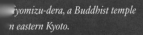

KYOTO

The former imperial capital was fortunately spared destruction during World War II and today retains pockets of Japan's elegant spiritual and architectural past.

Tokyo might have the national government and Osaka the entrepreneurial savvy, but **Kyoto**  defines traditional Japan and possesses an ingrained aristocratic bloodline, punctuated by a history unrivalled by any other Japanese city. Home to no less than 17 Unesco World Heritage Sites, Kyoto is the country's artistic and cultural repository, ranking with Athens, Cairo and Beijing as a living museum. Still, don't expect a quiet, idyllic place. Kyoto is Japan's sixth-largest city, with a population reaching nearly 1.5 million. It is a large metropolis, crowded and noisy and, like most other Japanese cities, lacking aesthetic appeal in its modern contours. Even the temples can feel claustrophobic with busloads of tourists and students doing the rounds.

Rapid post-war modernisation saw tens of thousands of old traditional houses lining Kyoto's narrow back-streets razed to the ground in favour of modern, convenient living spaces. These old houses – splendid *kyo-machiya* – were of simplistic wooden facades and dancing rectilinear patterns; sliding paper doors; window slats in clay walls; lattices, trellises, benches, and hanging blinds of reeds and bamboo; and *inuyarai*, curved bamboo fences, that protruded out from the houses to protect against street traffic and dogs.

Kyoto sits in a gradually sloping basin enclosed by a horseshoe of mountains on three sides, open southwards to the Nara plains, between the rivers Katsura-gawa to the west and Kamo-gawa to the east, and the Kitayama Mountains that stretch north to the Japan Sea.

Early April is when the cherry blossoms bloom, and by May, everything else has blossomed in ritual radiance. The rains of June offer a misty contrast to venerable temples and shrines, and also help to thin the crowds. The

Main Attractions
Nishi and Higashi Hongan-ji
Kyoto Imperial Palace
  (Gosho)
Nijo Castle
Kyoto National Museum
Kiyomizu-dera
Gion
Ginkaku-ji (Silver Pavilion)
Kinkaku-ji (Golden Pavilion)
Ryoan-ji
Fushimi Inari Taisha

Kinkakuji Pavilion and Gardens.

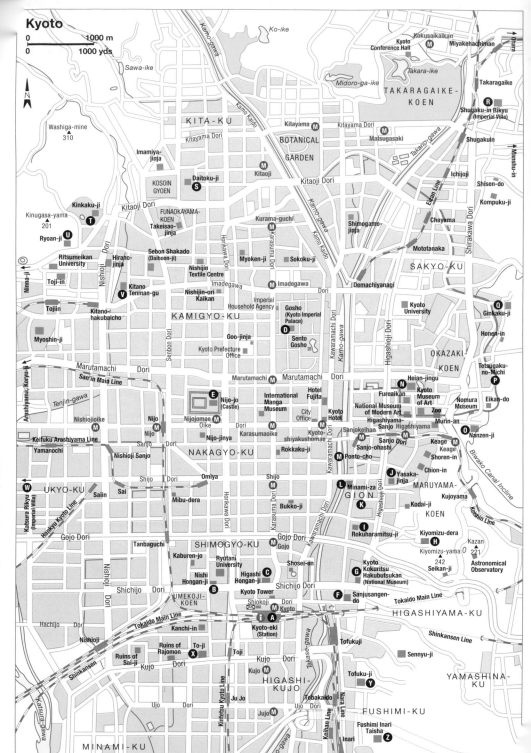

Kyoto

0 — 1000 m
0 — 1000 yds

N

Ko-ike

Sawa-ike

Washiga-mine
310

Kyoto
Conference Hall

Kokusaikaikan

M Miyakehachiman

Takara-ike

TAKARAGAIKE-
KOEN

Takaragaike

R

Shugaku-in Rikyu
(Imperial Villa)

Shugakuin

KITA-KU

Kitayama
M

Kitayama Dori

BOTANICAL
GARDEN

Matsugasaki
M

M Kitaoji

Kitaoji Dori

Shimogamo-
jinja

Manshu-in

Eizan Line

Ichijoji

Shisen-do

Kompuku-ji

Chayama

SAKYO-KU

Mototanaka

Imamiya-
jinja

KOSOIN
GYOEN

Daitoku-ji
M

S

Kinkaku-ji

Kitaoji Dori

Kinugasa-yama
201

T

FUNAOKAYAMA-
KOEN

Takeisao-
jinja

Kurama-guchi
M

Karasuma Dori

Myoken-ji
M

Sokoku-ji
M

Kamo Kaido

Demachiyanagi
M

Kyoto
University

Ginkaku-ji
Q

Honen-in

Ryoan-ji
U

Nijima-ji
⊙

Ritsumeikan
University

Sebon Shakado
(Daihoon-ji)

Nishijin
Textile Centre

Imadegawa
M

Imadegawa
M

Dori

Hirano-
jinja

Toji-in

Kitano
Tenman-gu
V

Nishijin-ori
Kaikan

Imperial
Household Agency

Gosho
(Kyoto Imperial
Palace)

D

Sento
Gosho

OKAZAKI-
KOEN

Tetsugaku-
no-Michi

P

Tojiin

Kitano-
hakubaicho

Goo-jinja

Kyoto Prefecture
Office

KAMIGYO-KU

Myoshin-ji

Heian-jingu

Fureaikan

N

Kyoto
Museum
of Art

Nomura
Museum

Eikan-do

Senbon Dori

Marutamachi

Dori

San'in Main Line

Tenjin-gawa

Marutamachi
M

Marutamachi
Dori

Hotel
Fujita

National Museum
of Modern Art

Higashiyama-
Sanjo Higashiyama

Zoo

Murin-an

Nanzen-ji
O

Nishiojiike

Nijo
M

E

Nijo-jo
(Castle)

Nijojomae
M

Oike

International
Manga
Museum

City
Office

Kyoto
Hotel

Sanjokeihan

Sanjo Dori

Keage

Keage

Shoren-in

Keifuku Arashiyama Line

Nijo-jinja

Karasumaoike
M

Kyoto-
shiyakushomae
M

Sanjo-
ohashi

Chion-in

Yamanochi

Nishioji Sanjo

NAKAGYO-KU

Rokkaku-ji

Ponto-cho

J Yasaka-
jinja

MARUYAMA-

Sai

Omiya

Shijo

Minami-za
L

GION

K

Kodai-ji

KOEN

Kujoyama

Shijo Dori

Bukko-ji
M

Kiyomizu-dera

I

Rokuharamitsu-ji

H

Kiyomizu-yama

Kazan
221

Mibu-dera

Gojo Dori

Gojo Dori

Gojo
M

242

Seikan-ji

Astronomical
Observatory

Tanbaguchi

Kaburen-jo

Ryutani
University

Shosei-en

Kyoto
Kokuritsu
Hakubutsukan
(National Museum)
G

SHIMOGYO-KU

Nishi
Hongan-ji

Higashi
Hongan-ji
C

Shichijo Dori

Sanjusangen-
do

Tokaido Main Line

Shichijo

Dori

B

UMEKOJI-
KOEN

Kyoto Tower

Shiokoji
Dori

F

HIGASHIYAMA-KU

Hachijo

Dori

Kanchi-in

Tokaido Main Line

Kyoto-eki
(Station)

M Kyoto
i

Shinkansen Line

Nishioji

Ruins of
Sai-ji

Ruins of
Rajomon

To-ji
X

Toji

Kujo

Dori

Tofukuji

Sennyu-ji

YAMASHINA-
KU

Shinkansen

Kujo

Kujo Dori
M

Tofuku-ji
Y

Ju Jo

HIGASHI-
KUJO

Tobakaido

Ujo

Dori

FUSHIMI-KU

MINAMI-KU

Jujo
M

Fushimi Inari
Taisha

Inari

Z

Uji ↓

sticky heat *(mushi atsusa)* of summer is cooled by breezes off the surrounding mountains, making the long July and August evenings some of the best. September and October deliver near-perfect temperatures for walking along Kyoto's temple paths. The autumn colours break out in earthy reds and oranges in November, making it one of the most popular times to visit.

The frigid, festive air of December and January is contagious all over town, while a light dusting of snow in February and March can cast Kyoto into a Zen-like state. Be aware that, at all the best times to visit Kyoto, most of Japan is doing likewise. Book well ahead for autumn and spring.

Kyoto's beginnings

For nearly 1,100 years, from AD 794 until 1868, Kyoto was home to the emperor, and thus was capital of the nation. Japan's first permanent capital was established in Nara in 710, but by 784, the intrigues of power-hungry Buddhist priests forced Emperor Kammu to move the capital to Nagaoka, a nearby suburb of present-day Kyoto.

Ten years later, in 794, Kammu relocated the capital again to the village of Uda, renaming it Heian-kyo – the Capital of Peace. It wasn't until 988 that the use of *kyoto* (capital) began to appear in official records. A century later, Kyoto was the city's proper name.

The arrival of Buddhism in Japan in the 6th century brought great Chinese influence to the archipelago, reaching its peak of cultural flowering during the Heian Period (794–1185). Heian-kyo was built to a scale model of the Chinese Tang dynasty's (618–906) capital of Chang'an (now Xi'an), in China. Heian-kyo extended in a grid pattern still in evidence today for 5.2km (3.2 miles) from north to south and 4.4km (2.7 miles) east to west. Walls with 18 gates and a double moat surrounded the city. And because of earlier and persistent trouble with priests in Nara, Buddhist temples were forbidden inside the capital, explaining in part why many of Kyoto's most venerated temples are isolated in the hills surrounding the city.

Frequently levelled by earthquakes, floods, fires and wars over the

Inside Kyoto Station.

Part of the Imperial Palace.

centuries, the buildings of Kyoto have been moved, rebuilt and enlarged, and now represent a mosaic of historical periods. As a result, a scant few structures in Kyoto pre-date 1600, though many temples and shrines faithfully reproduce the earlier styles. It is commonly understood that a decision by the Americans not to bomb Kyoto during World War II – its historical heritage was considered too valuable – assured that these ancient structures stand today. Kyoto today offers some 1,600 Buddhist temples, 400 Shinto shrines, dozens of museums, two imperial villas, a palace, castle and thousands of arts and crafts shops.

Around Kyoto Station

Most people first encounter Kyoto from inside the gargantuan **Kyoto-eki Ⓐ** (Kyoto Station), less than three hours from Tokyo by *shinkansen*. Construction of this futuristic 16-storey building, completed in 1997, created one of the hottest controversies in Kyoto's 1,200-year history. Preservationists, environmentalists, and much of the city's population were opposed to its

construction, especially for the sheer size of the complex, its obstruction of the mountain skyline, and because its modern glass structure lacked any resemblance to traditional architecture.

The station area, and tragically much of central Kyoto, displays the characterless, cluttered sprawl of all Japanese cities. But fortunately, amid the thoughtless creations that increasingly plague the city are a vast treasure of sights behind fading imperial walls, down narrow lanes and amid the surrounding hills.

Directly north of Kyoto Station are two notable temples, Nishi (West) Hongan-ji and Higashi (East) Hongan-ji. As was the case with many of Kyoto's historical treasures, Japan's great unifier, Toyotomi Hideyoshi (1536–98), was responsible for establishing **Nishi Hongan-ji Ⓑ** (daily, Mar–Apr and Sept–Oct 5.30am–5.30pm, May–Aug 5.30am–6pm, Nov–Feb 5.30am–5pm; free). In 1591, Toyotomi brought the Jodo-shinshu Buddhist sect to the temple's current location. Its Chinese influences are many, and historians sometimes consider it the best

example of Buddhist architecture still around. The *hondo*, or main hall, was rebuilt in 1760 after fire destroyed it. The founder's hall – *daishido* – contains a self-carved effigy of the sect's founder. Cremated after his death, his ashes were mixed with lacquer and then applied to the effigy. The study hall *(shoin)* contains a number of rooms named for their decorations: Wild Geese Chamber, Sparrow Chamber and Chrysanthemum Chamber.

To the east, **Higashi Hongan-ji** Ⓒ (www.higashihonganji.or.jp; daily, Mar–Oct 5.50am–5.30pm, Nov–Feb 6.20am–4.30pm; free) was established in 1603 when the first Tokugawa shogun, Ieyasu, wary of the Jodo-shinshu monks' power at nearby Nishi Hongan-ji, attempted to thwart their influence by establishing an offshoot of the sect. Only the main hall and founder's hall are open to the public. The present buildings were erected in 1895 after fire destroyed the predecessors. When these current structures were being built, female devotees cut and donated their hair, which was woven into 50 ropes used during construction; some of the ropes are on display between the main temple buildings. Just two blocks east, the temple's tranquil **Shosei-en** (daily 9am–4pm) is a garden sanctuary of water, rocks and moss.

Central Kyoto

Due west on the other side of the Kamo-gawa, the **Gosho** Ⓓ (Kyoto Imperial Palace; free tours Mon–Fri; apply at Imperial Household Agency: tel: 075-211-1215; http://sankan.kunaicho.go.jp) remains the emperor's residence in Kyoto and is thus under the control of the Imperial Household Agency, which dictates every nuance and moment of the imperial family's life. Originally built as a second palace for the emperor, the Kyoto Imperial Palace was used as a primary residence from 1331 until 1868, when Tokyo became the new residence with the fall of the hogunate and the Meiji restoration of the imperial system. The palace has

gone through many restorations over the centuries; the current buildings were constructed in the mid-1800s. Shishinden (the Enthronement Hall), standing with its sweeping cedar roof before a silent stone courtyard, is an impressive emblem of imperial rule. It was constructed in the *shinden* style, where all buildings are connected by covered walkways or galleries. The court town that once surrounded the hall is now **Kyoto Gyoen**, the public Kyoto Imperial Park.

From the palace, a few blocks west is **Nishijin**, the weavers' quarter. The **Nishijin Textile Centre** (www.nishijin.or.jp; daily 9am–5pm; free) has excellent displays of working looms and woven goods as well as several kimono shows every day. After browsing the centre, walk through the narrow side streets – the ancient crafts of weaving and dyeing are still practised in the old wooden buildings.

South is **Nijo-jo** Ⓔ (daily 8.45am–5pm, entry until 4pm; Jan, July, Aug and Dec – closed Tuesdays), a castle begun in 1569 by the warlord Oda Nobunaga and finished by Tokugawa

Nijo Castle is surrounded by two concentric rings of fortifications.

Workers at the Nishijin Textile Centre.

Statues of the Thousand Armed Kannon at Sanjusangen-do.

Ieyasu, ally to Oda Nobunaga, to demonstrate his military dominance over the city. In 1867, it served as the seat of government from where Emperor Meiji abolished the shogunate. Rectangular in shape, the castle's magnificent stone walls and gorgeous gold-leafed audience halls reflect the power of the Edo Period shoguns. The linking corridors of the castle's Ninomaru Palace feature "nightingale" (creaking) floors to warn of intruders, while the garden is a grand example of a lord's strolling garden.

Just south of the castle is **Nijo Jinya**, originally the home of a wealthy merchant and later used as an inn by visiting *daimyo*. The old manor house is full of trapdoors, secret passageways and hidden rooms. About 500 metres/yds east of Nijo-jo is the **Kyoto International Manga Museum** (www.kyotomm.jp; Thu–Tue 10am–6pm), which opened in 2006. Housed in an old elementary school, the museum has a vast collection of manga comics that covers every genre and which visitors can freely take off the shelves and read. It also holds regular manga art exhibitions and workshops.

Admiring the exhibits at Kyoto Manga Museum.

Eastern Kyoto

Just east of Kyoto Station and across the Kamo-gawa, **Sanjusangen-do** ⑥ (Sanjusangen Hall, also called Rengeo-in; daily, Apr–Nov 8am–5pm, Dec–Mar 9am–4pm) was last rebuilt in 1266. The temple houses 33 (*sanjusan*) alcoves nestled between 33 pillars under a 120-metre (200ft) long roof. Inside is a 1,000-handed Kannon, the *bodhisattva* of mercy and compassion, and her 1,000 disciples. Each of their faces is different; Japanese look for the face that resembles their own – or that of a relative – to whom to make an offering. A famed archery festival, first started in 1606, takes place at the temple on the Sunday closest to 15 January.

On the opposite side of Shichijo-dori to the north is the **Kyoto Kokuritsu Hakubutsukan** ⑥ (Kyoto National Museum; www.kyohaku.go.jp; Tue–Sun 9.30am–5pm, longer hours during special exhibitions), founded in 1897 and exhibiting artefacts of history, art and crafts. Several other temples are east of the museum. Up the Kiyomizu-zaka, a slope on the east side

of Higashioji-dori, is **Kiyomizu-dera**  (www.kiyomizudera.or.jp; daily from 6am until 5.30–6.30pm). The temple's main hall (*hondo*) sits perched out over the mountainside on massive wooden pilings. The veranda, or *butai* (dancing stage), juts out over the valley floor overlooking the city below. A popular Japanese proverb equates taking any big chance in life to jumping off the elevated stage at Kiyomizu. Founded in 788, Kiyomizu-dera predates Kyoto and is dedicated to the 11-faced Kannon. The two 3.6-metre (12ft) tall deva kings (*nio*) guarding the front gate speak the whole of Buddhist wisdom: the right one has lips pursed in the first letter of the Sanskrit alphabet, *a*, while the one on the left mouths *om*, the last letter. Behind the main hall with its dancing stage is Jishu, one of the most popular Shinto shrines in the country, and where the god of love and good marriage resides. (Most Buddhist temples in Japan also house some sort of Shinto shrine.) Don't trip over the "blind stones" (*mekura-ishi*) or the people walking between them with their eyes closed.

The belief is that if you can negotiate the 20 metres (60ft) between the stones with eyes shut, silently repeating the name of your loved one, love and marriage are assured.

Steps lead down from Kiyomizu's main hall to **Otowa-no-taki**, a waterfall where visitors sip water from a spring said to have many health benefits, if not sheer divine power for the true believer. A short walk leads up the other side of the valley to a small pagoda with a view encompassing the entire hillside.

From Kiyomizu, return down the slope and follow a flight of stone steps down to Sannen-zaka, a street meaning "three-year slope". It is said that any pilgrim who trips or stumbles along this slope will have three years of bad luck. Today, the cobbled lane is less superstitiously known as Teapot Lane for all of the pottery shops lining its path. Continue to the charming Ninen-zaka, or "two-year slope". The restaurants near here are good for *soba* or *udon* noodles.

Back across Higashioji-dori sits **Rokuharamitsu-ji** ❶ (www.rokuhara.

Walking by the Kamo River.

THE WATER CITY

Even in my sleep/ I hear the sound of water/Flowing beneath my pillow" – Yoshi Osamu. Of all Japanese cities, Kyoto, with its rivers, commercial canals, irrigation channels, artesian wells and garden ponds is perhaps the most aquatic of Japan's inland urban centres, though in such a discreet way that you would hardly notice.

At one time there were literally thousands of wells in Kyoto. Wells were, and still are to some degree, an integral part of Kyoto life. They acquired a social function in the community, becoming focal points for informal gatherings. This practice among the townspeople of Kyoto gave birth to the expression "*Ido bata kaigi*" – literally, "to have a meeting around a well". Some private houses, if they are old enough, will still have them.

Glasses of water are often placed along with rice cakes and other delectables, in front of the stone figure of Jizo, a popular Buddhist saint found at roadsides or junctions. Fountains at the gates of Shinto shrines and strips of dyed cloth being fastened in the current of the Kamo River are constant reminders of the everyday importance of water.

Stroll anywhere in Kyoto and you are rarely beyond its presence. Water continues to be one of the main leitmotifs defining the character of the old imperial city.

A devotee at Yasaka Shrine.

or.jp; daily 8am–5pm), one of Kyoto's gems. At the rear of the main hall, built in 1363, is a museum with two fine Kamakura Period (1185–1333) sculptures: Taira-no Kiyomori, of the Heike clan, and Kuya, founder of the temple. The eyes of Kiyomori, presaging the tragic destruction of his clan, sum up the anguish often seen in Kamakura Period art. Kuya, who popularised the chanting of the lotus *sutra*, is shown reciting magic syllables, each of which becomes Amida, the saviour.

North are the brilliant-orange buildings of **Yasaka-jinja** ❶ (www.yasaka-jinja.or.jp; always open; free), formerly called Gion-san, a name more commonly associated with the adjoining Gion pleasure quarter. One of the tallest granite *torii* in Japan, at 9 metres (30ft) in height, marks the portal to the shrine. From the shrine's back gate, one enters adjoining Maruyama-koen. The park is known for its beautiful garden and magnificent cherry blossoms in early April. Two interesting temples sit just beyond: **Chion-in** and **Shoren-in**.

Exploring the Ponto-cho district.

Geisha district

East of the Kamo-gawa in central Kyoto, **Gion** ❸ is Kyoto's famous pleasure quarter or geisha district, today an uncanny blend of traditional and modern architecture. In Kyoto, geisha are known as *maiko* and *geiko*, not geisha. The word geisha in Old Kyoto referred to male entertainers dressed as women; in Tokyo and Osaka, however, it came to mean women. *Maiko* debut at about 16 years old and wear distinctive long trailing *obi*. At about 21, they may advance to the ranks of *geiko*, with their highly ornate kimono.

Along Gion's narrow streets one will rarely see *geiko*, but there's a good chance to catch sight of a *maiko* hurrying to entertain a guest. The teahouses in the quarter are in the style of Kyoto's old *machiya* townhouses, but with added delicate touches such as the orange-pink plastered walls (*ichiriki-jaya*). The best place to see the houses is along the alleyways that splinter off Hamani-koji, south of Shijo-dori. Just north of here is Gion Shimbashi, another well-preserved neighbourhood of old wooden buildings. At

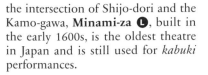

the intersection of Shijo-dori and the Kamo-gawa, **Minami-za** , built in the early 1600s, is the oldest theatre in Japan and is still used for *kabuki* performances.

Entertainment and nightlife

For the height of imperial drama, try a *noh* play, which developed in Kyoto in the 14th century. Rooted in *sarugaku* (ballad operas), the lyrical and melodramatic form became known as *sarugaku no noh*, later shortened to *noh*. A classical presentation includes five plays with several humorous interludes *(kyogen)*. Most presentations today show only two plays and two interludes. *Noh* greatly departs from Western ideas of drama by abandoning realism in favour of symbolism.

Noh developed in Kyoto as one of Japan's original art forms, along with *kabuki* and *bunraku* (puppet theatre). *Kabuki (ka-bu-ki*, or singing-dancing-performing) was the last purely Japanese art form to flourish, developing during the Edo Period as a commoner's entertainment. Originally dancing shows performed by women, *kabuki* turned to men as performers when the shogun declared the form immoral and forbidden to women. It has more variety and greater dynamic force than *noh* and appeals to a wider audience.

Other areas for traditional nightlife include traffic-free **Ponto-cho** along the west bank of Kamo-gawa and just across from Gion. The narrow street is lined with interesting bars, restaurants and *tayu* (top-ranked courtesan) houses. Kawaramachi is another busy shopping, eating and entertainment neighbourhood, also located beyond the Kamo's west bank. An excellent spot to dine in summer are the restaurants along Kamo-gawa, between Shijo and Sanjo streets.

Cross over Sanjo-dori and continue north to **Okazaki-koen**. This park holds museums, halls, a library and zoo. The best of the lot is the highly informative, visually stimulating **Fureaikan** (www.miyakomesse. jp/fureaika; daily 9am–5pm; free), a museum of traditional crafts housed in the basement of the Miyako Messe exhibition centre.

Maiko performing a Kyoto-style dance.

GEISHA

Few things are as emblematic of Japan as geisha. Although misconstrued by many in the West to be high-class prostitutes (something that never fails to annoy the Japanese), the geisha are in fact trained to be companions and entertainers, traditionally providing refined conversation and performing song and dance for well-heeled male customers. Today, however, you don't have to be aristocratic or rich to partake in a little geisha company. Many travel agents sell reasonably priced tickets to geisha evenings, and some hotels and *ryokan* organize their own geisha events for guests.

Time has changed in other ways for the geisha. It is estimated before World War II there were nearly 80,000 of them across Japan, a number that has since dwindled to just several thousand with the modernisation of the country. The few that hope to become a modern-day geisha, however, still face a long and arduous journey.

Training customarily begins at age 15 (although it is common nowadays to begin at a later age) and it then takes five years before the apprentice can be called a *geiko*, a fully fledged geisha. If you walk through Gion and catch a glimpse of a white-faced geisha in wooden *geta* sandals, shuffling awkwardly between teahouses, it will be one of these apprentices, or *maiko*. You can spot the *geiko* by the more elaborate design of their kimono.

The Shinto Heian shrine.

Heian-jingu

An arching 24-metre (80ft) high *torii* leads from Okazaki-koen to the vermilion-coloured gate of **Heian-jingu** Ⓝ (www.heianjingu.or.jp; daily, Mar–Nov 8.30am–5.30pm, Dec–Feb 8.30am–4.30pm; shrine – free), more of an architectural study than a Shinto centre. The shrine, dedicated to Kyoto's first and last emperors, is a replica of the original Imperial Palace built in 794 and last destroyed by fire in 1227. The shrine was erected in 1895 to commemorate Kyoto's 1,100th anniversary and displays architecture of the Heian Period, when Chinese influence was at its zenith. Shinto shrines took on Buddhist temple features during this period, when the plain wooden structures were first painted.

Passing through the shrine's massive gate, it's hard to imagine that the shrine is but a two-thirds-scale version of the original palace. The expansive, white-pebble courtyard leads the eye to the Daigoku-den, or main hall, where government business was conducted. The Blue Dragon and White Tiger pagodas dominate the view to the east

and west. To the left of the main hall is the entrance to the garden, designed in the spirit of the Heian Period for the pleasures of walking and boating. Mirror ponds, dragon stepping stones and a Chinese-style bridge are some of the beguiling features.

Tranquil shrines

From Heian-jingu walk southeast to **Murin-an** (Tue–Sun 9am–5pm), a 19th-century landscaped villa designed by the celebrated gardener Ogawa Jihei. The grass-covered grounds of this secluded garden, with its azalea-lined stream, incorporate an unspoilt view of Higashiyama. From the garden it is a short walk east to **Nanzen-ji** Ⓞ (www.nanzen.net; daily 8.40am–5pm, Dec–Feb until 4.30pm), which was originally the residence of 26-year-old Emperor Kameyama (1249–1305) after his abdication in 1274. Nanzen-ji sits nestled in a pine grove at the foot of Daimonji-yama and is part of the Rinzai school of Zen Buddhism, Zen's largest and best-known school. It's also one of Kyoto's most important Zen temples. The complex consists of the main temple and 12 sub-temples, of which only four are regularly open to the public.

Nanzen-ji provides an example of the Zen's belief in the relationship between all things. The pine grove influences the architecture, art influences the garden, and taken together they all influence the observer. The temple reflects the Chinese style *(kara-yo)* that arrived in Japan along with Zen. This style, evolving through the Ashikaga Period (1338–1573), achieved a near-perfect balance between the lordly Chinese style and the lightness of the native Japanese style. Exploring the two buildings of the abbots' quarters – Daiho-jo and Shoho-jo – reveals how garden architecture and landscape painting interrelate. The quarters are full of famous paintings, like *Tiger in the Bamboo Grove*, and the surrounding gardens are renowned as some of the best in

Japan. Here, the gardens are for sitting and contemplation, not strolling.

From Nanzen-ji, follow **Tetsugaku-no-Michi** ⓟ, or the Philosopher's Path, north past the Nomura Museum, Eikan-do temple and the intriguing hillside temple of Honen-in. The walk, named for the strolling path of Japanese philosopher Nishida Kitaro (1870–1945), snakes about 2km (1.2 miles) along the bank of a narrow canal to Ginkaku-ji. The quiet path – save for the crowds of tourists at times – is noted for its spring cherry blossoms and autumn foliage.

The walk ends at the Silver Pavilion, or **Ginkaku-ji** ⓠ (daily, Mar–Nov 8.30am–5pm, Mar–Dec 9am–4.30pm). The Ashikaga-era shogun who erected it in 1489 died before its completion and contrarily it remains without silver. However, its exquisite pavilion and Zen garden are not disappointing. The first floor of the pavilion was a residence and displays the Japanese *shinden* style. The second floor served as the altar room and shows a Chinese Buddhist style. The mound of white stones (*Kogetsudai*) in the garden was designed to reflect moonlight onto the garden. The quaint tearoom in the northeastern section of the pavilion is touted as the oldest in Japan.

A 20-minute walk away directly north of the Silver Temple is **Kompuku-ji**, the first of three exquisite gardens. A dry landscape arrangement with a steep bank of azaleas, this temple is affiliated with the Rinzai school of Zen, but also has literary associations with Basho and Buson, two of Japan's greatest haiku masters. The narrow, bamboo entrance to **Shisen-do**, a rustic hermitage with an adjacent stone garden bordered by azaleas, maples and persimmon, is a short walk from here. Northeast on foot takes you to the tranquil precincts of **Man-shu-in**, a hillside Tendai sect temple that dates from 1656.

To the northeast

In the northern foothills, the **Shu-gaku-in Rikyu** ⓡ (Shugaku-in Imperial Villa; free daily tours; apply at the Imperial Household Agency before visiting; tel: 75-211-1215; http://sankan. kunaicho.go.jp) was built in 1659 as an emperor's retreat. This imperial villa

A hanami at night.

THE SAKURA FORECAST

"On a journey / Resting beneath the cherry blossoms / I feel myself to be in a Noh play." The haiku poet Basho is one of countless Japanese to have been transfixed by the nation's favourite petals.

The *sakura* blossoms, which sweep northwards across the archipelago in spring, bring with them a wave of outdoor *hanami* (flower-viewing) parties, scheduled by groups of friends and co-workers to coincide with the peak of blossoming. To help with the planning, the Japan Weather Association issues a nationwide forecast for the start day, peak day and last day of the blossom period for each part of the country. If you want your trip to Kyoto to coincide with the best of the blossoms, you can check the forecast on the JNTO website (www.jnto.go.jp).

seems pure fantasy compared to Katsura Imperial Villa. It consists of three large, separate gardens and villas. In Rakushiken (Middle Villa) stands a cedar door with carp painted on both sides. It is said that the carp would escape each night to swim in the villa's pond. Not until golden nets were painted over them, in the 18th century, did they stay put.

Hiei-zan, an 850-metre (2,800ft) mountain northeast of Shugaku-in Imperial Villa, has long held historic and religious importance to Kyoto. Here, **Enryaku-ji** was founded to protect the new capital from evil northeast spirits. Apparently this exalted mission gave the temple's monks an inflated sense of importance. Over the decades, they became aggressive friars of the martial arts and swept into Kyoto on destructive raids. Their not-so-monastic rumbles were quenched by warlord Oda Nobunaga, who destroyed the temple in 1571. Today, there are three pagodas and 100 sub-temples, some offering accommodation and making Hiei-zan one of the area's most accessible hiking areas.

To the northwest and west

To the north and west of the city centre, skirting the foothills, are three renowned Zen temples that should not be missed. Established as a small monastery in 1315, the present buildings of **Daitoku-ji ⑤** were built after 1468 when one of the several fires in its history burned down the temple. It is the holy of holies, where Zen married art. The great Zen calligrapher Ikkyu (d. 1481), painter Soga Dasoku (d. 1483), and founders of the tea ceremony Murata Juko (d. 1502) and Sen-no Rikyu (d. 1591) all came from Daitoku-ji. The great warlord Oda Nobunaga is buried here. Although a brutal warrior, Nobunaga was fundamental to the 16th-century unification of Japan and was a leading patron of the arts.

Some eight of Daitoku-ji's 22 subsidiary temples are open to the public. The three best-known are Daisen, Zuiho and Koto. In **Daisen-in** (daily, Mar–Nov 9am–5pm, Dec–Feb 9am–4.30pm) is Kyoto's second most famous – maybe the best – Zen garden. Unlike the abstractions of other gardens, the Daisen garden more

The Silberner Pavilion at Ginkaku-ji.

Maps on pages
234, 238

closely resembles the ink-wash paintings of Zen art.

The Daitoku complex has been criticised for its commercialism, but it is still worth the visit. This is also one of the best places to sample authentic Zen-temple food, just like the monks eat.

Walk west along Kitaoji-dori past Funaokayama-koen to the best-known temple in Kyoto, if not all Japan: **Kinkaku-ji** ❶ (daily 9am–5pm), or the Golden Pavilion. It's a replica built in 1955 of a 15th-century structure and last re-covered in gold-leaf in 1987. Each of the pavilion's three storeys reflects a different architectural style. The first floor is of the palace style, the second floor of the samurai-house style, while the third floor reveals the Zen-temple style. The large pond in front of the pavilion and surrounding grounds give it a perfect setting.

The original temple was burned down in 1950 by a man who entered the Buddhist priesthood after being seduced by the pavilion's beauty. Thinking that his sense of aesthetics might approach perfection if he burned down the very object that had enchanted him in the first place, he did exactly that. The author and right-wing nationalist Mishima Yukio fictionalised the burning episode in his 1956 book, *Kinkakuji*.

Further west, visit **Ryoan-ji** ❶ (www.ryoanji.jp; daily, Mar–Nov 8am–5pm, Dec–Feb 8.30am–4.30pm), or Temple of the Peaceful Dragon, early in the day before the peace is shattered by the busloads of tourists and students. Here is the most famous Zen rock garden (*karesansui*, or dry landscape) in the world and one of Kyoto's main tourist attractions. The 16th-century garden is an abstract of an ink-wash painting executed in rock and stone. The sense of infinite space is said to lift the mind into a Zen state.

A little past Ryoan-ji to the west, **Ninna-ji**'s formidable gate with its fierce-looking *nio* guardians is one of the best in Japan. Returning east, **Myoshin-ji** was founded in 1337 on the site of an imperial villa. Cast in 698, Japan's oldest bell hangs here. Tenth-century **Kitano Tenmangu** ❶ is one of Kyoto's most earthy shrines and hosts a popular antiques

Katsura Rikyu.

The Garden of Daisen-in at Daitoku-ji.

TIP

Both Japanese and foreign visitors need special permission to visit one of the imperial villas. Bring your passport to the Imperial Household Agency office at the Kyoto Imperial Palace early on the day you wish to visit – or apply online up to three months in advance (www.kunaicho.go.jp).

market on the 25th of each month. Its restrained wooden architecture enshrines Sugawara Michizane, a 9th-century scholar and statesman. Small wooden votives, or *ema* – with a picture of a horse on one side and a wish or prayer (most for success in school exams) written on the other side – hang in the courtyard. The shrine also celebrates the first calligraphy of the year, when schoolchildren offer their writings to the shrine. The present shrine structure was built in 1607. Tenman-gu is known for its splendid plum trees that bloom in the snows of February, and for the geisha who serve tea under the flowering trees.

Uzamasa district

The Uzumasa district south of Ryoan-ji is home to two strikingly different sights: a temple of immense antiquity and cultural clout, and a cheesy but fun film studio.

Koryu-ji (daily 9am–5pm) traces its roots to 622, when either Prince Shotoku or Hata no Kawakatsu, an important family of Korean lineage, founded the temple. It's a disputed point, but

one that need not delay you in seeking out the treasures of this unique temple. The first building of note, the Kodo (Lecture Hall), is one of the oldest constructions in Kyoto, dating from 1165. The statues inside are even older, most dating from the 7th and 8th centuries. Impressive as they are, these are overshadowed by the collection housed in the contemporary Reiho-kan (Treasure House; daily 9am–5pm). The two most outstanding statues here are the image of Prince Shotoku at the age of 16, and Miroku Bosatsu, or Future Buddha.

For a more dramatic but decidedly lighter view of history, repair to the nearby Toei Uzumasa Eiga-mura (www.toei-eigamura.com; daily, Mar–Nov 9am–5pm, Aug and Sat–Sun until 6pm, Dec–Feb 9.30am–4.30pm, Sat–Sun until 5pm), a commercial studio renowned for churning out chambara-style, sword and Zen-flavoured samurai films and, now, TV dramas. Visitors can participate in acrobatic ninja shows and samurai sword fighting lessons.

One of Japan's most famous strolling gardens lies inside **Katsura Rikyu Ⓦ** (Katsura Imperial Villa; applications

The Japanese rock garden at Ryoan-ji.

for visits should be made to the Imperial Household Agency, which puts on several tours daily; tel: 75-211-1215; http://sankan.kunaicho.go.jp), due west of Kyoto Station on the west side of Katsura-gawa. Its garden features a number of splendid teahouses overlooking a large central pond. Katsura, with its severe refinement, has exercised more influence on contemporary architecture than perhaps any other building in the whole of Japan.

South of Kyoto Station

Just south of Kyoto Station, **To-ji** ⊗ (www.toji.or.jp; daily, mid-Mar–mid-Sept 8.30am–5.30pm, mid-Sept–mid-Mar 8.30am–4.30pm) boasts one of the nation's enduring postcard images: the five-storey Goju-no-to pagoda. Rebuilt in 1644, and standing at 55 metres (180ft), it is Japan's tallest pagoda. The temple itself was established in 796 and today draws large crowds to its flea markets. Built next to the old city's south gate, To-ji became Japan's main Buddhist temple. Its main hall (*kondo*) reflects Buddhist traditions from India, China and Japan.

To the east up against the hills, **Tofuku-ji** ⓨ (www.tofukuji.jp; daily 9am–4pm) contains Japan's oldest and most important Zen-style gate, from the 15th century. Yet its 25 subsidiary temples are rarely visited and the grounds are usually quiet. Walk through the abbot's quarters (*hojo*) to the platform over the ravine looking down on Tsuten Bridge – it's one of the most delightful views in Kyoto. During the last week of November, don't miss the festival of old brushes and pens where writers and painters cast their old tools into a sacred fire.

A few blocks south of Tofuku-ji, tunnel-like paths of hundreds of bright-red *torii* tempt walkers. Actually, there are over 10,000 *torii* covering the paths of **Fushimi Inari Taisha** ⓩ – the fox shrine founded in the 9th century in honour of the fox, which farmers believe is the messenger of the harvest god. Walk the full 4km (2.5-mile) course. Fushimi is renowned for its high-quality sake, and its famous brewery, Gakkien, is housed in an original Edo Period warehouse where visitors can sample products.

The many torii at Fushimi Inari Taisha.

AROUND KYOTO

Just beyond Kyoto's hilly boundaries is the cradle of its ancient agricultural life. Some surprising cultural highlights nestle in the midst of this rustic scenery.

Main Attractions
Enryaku-ji temple
The temples of Ohara
Hikone Castle
Lake Biwa
Miho Museum
Byodo-in
Arashiyama

Who would expect to find ancient Buddhist statuary and a paradise garden in a mist-filled valley less than an hour from Kyoto Station, or to enter a futuristic art gallery, concealed in the side of a mountain? How about the villa of a silent-movie icon set among bamboo groves, or the largest lake in the country, just a short train or bus ride away? Equally impressive is Hikone Castle, one of only a handful of original fortresses to have survived.

The remnants of Kyoto's 1,000-year reign as Japan's capital can be seen all over Kyoto Prefecture and neighbouring Shiga Prefecture. In ancient times, retinues of powerful lords and shoguns would make way for Uji's yearly procession of wooden chests, carrying Japan's most valuable green-tea harvest. The brew still ranks as the very best, but the journey now to Uji can be made in just 30 minutes. Using Kyoto as a base, you could easily spend a week exploring beyond the city, starting with the highlights that follow.

Ohara

A pleasant 50-minute bus ride through the northeastern suburbs of Kyoto crosses a fertile valley plain into the village of **Ohara**. The area has a strong association with ancient Kyoto aristocracy: emperors, empresses, imperial kin and consorts who repaired

here for respite and refuge. Retired aristocracy, peasants, high priests and monks coexisted in a simple but rarified atmosphere. Ohara has long been associated with the Buddhist faith. The legacy of beauty, calm and tradition clearly appeals to the handful of textile artists, potters and writers who have settled here.

An insight into the way that ordinary people lived in this naturally well-endowed area can be glimpsed in the **Ohara Kyodokan** (daily 9.30am–5pm), a 19th-century farmhouse that

Lake Biwa from Hikone Castle.

Green tea flavoured ice cream on sale in Uji.

You can sample the delights of green tea in shops in Uji.

the emperor's chief adviser. A closer glimpse of this era is found in Murasaki Shikibu's (a lady-in-waiting at the court) 11th-century narrative, *The Tale of Genji*, a tale of imperial court intrigue considered to be the world's first full-length novel. "He was obliged to move to Uji where fortunately he still possessed a small estate… after a time he began once more to take an interest in flowers and autumn woods, and would even spend hour after hour simply watching the river flow." Some years after Shikibu's work was completed, Yorimichi, the son of Fujiwara, converted the villa into a temple dedicated to Amida, the Buddha of the Western Paradise. The centrepiece of the project was the Amida Hall, commonly known as the Phoenix Hall, and the entire ensemble is known as Byodo-in. Amazingly, the building has survived centuries of weather, fire, earthquakes and years of neglect. In 1994 it was declared a Unesco World Heritage Site.

The best view of the perfectly balanced main building and its ornamental wings, seemingly floating on the surface of the water, can be had from across the pond that surrounds the complex, an image that appears on the reverse side of the ¥10 coin. When the doors to the hall are open, a gilded statue of Amida, floating on a bed of lotuses, is visible within. Some of the more valuable or vulnerable objects in the hall, such as wall murals, wooden statues and the original temple bell, have been preserved and are housed in a modern **museum** (Byodo-in Museum Hoshokan; daily 9am–5pm) located in the complex.

Uji's riverbank

Besides Byodo-in, Uji has several other features of interest, not least of which is the river itself and its series of bridges, islands, shrines and teahouses lining its banks. The journey into Uji's past begins at the "Bridge of Floating Dreams", the modern version of the original 7th-century structure that spans the river. A narrow shopping street runs from here to Byodo-in. The first thing you will notice here is the smell of roasting tea. Fragrant *uji-cha* was first planted in the 13th century,

and now Uji green tea is regarded as the finest in Japan. On summer evenings, demonstrations of cormorant fishing take place along the river, adding to the magic of fireworks, poetry readings and other events.

Arashiyama

Moving west from the centre of Kyoto, the **Arashiyama** district is where the dense urbanity begins to give way to a more pleasant semi-rural suburb, characterised by bamboo groves and the winding **Hozu-gawa River**. As with anywhere in and around Kyoto, Arashiyama has its fair share of temples, the most interesting visit being **Tenryu-ji** (daily 8.30am–5pm, late Mar–late Oct until 5.30pm). Built as a country home for the 13th-century emperor Kameyama, it ended up being converted into a temple in the 14th century. Most of the current buildings are modern reconstructions, but the temple's main garden – an exquisitely designed affair combining water and rock features set against a tree-covered hillside – supposedly dates back to Kameyama's day.

Near Tenryu-ji is the **Okochi Sanso** villa (daily 9am–5pm) that was once the home to a 1920s silent-movie star, Denjiro Okochi. As you wander through the villa's sprawling grounds, through moss and stone gardens and past tea ceremony pavilions, it soon becomes obvious that Denjiro must have been on a very tidy Hollywood-esque wage back in his day.

The other highlights of Arashiyama include the **Togetsu-kyo Bridge**, spanning the Hozu-gawa, the best place to see cherry blossoms in spring or the red leaves in autumn. The Hozu-gawa itself is a good place for taking a gentle boat tour, especially in spring or autumn when the trees along its banks are at their most colourful. South of the bridge, in the Arashiyama mountains, is the **Monkey Park Iwatayama** (www.kmpi.co.jp; daily 9am–4pm, mid-Mar–Oct until 5pm), where Japanese macaques roam freely on an observation deck, which also boasts good views down over the city. All of Arashiyama's sites can be taken in a single day trip from Kyoto.

Togetsu-kyo Bridge, Arashiyama.

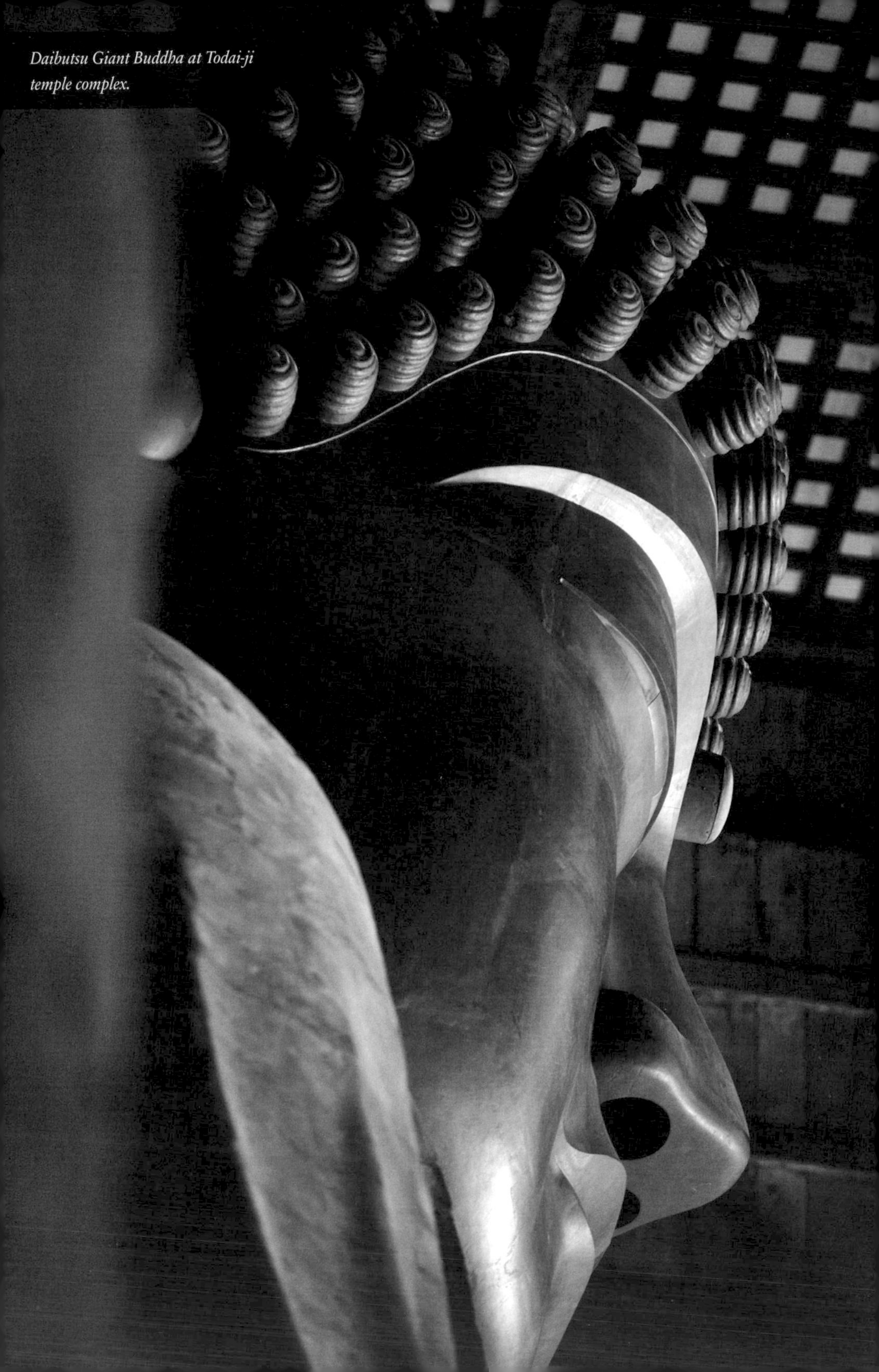

Daibutsu Giant Buddha at Todai-ji temple complex.

NARA

Japan's capital in the 8th century, Nara later escaped the civil wars that shook the country. A repository of ancient treasures, it embodies Chinese, Korean and even Middle Eastern styles.

The ancient site of **Nara** ❻ belongs to an era before Zen gardens and tea ceremonies, before Japan became Japan. Buddhist thought from India and arts from as far as Greece and Turkey flowed east along the Silk Road and Nara was the last stop. Preserved here long after extinction in their home countries are the finest examples of Tang-dynasty architecture from China, early Korean religious sculpture and treasures from Iran.

Japan had its capital at Nara from AD 710 to 784, after which the government moved to Kyoto, 35km (22 miles) to the north, and the Nara area lost political importance. This was Nara's great blessing. As a result, it avoided the wars that destroyed other ancient capitals of China, Korea and Japan. It has also avoided the worst of the tourist crowds that are drawn to the more illustrious Kyoto. Many people that visit Nara do so as a day trip, opting to be nearer Kyoto's selection of hotels and restaurants.

Nara Buddhism represented an early exuberant form of Buddhist thought, rich in symbolism. Everywhere in Nara are *mandala*, the diagrams or arrangements symbolising cosmic truth. Represented at the centre is the essence of the main god. Expanding outward in circles or squares are other gods exerting their powers to help the centre. *Mandala* can be interpreted in everything from the arrangement of statues on an altar to the layout of temple buildings. Every placement and gesture has meaning. For example, two guardian figures flank the gates to large temples. One has his mouth open, the other closed. These symbolise the sounds *a* and *om*, the first and last letters of the Sanskrit alphabet. Being first and last, they encompass all and hence have magical power to protect against evil.

Main Attractions

Nara Park
Kofuku-ji temple
Todai-ji temple
Kasuga Taisha
Shin Yakushi-ji temple
Horyu-ji temple
Asuka

Kofuku-ji.

Hand gestures, clothing and implements are significant. Most ornate are the *mandorla*, or haloes, in which can be seen the intercultural impact of the Silk Road. The haloes originated in Indian Buddhism and travelled east to Japan and west to Europe, where they were adopted by Christianity. The flames in the halos signify divine light.

Statues with great power were hidden from the public and became the so-called secret Buddhas, shown only on rare occasions. For instance, the Kuze Kannon of Horyu-ji was hidden from the public for 1,000 years before seeing the light of day in the late 19th century. Many statues, Kuze Kannon included, are still only shown in the spring or autumn or on religious holidays.

Old Nara

Old Nara, much larger than the city today, followed the traditional model of Chinese imperial cities: a sacred square with streets radiating from the central palace in a grid pattern. During the centuries of neglect after 784, the palaces of Nara disappeared, but the temples and shrines on the northeastern edge of the city survived. This corner of the city is now a public park, **Nara-koen** (Nara Park). Tame deer, sacred to the shrine of Kasuga Taisha, are its symbol.

A temple to the east of **Nara-eki** Ⓐ (Nara Station) is **Kofuku-ji** Ⓑ (www.kohfukuji.com; daily 9am–5pm), on the western side of Nara-koen. The patrons of Kofuku-ji were the Fujiwara clan, who gained power in the mid-7th century and succeeded in dominating the government for the next 500 years. Even after the capital moved to Kyoto, the Fujiwara continued to support Kofuku-ji as the family temple. Kofuku-ji is known for its two pagodas. The five-storey pagoda, built in 1426, is a copy of an original dating from 730 and is the second-tallest pagoda in Japan; the three-storey pagoda dates from 1114. The Central Golden Hall, which was destroyed in 1717, is currently being reconstructed and is due to be completed in 2018.

The adjacent **Kokuhokan** (Treasure House; daily 9am–5pm) – a dreary, concrete building – offers the best

introduction to Japanese sculpture available. Most famous is the set of guardians (734) with sweet, child-like faces moulded out of dry lacquer. Of these, the six-armed Ashura is one of the best-loved statues in Japan. In addition, the museum displays a cast bronze head of Yakushi Nyorai, practically Egyptian in its abstract simplicity, and massive heads of temple guardians originally from statues that must have been 15–20 metres (50–65ft) high. Nara developed in an age before Japan became the land of the miniature. The buildings and statues aimed to exceed even the grandeur of Imperial China.

From Kofuku-ji, cross the street east to **Kokuritsu Hakubutsukan ©** (National Museum; www.narahaku.go.jp; Tue–Sun 9.30am–5pm, May–Oct Fri until 7pm). The most interesting part of the museum is the East Gallery. At the end of October and the beginning of November, the normally stored treasures of Todai-ji are displayed to the public. Regular displays include an array of Buddha images from past centuries and archaeological artefacts excavated from ancient tombs.

Todai-ji and around

To the north across Nara-koen's central avenue is **Todai-ji ©** (www.todaiji.or.jp; daily, Apr–Sept 9.30am–5.30pm, Mar and Oct 9.30am–5pm, Nov–Feb 9.30am–4.30pm), founded in 743 and the most important temple in Nara. Walk north towards the temple and you will be met by the **Nandai-mon**, a gate dating from 1199. With its 18 pillars and elaborate roof construction, it is one of the outstanding monuments of the Kamakura Period. Inside the gate stand great wooden statues, called *nio*, who guard the entrance to Todai-ji. They were carved around the 13th century. As an aside here, to the west of the Nandai-mon is the **Isuien Garden**. Constructed in the Meiji era, Isuien encompasses two beautifully sculpted stroll gardens, each centred on a large pond and offering a peaceful break from Nara's more visited temples.

Straight ahead from the Nandai-mon is Todai-ji, with the **Daibutsu-den** (Hall of the Great Buddha). Enshrining a monumental bronze image of Vairocana, the Cosmic Buddha, the hall was meant to proclaim

TIP

The area south of Sarusawa Pond is an excellent place to find *ryokan*, traditonal Japanese inns. Note that rates at these tend to go up at weekends and in the peak spring and autumn seasons.

Feeding the deer in Nara Park.

Nandai-mon pillars and beams at Todai-ji temple complex.

Nigatsudo temple at Todai-ji.

the power of the imperial state. It was destroyed numerous times by fire; the present building dates from 1706. Although only two-thirds of its original size, Daibutsu-den is said to be the largest wooden structure in the world. The present building is not entirely a first-rate piece of architecture (note the pillars made of bound timbers, rather than single beams such as those of Nandai-mon). Still, the interior retains a sense of the medieval grandeur that was Nara.

The Buddha has been greatly altered in later restorations, but the petals of the lotus upon which the Buddha sits retain original engravings in fine lines showing Sakyamuni (the historical Buddha) as one of 110 billion avatars of Vairocana. The bronze statue is 16 metres (55ft) tall and weighs 500 tonnes. Like the statuary found in the nearby Sangatsu-do and Kaidan-in, it shows off Tempyo Period (729–764) art and craftsmanship.

To the east of Daibutsu-den is a road lined with picturesque stone lanterns leading up the hill to two temples.

Sangatsu-do ❸ (March Hall), built in 746, contains a large central statue of Fukukenjaku Kannon (the god of compassion) radiating light beams and surrounded by a *mandala* arrangement of attendants and guardian beings. Next door is **Nigatsu-do** (February Hall), the perfect place for a final view of the park. Raised high over the city, this pyramidal building was frequently burned and rebuilt, most recently in 1669. Every 13 March since its founding in 752, the emperor sends an emissary at midnight with water symbolising the coming of spring. The arrival of the water is the occasion for a fire festival, with monks carrying burning pine running around the veranda and spinning sparks into the night. The building is closed to the public.

Kasuga Taisha ❻ (www.kasugataisha. or.jp; daily Apr–Sept 6am–6pm, Oct–Mar 6.30am–5pm) was originally built in AD 710, but its buildings have been reconstructed numerous times following the Shinto tradition that sacred structures be thoroughly rebuilt at intervals, often every 20 years, as is also the case with the

shrines at Ise. Kasuga Taisha's treasure house is a modern structure housing the shrine's artefacts.

The city of Nara contains numerous other temples of historical importance. The most interesting temple outside Nara-koen is **Shin Yakushi-ji** G (daily 9am–5pm) built in 747 to the southeast. This, along with Sangatsu-do, is one of the few original Nara buildings. The central figure of Yakushi Nyorai (Healer) grants aid to those suffering from ailments of the eyes and ears. Most unusual is the set of 12 clay guardian images still standing intact. Shin Yakushi-ji, tucked away among crowded streets in a forgotten part of town, is a favourite. Just a few steps west of the temple is the **Irie Taikichi Memorial Museum of Photography Nara City** (http://irietaikichi.jp; Tue–Sun 9.30am–4.30pm), with a splendid collection of images of Nara by the late Irie Taikichi and others.

Northwest

Leaving Nara-koen behind, and heading a couple of kilometres northeastwards, is the old centre of the ancient city. The best place to begin here is **Hannya-ji** (www.hannyaji.com; daily 9am–5pm), the Temple of Wisdom. Surrounded by a garden of wild flowers, it has great charm. In the garden is a Kamakura-era gate with elegant upturned gables and a 13-storey Heian-era stone pagoda. The temple houses a Kamakura statue of Monju, the god of wisdom. Monju rides on his sacred lion, carrying in his hand the sword to cut through ignorance. A palace once stood near here, but today nothing survives but a large field with circular clipped hedges showing where the pillars used to stand. Just east of the palace field is **Hokke-ji** (www.hokkeji-nara.jp; daily 9am–5pm), a nunnery known for its 8th-century statue of Kannon.

North of Hokke-ji are imperial tomb mounds surrounded by moats, and beyond them to the northwest is **Akishino-dera** (daily 9am–5pm), patron temple of the arts. The original temple was founded in 775, but the present hall dates from the Kamakura Period. Inside is Gigeiten, god of the arts and a favourite of Nara

A miko (female attendant) at Kasugataisha.

Mochi (sticky rice snacks) on sale in Nara.

DIALECTICAL ROOTS

Japanese ranks ninth worldwide in number of native speakers, although no nation other than Japan has used Japanese as a language since World War II.

The origins of Japanese are not known with any certainty. A strong hypothesis connects Japanese to Korean, claiming that a language of southern Korea was imported into Kyushu over 2,000 years ago, along with the cultivation of rice.

Dialects abound in this archipelago punctuated by mountain peaks and deep valleys, not to mention the islands themselves. Some dialects – those of Kyushu and Tohoku come to mind – can be nearly unintelligible to many Japanese people when spoken by older generations. *Kyotsu-go*, or "common language", which is based on the Tokyo/Kanto dialect, linguistically unifies the islands.

Shin Yakushi-ji was founded in 747.

Yakushi-ji at sunset.

cognoscenti. The head is original Nara, with the delicacy of expression typical of dry lacquer. The body, a recreation from the Kamakura Period, has the S-curve of Chinese sculpture.

Southwest

Heading about 3km (1.8 miles) out of central Nara, the southwestern temples are a major destination for travellers. The first temple you reach heading from Nara-koen is **Toshodai-ji** (www.toshodaiji.jp; daily 8.30am–5pm), founded by the Chinese monk Ganjin in 751. The roof of the *kondo* (main hall) is the finest surviving example of Tang-dynasty architecture. Note the inward-curving fish tails on the roof, unique to Nara. **Yakushi-ji** (www.nara-yakushiji.com; daily 8.30am–5pm) is a 10-minute walk due south from Toshodai-ji. All of the original buildings have been destroyed by fires except the eastern pagoda, originally built in 698 and rebuilt 718. This is constructed of a harmonious arrangement of three roofs, with smaller roofs underneath creating the illusion of six storeys. Unfortunately,

the complex as a whole lacks the Nara charm due to modern reconstructions of the western pagoda (1981) and the main hall (1976). The main hall houses an original triad (considerably restored) of Yakushi flanked by Nikko, Light of the Sun, and Gakko, Light of the Moon.

Horyu-ji

To the southwest of Yakushi-ji, about 10km (6 miles) from Nara Station, is one of the region's standout sights: **Horyu-ji** (www.horyuji.or.jp; daily, late Feb–early Nov 8am–5pm, early Nov–late Feb 8am–4.30pm), home to the oldest wooden buildings in the world. Horyu-ji was founded in 607 by Prince Shotoku, the pivotal figure who established Chinese culture in Japan. The temple is something of a time capsule, preserving hundreds of art works from the 7th and 8th centuries. Horyu-ji is divided into two wings. Most visitors start from the western cloister. The main gate, dating from 1438, leads to an avenue lined by earthen walls characteristic of Horyu-ji. Note

the wood-grain patterns created by pressing the walls with boards, thought to make the walls earthquake resistant. At the end of the avenue is **Chu-mon** (Middle Gate). The pillars of the gate (dating from 607, rebuilt c.670) are famous for their entasis (outward curvature), a feature of Greek architecture that travelled to Japan via the Silk Road.

Inside the western cloister are the pagoda and *kondo* (main hall), built around 670. The *kondo* houses a rare group of bronzes dating from 620 in Wei style. They are distinguished by elongated faces, the "archaic smile" and the abstract, almost Art Deco lines of the falling drapery and the flames of the *mandorla*. In the centre is the Shaka Triad (Sakyamuni, the historical Buddha, with attendants). To the right is Yakushi and to the left is Amida, the Buddha of Paradise. Guardians, standing on demons, are Japan's oldest "Four Heavenly Kings".

One of the pleasures of Horyu-ji is the walk out through the cloister, an old example of a Chinese form that influenced temples and palaces throughout eastern Asia. Outside the cloister, walk east to the two concrete buildings of the museum, **Daihozod-en** (Great Treasure House). These buildings are even uglier than the museum of Kofuku-ji, but the treasures inside are important. Among the displays in the museum are the Kudara Kannon from Korea, the portable shrine of Lady Tachibana and the Hyakuman pagodas, which contain strips of paper printed with short prayers. Published in 764 in an edition of 1 million, they are the world's oldest printed material.

From the museum there is a walk bordered by temples and earthen walls to the eastern cloister. In the centre is an octagonal building of Chinese inspiration, surmounted by a flaming jewel and known as the **Yumedono**, Hall of Dreams. Built around 740, it commemorates a dream of Prince Shotoku in which an angel appeared to him while he was copying the sutras. The Yumedono contains a secret Buddha, the Kuze Kannon, which is only on view in the spring and autumn.

FACT

The statue of Kannon at Hokke-ji is one of the secret Buddhas, on view only from 20 Mar–7 Apr, 5–9 June, and 25 Oct–11 Nov each year.

Pagoda at the Horyu-ji temple complex.

SOUTHERN KANSAI

The rugged mountains and ancient forests of the southern part of Kansai are a far cry from the region's urban centre. Like Kyoto and Nara to the north, however, the region is rich in history.

Fanning southwest and southeast from Nara, the largely rural southern Kansai region has some outstanding sights, both historic and modern. From a base in Nara or even Osaka or Kyoto, no visit to Kansai would be complete without a couple of days exploring the more remote south. At Koya-san, the mountain home of the Shingon sect of Buddhism, the more than 100 temples within ancient cryptomeria forest create an almost mystical aura befitting one of Japan's holiest sites, while the ancient Kumano Kodo pilgrimage trails to the east of the region wind through breathtaking mountain and forest scenery. Off the western coast, in the Seto Inland Sea, the traditional has given way to cutting-edge art on Naoshima – dubbed "Japan's art island" for good reason.

Out of Nara

It's an easy run directly south of Nara to **Imai-cho** ❼, where the old quarter of the town is a 10-minute stroll from Yagi-nishiguchi Station. A thriving merchant town since the 17th century, Imai-cho has over 500 traditional wood-and-plaster houses, a half-dozen or so of which are open to the public. A real bonus is that most of the houses are occupied, making the town feel like a living entity rather than a stagey museum

Pilgrims at Kumano Kodo, Wakayama.

set. A single ticket admits you to all the *machiya*, as these residences are known. The most interesting is the **Imanashi Jyutaku** (www.imanishike. or.jp; Tue–Sun 10am–5pm), dating from 1650. Another notable building and Important Cultural Property is the Kawai Residence, which still functions as a private home and sake brewery.

The village of **Yoshino** ❽, a quiet getaway at most times, is awash with visitors during the spring cherry blossom season when an astonishing

Main Attractions
Imai-cho
The Kii Peninsula
Kumano Kodo
Koya-san
The Grand Shrines of Ise

Kumano Hongu Taisha is part of the Kumano Sanzan in the Wakayama Prefecture.

Yoshino-san in spring.

co.jp). Before following the trails through the cherry trees, spare some time for the nicely appointed temples and shrines along and off the main street. **Kimpusen-ji** temple (www.kinpusen.or.jp; daily 8.30am–4.30pm), with its fierce guardian statues and a main hall, said to be the second-largest wooden building in Japan (after Todai-ji's Daibutsu-den in Nara), is a designated National Treasure.

Chikurin-in (www.chikurin.co.jp), a beautifully designed and finished temple, operates primarily as an upmarket Japanese inn, but has a fetching and quite famous stroll garden, said to have been partly designed by the tea master Sen no Rikyu. The garden uses Yoshino-san to great effect as borrowed scenery. To get to Yoshino take the Kintetsu Nara Line, changing onto the Kintetsu Yoshino Line at Kashihara-jingu-mae.

100,000 trees are in bloom. Grown at different elevations on the slopes of **Yoshino-san**, the earliest to bloom are at the bottom, the last at the top, an effect that stretches the viewing season to a full month.

It's an easy enough ascent from Yoshino Station to the village, which sits on the side of the mountain, but there is also a convenient cable car (Yoshino Ropeway; www.yokb315.

The Kii Peninsula

The **Kii-hanto** ❾ (peninsula) at the southern end of the Kansai region is

Honshu's largest peninsula, an area known for the dense forests and rugged mountains of its interior and a dramatic Pacific-facing coastline. The warm Kuroshio Current here has created a distinctive ecosystem and climate. On the one hand, the warm waters have helped produce the most poleward living coral reefs in the world; on the other the Kuroshio is blamed for making Kii the wettest place in the subtropics, with annual rainfall in the southern mountains nearly 5 metres (16.5ft). When typhoons batter Honshu in late summer and early autumn, Kii often takes the brunt of the damage. No wonder the people here have a reputation for being hardy folk.

A highlight of the Kii region is the **Kumano Kodo**, a network of four historic pilgrimage routes that have been granted Unesco World Heritage status. The routes would lead pilgrims between Kumano and religious sites such as the Grand Shrines of Ise (see page 275) and Koya-san, but today the pious have largely been replaced by tourists who come

to gape at Kumano's sheer natural beauty – its remote mountains, tea fields and ancient woods – before soaking in the area's reportedly healing hot springs.

Koya-san

Surrounded by 117 temples concealed within the green and mysterious canopies of cryptomeria trees and moss, spending a night at a *shukubo*, or temple lodging, on **Koya-san** ❿ in the heart of the Kii-hanto is one of those quintessentially Japanese experiences not to be had with more conventional sights. Although easily accessed by train – take the Hashimoto and Nankai lines from Nara, about 40km (25 miles) to the east, to the terminus at Gokurakubashi Station and the cable car up to the mountain – Koya-san still manages to seem remote and isolated. The mountain became a major religious centre in 816, when the celebrated priest Kobo Daishi set up a temple here. Today it is a retreat, meditation centre and place of Buddhist study for trainee priests and monks, but it also offers simple lodgings for

TIP

The graceful buildings of Kongobu-ji temple at Koya-san are worth seeing for their religious and secular treasures, including screen paintings by the respected Kano school of artists. There is also an impressive stone garden here called the Banryu-tei, which you can contemplate from the veranda.

View of the mountains from Kumano Kodo, Wakayama.

Daito at Koya-san.

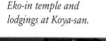

Eko-in temple and lodgings at Koya-san.

everyone from commoners to members of the imperial family to Kobo Daishi himself. Followers of the priest believe that when he ascends to meet the Buddha, those buried near him will also rise to glory, hence the jam of tombs. Kobo Daishi's mausoleum at the far end of the cemetery, the most sacred spot on Koya-san, is located behind the **Lantern Hall** (daily 6am–5.30pm; free), where thousands of lights are kept burning. On the other side of the small town that serves all Koya-san's needs is the central religious compound known as the **Garan** (grounds always open; free), and also the symbol of the mountain, a two-storey vermilion pagoda called the **Daito** (daily 8.30am–5pm), or Great Stupa.

The Reiho-kan (www.reihokan.or.jp; Treasure Museum; daily 8.30am–5pm, May–Oct until 5.30pm) at Koya-san has a first-rate collection of priceless Buddhist art, including painted scrolls, silk paintings and *mandalas*. The exhibits are changed regularly through the year.

travellers – mostly traditional Japanese rooms with tatami floors, sliding doors and shared toilets (for a list of temple accommodation, see www.shukubo.net).

Koya-san can be explored at random, but Ichinohashi, the entrance to **Okuno-in** cemetery, is a good starting point. In this veritable city of the dead, moss-covered tombstones mark the resting place of

The shrines of Ise

While not part of the Kansai district, Ise and its shrines, east from Nara and Kyoto, perhaps best exemplify the nature and purpose of the Japanese Shinto belief.

An excursion to Ise can be enlightening, but know beforehand that visitors are not allowed into the shrines' compounds under any circumstances.

No one can say exactly how long the two main shrines of what are collectively called the Grand Shrines of Ise have existed. Historical evidence suggests that **Naiku,** or the Inner Shrine, has been in place since around the 4th century, and **Geku**, or the Outer Shrine, since the late 5th century (www.isejingu.or.jp; both shrines: daily, Jan–Feb 5am–5.30pm, Mar, Apr, Sept and Nov 5am–6pm, May–Aug 4am–7pm, Nov–Dec 5am–5pm, free).

At Ise, the venerable cypress-wood *(hinoki)* shrine buildings stand today in perfect condition – almost new and mocking the ravages of time. The secret of the fine condition of these most sacred of Shinto shrines is *sengu*, or shrine removal, performed at Ise every 20 years over the past 13 centuries, the last and 62nd *sengu* took place in 2013. *Sengu* consists of the razing of the two main buildings of both shrines, along with 14 smaller auxiliary structures. In the *sengu*, before the existing structures are destroyed, new shrine buildings of identical scale and materials are erected on adjacent foundations set aside for that purpose. Then Japan's largest and most important Shinto festival, Jingu Shikinen Sengu, begins as the deities of the respective shrines are invited to pass from the old into the new structures. Later, the old structures are torn down and sections of the timbers sent to Shinto shrines throughout Japan. Visitors can learn more about the rebuilding of shrines in the recently opened Sengukan Museum (9am–4.30pm; closed 4th Tue of month), adjacent to Geku.

Why this work? First, the 20-year period can be viewed as a transition point. In human life, it is a line of demarcation between generations. Thus, *sengu* perpetuates an appreciation and an awareness of the cultural and religious significance of the shrines from age to age. Two decades is also perhaps the most logical period in terms of passing on from generation to generation the technological expertise needed for the reconstruction.

Geku is dedicated to Toyouke no Omikami, the goddess of agriculture. The grounds of Geku cover about 90 hectares (220 acres). A thatched gateway stands at the outermost of the three formidable fences, which is as close as anyone except imperial personages, envoys and shrine officials get to Shoden, the main hall. The clean, simple lines of the building are the very essence of Japanese architecture, showing nary a trace of the often bolder Chinese and Korean influences that dominate shrines elsewhere in Japan.

Naiku is a few kilometres from Geku. Here, as in the Outer Shrine, the object of attention is enclosed in a series of fences and can be viewed only from the front of a thatched-roof gate in the outermost fence.

Naiku is said to contain the *yata no kagami* (sacred mirror), which, along with a sword and a jewel, constitute the Three Sacred Treasures of the Japanese imperial throne. Mythology says that the mirror was handed by Amaterasu Omikami to her grandson when he descended from heaven to reign on earth. She gave him the gift of rice agriculture and a blessing for Japan.

One of the various facilities of the Ise Shrine.

Neon lights on Dotonbori Canal, Osaka.

OSAKA AND KOBE

Tokyo may be where the bureaucrat and banker confer, but Osaka is where the entrepreneur and marketeer huddle, making it Japan's centre of commerce, with a gritty, refreshing straightforwardness.

Kyoto can lay fair claim to be Kansai's cultural heart, but it's Osaka – and to a lesser extent Kobe – that really epitomise the hustle and bustle for which Kansai is best known. Osaka has its fair share of historic attractions (where in Japan doesn't?) with the mighty Osaka Castle and temples such as Shitenno-ji, but it's areas like the buzzing, neon-drenched Dotonbori entertainment district, with its restaurants, bars and theatres, that best represent the city. The entertainment continues out in Osaka Bay, where the Universal Studios Japan amusement park is a huge draw for Japanese travellers. Like Osaka, Kobe offers visitors a mixture of fun and tradition. The European architecture in the Kitano-cho area, not to mention the colourful Nankinmachi Chinatown, can trace their roots to the early days of Kobe Port, while the Rokko Island development is all modern amusements. Away from these two cities, Himeji makes for one of the most rewarding day trips in Japan for anyone with an interest in feudal history – Himeji-jo is without a doubt the finest original castle still standing in Japan.

Commerical conduit

Some Japanese look askance at **Osaka ⓫**, as if it belonged to another

somewhat unrelated part of the hemisphere. Its humour is different and a bit more rollicking than Tokyo. Even the language and intonation have a gritty, home-cooked flavour, raising eyebrows of disdain in sophisticated and bureaucratic Tokyo. Osaka is known for the character of its people: straightforward, business-savvy jaywalkers who know how to eat well. While sophisticated Kyotoites are said to spend their money on clothes, Osakans prefer to dispose of their hard-earned yen on culinary exploits.

Main Attractions

Osaka Castle
Semba
Dotonbori
America-mura
Shitenno-ji temple
Osaka Bay
Kitano-cho
Port Island and Rokko Island
Takarazuka
Himeji

Kita-ku, Osaka.

Arima at night, Hyogo.

stone coffins mined from nearby tombs can be seen in one part of the precinct. The contribution of a millstone, from a woman living in the town below the castle, is still remembered today.

The castle was never tested in battle, but walking up past the succession of defensive lines – three concentric moats surrounding high, curved ramparts punctuated by gates and watchtowers with arrow slits and gun ports – it seems an impregnable bastion. Roads within the castle grounds twist and turn, the better to confuse hostile forces if the outer defences were breached, and the uppermost floors of the castle contain hidden places where troops could continue to shoot at the enemy until the bitter end.

Himeji-jo is a hillock (as distinct from a mountain or flatland) castle atop a 45-metre (150ft) hill. There are spectacular views from the main *don-jon*, which rises 30 metres (100ft) from the castle grounds. *Shachihoko*, huge ornamental fish that were strategically placed on the roof as charms to ward off fire, can be seen close up from the top floor; some now support lightning rods.

Blossoms at Himeji-jo.

An attractive angle on Himeji-jo in any season is from the grounds of the surprisingly quiet **Himeji Koko-en** (daily, mid-Apr–Aug 9am–6pm, Sept–mid-Apr 9am–5pm), located next to the castle moat on the site of old samurai residences. Built in 1992, to celebrate the 100th anniversary of the Himeji receiving city status, Koko-en is a beautiful composite of nine separate Edo-style gardens with a teahouse and pools with carp. You can buy a combined ticket to the castle and gardens.

The **Hyogo-kenritsu Rekishi Hakubutsukan** (Hyogo Prefectural Museum of History; Tue–Sun 10am–5pm) nearby to the north contains informative displays about Japanese castles, including the most magnificent of them all, Himeji. It is the best of Himeji's several museums. For information on others, as well as on several worthwhile shrines, visit the **tourist office** (daily 9am–7pm) by the central exit of JR Himeji Station; the English-speaking staff here can help you plan a full day's worth of activities and also have free rental bicycles, which make for a great way to get around the city.

Earthquakes

From time to time over the centuries, major quakes have wreaked havoc on Japan, most recently the devastating earthquake in Tohoku on 11 March 2011.

Japan is highly prone to earthquakes. There are minor shakes recorded on seismological instruments almost every day, and bigger ones that startle people from their sleep, rattle dishes and knock objects off shelves occur several times a year.

The reason for the earthquakes is that the Japanese archipelago is at a place where three moving segments of the earth's crust – the Pacific Plate, the Philippine Plate and the Eurasian Plate – come into violent contact. This also explains Japan's volcanic activity and its many hot springs.

The Philippine Plate is the prime culprit, sliding in under central Honshu in a northeastern direction at about 3cm (1.25in) a year. The movement, in turn, puts stress on the primary fault that affects Tokyo and other earthquake-prone regions. Add to this a nest of faults spread widely under the islands, sometimes as deep as 100km (60 miles).

In Tokyo, the danger from earthquakes is made worse because much of the city is on unconsolidated alluvial soil and on landfill. This is a very poor foundation, which makes buildings tremble and oscillate more than they would on solid ground. Much of the waterfront damage during the 1995 Kobe earthquake was also because of landfill liquification, and a great deal of the remaining damage was due to fire from burst gas mains.

A country at risk

A major tremor whiplashes the Tokyo area every 60 or 70 years on average, and the last one, the Great Kanto Earthquake – a 7.9-magnitude jolt on the Richter scale – took place in 1923. At that time, most of the central part of the city was levelled and totally destroyed by fire, and more than 100,000 people were killed. Close to Ryogoku Station, 40,000 people were incinerated when a fire tornado swept across an open area where they had sought safety. More recently, in Kobe, earthquake-proof structures collapsed like jelly during a 7.2-magnitude earthquake in 1995. Rescue and relief plans proved unworkable, and government response, both on the local and national levels, was inept and embarrassingly inadequate. Nearly 6,000 people died.

Experts say that Tokyo is now much safer than it was in 1923, and far safer than Kobe in 1995. Buildings, bridges and elevated highways are reinforced and built according to the latest techniques, something in which Japan has invested heavily in recent decades. In addition, much of the city is been made fireproof. There are also shelters and elaborate plans to provide help should the worst happen.

But there are still concerns about whether or not Japan – and the world's largest metropolitan area, Tokyo – can ever be fully prepared.

Tokyo is the world's most populated city, with extensive underground networks of subways and gas lines, and above ground, glass-covered buildings and many flimsily constructed residences. In a reassessment of Tokyo's preparedness after the catastrophic earthquake of 3/11, experts believe a 7.3-magnitude earthquake (with a *shindo* intensity level of 7) directly under northern Tokyo Bay could destroy some 390,000 buildings and kill 9,600 people in the Greater Tokyo area.

Nishinomiya after the Kobe earthquake in 1995.

KIMONOS FOR ALL SEASONS AND STYLES

Adopted from ancient Chinese court attire, the Japanese kimono today is mostly a ceremonial dress of exquisite textures and appeal.

Western dress is the norm amongst today's Japanese, and few wear traditional attire except on special occasions such as weddings or festivals. But when a busy street of suited businessmen and trendy schoolgirls is punctuated by the colours and elegance of a kimono, Japan momentarily reverts to another time and place.

Contrary to popular belief, the kimono did not originate in Japan. Like many things "distinctly" Japanese, the kimono has its roots in China – the Chinese court. During the Nara Period (710–84), the Japanese imperial court adopted the Chinese-style *p'ao*, a long, kimono-like gown brilliant with colours and embellishment; kimono styles used by Japanese women during this time were similar to the *p'ao* garments of women in Tang-dynasty China. Indeed, the Heian-era court dress worn by Japan's emperor and empress today during special occasions displays Chinese characteristics unchanged since the 12th century.

As did most things adopted by the Japanese over the centuries, the kimono underwent changes that eventually made it distinctly Japanese. During the Muromachi Period (1338–1573), for example, women introduced the *obi* (sash), and adapted the kimono sleeves to fit Japanese climate and styles.

Visit a shrine in November and you might see kids – girls aged 3 or 7 and boys aged 5 – in kimono as part of the Shichi-go-san rituals.

Kyoto is a great place to discover kimono. You could wander about Gion hoping for a glimpse of a geisha, or better yet take a trip to the Nishijin Textile Centre for the daily kimono fashion show.

Geisha and maiko are the most obvious examples of kimono being worn for work, but the traditional attire is also worn by staff at ryokan and in some traditional restaurants.

The obi (sash) – often ornate and made of embroidered silk – today is about 25 cm (10 in) wide and 3.7 m (12 ft) long.

THE OBI: SIMPLE AND EXQUISITE

Once a simple and narrow sash introduced by Muromachi Period women, the *obi* has evolved into one of the most beautiful – and complicated – aspects of the kimono today.

The *obi*'s need came about when the Japanese made changes to the adopted Chinese-court *p'ao*. A short-sleeved form of kimono *(kosode)* began to be worn as an outer garment, constrained by the *obi*. Later, the *obi* took on increased importance when women of the feudal estates wore an elaborate and exquisite outer kimono called *uchikake*. As centuries passed, only married women wore the *kosode*, while unmarried women wore the long-sleeved *furisode*.

The wider and more embellished silk sash seen today developed in the early 1700s during the Edo Period. This *obi* can be tied in a number of ways and may be embellished with *netsuke*, beautifully carved images used to cinch cords and fasten the details of the woman's *obi*.

Most young Japanese rarely, if ever, wear traditional kimono like these – more commonly they might wear a light cotton yukata to a summer festival or at an onsen.

While the basic kimono design is consistent and often features seasonal motifs, regional and ceremonial differences abound. There are even subtle differences between kimono for single and married women.

It's not just the kimono itself that has to be immaculate. A lot of time and effort also has to go into the accompanying hair and make-up.

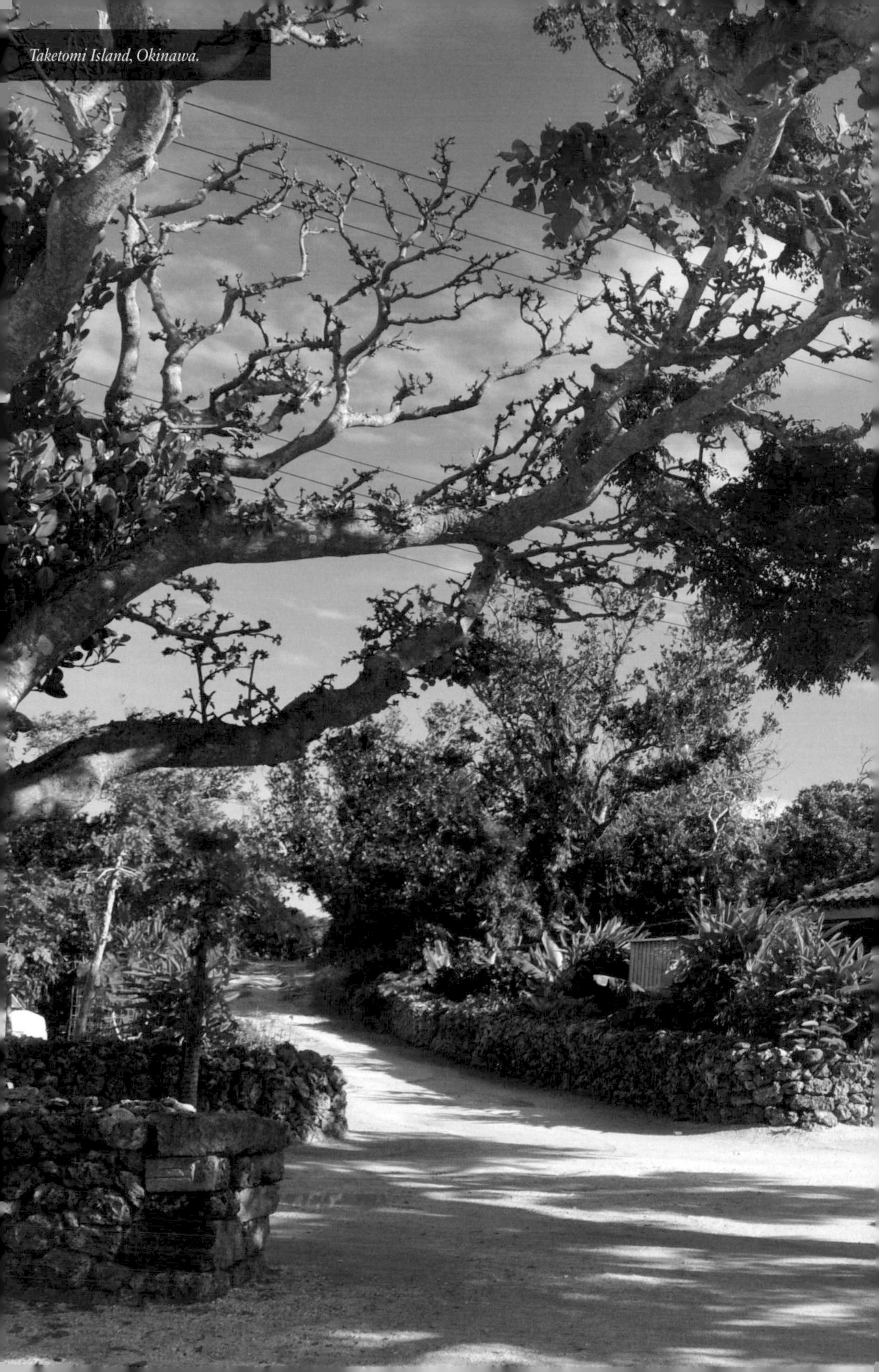

Taketomi Island, Okinawa.

THE SOUTH

Southern Japan includes western Honshu and two main islands, Kyushu and Shikoku, along with Okinawa.

Itsukushima-jinja, Hiroshima.

The "south" is called "western" Japan by the Japanese, although this part of the archipelago does extend southwards. Chugoku (Western Honshu), Shikoku and Kyushu are all very different, yet have one element in common: Seto Naikai, or the Inland Sea. All three regions also face the open ocean, and as a result, each area has widely varying climates and local qualities.

The Honshu coast along the Inland Sea, where you will find Hiroshima, is markedly different from the Sea of Japan (East Sea) side. Likewise, Shikoku, the smallest of Japan's four main islands, could as well be in a different hemisphere from the one occupied by the islands of Okinawa. As for Kyushu, there are those who believe this large island, particularly the southern part, is a nation unto itself and who cite the long tradition of fierce independence stemming from the Satsuma clans, not to mention Kyushu's thick dialect, as proof.

Even in the most populous and industrial cities of Kyushu and Shikoku, and even Chugoku, the pace is mellow compared with Tokyo and Osaka. Not all is idyllic down this way, however. The southern parts lie in the path of seasonal typhoons and thus are regularly given good soakings by torrential rains. Moreover, there are more active volcanoes on Kyushu than on any other Japanese island.

Ibusuki public hot spring, Kyushu.

These volcanoes have given the archipelago an unlimited variety of ceramic-quality clays, along with natural chemicals for glazes. Kyushu and parts of Chugoku are noted for their hearty pottery, an art form with a considerable amount of Korean influence.

Shikoku, Chugoku and Kyushu are large enough to keep travellers occupied for quite some time. Smaller gems await even further south, however. Like pearls upon the ocean, islands drip away from Kyushu's southern tip and stretch down to within 200km (125 miles) of Taiwan. This string of islands, Nansai-shoto, is over 1,200km (750 miles) in length. Best known by foreigners is Okinawa for its historical importance in World War II and also for its cultural uniqueness.

Chugoku and Shikoku

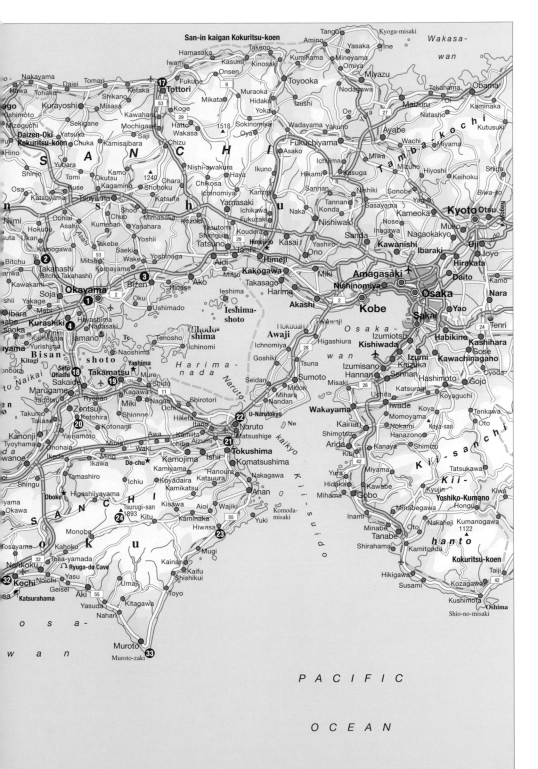

San-in kaigan Kokuritsu-koen

PACIFIC

OCEAN

CHUGOKU

Chugoku means "centre country", and this varied region was once Japan's heartland, with the historic towns and shrines to prove it – as well as the evocative city of Hiroshima and its altogether more recent associations.

Main Attractions

Okayama
Takahashi
Kurashiki
Tomonoura
Hiroshima
Miyajima
Yamaguchi
Tsuwano
Hagi
Matsue

Most travellers would look at a map of Japan's main island of Honshu and consider Chugoku to be the southern part. The Japanese, however, consider it to be the western part. In fact, of course, it is southwest. Compass directions aside, the Chugoku region spreads over the bottom third of Honshu, bounded by Seto Naikai (Inland Sea) to the south and the Sea of Japan (East Sea) to the north. Not many foreign travellers get to Chugoku other than to its main cities of Okayama and Hiroshima. The region includes the prefectures of Okayama, Hiroshima, Yamaguchi, Shimane and Tottori, and it offers some splendid views of rustic Japan, especially along the Sea of Japan (East Sea) coast.

Seto Naikai, or the Seto Inland Sea, is a 9,500-sq km (3,700-sq mile) body of water surrounded by Kyushu, Shikoku and the western extent of Honshu, dotted with more than 1,000 small islands. Osaka, Kobe and Hiroshima are all on the sea's coast. Although largely industrialised these days, the sea coast still retains some exquisite vistas, enough for the area to have been designated Japan's first national park in 1934 (for more about the different islands in the Inland Sea, see page 305).

The Chugoku region's most visited sites are Hiroshima, with its Gempaku Dome and Peace Memorial Park a

testament to the horrors of nuclear conflict, and the nearby floating shrine at Miyajima. But the region offers more than its most common postcard images. On the Seto Naikai coast, the town of Kurashiki reveals a sophisticated tradition of crafts and art, while towns like Tsuwano are rich with remnants of medieval Japan. Take time to explore the whole region and you will be treated to the intriguing mix of rural traditions, Edo-era history, ancient myth and Western influences that make Chugoku so diverse.

Genbaku Dome and Cenotaph, Hiroshima.

FACT

Though the trams themselves are modern, iron tracks and worn stone are part of Okayama's endearingly aged streetcar system. Called *chin chin densha* in Japanese – a euphonic rendering of the sound made by the starting bell – Okayama has a system that is both efficient, cheap and well supported.

Koraku-en, Okayama.

Okayama

The rapidly growing city of **Okayama** ❶ has asserted itself as the region's most dynamic metropolis. For this reason it often finds itself playing host to visiting foreigners, mostly on business and not for sightseeing, although it does have a handful of worthwhile attractions. The most notable of these, the **Koraku-en** (Koraku Garden; www.okayama-korakuen.jp; daily, 20 Mar–Sept 7.30am–6pm, Oct–19 Mar 8am–5pm) was originally laid out in 1686 for the warlord Ikeda. Located on an island in the Asahi-gawa across from **Okayama-jo** (Okayama or Crow Castle because of its black exterior; daily 9am–5.30pm), Koraku-en is unusual for its large grassy areas and the cultivation of such crops as rice and wheat. Tea is also grown and harvested here and teahouses are scattered throughout the fine strolling garden, which Japan ranks among its top three.

Other sights in Okayama include the **Orient Museum**, with exhibits tracing the impact of Near Eastern civilisation on Japan; the **Okayama Prefectural Museum of Art**; and the compact **Yumeji Art Museum**, with works by Yumeji Takehisa (all Tue–Sun 9am–5pm).

Takahashi

Takahashi ❷ is one of those towns it is easy to overlook. Lying 40km (25 miles) northwest of Okayama, it takes just under one hour to get here by rail on the JR Hakubi Line, a pleasant journey along the attractive, well-contoured Takahashi-gawa. The shallow, winding river is well stocked with *ayu* (sweetfish), a local speciality found on the menus of most of the town's traditional restaurants or, sprinkled with salt and smoked over a charcoal brazier, served from roadside stalls.

Takahashi enjoys a modest celebrity among travellers and cognoscenti of curious and obscure places. A provincial town with mountain and valley setting, its cultural credentials are unimpeachable, and most of its sights are conveniently located within walking distance of the station.

Pausing to pick up a local map at the information office (Mon–Fri 8am–6pm, Sat 8.30am–5pm) at the bus terminus beside the station, make your way to **Raikyu-ji** (daily 9am–5pm), a Rinzai school of Zen temple; the temple's date of origin is disputed, but most historians concur that a rebuilding took place under the orders of the shogun Ankoku in 1339. However illustrious the temple and its collection of hanging scrolls and sutras may be, it is its magnificent garden that sets the site apart.

Created by Kobori Enshu, a member of the local nobility who would go on to become one of the foremost designers of gardens in Japanese landscape history, the small but dynamic balanced asymmetry of the garden is classified as a *karesansui* (dry landscape) type. Enshu finished the garden, also known as "Tsurukame Garden" on account of its crane- and turtle-shaped islands (signifying longevity), in 1609. Mount Atago can be glimpsed in the distance beyond the garden proper, forming the classic "borrowed view" frequently incorporated into such designs.

If Raikyu-ji represents Takahashi's spiritual and artistic heritage, **Takahashi-jo** (also known as Bitchu-Matsuyama-jo; daily, Apr–Sept 9am–5.30pm, Oct–Mar 9am–4.30pm), the town's castle, stands for its martial traditions. This well-appointed fortress, constructed on the peak of Gagyuzan-san, is at 430 metres (1,400ft) Japan's highest castle, something of a tourist draw for the town. Adding to elevation as a formidable defence, the lower and middle levels of the mountain were further fortified with samurai villas and farmhouses designed to act as a second line of defence in the event (tested on several occasions) of attack. Interestingly enough, many of the homes here in the district of **Ishibiya-cho**, grand constructions sitting on raised ground above stone walls and foundations, are still occupied by the descendants of Takahashi's old samurai families.

Meiji- and Taisho-era wooden buildings and private estates face the Kouyagawa as it runs through the centre of Takahashi, their Japanese features mixing effortlessly with the occidental experimentation in architecture associated with the time. The Takahashi church and the wooden Takahashi Elementary School, now serving, along with the **Haibara Samurai House** (daily 9am–5pm) in Ishibiya-cho as local history museums, are good examples of this blending. Like the Haibara Samurai House, the **Takahashi History Museum** (Wed–Mon 9am–5pm) houses items closely associated with this period of contact with the West, expressing Japan's fascination with Western science, design and the new technology that would lead to the transformation of Japan from a feudal backwater to an advanced nation. Exhibits include an old Morse code set, a symbol and harbinger of modernity, period clocks and a microscope. There are also local exhibits pre-dating this period, and a fine collection of black-and-white photos of the town.

Bizen ❸, about 45 minutes by train east along the coast from Okayama, is famous for its unglazed, coarse pottery that is frequently enhanced by

Raikyu-ji Zen Garden, Takahashi.

Making Bizen pottery.

Takahashi Castle.

kiln "accidents", such as a stray leaf or a bit of straw sticking to the side of a pot that leaves an interesting pattern after firing. There are more than 100 kilns in Imbe, the 700-year-old pottery-making section of Bizen, along with several museums, including the **Bizen Togei Bijutsukan** (Ceramics Museum; Tue–Sun 9.30am–5pm) and Fujiwara Kei Kinenkan gallery.

Kurashiki

West of Okayama, **Kurashiki ❹** is a textile-producing city containing the pearl of Japanese tourist attractions: an arts district that brings world-class Japanese and international art and traditional crafts together in an exquisite setting. Some 13.5 hectares (33 acres) of 300-year-old rice warehouses, Meiji-era factories, and the homes of samurai and wealthy merchant families have been elegantly preserved and converted into museums, craft shops and art galleries. Kurashiki is for walkers, with most of the attractions within a block or two of the central canal. The streets and alleys bordering on this canal look much as they did during the

town's cultural and economic zenith in the 18th century. Automobiles are not allowed to disturb the atmosphere of its preserved quarter.

During the Edo Period, Kurashiki was a central collection and storage site for the shogun's taxes and tribute – paid in rice – from communities throughout western Honshu, Seto Naikai and Shikoku. Numerous stone rice warehouses *(kura)* are clustered around willow-lined canals, thus giving the town its name. Their striking designs employ black tiles deeply set in bright-white mortar, capped by roofs of black tile. Stone bridges, arched so that barges piled high with sacks of rice from the hinterland could pass below them, span the waterways. Kurashiki's preservation was largely the work of Ohara Magosaburo, the wealthy scion of Kurashiki's leading family. The Ohara family's textile mills were the primary source of employment in Kurashiki during the Meiji Period, by which time rice levies had been replaced by cash taxes, thus making the city's huge rice warehouses redundant.

Ohara Magosaburo built the nation's first museum of Western art in 1930, the **Ohara Museum of Art** (www.ohara. or.jp; Tue–Sun 9am–5pm), and stocked it with works by El Greco, Monet, Matisse, Renoir, Gauguin and Picasso. The neoclassical building remains the city's centrepiece, although new galleries have proliferated around it over the years. The restored *kura* next to the main gallery are likely to be of more interest to visitors already familiar with European art as they contain Japanese folk art and a fine collection of ancient Chinese art. Other rooms are devoted to the works of the great *mingei* (Japanese folk art) potters such as Hamada Shoji, Kawai Kanjiro and Tomimoto Kenkichi.

Many of Kurashiki's warehouses-turned-art-houses are devoted to preserving and revitalising *mingei*. Among the most interesting is the **Japanese Rural Toy Museum** (daily 9am–5pm). The first floor is packed

with traditional Japanese toys, dolls and kites, while a collection of toys from around the world can be seen on the second floor. In all there are over 5,000 toys on display. The adjacent toy store is as interesting as the museum. Next door, the **Kurashiki Mingei-kan** (Museum of Folk Craft; Tue–Sun, Mar–Nov 9am–5pm, Dec–Feb 9am–4.15pm) displays around 4,000 simple, hand-made objects that are or were used in everyday life. The building that houses this museum was remodelled from four two-storey wooden rice granaries.

Visitors can learn about the daily life of one of Kurashiki's leading families at the **Ohashi House** (Tue–Sun 9am–5pm, Apr–Oct Sat until 6pm), constructed in 1796 for a merchant family. Of samurai status, the house is much larger than typical merchant houses of that time. Note the unusual roof tiles. Ivy Square, an arts complex created out of the red-brick textile factories that brought about the Ohara family fortune, houses the Kurabo Memorial Hall, with displays on the textile industry as well as scores of shops and restaurants.

Tomonoura

Some 14km (9 miles) south of the JR *shinkansen* stop at Fukuyama, a 30-minute bus ride from outside the station takes you to the delightful fishing port of **Tomonoura ⑤**. In this well-preserved but working town at the very extremity of the Numakuma Peninsula, southern enough for garden cacti, one may savour the smell of the sea, squawking gulls and the sight of kites wheeling over temple roofs. And fleeting images of history. The warrior Masashige passed through here on his way to Kyushu, as did the Empress Jingu.

Succoured, as it always has been by the sea, Tomonoura has not entirely escaped Japan's post-war uglification programme, as some of its cement installations testify. The town seems to have had its last flirt with concrete in the 1980s, however, and then mercifully left it at that.

The waters here are abundant in sea bream, a local speciality. You'll also see octopus, caught on lines rather than in pots or nets, being hauled from the water just below the sea walls, gleaming

The port town of Tomonoura.

Punting at Bikan District, Kurashiki, Okayama.

and full of life. The raised bund along the port also provides space for women to set up stalls under temporary plastic roofing, where the local catch is displayed and tasty fare sold. Shrimps are sold directly from their drying frames, from street stalls or from the doorways and entrance halls of private homes, conveying the largely accurate impression that most of the inhabitants of this village are engaged in one way or another with the sea.

The sea bream netting methods can be glimpsed in simulated form in the models and photographs at the **Tomonoura Museum of History** (Tue–Sun 10am–5pm). From the museum grounds, a commanding view of grey, undulating ceramic roofs, their eaves interlocking, suggests a community that is also tightly knit. Donald Richie (see Further Reading, page 397), a profoundly attentive traveller, described the town at the end of the 1960s as having "the casual look of most towns where progress has been late in arriving. It is a crosswork of little streets like those in Italian mountain villages."

Tomonoura fishing village.

Tagashima-jo, the ruins of an old castle that once stood on the headland above the harbour, and its adjacent temple, Empuku-ji, offer another angle on the town. Here you can glimpse the harbour to the west, and **Benten-jima**, a tiny island, to the east. Of Indian provenance, the goddess Benten is a sensuous figure, now firmly inducted into the Shinto pantheon and serving as the patroness of music, the arts and beauty.

Half the enjoyment of this little town, where it is still possible to lose your bearings, is to explore its labyrinth of lanes and stone alleys, noting the old wooden houses, ship's chandlers, and the bijoux gardens that can be glimpsed behind timeworn fences. One area of streets near the harbour contains the **Shichikyo-ochi Ruins**, a misleading name for what is in fact a graceful ensemble of wood-and-plaster sake breweries and warehouses dating from the mid-18th to the 19th century.

Despite its diminutive scale, there are several temples of note in Tomonoura. **Io-ji** was supposedly founded by Kobo Daishi, a priest who, if only half

the temples that claim a connection are true, must have been one of Buddhism's most itinerant pilgrims. **Fukuzen-ji** (daily 8am–5pm), a reception hall located near the ferry terminus and once used to receive Korean missions, inspired flights of calligraphy from envoys, such as the man of letters I-pan-o, who were overcome with the beauty of the view. Only slightly disfigured by small concrete installations and power lines, it remains largely intact.

Moving west along the coast, **Onomichi** ➏ was an important commercial port 800 years ago. Wealthy merchants flocked to the city during the Edo Period, building 81 temples on the steep slopes overlooking the sea to celebrate their prosperity. With the coming of the railway in the late 19th century, however, commerce literally passed the city by. Because of its relative lack of importance, American bombers also passed by Onomichi, and when the *shinkansen* route was mapped, Onomichi was passed over again. As a result of its slide into relative obscurity, the city has retained

much of its pre-Meiji heritage. Some 25 of the old temples remain, the most interesting being the 1,100-year-old **Senko-ji**, which is best reached via the tram. From here, walk down the hill towards town, taking in as many temples as you can stand.

Hiroshima

One moment – 8.15am, 6 August 1945 – irrevocably changed world history. An atomic flash signalled the instant destruction of **Hiroshima** ➐, the eventual loss of over 200,000 lives, and for ever linked the city's name with nuclear holocaust and mass killings. The immediate and lasting impact on Hiroshima gives concrete reality to the horrors of atomic and nuclear war. Unlike Nagasaki, the second city to receive such an attack but which doesn't dwell much on past history, there seem to be reminders of Hiroshima's atomic bombing around virtually every corner in the city.

Amazingly, Hiroshima's people quickly rebuilt a vibrant city from the ashes, making it larger and more prosperous than the old one and

TIP

The best way to see Hiroshima is from a tram. As other Japanese cities tore up their tram lines after World War II, their cars were sent to Hiroshima; as a result, the city acquired an eclectic collection of tram cars, many dating back to the 1940s.

People in front of Yayoi Kusama's art installation on Naoshima Island.

ISLANDS OF THE SETO NAIKAI

The islands that bejewel the Seto Inland Sea have a diversity of riches. The most prominent of the islands, **Naoshima** (see page 319), has risen to international attention for the contemporary art galleries that have transformed it from a collection of sleepy fishing communities to an undoubted high point on Japan's art scene. Often overlooked, however, are smaller islands nearby, such as **Teshima** and its picturesque rice terraces and the quiet **Inu-jima** – both have had less dramatic, but nonetheless impressive, art renaissances.

Naoshima's larger neighbour, **Shodoshima** (see page 320), is an altogether different affair. Head here not for art, but to soak up the slow-paced, traditional way of life. Many of the islanders are still involved in Shodoshima's traditional industries of fishing, soy sauce production and making sesame oil.

Away to the west, off the coast off Onomichi, **Ikuchi-jima** reveals another side of the Seto Naikai. Palm-lined beaches and citrus groves make it a beautiful setting for one of Japan's most distinctive temples, Kosan-ji – known as the "Nikko of the west" because of its flamboyant design. Rounding out the variety is **Omishima** next door, which has one of the oldest shrines in the country, the Kamakura-era Oyamazumi-jinja. You could easily amuse yourself for weeks hopping from island to island.

Hiroshima Castle.

*Peace Memorial
Museum in Hiroshima.*

leaving a few carefully chosen scars to memorialise its abiding atomic legacy. Hiroshima was chosen for the first atomic-bomb attack because of its military importance. The city was one of Japan's most vital military depots and industrial areas (a fact that goes unmentioned in the atomic bomb museum). However, Hiroshima's military significance pre-dates World War II by several hundred years: troops were staged here in preparation for the invasion of Korea in 1582. A castle incorporating the latest construction and defensive techniques was built here seven years later by the Mori clan. It rested on pilings driven into reclaimed swampland, and the outer moats were built above the level of the surrounding land so that their walls could be breached, flooding the plain where siege troops would likely mass. The castle was an important bastion of the Tokugawa shogun's forces, a western outpost facing the often hostile Choshu and Satsuma clans.

In the 19th century, **Hiroshima-jo Ⓐ** (Hiroshima Castle; daily, Mar–Nov 9am–6pm, Dec–Feb 9am–5pm) was occupied by the emperor during the occupation of Manchuria. The castle also served as an important Japanese Army headquarters during World War II and was completely destroyed by the atomic bomb. Reconstructed in 1958, the castle contains an excellent museum.

A few blocks east of the castle, **Shukkei-en Ⓑ** (Shukkei Garden; http://shukkeien.jp; daily, Apr–Sept 9am–6pm, Oct–Mar 9am–5pm) was built on the banks of the Kyobashi-gawa in 1620 in emulation of a famous Chinese lake. Early spring brings cherry blossoms to the garden, while azaleas bloom a little later, and multicoloured carp inhabit the garden's central pond throughout the year.

The **Heiwa Kinen-koen Ⓒ** (Peace Memorial Park), southwest of the castle and wedged between the Motoyasu and Ota rivers, is adjacent to the **Genbaku Domu Ⓓ** (Atomic Dome), a World Heritage site that marks ground zero of Hiroshima's atomic explosion. At its maximum intensity, the temperature approached that on the sun's surface and almost everything within sight was

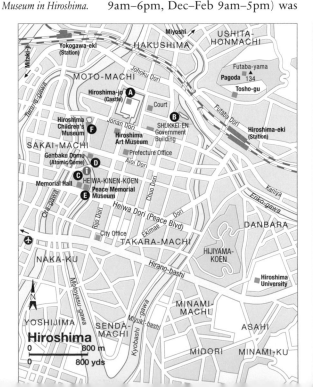

vapourised instantly. The famous building with the carefully maintained skeletal dome once housed the Industrial Promotion Hall and was one of the few surviving vertical structures. Today the park has a serene air; men perhaps old enough to remember the explosion sit meditatively on benches, the sonorous tones of the Peace Bell echo through the trees, and the solemnity is disturbed only by the exuberance of children who dash about with clipboards in hand for their school projects and then stand silent in prayer before the many shrines.

Tange Kenzo designed the heart of the park complex, which comprises the **Peace Memorial Museum** Ⓔ (www.pcf.city.hiroshima.jp; daily, Mar–Nov 8.30am–6pm, Aug 8.30am–7pm, Dec–Feb 8.30am–5pm), Peace Memorial Hall, the Cenotaph and Peace Flame. The museum contains graphic portrayals of the bombing. Although the museum is filled with powerful images of terrible suffering, it certainly is not the hall of horrors one might expect. A visit is nonetheless an emotional experience, even though the museum has been accused of failing to place the bombing in historical perspective, mainly as a result of right-wing nationalist opposition – it seems to suggest that the bomb fell on Hiroshima, figuratively as well as literally, out of the blue. There is little mention of Japan's brutal war record, and the suffering meted out on other peoples. However, all this may change significantly as exhibits and viewing routes were being revised at the time of writing. The work at the museum's east building will be completed in spring 2016, while the main building will be closed for renovation until 2018.

The **Cenotaph**'s inverted U-shape reflects the design of the thatched-roof houses of Japanese antiquity. It contains a stone chest with the names of the victims of the atomic bombing and bears an inscription, "Sleep in peace: the error will not be repeated". The **Peace Flame** and Atomic Dome can be seen through it. The statue of the children killed by the bombing is dedicated to Sasaki Sadako, who died of leukemia caused by radiation when she was just 12 years old. She

Photograph of the injured on the day of the atomic bomb in Hiroshima.

BLACK RAIN

"It was like a white magnesium flash… We first thought to escape to the parade grounds, but we couldn't because there was a huge sheet of fire in front of us… Hiroshima was completely enveloped in flames. We felt terribly hot and could not breathe well at all. After a while, a whirlpool of fire approached us from the south. It was like a big tornado of fire spreading over the full width of the street. Whenever the fire touched, wherever the fire touched, it burned… After a while, it began to rain. The fire and the smoke made us so thirsty… As it began to rain, people opened their mouths and turned their faces towards the sky and tried to drink the rain… It was a black rain with big drops."

Takakura Akiko

300 metres (1,000ft) from ground zero

believed that if she could fold 1,000 paper cranes – a symbol of happiness and longevity for Japanese – she would be cured. Despite her illness, she managed to complete folding 1,000 cranes. As she did not get better, she started on a second thousand. She had reached some 1,500 when she finally died in 1955, 10 years after the atomic bomb exploded. Her spirited actions inspired an outpouring of national feeling and her classmates completed the second thousand paper cranes. Today, schoolchildren from all over the country bring paper cranes by the tens of thousands to lay around Sadako's memorial, a tribute that is simultaneously heart-rending, beautiful, and a terrible condemnation of militarism.

Many visitors ring the Peace Bell before crossing the Motoyasu-gawa to the dome. Colourful rowing boats can be rented by the hour near the **Heiwa Ohashi** (Peace Bridge), offering a more cheerful perspective on Hiroshima. Sightseeing cruises depart from the nearby pier. By the river, and just east of the Peace Memorial Museum, is

Peace Memorial Park and Cenotaph, Hiroshima.

the **Hiroshima Children's Museum** **F** (www.pyonta.city.hiroshima.jp; Tue–Sun 9am–5pm; free except for planetarium). It offers a refreshing break from the sombre park, with a planetarium and plenty of fun, hands-on science exhibits.

Half an hour away and northwest of central Hiroshima, **Mitaki-ji** is set in a lush forest with three waterfalls. Buddhas adorn the hillsides, and a fierce, life-size baby-killing devil statue of wood hangs out on the temple's porch. A friendly dog often welcomes visitors to the teahouse, which is decorated with a colourful collection of masks and kites. The walk from the central train station to the temple grounds passes a group of graves belonging to many unknown atomic-bomb victims.

Miyajima

Though it is formally called **Itsukushima** (Strict Island), this major Hiroshima-area tourist attraction, which boasts World Heritage status, is better known as **Miyajima** **8**, the Island of Shrines. To find the spirit and splendour of Miyajima, one of the country's

holiest sites, visitors must make their way through herds of tame deer and the litter left by thousands of tourists. Most of the island is covered with uninhabited virgin forest. A good way to see it is from the 1.6km (1-mile) long cable car (http://miyajima-ropeway.info; daily, Mar–Oct 9am–5pm, Nov 8am–5pm, Dec–Feb 9am–4.30pm) that runs over Momijidani-koen to the top of Misen.

The large crimson *torii* (shrine gate), rising out of the sea in front of the **Itsukushima-jinja** (daily sunrise–sunset), is probably the most familiar Japanese cultural icon and representative of Shintoism. But this *torii*, which is plastered on nearly every travel poster and guidebook that has anything to do with Japan, hasn't suffered from the overexposure. For those who stay overnight on the island, it is especially breathtaking in the evening, when the crowds have returned to the mainland.

The current gate was built in 1874, but a similar *torii* has lured visitors for seven centuries. The island's spiritual roots are much older, however. The first shrine, honouring Amaterasu's three daughters – goddesses of the sea – was built in the 6th century. To maintain the island's "purity", births and deaths have been prohibited on Miyajima from the earliest times. The entire island was dedicated as a sanctuary by Taira no Kiyomori, who ordered the Itsukushima-jinga completely rebuilt in 1168.

Itsukushima-jinga itself rests on stilts and seems to float like a giant ship when the tide comes in. Costumes and masks used in the *bugaku* dance festival (first week of January) and the *noh* plays, performed in mid-April, are on display in the Asazaya (morning prayer room), which is reached via a bridge. Next to Itsukushima, one of the oldest *noh* theatres in Japan, built in 1568, also seems to float a few inches above the sea. A nearby building contains hundreds of government-designated National Treasures and Important Cultural Objects, including illuminated sutras made by the Taira clan in the 1160s.

A five-storey pagoda, built in 1407, and the hall of **Senjokaku** (A

The Yamaguchi-go steam train in Yamaguchi.

Torii at Miyajima.

Thousand Mats) are at the top of a hill behind Itsukushima-jinga. Senjokaku, built in 1587, is the great warlord Toyotomi Hideyoshi's contribution to Miyajima. The island has a number of noteworthy *matsuri*, like its February **Oyster Festival** and a pine torch parade in December. The best of these utilise the island and shrine's stunning setting. Look out for the 17 June Kangensai with its traditional music and boat parade, and on 14 August, the **Hanabi Matsuri**, a huge firework display in front of the shrine.

To the west

Iwakuni , 44km (27 miles) west of Hiroshima, is on both the *shinkansen* and JR San-yo Line. The stations are located to the west and east of the central area, where most of the sights are. Each has a useful tourist information office with handouts in English.

Iwakuni's premier sight is, without question, **Kintai-kyo** (http://kintai-kyo.iwakuni-city.net), the Brocade Sash Bridge, a graceful span that undulates between five steep arches, a popular image with tourist promoters and directors of TV samurai dramas looking for instant image bites. The original bridge, built in 1673, was destroyed in a flood in 1950. Rebuilt a few years later, the present construction is almost indistinguishable from the original. There's a small toll charge to cross the bridge.

On the far side of the bridge, **Kikko-koen**, a pleasant parkland area, includes the surviving residences of an old samurai district and a ruined moat that once served a castle, **Iwakuni-jo** (daily 9am–4.45pm; closed final two weeks of Dec). The castle was relocated into a more commanding and picturesque spot when it was rebuilt in 1960. There's a cable car to take you to the top of the hill, but the walk is hardly strenuous.

If you happen to be in Iwakuni during the summer months from June to August, you can, for a fee, board a night boat to observe *ukai*, a visually exciting, traditional method of fishing using cormorants and baskets of burning flames that light up the river surfaces.

Kintai-kyo, Iwakuni, Yamaguchi.

Yamaguchi

The bullet train does not number the provincial city of **Yamaguchi** ❿ among its stops, sparing it both excessive development and crowds of visitors. Just 30 minutes on the JR Yamaguchi Line from Ogori, the city's best-known form of transport is a 1937 locomotive, one of the few in Japan to remain in regular service. Operating during weekends and holidays from late March to November, the gleaming steam engine, called the **SL Yamaguchi-go**, runs between the castle town of Tsuwano and Shin-Yamaguchi. Tickets sell fast and need booking well in advance.

During the Sengoku era (1467–1573), Japan's century of anarchy, much of the cultural and political life of the country shifted to the relative security of Yamaguchi. Many literati, noblemen and their retinues sought refuge here, bringing with them the sensibilities and tastes of the imperial capital, Kyoto. Several of Yamaguchi's easily sought-out temples and shrines date from this period.

Japan's first Christian missionary, the Basque priest Francis Xavier, stayed in Yamaguchi for two months trying, without much success, to convert the locals. Xavier and his mission are still remembered with affection in Yamaguchi, though, where there is a gleaming **Yamaguchi Xavier Memorial Church**. A strikingly modern structure, a pyramid of silver and eggshell white, it is crowned with metallic towers, sculptures and a brace of suspended bells. Its stained-glass windows and coloured jars of burning candles create the effect of a slightly dimmed café-gallery.

Were the Yamaguchi Post Office to be looking for an image to place on a commemorative stamp of their prefectural capital, they would no doubt choose the city's magisterial five-storey pagoda, built in the grounds of the **Ruriko-ji** temple (grounds always open; free; pagoda museum: daily 9am–5pm). Made from Japanese cypress, each roof a fraction steeper than the one below it, the pagoda, typical of the Muromachi-era Zen Kyoto style, is strikingly situated beside an ornamental pond graced by bushes and topiary, the effect only slightly marred by a tape recording giving an account of the history of the building.

Sesshu-tei garden

A kilometre (0.6 miles) or so northeast of the pagoda, the **Sesshu-tei** (daily 8am–4.30pm, Apr–Sept until 5pm), named after its designer, the master painter and priest Sesshu, is a Zen-inspired garden, a combination of dry landscape and moss, an arrangement of stones, rocks, lawn and lily-pad pond. It's best viewed in its intended entirety from the broad wooden veranda at the rear of the temple, from where the garden resembles a horizontal scroll.

Transected by the only moderately busy Route 9, it is possible to preserve some of the serenity of Sesshu's garden by following a path along the **Ichinosaka-gawa** as it makes a sinuous course back to the town centre.

FACT

Yasaka-jinja is best known for its *Sagi-Mai*, a heron dance performed on 20 and 27 July by men dressed in plumes and heron-beaked headdresses. It is a little similar to a spring and autumn event performed by women at Asakusa's Senso-ji shrine in Tokyo.

Koi pond in Tsuwano.

TIP

The port of Shimonoseki provides a nightly ferry connection to Busan in Korea. With prices from just ¥9,000, the eight-hour crossing is an extremely cheap option if you are travelling around Asia. There are also low-cost ferry connections to parts of China. Check www.shimonoseki-port.com/e for details.

Crossed by pedestrian bridges, the banks of the stream, a place of water reeds and azaleas, is a popular walk in springtime when its cherry trees are in full blossom, while in the summer there are swarms of fireflies.

Tsuwano

Easily accessed from either Yamaguchi City or Hagi, **Tsuwano** ⓫ is one of the best-preserved medieval towns in Japan, and another of its "Little Kyotos" – but, unlike many other self-titled "Little Kyotos", Tsuwano really does live up to the billing. Its exquisite samurai and merchant houses, temples and museums are located in a narrow, photogenic ravine. An extraordinary 80,000 colourful carp live in shallow streams and culverts that run between the main road, Tonomachi-dori and the walls of the samurai residences. The fish were stocked as a food resource in case of a siege, and the streams would provide ready water in the event of fire.

The tourist information centre (daily 9am–5pm) near the station has a very decent English guidebook to the town. The centre is a good starting point to explore the old district of Tonomachi, beginning with the **Katsushika Hokusai Museum of Art** (daily 9.30–5pm), which has an exquisite collection of woodblock prints, paintings and illustrations by Hokusai Katsushika, arguably the 19th century's foremost Japanese artist, and known in particular for his depictions of Mount Fuji.

Following Tonomachi-dori southeast of the museum, the spire of Tsuwano's 1931 **Catholic Church** is visible. It's a modest sight, but worth a few minutes to view the stained-glass windows. A moderately interesting folk museum (Tsuwano Minzoku Museum; daily 8.30am–5pm) stands nearby on the banks of the Tsuwano-gawa. The building, known as the **Yorokan**, once served as a school for young samurai.

On the other side of the rail tracks from here are two shrines of interest – **Yasaka-jinja**, known for its July Heron Dance festival, and, further on, **Taikodani Inari-jinja**, an Inari fox shrine with a tunnel of bright-red *torii*

Castle town of Hagi, Yamaguchi.

gates wending its way uphill to the main shrine and its colourful Shinto paraphernalia.

Climb or take the cable car from here up to the site of **Tsuwano-jo**, remains of another hilltop castle with the best views of the town. The original castle was built in 1295 as a bulwark against a possible Mongol attack, a very real threat at that time. Ironically, it was the Meiji era's passion for reckless modernisation, and dismantling feudal castles, that reduced Tsuwano-jo to a ruin.

Crossing back over the river to the southeast end of town, the last sight of note, especially for those interested in Japanese literature, is the **Old House of Ogai Mori** (Tue–Sun 9am–5pm). A major novelist and essayist of the Meiji Period, Mori was born in Tsuwano in 1862. This house and museum, containing original manuscripts and personal effects, is very evocative of the period. Several of Ogai's works, including the novels *The Wild Geese* and *Vita Sexualis*, are available in English.

Shimonoseki

At the western limit of Honshu, **Shimonoseki** ⑫ is the gateway to Kyushu and to Korea as well, with *shinkansen* (bullet train) service to Hakata Station in Fukuoka and daily overnight ferries to Busan, South Korea. There isn't much reason to linger here, but one of the largest aquariums in Asia, the **Shimonoseki Kaikyokan** (www.kaikyokan.com; daily 9.30am–5.30pm), and the Akama shrine may be of interest to those waiting for a boat to Korea.

Shimonoseki has been an important port over many centuries, although today it is less so. The area was also the site of some of Japan's most important sea battles. History and literature students will recall that the final scenes of *Tale of the Heike* were set here. It is where the exiled empress dowager hurled herself and the infant emperor into the swirling tides. Several spots in the area claim

to be the actual location, but, in fact, any would do, as the cliffs are high and the waters do swirl frighteningly as the Sea of Japan (East Sea) meets the Seto Naikai.

Hagi

From Shimonoseki, the coastal road loops back east along the northern coast of Honshu and the Sea of Japan (East Sea). Samurai footsteps echo through the narrow streets in the heart of **Hagi** ⑬, and indeed the whole town resounds to the beat of historical events that have shaped Japan as it is today. If there is one reason to journey to this part of the coast, it is here in Hagi – a place that is as picturesque as it is fascinating.

Many of the statesmen who played significant parts in the Meiji Restoration came from here, Korean potters brought their art and flourished in Hagi, and it is the site of some of the earliest steps taken in glass-making.

Start where Hagi itself started, at the castle site at the foot of **Shizuki-san**. Built on the orders of Terumoto Mori in 1604, who then presided over the

FACT

Hagi pottery came to Japan in the wake of the warlord Toyotomi Hideyoshi's invasion of Korea in the 16th century. Two Korean potters were brought with the returning armies to practise their craft. Today there are some 100 kilns scattered about the city.

Hagi pottery.

Izumo-taisha, Shimane.

area that is now Yamaguchi Prefecture, the castle stood until 1874, when it was pulled down to express allegiance to the new Meiji government, which had returned the emperor to power. Parts of the walls and the former dungeon remain today (castle ruins: daily, Mar 8.30am–6pm, Apr–Oct 8am–6.30am, Nov–Feb 8.30am–4.30pm), and there's a Japanese teahouse in the adjacent gardens.

From here, head to the Asa Mori clan residence, the largest of the surviving samurai houses that arose in Hagi beyond the castle walls, or, just a few steps away beyond a natural, grassy sea wall, **Kikugahama beach**, a sandy curve with clean water for a pleasant swim. The streets of the castle town, or Jokamachi, were divided into three sections: one for lower-ranking samurai, a second for rich politicians and the third for merchants. As you wander its lanes – particularly Edoya, Iseya and Kikuya – every turn reveals another pocket of days gone by. Doctor's son Kido Takayoshi, one of the Meiji Restoration's dynamos, grew up in a house

on Edoya. Another prominent Restoration figure, Takasugi Shinsaku, lived on Kikuya and was cured of smallpox by Dr Aoki Shusuke, another inhabitant of Edoya. All their residences are on view to the public. After the Meiji Restoration, a number of *natsu mikan* (orange or tangerine) trees were planted in Hagi, mainly to provide some relief to the unemployed samurai. Many trees dot the Horiuchi (inner moat) district, and in May and June the scent of the blossoms is almost intoxicating.

Hagi's other great influence on Japan is its pottery, ranked the second-most beautiful in the country after that of Kyoto. At first glance it can appear deceptively simple and rustic, but closer examination reveals subdued colours and classical features, especially in the glazing that is exceptionally clear and vivid.

Lesser known is Hagi's glass, introduced around 1860 as the Edo Period drew to a close and using European techniques. After a century-long hiatus, the old techniques are now being used again to make Hagi glass.

Along the Sea of Japan (East Sea)

Further on along the coast, **Shimane** and its modest peninsula consist of three ancient districts: Izumo, Iwami and the islands of Oki-shoto. It is one of the longest-inhabited areas of Japan and offers special insights into the cultural heritage of the nation. **Izumo** ⑭ covers the eastern part of the prefecture and is known as the mythical province where the history of Japan began. Several shrines, temples and ancient buildings can be seen around the prefecture, including the **Taisha** ⑮ (shrine: always open, free; museum: daily 8.30am–4.30pm), the oldest Shinto shrine in the country. Dedicated to the spirit god of marriage, it is paid particular heed by couples.

Shinji ko sits at the eastern end of the prefecture. The lake's 45km (30-mile) coastline offers beautiful sights throughout the year, and sunset over the lake is one of the finest evening scenes in Japan. At the eastern end of the lake sits **Matsue-jo** (daily, Apr–Sept 8.30am–6.30pm, Oct–Mar 8.30am–5pm). Often called Plover Castle because of its shape, the castle was built in 1611 by Yoshiharu Horio, a samurai general. It is the only remaining castle in the Izumo area and very little has been done to modernise it, so the feeling inside is truly authentic. Across the castle moat to the north lies Shiominawate, an area where ranking samurai once lived.

Matsue ⑯ was also the home of a renowned writer and observer of Japan, Lafcadio Hearn (1850–1904). Greek-born Hearn was raised in the US and went to Japan in 1891 as a *Harper's* magazine reporter. In his many years in Japan, he wrote numerous works, including *Kwaidan: Stories and Studies of Strange Things*; *Shadowings, Japan: An Attempt at Interpretation*; *Bushido: The Soul of Japan*; and *A Daughter of the Samurai*. Although written over a century ago, his observations carry well over time. Along with Matsue's other cultural credentials, such as its samurai dwellings, history museum and the interesting Karakoro Art Studio with its exhibits of local crafts, is the **Lafcadio Hearn Memorial Museum** (daily, Apr–Sept 8.30am–6.30pm, Oct–Mar 8.30am–5pm). Also in Matsue is the ancient shrine of **Kamosu**. Its unique architectural style, *taisha-zukuri*, is the oldest architectural style in Japan.

About 20km (13 miles) east of Matsue, the **Adachi Museum of Art** (www.adachi-museum.or.jp; daily, Apr–Sept 9am–5.30pm, Oct–Mar 9am–5pm) is well worth a detour. The collection covers Japanese art from the Meiji era through to the present, and while that is impressive enough in its own right, it's almost secondary to the pristine gardens, complete with teahouses, that make up the museum's 43,000 sq metres (465,000 sq ft) of grounds.

Continuing east along the coast brings one to **Tottori** Prefecture, with a rural reputation not too dissimilar to Tohoku's. Though its tourist attractions are few and far between, Tottori does lure visitors with one thing very un-Japanese – large **sand dunes** *(sakyu)* on the coast by **Tottori City** ⑰ that attract nearly 2 million tourists annually.

The Tottori dunes.

Rock garden at the Adachi Museum of Art.

A pilgrim on the route of 88 Temples.

SHIKOKU

Until 1988, the only way to reach Japan's fourth-largest island was by air or water. It's an island of rugged terrain and open exposure to Pacific typhoons, and its people are fiercely independent.

The least developed and rarely visited of Japan's four main islands, Shikoku's attractions (and drawbacks) are attendant on its relative isolation. The island can provide a more "Japanese" experience than either Honshu or Kyushu. Its people are less familiar with foreigners and its atmosphere has been less influenced by the homogenising aspects of modern culture. It is also more diffused. Places likely to be of interest to travellers are relatively far apart and more difficult to get to than on more widely travelled pathways.

Shikoku's separate identity is not as isolated as before. The smallest of Japan's main islands, it was the last to be linked by bridge with Honshu, the largest and most populated of Japan's islands. In 1988 the completion of the **Seto Ohashi** ⑱ bridge, which took 10 years and nearly US$1 billion to build, gave Shikoku a ground transport link to the rest of Japan. At 12.3km (7.5 miles) in length, it is one of the longer double-deck bridges in the world, carrying four lanes of traffic above dual rail tracks. Since its completion another two bridges have been added to improve further Shikoku's connections with the main island.

The most numerous and distinctive visitors crossing into Shikoku today are *ohenrosan* – devout Buddhist pilgrims making the rounds

of the 88 holy temples and shrines established on Shikoku by the priest Kobo Daishi some 1,200 years ago. In the feudal period, it was common for white-robed pilgrims carrying staffs to complete the circuit on foot, a feat requiring more than two months. Today's similarly adorned pilgrims usually make the rounds in two weeks or less via air-conditioned buses.

Shikoku is split into northern and southern sections by steep, rugged mountains. The relatively dry northern part, facing the **Seto Naikai**

Main Attractions
Takamatsu
Kotohira
Tokushima
Naruto
Matsuyama
Dogo Onsen Honkan
Uchiko and Ozu
Ashizuri-misaki
Kochi

The Great Seto Bridge.

The Konpira-san temple complex has a nautical theme, as sailors, in particular, believe this temple brings good fortune.

Ritsurin Garden, Takamatsu.

(Inland Sea), is more industrialised, and in cities like the fairly cosmopolitan Takamatsu feels really no different from Honshu. The south is wilder, warmer and wetter, offering opportunities to experience Japan at its most rugged and rural, especially in the small fishing and farming communities towards the southern capes. The weather here is most favourable in early spring and at the beginning of the autumn.

Takamatsu

The capital of Kagawa Prefecture, **Takamatsu** ❶ is the main railway terminal and ferry port in eastern Shikoku. **Ritsurin-koen** (Ritsurin Park; http://ritsuringarden.jp; daily from 5.30–7am until 5–7pm, depending on the season) contains one of the finest traditional gardens in Japan, with 54 hectares (133 acres) of ponds, hills, pine forests and a botanical garden. One of the garden's best rewards is a cup of tea at the beautiful Kikugetsutei teahouse. The **Kagawa Museum** (www.pref.kagawa.jp/kmuseum; Tue–Sun 9am–5pm), near the entrance to the park,

displays comprehensive collections of crafts from Shikoku and throughout Japan. However, the region's most popular craft are the distinctive *sanuki-udon* noodles, served daily at thousands of *udon* restaurants throughout the area.

A few kilometres east by train from the centre of Takamatsu is **Yashima**. It was one of the seemingly countless battlefields of the Gempei War (1180–85) between the Minamoto and Taira clans. The architectural embodiments of Shikoku's past – an open-air *kabuki* theatre, a vine suspension bridge, thatch-roofed farmhouses and a variety of other traditional buildings – have been collected and preserved in **Shikoku-mura** (Shikoku Village; daily, Apr–Oct 8.30am–6pm, Nov–Mar 8.30am–5.30pm). This tiny part of Shikoku Island was itself once an island; now a narrow strip connects it to the mainland. It juts out into the Seto Naikai and provides extensive views, particularly from Yashima's lofty temple on the hill. In addition to the temple's beautiful garden you can visit its Treasure House, stuffed with

interesting relics and local art and craft objects.

Southwest of Takamatsu, **Koto-hira ㉑** is home to one of the most famous and popular shrines in Japan, **Kotohira-gu** (also called Konpira-san; the main precinct is free, but some buildings require an entrance fee). Dedicated to Okuninushi no Mikoto, the guardian of seafarers, the shrine has lured sailors and fishermen seeking propitious sailing since the shrine's inception in the 11th century. In recent years, their numbers have been swelled by the 4 million tourists arriving each year. The main shrine is at the end of a long, steep path lined with stone lanterns. A trip to the top of the 785 stairs and back takes at least an hour.

The **Kanamaru-za** (www.konpiraka buki.jp), restored to its original early 19th-century condition, is the oldest existing *kabuki* theatre in Japan. Its stage, resonating with the fading echoes of thousands of performances, is exciting to visit even when empty. In the third week of April, the nation's best *kabuki* actors bring it alive. The revolving section is turned by strong men pushing the 150-year-old mechanism under the stage, and the audience is seated on cushions on *tatami*.

Off the coast of Takamatsu, in the Seto Naikai, are two islands worth a day trip or overnight visit. **Naoshima Island**, a 20-minute ferry ride from Takamatsu's port (also accessible by ferry from Okayama), is nationally renowned for its collection of contemporary art galleries. Until the 1990s, the small fishing island had seen several decades of decline, its population shrinking as the island's youth shunned the traditional island life for modern distractions on the mainland. Then along came the publishing group Benesse, who chose Naoshima's idyllic setting for its Art Site Naoshima contemporary art initiative.

Naoshima's three major and very sleek contemporary art galleries – **Benesse House Museum** (www.benesse-artsite.jp/benessehouse; daily 8am–9pm), **Lee Ufan Museum** (www.benesse-artsite.jp/lee-ufan; Tue–Sun 10am–5pm, Mar–Sept until 6pm) and

Bar sign in Naruto.

Naoshima Island.

TIP

Tokushima Prefecture's southern end is surfing country. The place to head to is Kaifu, about 25km (15.5 miles) south of Hiwasa on the JR line – there are plenty of surf shops here for renting gear before heading out to ride the breakers at Kaifu Point or moving to the equally good Shishikui beach a few kilometres further south.

Chichu Art Museum (www.benesse-artsite.jp/chichu; Tue–Sun 10am–5pm, Mar–Sept until 6pm) – feature work by local artists and international stars such as Pollock, Warhol, Walter de Maria, Lee Ufan, and James Turrell. Naoshima's **Art House Project** (most installation: Tue–Sun 10am–4.30pm) has also seen several traditional houses and other structures in Honmura Village transformed into art installations, while art can also be found in other unexpected places. Some 20 installations dot the beaches and cliff tops near Benesse House and the even the local public bath (**I Love Yu**; Tue–Fri 2–9pm, Sat–Sun 10am–9pm) has been bombed inside and out with pop art and erotica. The **Ando Museum** (www.benesse-artsite.jp/ando-museum; Tue–Sun 10am–4.30pm), opened in 2013 and dedicated to the world-renowned architect Tadao Ando's work, is the most recent addition.

An hour by ferry is **Shodoshima**, which among its attractions has several soy-sauce plants that can be toured and great views of the Inland Sea from its mountainous interior.

The Awa Odori dance festival in Tokushima.

Eastern Shikoku

Tokushima Prefecture faces Osaka Bay and the Pacific Ocean along the western end of Shikoku. In ancient times, Tokushima was known as Awa no Kuni – Millet Country. Today, most of the prefecture's traditional arts still use the Chinese characters for Awa no Kuni. The Awa Odori – the summer "crazy dance" festival – is held in mid-August and is perhaps the most humorous of Japanese festivals, with residents and tourists joining in processional dances and contests for the "biggest fool of all". Another home-grown entertainment are puppet shows featuring giant puppets accompanied by *shamisen* and performed by farmers between growing seasons.

The garden of the old castle of **Tokushima** ㉑ is set against the backdrop of forest-covered Shiro-yama. The garden consists of a traditional landscaped area with a fountain. Over a quarter of the 88 Kobo Daishi temples are in the immediate vicinity of Tokushima. Along the once prosperous and busy main highway through the centre of town are several old,

JAPAN'S CARNIVAL

"You're a fool if you dance and a fool if you don't, so dance, fool!" goes the rallying cry of the centuries-old Awa Odori dance festival in Tokushima. Over four days every 12–15 August, more than 1 million people descend on the city to watch some 80,000 dancers prance through the streets like lunatics on the run. Dressed in colourful *yukata* and driven by a pounding two-beat drum rhythm accompanied by *shamisen* and flute, the dancers produce an intoxicating display that invariably goes on long into the night and has spectators starting their own impromptu dance parties across the city.

You can get a taste of the Awa Odori year-round at the Awa Odori Museum (www.awaodori-kaikan.jp; daily 9am–5pm), where local dance troupes also put on several displays daily.

fire-resistant *kura* (warehouses) used by merchants to store their goods in earlier times.

About 20km (12 miles) to the north, **Naruto** ㉒ faces the **Naruto-kaikyo** (Naruto Straits), where the **O-Narutokyo** (Great Naruto Bridge) connects Tokushima with Awaji-shima and is one of the longer suspension bridges in Asia. The attraction to travellers is not the bridge, however, but rather the countless whirlpools, some as large as 20 metres (60ft) in diameter, that swirl in the Naruto Straits flowing beneath the bridge. The whirlpools are largest in the spring and autumn, when tides reach a speed of 20kmh (12mph). Sightseeing boats chug right up to the whirlpools during peak tourism season.

The 100km (60-mile) coastline of Tokushima Prefecture holds some of the best beaches in Japan. Along the centre of the coast, **Komoda-misaki** (Cape Komoda) stretches out into the Pacific. The peninsula is noted for its luxuriant subtropical flora. The offshore reefs, washed by the warm Japan Current, are the site of some of the best surf-fishing in Japan. The area is also noted as an egg-laying location for giant loggerhead turtles. In **Hiwasa** ㉓ to the south is a sea turtle museum. Also in Hiwasa is **Yakuo-ji**, the 23rd temple on the great Shikoku pilgrimage and famous for its series of paintings of the miseries of the Buddhist hell. The temple is thought to ward off evil. Men and women in their *yakudoshi* (unlucky years) visit here to ask for divine help by placing a one-yen coin on each step as they climb up to the temple. The grounds of Yakuo-ji afford fine views of Hiwasa harbour.

Oku-Iya double vine bridges (kazura-bashi).

Inland Shikoku

Tsurugi-san ㉔ (1,893 metres/6,200ft) dominates the interior of eastern Shikoku and is one of the main peaks of Shikoku. In contrast to its name – meaning "broadsword" – the crest of the mountain slopes gently. A lift brings visitors up to near the summit, followed by a 40-minute hike to the peak. A lodging house, skiing area and old shrines make Tsurugi a major recreation area.

Oboke Gorge.

Train in Matsuyama.

Matsuyama's Dogo Onsen.

South of Tsurugi-san, the gorge of **Konose** lies deep in the mountains at the source of the Naka-gawa. It is a site of magnificent natural beauty, and in autumn, red and yellow foliage covers the surrounding mountains.

To the west of Tsurugi-san is the gorge at **Oboke**, formed by the upper reaches of the Yoshino-gawa. The site is noted for towering cliffs and giant rocks polished like marble from the cascading waters. Spring and autumn are the best times to see the gorge, which is also visited by busloads of tourists, however. The **Iya Valley**, with its hot springs, river rafting, and the much-photographed pair of unique vine bridges, are a little east of Oboke.

The **Yoshino-gawa Valley**, north of Tsurugi-san and running due west from Tokushima, holds most of the area's main attractions. The valley is full of ancient temples, shrines, museums and cultural sites. The area is also peppered with *ai yashiki* (indigo-dyeing plants); *Awa*-style indigo dyeing has flourished as the main industry of Tokushima for centuries.

About 30km (20 miles) up the Yoshino-gawa from Tokushima is **Do-chu** (Earthen Pillars). The strangely shaped pillars were formed over millions of years as the result of soil erosion. Nearby are the historic streets of Udatsu and the Awagami traditional paper factory. The entire valley is served by the JR Yoshinogawa rail line from Tokushima.

Western Shikoku

Facing the Seto Naikai along Shikoku's northeastern shore, Ehime Prefecture was described as early as AD 712 in the *Kojiki*, Japan's first chronicle of historical events and legends. Ehime has many historical places, hot springs and festivals.

Several castles dot the Ehime landscape, **Imabari-jo** in **Imabari** ㉕ being one of them. It is a rare coastal castle built in 1604 by Takatora Todo. The massive walls and moats, filled by water from the sea, let its masters fight attacks by land or sea. Shikoku's best-known castle is **Matsuyama-jo** (www.matsuyamajo.jp; daily 9am–5pm, Aug until 5.30pm, Dec–Jan until

4.30pm), which stands in the middle of the city of **Matsuyama** ㉖, with a slightly incongruous baseball park and athletic stadium at its base. It was completed in 1603, burned down but was rebuilt on a slightly smaller scale in 1642, struck by lightning and razed to the ground in 1784, and then not fully rebuilt until 1854. The present-day edifice is a result of restoration work completed in 1986, so it's not exactly an original, but the cable-car ride up to it is fun, and this is a good place to get your bearings.

Away to the west near **Dogo-koen** stands the **Dogo Onsen Honkan** (www.dogo.or.jp). People in Matsuyama have been coming to Dogo for more than a century, taking off their shoes at the entrance to the rambling three-storey castle affair topped with a white heron and leaving their clothes and cares behind as they wallow in the glory of the alkaline hot spas. It is thought that they've been doing so for as long as 3,000 years – Dogo Onsen is reckoned to be the oldest hot spring in use in Japan. It was first mentioned in the early 8th-century *Kojiki* ('record of ancient matters') and also in the mid-8th-century *Manyoshu* book of poetry.

One can get a basic soak in **Kaminyu** (Water of the Gods; daily 6am–11pm) for a few hundred yen, but that would be like going to a Michelin-starred restaurant and merely nibbling on the breadsticks. Pay the full price and head up Dogo's precipitous stairways to **Tamano-yu** (Water of the Spirits; daily 6am–10pm). Language is not a problem as smiling ladies point the way to a private *tatami* room where you can leave clothes in a locker, don a *yukata* and head for the bath itself.

Males and females go their separate ways at this point, and then, as in all *onsen*, you soap and thoroughly rinse off, sitting on a little wooden stool and dousing your body from a wooden bucket. Then it's time to lower yourself inch by inch into the waters (hot but not scalding) and let the body gradually adjust. It's a tingling cleanliness that washes over you, penetrates beneath the skin and drowsily wafts over the mind. After 10 or 20 minutes, heave yourself out, dry off, dress and

Kabuki Theatre, Uchiko.

TIP

Remember that in the Japanese *onsen*, or hot spring, no clothes are worn (though a small hand towel offers a little modesty while walking around), and you should thoroughly wash and rinse before entering the water, as the pools are communal and used only for soaking.

Cape Ashizuri-Misaki.

climb back up to the *tatami* room. The maid will pull out your sitting pillows and serve tea and marzipan balls. The balcony looks out over tiled roofs and trees, and laughter and the contented buzz of conversation drifts over from adjoining rooms.

Also in Dogo, **Ishite-ji**, the 51st temple on Shikoku's 88-temple pilgrimage, was built by the decree of Emperor Shomu in 728. It was restored by the great priest Kobo in the early 9th century. Its treasure hall (daily 8am–5pm) holds some 300 important historical articles.

One of Ehime's more interesting historical sites is the *kabuki* theatre in **Uchiko** . This full-scale *kabuki* theatre was built in 1916 in the Irimoya zukuri style, its tiled roof typical of the housing style of the 1800s. Its restoration in 1985 preserved the oldstyle drum tower on the top floor, a rotating stage, an elevated passageway and box seats. Ten kilometres (6 miles) southwest of Uchiko, the small town of **Ozu** ❷ calls itself "mini Kyoto". Among the traditional attractions that have helped give it that tag are

summer **cormorant fishing** *(ukai)* displays along Ozu's Hiji-kawa River and several old *sukiya*-style villas about town. Ozu also has Japan's newest castle, an impressive 2004 reconstruction of the original 16th-century, four-storey **Ozu-jo**.

Continuing south, **Uwajima-jo** was built in 1595 by Takatora Todo. The castle's three-storeyed tower stands atop an 80-metre (260ft) hill overlooking the city of **Uwajima** ❷, noted throughout Japan for bullfights. The curious visitor drawn to Uwajima by tales of **Taga-jinja** and its sex museum (daily 8am–5pm) should be aware that many of the more tantalising exhibits within this shrine are locked away in glass cases and there is little interpretation in English, although, of course, most of the items on display – from lurid photos to well-proportioned fertility sculptures – are self-explanatory.

To the south in **Tsushima** ❸ is a strolling garden, **Nanrakuen-koen**, covering more than 15 hectares (37 acres) and the largest on Shikoku. Developed in 1985, the garden has four theme areas: mountains, villages, towns and the sea. Some 30,000 irises, which bloom in early May, cover most of the gardens. Near Nanrakuen-koen is a gorge, **Nametoko**, carved out by the Shimanto-gawa, which is reported to be the last clear river in Japan. The gorge runs through Ashizuri-Uwakai National Park.

Ehime Prefecture is also noted for its many and varied festivals: the Ikazaki Kite Festival in May displays Ehime's 300-year history of kite-making; the Saijo Festival in October features 80 moveable shrines; the Niihama Drum Festival in October includes a competition between 33 massive drums, or *taiko*. Other festivals include bullfights, samba competitions and the Matsuyama Spring Festival in April.

Southern Shikoku

Two large capes frame Kochi Prefecture. On the far western side of Kochi

lies **Ashizuri-misaki ㉛**. This cape is noted for towering marble cliffs and Japan's first underwater park. In early spring, camellias cover the cape in a dazzling red carpet of blossoms.

The prefecture of Kochi broadly encircles the wide **Tosa-wan** (Tosa Bay), with its capital of **Kochi ㉜** facing the south on a flat plain. Kochi is best known for the role its leading families played in forging the alliance between the Satsuma and Choshu clans and the ensuing imperial Meiji Restoration of 1868. Its most renowned citizen from this period is Sakamoto Ryoma. Sakamoto – from a half-merchant, half-samurai family – left the class system and set up a trading company in Nagasaki.

While there, he helped establish a network of anti-Tokugawa samurai but was assassinated in Kyoto in 1867 – just a year before the overthrow of the shogun and restoration of the emperor to legitimate rule. He is remembered in the museum at **Kochi-jo** (Kochi Castle; daily 9am– 5pm), an elegant castle built in the 17th century and rebuilt in the 18th. A market is held every Sunday on the road leading to the castle's Ote gate. The market is popular with local residents, with as many as 700 small stalls selling vegetables, antiques, plants and just about everything else imaginable; it runs for about 1km (0.6 miles) along both sides of the road. A statue of Sakamoto Ryoma graces the beach at **Katsurahama**, more famous as one of the few locations in Japan where dog-fighting is legal. This beautiful beach is also a popular spot for admiring the moon. Katsurahama-koen is nearby, and there are many places of interest, such as the **Tosa Dog Museum** (www.tosa.or.jp; daily 9am– 4.30pm) featuring the Tosa breed that participates in dog-fighting (not to everyone's tastes), and an aquarium (http://katurahama-aq.jp).

Ryuga-do (daily, Mar–Nov 8.30am–5pm, Dec–Feb 8.30am– 4.30pm), a limestone cave 25km (15

miles) east of Kochi and gradually moulded over a period of 50 million years, boasts a mysterious natural beauty that enthrals everyone who visits. The scenic Skyline Drive to the top of the mountain where the cave is buried offers a wonderful vista of the Pacific Ocean.

A few kilometres west of Kochi, in **Ino**, is a fabulous paper museum. Ino has a long history of paper-making, and Kochi paper is famous throughout Japan. (For a place to be viable in Japan's domestic tourism industry, it must be "famous" for something, no matter how insignificant.) In the museum, visitors can try their hand at paper-making in addition to observing the paper-making process.

On the far eastern side of Kochi from Ashizuri-misaki, **Muroto-zaki ㉝** points out southwards into the Pacific Ocean. The cape is warm year-round, and at its tip the towering waves of the Pacific have eroded the rocks and reefs into strange shapes. The area is also noted for its connection with the venerable Kobo Daishi, founder of the Shingon sect of Buddhism.

Statue of Kobo Daishi in Shikoku.

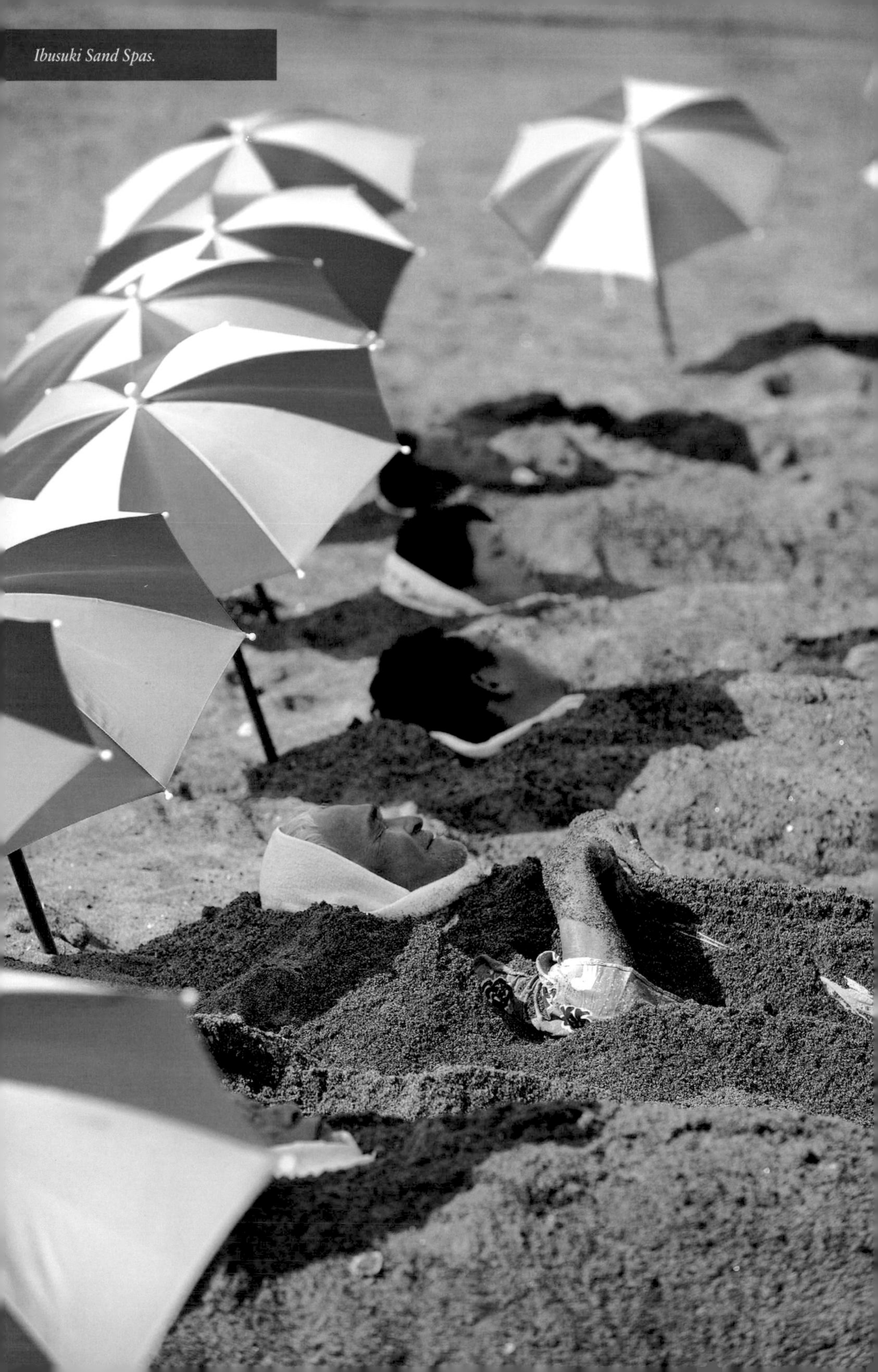

Ibusuki Sand Spas.

KYUSHU

An erupting volcano next to a large city, Kagoshima, and the history of a port city, Nagasaki, are unique to Kyushu, as are some of Japan's most independently minded leaders.

Kyushu is far to the south and, it seems at times, almost forgotten by the rest of Japan. Yet the region has always been in the vanguard of development and change. Kyushu is where the Yamato tribe – and thus the Japanese people – first took root in what was to become their homeland. It was Kyushu that withstood the onslaught of the Mongols from the mainland. It is also from where the Japanese first struck out on foreign conquest – the invasion of Korea in 1594 – and where ancient Chinese and Korean culture entered the archipelago as foundations for Japanese art and philosophy. In later years, it was one of the few places where Westerners had a foothold in the xenophobic islands. Kyushu's main cities aren't as cosmopolitan as Tokyo or Osaka, but there is a more welcoming warmth here for visitors, possibly related to the island's long history of openness to outsiders.

Any traveller coming from the north usually enters Kyushu at **Kitakyushu ❶**, considered by some as a city in search of a soul – it is an amalgamation of five cities (Moji, Kokura, Yawata, Tobata and Wakamatsu) with a combined population of over 1 million. The civic marriage was arranged by Tokyo bureaucrats in 1963, but it has yet to be

consummated by a blending of culture or politics. It is a lacklustre city with little of interest for travellers. Kitakyushu is linked to Shimonoseki on Honshu by a bridge across the Kanmon Strait. Immense steel mills (now an endangered species) and factories were built here to take advantage of the region's rich coal deposits.

Don't, however, let Kitakyushu put you off – Kyushu has so much else to offer, from the hot springs of Beppu and subtropical islands like Yakushima, to charming cities such as Nagasaki,

Main Attractions

Fukuoka
Dazaifu
Yanagawa
Nagasaki
Shimabara Peninsula
Beppu hot springs
Kagoshima and Sakura-jima
Yaku-shima Island

Businessmen in Fukuoka.

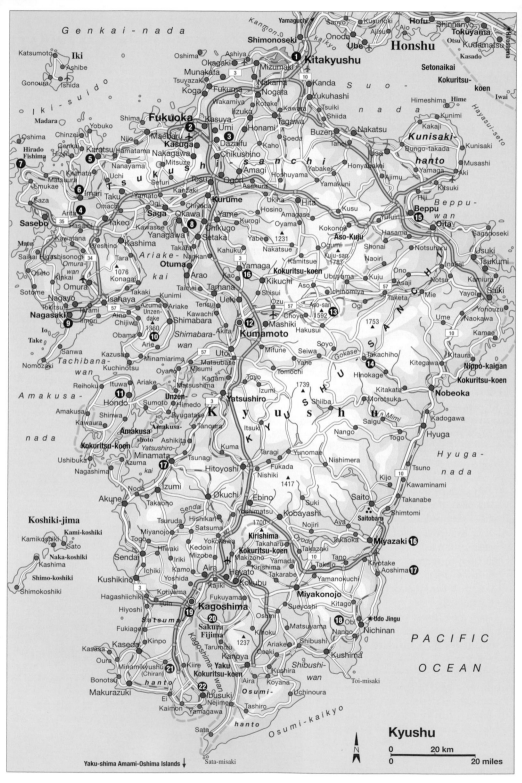

Kyushu

0   20 km

0   20 miles

and the fine ceramics of Arita. And that's just scratching the surface.

Fukuoka

Northern Kyushu has a long history of overseas influence. In the 13th century it was targeted by foreign invaders, but other "imports" have been of a more peaceful nature. **Fukuoka** ❷ is reportedly where both tea and Buddhism were introduced to Japan, and Korean captives brought back here were responsible for starting up a sizeable pottery industry. Today, with a population of over 1.4 million, Fukuoka competes with Kitakyushu as the largest city on Kyushu. It certainly has more soul.

The city remains an important hub in regional trade and commerce, but while shopping and hotel complexes such as the glistening Canal City dominate the skyline, Fukuoka still retains a lot of charm at ground level. Canals crisscross the central urban area and in the evenings and at weekends small stalls selling snacks and alcohol are set up on the paths beside the water, each an oasis of relaxation and merriment for the hordes of harried *sararimen* ("salarymen") wending their way home from work.

Fukuoka's history has not always been benign. During the Nara and Heian periods, the area was the principal Japanese port for trade with China and Korea, but in 1274 a reconnaissance force of some 30,000 Mongols landed near Fukuoka after annihilating garrisons on the islands of Tsushima and Iki, just to the north of Kyushu in the Korea Strait. The invaders enjoyed similar success on Kyushu, but the death of their commander, along with serious storms that threatened their ships, forced them to retreat. Seven years later, in 1281, Kublai Khan dispatched another Mongol expeditionary force of 150,000 troops, the largest amphibious assault recorded in history prior to World War II. Backed by a ferocious armoury of catapults and cannons, the Mongols gradually wore down the tenacious Japanese resistance, but when they were on the brink of victory after 53 days of fighting, a terrific typhoon – *kami-kaze* (literally, divine wind) – sent most of the

Stall selling ramen, Fukuoka.

FUKUOKA'S YATAI

Yatai – food street stalls – aren't by any means unique to Fukuoka. In fact, most cities have them somewhere. It is doubtful, however, that any have as many of these little mobile kitchens, or indeed as vibrant a *yatai* scene, as Fukuoka, where they have become one of the best known city symbols. Usually open from nightfall to early morning, and covered by cheap plastic tenting that creates something akin to a mini, ramshackle *izakaya* just big enough for a small handful of customers, there are *yatai* specialising in all manner of cuisine – from staples such as *ramen, oden* and *yakitori* to more unusual *yatai* fare like French cuisine. The best places to go *yatai* hunting are Tenjin and Nakasu. Some stalls also sell alcoholic beverages.

TIP

Fukuoka International Association (www.rainbowfia.or.jp; daily 10am–8pm, closed third Tue of each month), located on the eighth floor of the IMS Building in Tenjin, is an excellent information centre with noticeboards, events calendars, brochures and newspapers in English.

invading fleet to the bottom of the sea. Remnants of the defensive wall built to repel the Mongols can still be seen on the outskirts of Fukuoka, although nowadays they are rather unimpressive.

Modern Fukuoka traces its roots to 1601, when a castle was built on the west side of the **Naka-gawa** in what is today Ohori Park, and the town that grew up around the castle took the same name of Fukuoka. Only the castle's walls survive nowadays, but they provide an excellent view over the city. Hakata, a town for merchants who enjoyed a less important status than the ruling samurai, was built on the other side of the river. Hakata-ku has been a ward within Fukuoka since 1889, but the name remains – **Hakata-eki** (Hakata Station), the southern terminus of the *shinkansen* line; Hakata clay dolls; and the popular Hakata Yamagasa festival are all named after the merchant city. In its role as the crossroads between Japan and China, Fukuoka was the place where Zen Buddhism first touched the archipelago's shores. Located northwest of Hakata Station near Mikasa-gawa, **Shofuku-ji** (always

open; free) is the oldest Zen temple in Japan, founded in 1195 by Eisai after years of study in China. Sadly, much of the temple suffered bomb damage during World War II and the current complex is only a fraction of its former self. Eisai is also credited with bringing the first tea seeds into the country.

The **Sumiyoshi-jinja**, the oldest extant Shinto shrine on Kyushu, was built in 1623. South of Shofuku-ji and due west of the train station, it sits atop a hill that provides an excellent city view. A museum, **Hakata Machiya Furusato-kan** (www.hakatamachiya.com; daily 10am–6pm), chronicling the history of the city, is located on a street running almost opposite **Kushida-jinja** (daily 9am–5pm; free, but charge for the shrine's small museum) in the central district of Nakasu, the city's most important shrine.

All in all, Fukuoka today is still very much open to outside influence and sees itself as the cultural crossroads of this part of Asia. The downtown **ACROS Centre** (www.acros.or.jp), easily recognisable for its imaginative stepped-garden exterior, stages

Canal City Mall.

CANAL DREAMS

Fukuoka's modernity and willingness to experiment is exemplified by the Canal City shopping and entertainment complex (http://canalcity.co.jp). Canal City was created by California architect Jon Jerde, who also designed Universal Studios' cartoon-like City Walk, and the giant Mall of America. Opened in 1996, it was the first mall of its kind in Kyushu to mix shopping and leisure activities in one unified space. Curvaceous walls, like opera or window balconies, with overhanging plants, overlook an artificial canal, with outdoor retail booths and a performance space. Sleek cafés, restaurants and a number of import clothing stores are represented here, along with a 13-theatre IMAX cinema. Canal City's fountains use rain and waste water, which is treated within the complex.

international opera, ballet, symphony orchestras and popular musical extravaganzas, as well as more traditional Japanese performances.

Two other significant structures overlook life in the city. A mammoth seaside stadium, **Hawks Town**, whose retractable dome is the first of its kind in Japan, is home to the local baseball team as well as a hotel and shopping mall. And a little further along the coast above Momochi-koen stands the 234-metre (768ft) **Fukuoka Tower** (www.fukuokatower.co.jp; daily 9.30am–10pm), with two observation towers that provide stunning views over the surrounding area.

Other points of interest in Fukuoka include **Fukuoka-shi Bijutsukan** (Fukuoka Art Museum; www.fukuoka-art-museum.jp; Tue–Sun July–Aug 9.30am–7.30pm, Sept–June 9.30am–5.30pm; closed for renovation from Sept 2016 until 2019), a museum housing a collection of Japanese art, and **Ohori-koen** (Ohori Park), a pleasant park harbouring the remains of Fukuoka-jo (Fukuoka Castle) and reconstructions of its turret and gates.

Dazaifu and around

Forty minutes from Fukuoka and inland to the southeast, **Dazaifu** ❸ is home to **Tenman-gu** (www.dazaifu tenmangu.or.jp; main hall: daily 6am–7pm, June–Aug until 8pm, winter from 6.30am; free), a shrine built in 1591 to commemorate the poet-scholar Sugawara Michizane, who died in AD 903 after being unjustly exiled from the court in Kyoto. Successive mishaps befell Kyoto supposedly because of Sugawara's banishment. As a result, he gradually came to be acknowledged as *Tenman*, a deity of culture and scholars.

Nowadays, students of all ages tramp over the bright-orange shrine's arched bridge to beseech his help in passing school examinations, which can make or break careers and lives in Japan. Sections of defensive walls built after the first Mongol invasion can still be seen on the road to Dazaifu.

Dazaifu offers a lot more than just a simple pilgrimage to Tenman-gu and its commercial offerings. Rather than bearing left at the end of the approach road to the shrine, turn right and, tucked into a small lane, you will come across a stark Zen garden fronting the grounds of **Komyozen-ji** temple (daily 8am–5pm). Remove your shoes to enter its dimly lit wooden corridors, where Buddhist art and other treasures lurk in the unlit rooms that the temple's trickle of visitors file past. You have to look twice, surprising yourself with a small camphor statue, Korean bowl or earth-coloured teacup, objects that have been sitting in the shadows for centuries. The rear walkways provide a slightly elevated view of another rock, gravel and moss garden below. Also near Tenmangu is the **Kyushu National Museum** (www.kyuhaku.com; Tue–Sun 9.30am–5pm), which houses a fine collection of artefacts from around Asia and details the influences other Asian cultures have had on Japanese art and crafts.

The **Kanzeon-ji** temple (grounds: always open, free; Treasure Hall: daily

Dazaifu temple Rock Garden.

Fukuoka Dome is home of the Softbank Hawks baseball team.

Ceramics made in Arita.

9am–5pm), with its rare ordination stage and great bell, is a 15-minute walk from here. Its Treasure House contains a number of highly prized statues, some of the figures masked, including an unusual horse-headed Kannon. A short walk further on, near a small museum to the site, are the remains of the Tofuro, or City Tower, a lookout post used during the Yamato Period when rebellious tribes, like the Kumaso in southern Kyushu, threatened the realm. There are several axially arranged foundation stones here of former administrative buildings.

Dazaifu's heady blend of religion, historical relics and academia dissolve in the curative waters of **Futsukai-chi Onsen**, just 3km (2 miles) south. Although this is the closest spa town to Fukuoka, Kyushu's largest city, it rarely gets crowded even at weekends. There are three hot springs here, conveniently lumped together – the perfect place to nurse out the day's aches and pains.

Ceramic cities

When Ri Simpei, an ordinary Korean potter, first chanced upon *kaolin* clay – the essential ingredient for producing fine porcelain – in **Arita** ④, 50km (30 miles) west of Fukuoka around the turn of the 17th century, he probably had little notion of the ramifications of his discovery.

Nearly 400 years later, Arita and its neighbours **Karatsu** ⑤ and **Imari** ⑥ are the hub of a thriving pottery industry. The delicate craftsmanship and brightly coloured glazes that are the hallmarks of pottery from this region are prized all over Japan, and further afield, too. Simpei and the other potters who were brought over from Korea as prisoners of the Nabeshima *daimyo* were kept under close guard so their trade secrets did not slip out.

To understand something about those times, the **Nabeshima Hanyo-koen** at Okawachiyama (a short bus ride from Imari) portrays the sort of techniques Simpei and his fellow workers used and the conditions in which they lived. There are plenty of working potteries in the area as well, but **Kyushu Toji Bunkakan** (Kyushu Ceramic Museum; http://saga-museum.jp/ceramic; Tue–Sun 9am–5pm) in Arita is the best place to

view the full range of Kyushu pottery. Imaizumi Imaemon and Sakaida Kakiemon are celebrated workshops with galleries and shops open to the public.

Karatsu is also highly regarded for its stoneware. Several galleries and workshops, including the Nakazato Taroemon and the Ryuta kilns, are open to visitors. The Hikiyama Tenijo museum exhibits 19th-century Karatsu *kunchi* festival floats, which are paraded through the town every 2–4 November. **Saga**, a pottery town in its own right, is an excellent base from which to explore the three principal ceramic centres of Arita, Imari and Karatsu.

For a breath of ocean air, take a stroll or hire a bike to explore the pine groves of **Niji-no-Matsubara**, which stretch along the beach found at Matsuragate.

Hirado

Some 40km (25 miles) west of Imari, the focus shifts to Japan's early Christians. The first foreign settlement in Japan was established by Dutch traders on **Hirado-shima** ❼ (Hirado Island) in 1550, although the one-time island is now connected to the mainland by a bridge. The Francis Xavier Memorial Chapel consecrates the Spanish saint's visit to Hirado after he was expelled from Kagoshima in southern Kyushu. European activity here ended when the Dutch were forced to move to Dejima, in Nagasaki harbour, in 1641. But secretive Christians maintained a version of the faith here for centuries afterwards, often under the threat of imprisonment and death. This bit of historical lore has provided the basis for a thriving domestic tourist industry here, with "real" icons for sale.

Yanagawa

Like Kyoto, **Yanagawa** ❽, under an hour on the Nishitetsu Omuta Line from Fukuoka Station, is a water city. The angularity of Yanagawa's grid of canals contrasts intriguingly with the winding lanes of the Old Town that transects it. An aerial view would no doubt reveal something like an octopus on a chequerboard.

Yanagawa was founded by the Kamachi clan in the 16th century. Its water sources, however, are far older, dating back to the Yayoi Period, when an area of damp lowland existed near the mouth of several rivers that funnelled into the nearby Ariake Sea. Canals were dug to drain the land and improve its agricultural prospects. The canals remain more or less intact, covering a total length of 470km (290 miles). In fact, 12 percent of the town's surface area is water.

It's a comfortable place to stroll through, though many visitors elect to view the town, its willow-lined canals flowing by old samurai villas, luxuriating back gardens and old brick storehouses, from the comfort of a canal barge. The vessels are propelled by boatmen who, like Oxbridge punters, use poles to propel the barges along the currentless waterways. During winter months the boats install quilts with heaters placed underneath.

If you opt to walk, one building in particular worth checking out is the

Dazaifu shrine.

Hirado with Xavier Memorial Chapel in the background.

Fugu/blowfish sashimi.

Former Residence of the Toshima Family (Wed–Mon 9am–5pm), which is built in sukiya style, complete with thatched roof and pretty ornamental garden. Pick up a free copy of the "strolling map" from Yanagawa's tourist office (or download it from www.yanagawa-net.com), and it will lead you to many more intriguing buildings.

Eating baked and steamed *unagi no seiromushi*, rice and eel steamed with a sauce made from sugar and soy, with a finely sliced omelette on top, is part of the Yanagawa experience. The fish is said to increase a person's stamina and virility, especially during the dog days of summer. At lunchtime the whole town seems to smell of baked eel, as charcoal-coloured smoke billows out into the street from vents at the side of restaurants. In winter, visitors can sample duck. *Yanagawa nabe*, small fish cooked with local vegetables and egg in an earthenware pot, is another local speciality.

Nagasaki

Pleasure boats exploring Yanagawa's canals.

Like Hiroshima, **Nagasaki** ❾ is a name automatically associated with the atomic bomb that brought World War II to its terrible and tumultuous climax. It is particularly ironic that this devastating manifestation of Western technology should have been detonated in a city that was one of the first to open up to the outside world and where foreign inventions and ways were once eagerly adopted.

The path was not always smooth, of course, and many early Christian converts were brutally executed and foreign residents were expelled from time to time. But Nagasaki was one of the first Japanese cities to take a serious interest in Western medicine. It was here, too, that the first railway and modern shipyard in Japan were established.

Now home to nearly half a million people, Nagasaki clings to steep hills wrapped around a very active deepwater harbour, competing with Kobe for designation as Japan's San Francisco. Like San Francisco, it has a lively Chinatown and a continuing spirit of receptiveness to novel ideas. As it is one of the most interesting cities in Japan, even travellers on a restricted time budget should allow for two days or more to explore Nagasaki and its surroundings.

Nagasaki's harbour has played a prominent role in Japan's relations with the outside world. Dutch traders initiated the first sustained European presence here, on an island in the harbour that also acted as a conduit for most of the early Christian missionaries. The port at Nagasaki was established in 1571 to serve Portuguese traders. A decade later, Omura Sumitada, a local *daimyo* who had grown rich on trade with the foreigners, turned over partial administration of the port to the Jesuit missionaries who followed in the merchants' wake.

A generation later, fearing that the Christians and their converts would subvert his authority, the shogun Toyotomi Hideyoshi banned Christianity. He ordered six Spanish priests and 20 Japanese Christians, including two teenage boys, to be rounded up in

Kyoto and Osaka. They were brought to Nagasaki and crucified in 1597 as a warning to Japan's largest Christian community. A memorial constructed in 1962 and related Memorial Hall (daily 9am–5pm) stands in **Nishi-zaka-koen** (Nishizaka Park) on the spot of the crucifixions, near **Naga-saki-eki Ⓐ** (Nagasaki Station) at the north end of downtown.

Christianity was utterly and viciously suppressed following the Christian-led Shimbara Rebellion of 40,000 peasants south of Nagasaki in 1637. As a result, Japan's sole officially sanctioned contact with Europeans for the next two centuries was through a settlement on **Dejima Ⓑ**, in Nagasaki harbour and south of the present-day Nagasaki Station. The artificial island – now part of the mainland – was built for Portuguese traders but it was occupied by the Dutch after the Portuguese were banished in 1638. Its occupants were confined to a small, walled area and contact with Japanese was limited to a small circle of officials, traders, prostitutes and, in the later years, scholars.

As no other Europeans were permitted in Japan until 1854, whatever news of European technology and culture filtered into Japan came through this settlement. The **Shiryokan** (Dejima Museum; daily 9am–5pm) near the site preserves relics of the settlement.

Like the Dutch, Nagasaki's Chinese, mostly from Fujian along China's southern coast, were officially confined to a walled ghetto, but restrictions on their movements were not as strictly enforced. The Chinese in Nagasaki left the only pure Chinese architecture to be found in Japan, along with one of the country's three remaining Chinatowns (the others are in Yokohama and Kobe). The narrow and winding streets of **Shinchimachi** are filled with Chinese restaurants catering to tourists, as there are very few Chinese remaining in Nagasaki.

Two popular "Chinese" dishes in Japan, *saraudon* (meat, seafood and vegetables served on a bed of crispy noodles) and *champpon* (similar, except served in broth instead of with crispy noodles), were invented in Shinchi-machi. Like most of the foreign food

Peace Statue in Peace Park, Nagasaki.

served in Japan, they bear only a passing resemblance to the original but they are still quite palatable. On the subject of food, the other "foreign" delicacy that survives in Nagasaki is the *kasutera*, or sponge cake, that is supposedly baked to an old Portuguese recipe and sold (in exquisitely wrapped packages) in bakeries around town.

The Chinese community was granted permission to build its own temples. Teramachi (Temple Town) contains two of the oldest Chinese temples in Japan, as well as numerous Japanese Buddhist temples and graveyards. **Kofuku-ji** (www.kohfukuji.com; daily 6am–5pm), founded in 1620, was built on the edge of the original Chinatown in the northeast part of town. The Chinese quarters burned down in 1698; the current Shinchimachi occupies land designated for Chinese merchants following the fire. Centrally located, **Sofuku-ji** (daily 8am–5pm) is a bright, elaborate Ming-style temple and is in better condition than most Ming-era temples in China. The Masodo (Hall of the Bodhisattva) contains an image of the goddess of the seas, flanked by fierce guardians reputed to have thousand-mile vision. Nagasaki's premier shrine, **Suwa-jinja**, is a 10-minute walk north. Points of interest include a graceful main hall, a curious collection of guardian lions and an imposing horse statue, and the shrine's dynamic festival, the Kunchi Matsuri, held annually on 7–9 October. A few blocks west of Suwa is the **Nagasaki Museum of History and Culture** (www.nmhc.jp; daily 8.30am–7pm; closed third Tue of each month), which gives insights into Nagasaki's role as a meeting point between Japan and other cultures.

Within walking distance of the temples, the **Nakashima-gawa** (Nakashima River) is spanned by a picturesque range of bridges. The best known and most photographed is **Megane-bashi**, whose English translation of Spectacles Bridge makes immediate sense when there is enough water in the river to ensure a good reflection. The original bridge was the oldest stone arch bridge in Japan, built in 1634 by a priest from Kofuku-ji. However, a flood in 1962 destroyed it and the present structure is a carbon-copy restoration.

Spectacles Bridge, Nagasaki.

True to its traditional receptiveness to new ideas, Nagasaki embarked on an aggressive modernisation campaign in the latter part of the 19th century. Thomas Glover, a Scotsman, was one of the first and most significant of the European traders who arrived soon after Commodore Matthew Perry's Black Ships reopened the country. Glover helped Nagasaki achieve many Japanese firsts: the first railway, the first mint and the first printing press with movable type were all built in Nagasaki as a result of his efforts. He was also very active in supporting the rebels who defeated the shogun's forces – mainly through a profitable line in gun-running – and re-established the emperor's rule in 1868 in the Meiji Restoration. There is considerable controversy over whether Glover's marriage to a geisha did, as many guidebooks assert, inspire Puccini's opera *Madame Butterfly*. Glover also built the first Western-style mansion in Japan.

At the southern end of the city, **Glover-en** ❻ (Glover Gardens; www.glover-garden.jp; daily, late Apr–early-Oct 8am–9.30pm, early Oct–late Apr 8am–6pm) contains this mansion, built in 1863, and several other early Meiji-era, Western-style houses – elegant mixtures of Japanese and European architecture plus the inevitable statues of Puccini and his tragic Japanese heroine. It is amusing to wander around the grounds today, which now have vending machines, covered escalators and recorded announcements, and speculate that these are technological innovations of which Glover himself would have approved.

If your trip does not coincide with the annual Kunchi Festival in early October, when Chinese-style dragon dances and parades are held in the vicinity of Suwa-jinja, a trip to the **Kunchi Shiryokan** (Kunchi Museum; daily 8am–6pm) near Glover Garden will at least give a visitor some idea of the floats and costumes involved.

Nearby in the same neighbourhood is **Oura Tenshu-do** (Oura Catholic Church; daily 8am–6pm), said to be the oldest Gothic-style structure in Japan. Completed in 1865, it is dedicated to the 26 Christian martyrs who

Sofoku-ji Temple.

Nagasaki City Temple.

Atomic Bomb Museum.

were crucified in the 16th century and has some fine examples of stained glass. Signposts point along a paved footpath east of the church to an interesting enclave of foreign influence, the **Dutch Slopes**.

The highly conspicuous **Koshi-byo**, a red and orange lacquered Confucian temple (daily 8.30am–5pm), lies close by the slopes. It's one of just a handful of Confucian temples in Japan, and the treasures within its sanctuary are sumptuous.

A city remembers

A simple stone obelisk stands at the epicentre ("hypocentre" in Japan) of the atomic blast that devastated much of Nagasaki on the morning of 9 August 1945. The plutonium bomb, which was nearly twice as powerful as the uranium bomb dropped earlier over Hiroshima, landed about 3km (2 miles) off course over **Urakami**, a Christian village just to the north of downtown. (The Mitsubishi Heavy Industry shipyard, on the west side of the port and the first modern ship-building facility in Japan, was the intended target; the pilot's vision was hampered by poor visibility.)

Urakami Roman Catholic Church, the largest Christian church in Japan, stood a few hundred metres from the epicentre; it was rebuilt in 1958. Headless statues of saints scorched in the blast remain as mute witnesses to the tragedy. A similarly poignant memorial is the small hut used by Dr Takashi Nagai, who struggled to treat bomb victims as best he could until he himself succumbed to radiation sickness in 1951.

The **Atomic Bomb Museum ⓖ** (daily, May–Aug 8.30am–6.30pm, Sept–Apr 8.30am–5.30pm) at the International Culture Hall contains photos, relics and poignant details of the blast and its 150,000 victims. Simple objects – a melted bottle, the charred remains of a kimono – as well as photos of victims provide stark evidence of the bomb's destructive powers.

As important as its displays are, the museum fails to provide historical context or background to the bombing. Arguments for and against this revolve around whether it is appropriate to include Japan's appalling war record, and thereby attribute partial blame for the bombing to the Japanese, or whether this undoubted atrocity against humanity should be allowed to stand for itself.

Heiwa-koen ⓗ (Peace Park) is dominated by the Peace Statue – a man with right hand pointing to the sky (signalling the threat from the atomic bomb) and left hand extended (symbolising world peace). The Peace Fountain, on the south side of the park, was built in remembrance of the bomb victims who died crying for water. Heiwa-koen was built on the site of a former jail, whose occupants and warders were all killed in the blast. On the other side of the harbour, the cable car (Nagasaki Ropeway; daily 9am–9pm, Mar–Nov until 10pm) climbing the 332-metre (1,089ft) peak of **Inasa-yama ⓘ**

provides fantastic vistas of the harbour and surrounding hills, especially at night. Further south is the Mitsubishi shipyard, the intended target for the atomic bomb.

An hour out of Nagasaki stands **Huis Ten Bosch** (www.huistenbosch.co.jp; daily, closing times varying often, but at least 9am–7pm last admission), one of the most graceful theme parks in Japan with many replicas of Dutch buildings and windmills, canals and clogs galore. Theme park is perhaps an inaccurate description, as Huis Ten Bosch has been carefully constructed on environmentally friendly lines and stands as a modern-day testimony to the area's close links with the Dutch. There is something particularly Japanese about the place in the way that the replicas are built to look precisely like the originals, even to the point of making the Amsterdam canal houses lean out at an angle over the water. Once through the pricey gate most attractions are free, and watching the Japanese tourists dressing up in traditional Dutch clothing for photos is as much fun as examining the architecture.

Shimabara Peninsula

Leaving Nagasaki a scenic route takes travellers through **Shimabara Peninsula** and the Amakusa Islands to Kumamoto on a combination of buses and ferries. Down the peninsula, roughly midway between Nagasaki and Kumamoto, is **Unzen-dake** ⑩, whose *jigoku* (hell) pits of boiling mud and coloured mineral waters are less dramatic but less commercialised than those in Beppu, on the east coast of Kyushu. In the 17th century, Christians who refused to renounce their faith were thrown into these *jigoku*. The town is named after the 1,360-metre (4,460ft) volcano Unzen-dake, on the peninsula and in **Unzen-Amakusa Kokuritsu-koen** (Unzen-Amakusa National Park). Unzen erupted in 1991, causing widespread death and damage. **Shimabara-jo** (Shimabara Castle; daily 9am–5.30pm), destroyed in a 1637 Christian rebellion, was reconstructed in 1964. The castle houses a museum displaying the *fumi-e* Christian images, which suspected believers were forced to walk upon. **Amakusa-shoto** (Amakusa Islands), about 70

FACT

Kyushu cuisine is no less feisty than its inhabitants, typical preparations being slices of sashimi horse meat, grilled sparrow and *karashi renkon*, deep-fried lotus root stuffed with *miso* and mustard, washed down with *shochu*, a firewater distilled from sweet potato and a speciality of Kagoshima.

Huis Ten Bosch.

MINAMATA

The bay near **Minamata**, in the southern part of Kumamoto Prefecture, is a monument to the excesses of industry. A severely debilitating and often fatal ailment known as Minamata disease was traced to shellfish and other products taken from its waters, into which industries had been discharging mercury and other wastes for decades. Legislation hurriedly passed by the Diet soon after the disease's discovery in the 1970s now constitutes the basis of Japan's still weak pollution controls. Nevertheless, litigation regarding the responsibility for the mercury dumping was dragged out until the mid-1990s, with no entity admitting responsibility. Minamata Bay itself is being reclaimed and turned into an ecological park.

FACT

The restored Edo-style Yachiyo-za (www.yachiyo za.com), in Yamaga, 50 minutes by bus from Kumamoto, is one of 10 *kabuki* theatres in Japan. Built in 1910, it is a mixture of traditional Japanese and imported innovations, including a revolving stage and concealed trapdoors. Patrons sit on *tatami*, warming themselves with a *hibachi* (porcelain bowl containing burning charcoal) in winter. Around the corner, a lantern museum displays hundreds of handmade lantern headdresses.

islands in all, lie between Unzen and Kumamoto. The Kirishitankan in **Hondo ⓫** is a museum with relics of the Amakusa Christians.

Kumamoto

Although it isn't a popular tourist destination, **Kumamoto ⓬** is an interesting and dynamic provincial capital. This city of over 0.7 million people is best known for its 17th-century castle, 350-year-old **Suizenji-jojuen** (Suizenji Park), and its horse-meat sashimi. Kumamoto also has the most successful technical research park (adjacent to the airport) in Japan. Kumamoto Prefecture has a sister-state relationship with the American state of Montana, due more to the power and influence of the former American ambassador to Japan, Mike Mansfield, a Montanan, than to any similarity between the two places.

    Kumamoto-jo (Kumamoto Castle; daily, Apr–Oct 8.30am–6pm, Nov–Mar 8.30am–5pm) was built in 1607 by Kato Kiyomasa. Unfortunately, the castle's 49 towers were made of wood and most were incinerated in an 1877

Shimabara-jo.

siege. The restored *donjon*, housing a museum as well as original turrets, moats and stone palisades, evoke the grandeur of what was one of Japan's most impressive castles.

    Honmyo-ji (daily 9am–4.30pm), a Nichiren temple housing Kato's tomb, can be seen from the castle's towers. The basement of the **Kumamoto Prefectural Traditional Crafts Centre** (http://kumamoto-kougeikan.jp;Tue–Sun 9am–5pm), across the street from the castle, is a good place to enjoy a cup of tea, while the first floor has a colourful collection of toys, tools, jewellery and ceramics produced by Kumamoto craftsmen. The museum is part of the prefecture's efforts to sustain traditional crafts, largely abandoned after World War II. **Suizenji-Jojuen** (daily, Mar–Oct 7.30am–6pm, Nov–Feb 8.30am–5pm), designed in 1632 and south of the modern city, contains in its lush, sprawling grounds landscaped models of Mount Fuji and a 400-year-old teahouse that serves *matcha* and sweets.

    The Kyushu Kokusai Kanko Bus has regular departures for **Aso-Kuju Kokuritsu-koen** (Aso-Kuju National Park), but the JR Hohi Line switchback train from Kumamoto to Aso affords great views.

    Signposts along the roads welcome visitors to *Hi-no-Kuni*, the "Land of Fire". **Mount Aso ⓭** is actually a series of five volcanic cones, its massive caldera stretching to a circumference of 128km (80 miles). Of the five peaks, Daikanbo, at 936 metres (3,070ft), is the highest. **Nakadake**, the massive, highly active crater, which is the highlight of an Aso trip for many, emits sulphurous fumes and high-temperature gases that occasionally bring hiking above the basin to an abrupt halt. It last erupted in 2014, and the area within 1km of the crater was still off-limits at the time of writing (check the latest information on www.aso.ne.jp/~volcano/eng/index. html). The ideal way to explore the area beyond the main road connecting the caldera with the town would

normally be by bicycle – a steep ride up, a blissful one down – or time permitting, on foot. You could also get to Mount Aso's crater edge by cable car (however, due to increased volcanic activity, the service was suspended at the time of writing).

Once in the caldera, a striking shape materialises on the right-hand side of the road. This is the grass-covered hill known as **Komezuka**, the name meaning "inverted rice-bowl". Equally suggestive of the ziggurat or burial mound of some ancient nature cult, it is a configuration of great beauty.

Buses en route for Nakadake stop a little further on at Kusasenri-ga-Hama, a circular plain that was originally a minor crater. A large pond at its centre serves as a watering hole for cattle and horses. The **Aso Volcano Museum** (www.asomuse.jp; daily 9am–5pm), with its 170-degree multi-screens relaying images of the crater and its catchment area, is also here. All this subterranean activity means superb hot springs, most found in the caldera itself, though there are *onsen* retreats tucked away in the highlands nearby as well.

East of Kumamoto and on the other side of Aso, the shrine at **Takachiho** ⑭ is where the *iwato kagura*, a sacred dance, is performed for tourists every night (daily 8pm). **Takachiho-kyo** (Takachiho Gorge), with its 80-metre (260ft) cliffs, is another one of the many spots where the Sun Goddess Amaterasu is said to have emerged from her cave to create the islands and people of the archipelago. A cave near the shrine at Iwato is touted as the very one.

Hot springs

If seeking to go to hell and then come back, head for **Beppu** ⑮ on the northeastern coast of Kyushu. The resort town is famous – and thus highly commercialised – for its *jigoku*, or variously coloured ponds of water and mud that steam and boil, as well as its hot springs. A popular destination

for Japanese tourists, Beppu is gaudy and rather tacky and a far cry from the serene elegance of Japanese travel posters. Besides the hype, there are other hells, more than can be experienced in a lifetime, including: Blood Pond Hell, a vermillion-coloured boiling pond; Sea Hell, a boiling mud pond 120 metres (400ft) deep; and Mountain Hell, a mud pond in the hills, complete with statues of gorillas. All these are far too hot for bathing, but in the many *onsen* inns, comfortable hot-sand and hot-mud baths are available.

A more serene and sophisticated hot-spring resort, **Yufuin**, less than an hour inland from Beppu, is known for its galleries, elegant country inns, fashionable guesthouses, and the beautiful morning mists that rise from the warm, thermal waters of **Lake Kinrin**. Bicycles can be rented for a circuit of the lake, and hiking trails taken up nearby Mount Yufu or through the woods.

About 40km (25 miles) south along the coast from Beppu, the **Usuki Sekibutsu** (daily 6am–6pm, Apr–Sept until 7pm), a collection of more than

Kumamoto-jo.

Standing 30km (18 miles) south of Aoshima is the vermilion-coloured shrine of Udo Jingu. It occupies an unusual and spectacular setting in the mouth of a cave beside the ocean. Legend has it that this is the spot where Emperor Jimmu's father, Yamasachihiko, was born; the rounded breasts in front of the cave represent his mother's breasts.

Minamata Memorial.

60 stone Buddhas, is all that remains of the **Mangetsu-ji**, once an important temple. The stone images are some of the most exquisite and mysterious Buddhist images in Japan. It takes less than an hour to take in the statues, but it's still worth the jaunt here and back from Beppu.

Descending Kyushu's rugged east coast to its southern end, the pleasant provincial city of **Miyazaki** ⓰, with its locally grown mangoes, palm-lined streets and indoor water theme park called Seagaia, or Ocean Dome, is a convenient stopover on the way to the Nichinan coast that stretches south of the city. The delightfully rural Nichinan Line train follows the shore, taking a slightly inland route.

Aoshima ⓱, a seaside resort with plenty of action and animation of the modern kind at its beaches, cafés, hotels and amusement arcades, is the most popular stop on the line. Patronised by sun-worshippers and weekend surfers, Aoshima's main draw is its tiny subtropical island of the same name, surrounded by great platforms of "devil's washboard"

– eroded rock formations with row upon row of shallow pools and indented octopus-shaped rings sunk into long furrows of basalt – which disappear at high tide.

Obi and its castle

The crowds rarely make it as far as the old samurai town of **Obi** ⓲, a few stops slightly inland on the Nichinan Line and another town that has taken to calling itself "Little Kyoto". A few discerning Japanese, a quiet trickle of visitors (virtually no foreigners as yet), file in and out of its gardens and samurai villas, though you will often find yourself left alone.

At the core of the old quarter, 15 minutes on foot from Obi Station, Otemon-dori, a ramrod-straight avenue lined with old houses, plaster storerooms and stone and clay walls topped with ceramic tiles, leads to the superbly restored Ote-mon, or main gate, the entrance to the **Obi Castle** grounds (daily 9.30am–4.30pm).

Destroyed in 1870, only its walls, carefully reconstructed in the original style using joinery rather than nails, and a whitewashed history museum, remain. Up a further flight of steps in the castle precincts, the Edo Period **Matsu-no-Maru** (daily 9am–4.30pm), the residence of Lord Ito's most senior wife (yes, he had a few!), is a faithful replica of the original, complete with women's quarters, reception rooms and the Gozaemon, a beautifully stark tea-ceremony room.

The wooden gate to the **Yosho-kan** (daily 9.30am–4.30pm), former residence of the Ito clan, is just to the left of the Ote-mon. Obi's most graceful samurai residence, this airy construction was built for the family's chief retainer and then requisitioned for their own use after feudal holdings were abolished in the Meiji era. All the rooms in the Yoshokan face south in conformity with tradition and the rules of geomancy. Each chamber overlooks a fine dry landscape garden with the ultimate

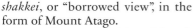

shakkei, or "borrowed view", in the form of Mount Atago.

Proceeding south, **Ishinami beach** is one of the finest stretches of unspoilt white sand along the Nichinan coast. **Kojima**, at the southern end of the cove, is inhabited by wild monkeys. A cluster of rustic farmhouses, doubling in the summer months as *minshuku* (*lodgings*), lie within a short stroll of the beach. **Toi Misaki**, a scenic but overdeveloped cape marred by tacky hotels and other resort facilities, marks the southern tip of this extraordinary, timeworn coast.

Kagoshima

This prefecture in the far south of Kyushu consists of two peninsulas, Satsuma and Osumi, that encircle **Kagoshima-wan** (Kagoshima Bay), and also a chain of islands stretching south towards Okinawa. **Kagoshima ⓳**, on the interior side of Satsuma-hanto and the southernmost metropolis in Kyushu, is situated on large Kagoshima Bay. It is famous for being Japan's most polluted city. The pollution comes from **Sakura-jima ⓴**

(Cherry Blossom Island), the very active volcano east across the bay that rises 1,120 metres (3,670ft) directly above the water. The mountain has erupted more than 5,000 times since 1955, sending clouds of ash and often large boulders raining down on Kagoshima. (Umbrellas are used as much against ash as against rain.) More than half a million people live within 10km (6 miles) of Sakura-jima's crater. No other major city is as precariously positioned; Naples, Kagoshima's sister city, is twice as far from Vesuvius.

Sakura-jima itself can be reached via a short ferry ride from Kagoshima or by road around the periphery of the bay. As the name indicates, it was once an island, but an eruption in 1914 spilled some 3 billion tonnes of lava down its southeast flank, joining it to the peninsula. There are dramatic views from the **Yogan Tenbodai** on the southeast side of Sakura-jima. Extra-large *daikon* (Japanese radishes) grow in the rich volcanic soil, along with kumquats, summer oranges and other fruits.

Beppu Hot Springs.

Satsuma clans

Aside from the ash and sometimes polluted air of Kagoshima, the city itself is delightful and retains the spirit of the once-powerful Satsuma clans, from whom the area takes its name. The Satsumas were ruled by the Shimazu *daimyo*, among the most dynamic of the Japanese hereditary rulers, for seven centuries. The Shimazu's distance from Edo Tokyo bred a fierce independence here in southern Kyushu. The Shimazu were open to new ideas from abroad. They welcomed Francis Xavier to Kagoshima, the first Japanese city he visited, in 1549. Returning from Japan's ill-fated invasion of the Korean peninsula in the early 17th century, the Shimazu brought captive Korean potters to Kagoshima, where they developed Satsuma-ware.

Despite their receptiveness to outsiders, the Satsuma clans opposed the Edo shogunate's capitulation to European demands that Japan open its ports to trade. Demonstrating resistance to the shogun's edicts, Shimazu retainers killed an Englishman near Edo in

1862. The British retaliated the following year by sending a squadron of ships to bombard Kagoshima. To the British sailors' surprise, the lords of Satsuma admired this demonstration of modern naval power. They welcomed Her Majesty's officers to the still smoking city and purchased some of their ships. In 1866, the Satsuma clans joined with the rival Choshu clan in a successful military coup against the shogun, which restored imperial rule with the Meiji Restoration in 1868. (Close relations between the Japanese and British navies lasted until the 1920s, and Satsuma clansmen dominated Japan's navy until World War II.)

Satsuma-ware and the more rustic Kuro-Satsuma pottery can be purchased in **Naeshirogawa**, a village that was settled by Korean potters in the 1600s. In addition to pottery, Kagoshima is known for *kiriko* cut glass.

Iso-koen, containing a garden laid out in 1661, provides excellent views of Sakura-jima. Just outside the park, the **Shoko Shuseikan** (History Museum; www.shuseikan.jp; daily 8.30am–5.30pm) houses one of the first Western-style factories in Japan. It contains exhibits on the factory and the Shimazu family, whose mansion has also been preserved.

The cemetery of Nanshu holds the remains of Saigo Takamori (1827–77), who led the forces that defeated the shogun. Saigo later perished after leading the 1877 rebellion against the Meiji regime he had created. Saigo made his last stand at the hill called Shiroyama. With defeat inevitable, he had a loyal follower decapitate him.

Twelve buses leave Kagoshima every day for the near-1.5-hour ride south to **Minamikyushu** (formerly **Chiran**) ㉑, a charming samurai town set in a pastoral landscape of striking warmth, a concentration of green volcanic peaks, tea plantations and white stucco-faced houses.

The *tokko-tai*, better known in the West as kamikaze pilots, flew from what was then called Chiran and other

Sakurajima Volcano.

bases in southern Kyushu, on the first leg of their one-way missions. Visitors should view the **Tokko Heiwa Kaikan** (Peace Museum for Kamikaze Pilots; www.chiran-tokkou.jp; 9am–5pm), a 3–4km (2–3-mile) taxi or bus ride into the hills north of town. A rather splendid plane, superior to the hastily refurbished trainers most flew, greets visitors to the open space beside the museum. The museum's centrepiece, its **Peace Hall**, was completed in 1975. Its collection, though chilling, is more sentimental than gruesome, with drawers full of uniforms, flying gear and adolescent mascots, its walls and cabinets bristling with letters and photos. In one image, a pilot tightens the rising-sun *hachimaki* bandanna of a comrade, a symbol of samurai valour and pre-battle composure, around the head of a doomed but smiling youth.

Ibusuki ㉒, a spa town southeast of Minamikyushu with hot-sand baths near **Kaimon-dake**, a 900-metre (3,000ft) volcano looking much like Fuji.

Yaku-shima

A circular island 1,000km (600 miles) south of Tokyo and 135km (80 miles) from Kagoshima, **Yaku-shima** is a naturalist's fantasy, declared a UN World Heritage Site in 1993 for its flora. There is the rare Yakushima rhododendron, and the *Yaku-sugi* cedar trees that are over 1,000 years old. (Youthful cedar trees less than 1,000 years old are *ko-sugi*.) Existing at 700 to 1,500 metres (2,300–5,000ft) on the slopes of some of Yaku-shima's 40 peaks that are higher than 1,000 metres (600ft), the cedar trees are like elderly sages amidst the dense foliage. The largest cedar is said to be the world's biggest, with a circumference of 43 metres (141ft) at its roots, a trunk circumference of 16.4 metres (54ft) and a height of 25 metres (80ft). The Japanese also claim that it is the oldest in the world at 7,200 years, but there is some dispute about this.

Waterfalls and lush hiking trails lace this ancient volcanic island, which is nearly 30km (20 miles) in diameter. Once you are done exploring them, head to the island's coast, where you will find several good dive spots and places worth snorkelling. The two small towns of **Anbo** and **Miyanoura** are home to most of the island's 13,000 people and have accommodation and places to rent dive gear.

Amami Islands

Just before Kyushu gives way to Okinawa, and some 300km (200 miles) south of Yaku-shima, are the **Amami Islands**. The largest of these eight islands, **Amami Oshima**, reached by air or ferry from Kyushu, has some great diving spots that take divers to vivid coral in a rich ocean ecosystem. On land, which is 95 percent covered by forest and thick mangrove, the island's wildlife is on a par with Yakushima – it's home to a rare species of hare and a ray jaybird. Less travelled than many of the Okinawan Islands, with which it shares a Ryukyuan cultural heritage, a trip here is something you will share with few other foreign travellers.

A Yaku-shima cedar.

Scuba diving in Okinawa water.

OKINAWA

Once an independent kingdom called Ryukyu, Okinawa is a world of its own. Bloodied by World War II, tropical Okinawa is today Japan's domestic resort escape.

Extending for 1,200km (746 miles) southwest from Kyushu, the 70-plus islands of the Ryukyus, or **Nansei-shoto**, stretch across the ocean to within 200km (125 miles) of Taiwan. For centuries, the Okinawans minded their own business and accommodated themselves to outsiders. But during the age of imperialism in the late 19th century, their independence fell prey to the ambitions of powerful neighbours.

Ryukyu is the Japanese pronunciation of the Chinese name Liugiu, which is what the Ming-dynasty Chinese called the islands. Taken over by Japan, which then long ignored the islands like a faraway province, Okinawa was the final beachhead for a planned Allied invasion of the Japanese archipelago in World War II. The battle for Okinawa was bloody for both sides and for the Okinawan civilians. Placed under American control by the UN following the end of World War II, the islands reverted to Japanese sovereignty in 1972. Now, all islands north of the main island of Okinawa are part of Kyushu, and the main island and islands to the south are in Okinawa Prefecture.

Okinawa sits in a subtropical belt, blessed with average temperatures of around 23°C (73°F). A short rainy season blankets the area in heavy rains during May and June. Spring and autumn are enjoyable, typhoons in September and October notwithstanding.

There are the exquisite white-sand beaches and azure waters of the Yaeyama and Kerama Islands, not to mention some unusual flora and fauna – no wonder Okinawa is, along with Guam, Japan's backyard resort escape. Not that Okinawa is only about beaches – Unesco recognised the local Ryukyu culture in 2000, when they designated a group of historic Ryukyuan sites, including Shuri Castle, as Japan's 11th World Heritage Site.

Okinawans are proud of their heritage and will often remind travellers

Main Attractions

Naha
Himeyuri-no-To
Okinawa World
Nakagusuku
Motobu Peninsula
Zamami Island
Miyako Island
Ishigaki Island
Taketomi Island

Shisa figurine, Taketomi Island.

Awamori cup and jar.

Making sanshin, an Okinawan musical instrument.

that they are not Japanese. A fine and relaxing manner in which to gauge the differences between Okinawa and the rest of Japan is a visit to a local pub to listen to the frequently plaintive sounds of the *sanshin*, the three-stringed, snakeskin-covered Okinawan banjo known elsewhere as the *shamisen*. Traditional Okinawan dance and theatre differ considerably from their Japanese counterparts.

Okinawans are also quite proud of their exquisite textiles, which are typically hand-woven from linen and silk and feature beautiful designs created with painted-on dyes. The designs traditionally differed by area, and the *bingata* stencil-dyed fabric, originally made exclusively for aristocrats, is the most highly prized of the fabrics.

And no visit to Okinawa would be complete without sampling Okinawa's distinctive food and drink, ranging from "delicacies" such as pig ears and trotters to the fiery Okinawan version of shochu, *awamori*, which packs a vodka-like punch.

Naha

The centre of Okinawa's tourism is the city of **Naha ❶**, and Naha's centre of tourist activity is Kokusai-dori (International Road), which is a jangle of typical Japanese urban architecture – cluttered and without aesthetic appeal – and crowds of walkers and swarms of vehicles. Yet only a short distance away are typically Okinawan neighbourhoods. **Naminou-gu**, a small Confucian shrine, and the **Gokoku-ji**, a temple that was once considered a national religious centre, are along the waterfront not far from the central post office and just north of an old pleasure quarter that retains its fair share of bars, cabarets and steakhouses.

Okinawan crafts are a delight. Active since 1617, the **Tsuboya** pottery district, off Himeyuri-dori and southeast of Kokusai-dori, houses two dozen kilns that make everything from the *kara-kara* flasks once carried by country gentlemen to the fearsome *shisa* figures that guard dwellings. Tsuboya's pottery history began in the early 1600s when a Korean potter was forced to settle here after being taken

prisoner. Pottery made in Tsuboya bears 17th-century Korean characteristics, as is also the case in Kyushu. The **Tsuboya Ceramic Museum** (Tue–Sun 10am–6pm), built in the late 1990s, with pottery displays and models of reconstructed local buildings, is an excellent introduction to the history of the area.

Naha is the perfect spot for first experiments with Okinawan cuisine. Now familiar with the sashimi, *unagi*, *yabisoba* and other delicacies of central Japan, travellers might brave *mimiga* (sliced pig ears with vinegar), *ashite-bichi* (stewed pig legs), *rafutei* (pork simmered in miso, sugar, rice wine and soy sauce), *goya champuru* (stir-fried meat and melon), or one of the many kinds of local *somen* noodles. *Awamori*, the local distilled rice brew served with ice and water, packs a wallop that puts all else to shame.

Shuri

The first castle on **Shuri**, west of downtown on a hill overlooking Naha and the oceans beyond, was established in 1237. Under the second Sho dynasty, established in 1469 by King Sho En, Shuri became a mighty palace and temple complex. Shuri remained the political and cultural centre of the Ryukyus until 1879, when the last Okinawan king, Sho Tai, was forced to abdicate by the Meiji government in Tokyo. During the 82-day battle of Okinawa in 1945, when the Japanese Army chose Okinawa as the last stand against the Allies before an anticipated invasion of the main Japanese islands, **Shuri-jo** (Shuri Castle; http://oki-park. jp; daily 8.30am–6pm, Apr–June and Oct–Nov until 7pm, July–Aug until 8pm) was the headquarters of the Japanese forces. It was destroyed in the fighting. Pre-war accounts describe a marvel on a par in architectural and artistic interest with Kyoto, Nara and Nikko. Much of the castle's stonework has now been rebuilt.

Nearby, **Ryutan-koen** is an expansive park barely able to absorb the hordes of tour buses or the clusters of tour groups posing for photographs with classically attired Okinawan women in front of **Shuri no Mon**, the traditional gate to the castle grounds.

Shaping terracotta in Tsuboya.

The **Tama-udon**, minutes from the gate, contains the bodies of Sho En and other members of his family. The nearby **Okinawa Prefectural Museum** (Sun–Thu 9am–6pm, Fri–Sat 9am–7pm), is a very slick facility that presents a good digest of Okinawa's rich history and culture.

South of Naha

Southern Okinawa is noted for caves. The most famous caves are the tunnel labyrinths at **Tomigusuku**, near the Naha airport and the last headquarters of the Imperial Navy. The military commanders refused to surrender as the Allies pounded the island's south with naval bombardments; over 4,000 Japanese men committed suicide. Reminders and memorials of the bloodiest battle of the Pacific war that cost the lives of 13,000 Americans, 110,000 Japanese and 140,000 Okinawan civilians (one-eighth of the population) are numerous throughout the south of the island.

The coastal highway south past the international airport leads to **Itoman**, claimed to be the home of some of

US Marine Corps' Futemma Air Station in Ginowan.

the most fearless sailors in the world. Itoman's mid-August tug-of-war with intertwined "male" and "female" ropes draws crowds from afar. Several heavily promoted and developed caverns pepper the southern coastline, including **Hakugin-do**, a cavern with a shrine dedicated to the guardian deity of Itoman.

The story of **Himeyuri-no-To** ❷ (Lily of the Valley Tower) is famous: it involves a deep pit where a group of high-school girls and their teachers committed suicide – rather than endure the possibility of capture by Americans – after singing their school song. **Mabuniga-oka**, on a promontory overlooking the ocean, is the site of the last resistance of the Japanese Army. Just east of here is the **Okinawa Prefecture Peace Memorial Museum** (daily 9am–5pm), which documents the Battle of Okinawa and the suffering of the people of the islands during World War II.

Gyokusen-do is said to be East Asia's largest cave. Only about one-fifth of it is open to the public; unfortunately, in this part visitors have

US BASES

It's impossible to talk about Okinawa without the long-running debate over US military bases on the islands cropping up. For locals, it's certainly an emotive subject – while the bases contribute greatly to the local economy, the majority of islanders want no US military presence at all on the islands. The noise and disturbances caused by major bases such as Kadena and Futenma, both north of Naha, is one reason. Cases of US military personnel making a nuisance of themselves is another; although with the subject of the bases being so sensitive (and political), it isn't unheard of for incidents to get blown out of proportion.

One common complaint from Okinawans is this: why, when they represent only 1 percent of the country's landmass, do they get almost 75 percent of US bases? Part of the answer is that nowhere else in Japan wants them to be relocated to their front step. The only way for Okinawa to be rid of the bases is for them to move overseas.

In December 2013, the relocation of Futenma airbase (with its busy runway) was approved by the governor of Okinawa. According to the agreement, 9,000 marines will be moved to Guam, Hawaii or Australia, while 10,000 will stay on the island in a new base in Henoko. However, the latter has become another bone of contention. Okinawan people are against the construction of a new facility and would like to see all American bases simply moved off the island.

broken off most of the stalactites and stalagmites, and the cave's floor has been pockmarked by footprints. Not to worry, though, as the caves are part of the larger **Okinawa World** ❸ (www.gyokusendo.co.jp/okinawaworld; daily 9am–6pm), a "village" with extensive attractions related to local culture, arts and crafts. One of the quirkier places here is **Habu-koen** (Snake Park; www.habu-park.com; daily 9am–6pm), where there are displays of fights between mongooses and *habu* snakes, whose venom is strong enough to fell a horse.

A 5km (3-mile) ferry ride from **Chinen** ❹ on Okinawa's southeast coast brings visitors to small and flat **Kudaka-jima**, the so-called island of the gods. This is where the great ancestress of the Ryukyuan people, Amamikiyo, is said to have descended from heaven and bestowed on them the five grains. The people of these isolated, storm-swept islands came to believe that their fate rested in the hands of the gods, and an arcane priestess cult still survives, albeit only just. Covered with sugar cane and *fukugi* trees, Kudaka-jima, which has a resident population of about 200 people, is a somnolent place. Until the 1990s, it transformed in mid-November every 12th year for the five-day Izaiho Festival, in which local women served collectively as *noro*, or priestesses, to perform rites and communicate with the gods. The *noro* are still on the island, but because of a dwindling female population, the festival has been in hiatus since 1990. Kudaka still has its charms though. Like other *utaki*, or sacred places throughout Okinawa, visitors often remark that the sounds of the sea, wind and the singing birds seem strangely louder here.

Central and northern Okinawa

About 15km (9 miles) north of Shuri are the ruins of the castle at **Nakagusuku** ❺, built in the 15th century, and the largest in Okinawa. These ruins are part of the same World Heritage

package as Shuri, but they aren't the only worthwhile attraction here. The Nakamura home in Nakagusuku offers an insight into how an 18th-century gentry family lived.

Back on the west coast, the main road north of Naha, towards Moon Bay, passes **Ryukyu-mura** (www.ryukyumura.co.jp; daily 8.30am–5.30pm), a cultural heritage village that has preserved some genuine traditional farmhouses and other tangible features of Okinawan culture. Despite the souvenir-dominated entrance and exit areas, the "village" is an intriguing digest that includes displays of Okinawan crafts like textile weaving and dyeing, Eisa dancing and performances on the sanshin. Okinawan dishes and sweets made from the local brown sugar are readily available. You could easily spend half a day here, soaking up the Ryukyu culture.

Jutting out from the west coast about two-thirds of the way to the northern tip of Okinawa, **Motobu-hanto** ❻ (Motobu Peninsula) was the site of an ocean exposition in the 1970s. Most of the tourist-focused

Shuri Castle.

TIP

Okinawa has plenty of excellent diving opportunities. The best three places to check out are Zamami-jima in the Kerama Islands, Irabu off Miyako-jima, and Shiraho-no-umi on Ishigaki, home to the world's longest blue coral reef.

offerings are on the exposition's former site, Exposition Memorial Park, including several exhibitions about Okinawan culture and the ocean. The restored ruins of **Nakijin-jo** (Nakijin Castle; http://nakijinjo.jp; daily 8am–6pm last entry), on the peninsula's northern tip, are a fine place to watch a sunset. Offshore, tiny **Ie-jima** is where a famous US war correspondent, Ernie Pyle, was killed in World War II. Also on the Motobu-hanto is the **Ocean Expo Park** (http://oki-park.jp; daily, Mar–Sept 8am–7.30pm Oct–Feb 8am–6pm). Among the attractions that make this a good family trip are a fine aquarium, a planetarium, a museum documenting the lives of fishing communities in Southeast Asia, several small beaches, local crafts and arts, and a small kids' adventure area.

A visit to the far north of Okinawa, or *yanbaru*, will reward the adventurous with rugged hills, beaches and secluded fishing villages, along with some of the friendliest people anywhere. In the village of **Kijoka** ****, you can watch the various steps required

View from Nakijin Castle.

to produce the plantain-fibre textile *bashofu*. The view at **Hedo-misaki** ❽, the cape at the northern tip of the island, is stunning. But don't go wandering off in the bush in *yanbaru*, as this is *habu* – the deadly poisonous snake found in Okinawa – country.

One of the Ryukyu's sacred islands is **Iheya-jima** ❾, to the northeast of Okinawa. According to Okinawan legend, King Jimmu Tenno began his conquest of Japan from here. Moreover, a huge cave on the island, referred to as the "Hiding Place", is said to be the very cave where the Sun Goddess Amaterasu hid herself until the other deities could coax her out, thereby restoring light to the world.

Outer islands

The best way to experience the Ryukyuan way of life is to visit the outer islands, or *saki-shima*, reached by ferry or air from Naha. The 20 **Kerama Islands** ❿ are only 35km (20 miles) west of Naha, and the coral reefs in the surrounding waters provide excellent scuba-diving. A favourite diving and beach spot, **Zamami-jima** is a largely unspoilt island with its own dialect and customs. The **tourist information office** (daily 8.30am–5.30pm) in the harbour has a good map in English of the island. Zamami is a major centre for whale-watching. It may surprise foreigners to learn that a good many Japanese are just as concerned as they are about preserving whales – Japan's pro-whaling lobby is a minority, but one with powerful connections. The tourist office includes the Zamami Whale-Watching Association, which runs two-and-a-half-hour boat trips daily at 10.30am and 1pm, from January through to the end of March.

Further afield is the Miyako group of eight islands. **Miyako-jima** ⓫, the main island, is an hour by air or 10 hours by boat from Naha. The beaches here are some of the finest in Japan, most notably **Yonaha Maihama beach** on Miyako-jima (known as Maibama by locals). This 7km (4.5-mile)

strip of mostly undeveloped (save for a large Tokyu Resort) white sand is sandwiched by azure waters and subtropical trees, and is a good place to look for marine sports or just relax in relative peace and quiet. Nearby **Irabu**, an island that can be reached by boat from Miyako-Jima, offers attractive scenery and fine diving.

At Miyako-jima's port of **Hirara** are the *o-honoyama* (tax stones). After the samurai of Satsuma (now Kagoshima) on Kyushu invaded the Ryukyu kingdom in 1609, it became in everything but name a tributary to that fief's lord, even though the country also continued to pay tribute to the Ming dynasty in China. At the time, all children on Miyako-jima were paraded once a year before the *ninto-zeiseki*. Those taller than the stone had to pay the tax or else were shipped off to work as forced labour. This system was only abolished in 1918. Miyako-jima earned a place in Japanese school books when five local fishermen spotted the Czarist fleet steaming towards Japan during the Russo-Japanese War (1904–5). The timely warning allowed the Imperial Navy, under Admiral Togo Shigenori, to surprise and annihilate the Russians in the Battle of Tsushima Straits.

Yaeyama Islands

The narrator of Kushi Fusako's short story *Memoirs of a Declining Ryukyuan Woman* observes, "We always seem to be at the tail end of history, dragged along roads already ruined by others." Efforts to stamp out traditional Okinawan customs by the mainland Japanese government were only partially successful in the **Yaeyama Islands**, where the indigenous beliefs of these parts, the animism and shamanistic practices that predated the Japanese acquisition of the islands, survive and serve as the prime reason for paying a visit – nowhere is Ryukyu culture better felt than here. Further from Tokyo than from Taipei, the Yaeyamas assimilated both Chinese and Japanese influences. These remote islanders have also been influenced by Southeast Asians, allowing for other, more exotic influences to creep in. Being out of the mainstream has benefited the islands in a number of other ways. The Yaeyamas were fortunate enough to be left comparatively unaffected by Japanese colonial policies of the last century and to have emerged unscathed from both the pitched battles of World War II and the effects of the subsequent American Occupation of Okinawa, which only ended in 1972.

Ishigaki

Ishigaki-jima ⑫ is the main island of the Yaeyama chain and its administrative centre. Its name signifies "stone walls", a derivation from the local dialect *"Ishiagira"*, meaning "a place of many stones". Its airport and harbour serve the other outlying islands in the group. Ishigaki offers visitors more creature comforts than are normally found on the other islands, and a

FACT

An undersea earthquake occurred near Ishigaki Island in 1776, resulting in a massive tsunami. In 1924, underwater volcanic activity in the oceanic area north of Iriomote Island caused the sea to boil for several days.

Yaeyama Islands

0   20 km
0   20 miles

FACT

Iriomote is noted for its rare flora and fauna. The Iriomote wildcat, a nocturnal feline, was discovered in 1965 and is endemic to the island. Other rare species include the atlas moth, the yellow-margined box turtle and the crested serpent eagle.

The Kerama Islands.

larger number of conventional sights, but also makes an excellent base from which to explore islands whose names and locations are unfamiliar even to many Japanese people.

Ishigaki's island feel is intensified by the roadside presence of colourful dugout canoes, more suggestive of Polynesia than Japan. Samples of the region's unique culture can be seen at the **Yaeyama Museum** (Tue–Sun 9am–5pm), where good examples of ancient Panori ceramics, old Yaeyama-*jofu* textiles and more canoes can be found. Also of interest in the town itself is the beautifully preserved **Miyara Donchi** (Wed–Mon 9am–5pm), the ancestral home of the Matsushige family. Modelled on aristocratic buildings at the royal capital of Shuri in Naha, it is the only such house left in Okinawa. Built in 1819, its stone garden, made from pitted coral in the Chinese manner, and sprouting with myriad tropical plants, sets it far apart from mainland Japanese dry landscape arrangements.

The white beaches, clear blue waters, coral and tropical fish are ideal for snorkelling and diving. A bus ride from the port, protected **Shiraho-no-umi** on the southeast coast boasts the world's largest blue coral reef. Heading north along the western shore, the **Ishigaki Yaima Village** (www.yaimamura.com; daily 9am–5.30pm), a cultural heritage village in a lovely setting on a hill above Nagura Bay, has well-preserved Okinawan buildings, gardens and an exhibition on the history of the islands' weaving styles. Ishigaki is of considerable ecological importance. **Kabira Bay** on the north shore is unquestionably the island's most spectacular marine landscape. Here, green islets rise like loaves of bread from crystal-clear, steeply shelving emerald waters. But be warned that Japan's best views often come with an excess of tourist stalls – Kabira is no exception, but is still well worth a visit. Just 5km (3 miles) east of Kabira Bay, **Yonehara beach** is a wonderful place to snorkel the teeming coral.

Although **Taketomi-jima** can be reached by ferry in just 12 minutes from Ishigaki's port, it remains a time capsule among these southern seas, the hospitality of its 400 or so inhabitants a measure of how well it has retained its identity. The name Taketomi signifies "prosperous bamboo", stands of which can be seen at the roadsides or in the centre of this island, whose circumference stretches to little more than 9km (5.5 miles). These days the island is noted for its sumptuous flowers and plant life. Bougainvillea and hibiscus, traditionally used in this part of Okinawa to decorate graves and Buddhist altars, spill over walls made from volcanic rock, built as a defence against the furious typhoons that strike the islands from late September to early October.

Kondoi Misaki, the island's finest beach, located along the southwestern shore, is known for its star-shaped sand grains, actually the remains of tiny, fossilised sea creatures. Taketomi is also famous as the source of *minsa*, an indigo fabric often used as a belt for a women's kimono. *Minsa* is only produced on Taketomi. Strips of the material can be seen drying on the stone walls of the village, or at the **Mingei-kan**, a weaving centre where you can observe women at work on the fabrics.

A ferry also goes to the large island of **Iriomote** , which is no doubt the most unusual island in the Japanese archipelago – a touch of New Guinea in Japan. Except for the towns of Ohara in the southeast and Funaura in the north, the island is mostly tropical rainforest. Thankfully, development on the island has so far not run amok, and the majority of accommodation are hostels, *minshuku* (lodgings) or small developments. River trips along the broad, Amazonian-like **Urauchi-gawa** on Iriomote Island include trekking through the jungle to a series of natural waterfalls. The island is home to the nocturnal Iriomote lynx, one of the world's rarest species of cat.

Yonaguni-jima ⓮, a forested island with some of the chain's most spectacular diving and snorkelling offerings, is now accessible by plane. Yonaguni is Okinawa's most westerly island, a mere 125km (78 miles) from Taiwan.

Southernmost point

It is worth making the sometimes choppy, 50-minute crossing from Ishigaki port to **Hateruma-jima** ⓯, a rustic island out on a limb among the southern Yaeyamas, a place where empty roads lead not to hotels and shops, but to an infinity of sea and sky. The name "Hateruma" means "the end of the coral", an indication that this is Japan's southernmost island, its last landmass. Local maps to the island's **Southernmost Point Monument**, a cement and rock affair stuck on top of a bluff above the cliffs, read "Beyond here, the Philippines." Renting a bicycle for the day nicely matches the rhythm and pace of this small, 6km (4-mile) long island.

Ghostly banyan trees, *fukugi* and Indian almond trees dot the island. Among the island flowers are bamboo orchids, hibiscus and plumeria. Taking root also in the sand of Hateruma's superb **Nishi-no-Hama**, or West Beach, are pineapple-like *pandanus* trees. For divers, underwater Hateruma is a glorious filigree of coral, stone holes, rock arches and deep-blue silhouettes.

Mangrove forest, Iriomote-jima.

Kabira Bay, Ishigaki-jima.

A surfer carrying his board to Enoshima Beach.

TRAVEL TIPS
JAPAN

TRANSPORT

GETTING THERE AND GETTING AROUND

GETTING THERE

By air

Tokyo, the main gateway to Japan, is served by two main airports: **New Tokyo International Airport** (Narita), 66km (41 miles) east of the city, and **Tokyo International Airport** (Haneda), 20km (12 miles) to the south of the city centre. The airports are usually simply referred to as Narita and Haneda. Narita is the main international airport serving the Kanto region. While Haneda has been increasing its international routes in recent years, its main function is still as Tokyo's domestic hub.

Narita Airport

Although it is a little inconveniently located, Narita Airport's services have vastly improved since its renewal and extension, completed in 2009. It has two terminals and two runways. Both terminals have currency-exchange counters, ATMs, restaurants and cafés, internet facilities, post offices and health clinics, and a range of shops including duty-free. Terminal 2 has a children's playroom, day rooms for taking a nap, and showers. **General and flight info**: 0476-34-8000; www.narita-airport.jp/en **Tourist info**: 0476-30-3383 (Terminal 1); 0476-34-5877 (Terminal 2)

Haneda Airport

Haneda is Tokyo's hub for domestic flights. Both domestic airlines – Japan Air Lines (JAL) and All Nippon Airways (ANA) – operate flights throughout Japan from Haneda. Since the opening of its new international terminal in 2010 and the launch of long-haul daytime services in 2014, Haneda has also offered flights to many major cities overseas, including London, New York, Paris, Bangkok and Beijing.

Haneda's two domestic terminals are well designed, with Japanese, Western and Chinese restaurants, cafés, shops, a post office, information desks and a bookstore. The sleek international terminal has a similarly good selection of facilities, in addition to one floor designed to look like an Edo-era town.

Airport info: 03-5757-8111; www.haneda-airport.jp (international); www.tokyo-airport-bldg.co.jp (domestic)

Osaka-Kansai Airport

Kansai International Airport (www.kansai-airport.or.jp/en) in Osaka serves the entire Kansai region, especially Osaka, Kyoto and Kobe. Airport facilities are good, city transport rapid and efficient.

Central Japan International Airport, Nagoya

This international airport (www.centrair.jp/en), commonly known as Centrair, is handily located between Tokyo and Osaka. Flight routes include those to and from the USA, Continental Europe and numerous Asian destinations, including Singapore, Thailand and Hong Kong.

Fukuoka Airport

Western Japan's main arrival and departure point from overseas, this international airport (www.fuk-ab.co.jp/english) provides flights to Asian destinations, as well as domestic routes.

Naha Airport

The main gateway to Okinawa, Naha International Airport's (www.naha-airport.co.jp/en) main overseas destinations is Hong Kong, Shanghai, Taipei and Seoul.

Niigata Airport

The main international airport in northern Japan (www.niigata-airport.gr.jp), Niigata provides useful links to Harbin, Shanghai, Xian, Guam, Vladivostok and other Asian airports, in addition to domestic routes.

New Chitose Airport, Sapporo

The main gateway to Hokkaido, New Chitose (http://www.new-chitose-

Key airlines

American Airlines
2-4-11, Higashi-Shinagawa,
Shinagawa-ku, Tokyo
Tel: 03-4333-7675
www.aa.com
British Airways
Tel: 03-3298-5238
www.britishairways.com
Qantas Airways
Tel: 03-6833-7000 (in Tokyo), 0120-207 020 (toll free, outside of Tokyo)

www.qantas.com.au
Singapore Airlines
1-10-1 Yurakucho, Chiyoda-ku,
Tokyo
Tel: 03-3213-3431
www.singaporeair.com
United Airlines
Tel: 03-6732-5011
www.united.com
Virgin Atlantic Airways
www.virgin-atlantic.com

airport.jp/en), just outside Sapporo, provides numerous domestic connections, as well as handy links to Seoul, Taipei, Beijing, Shanghai, Hong Kong and Bangkok.

More gateways

A number of smaller airports, including those in Nagasaki, Kumamoto and Kagoshima, may be worth checking out for their connections to and from Asian destinations in South Korea, Hong Kong, China and other East Asian destinations.

Flying from the UK and the US

The four big-name airlines serving Tokyo from the UK are British Airways, JAL, ANA and Virgin Atlantic. Flying time direct from London is 11–13 hours.

Coming from the US or Canada, you are spoilt for choice. Besides JAL and ANA, among the better-known airlines are Delta, United Airlines and American Airlines. Flying time from the US west coast is 12–13 hours; from the east coast it is 18–20 hours, including stopovers, though there are now some non-stop flights, for example from New York.

Tokyo is an increasingly important transport hub for direct flights from major destinations like Beijing, Shanghai, Hong Kong, Bangkok and further afield from Singapore, Bali and Sydney.

While fares vary between airlines, April, August and December tend to be the most expensive times to fly to Japan from the UK or US as they coincide with the country's Golden Week, O-Bon and Year End–New Year holidays. Flying a few days either side of these peak periods can result in huge savings.

Other departure points

JAL and Qantas have daily flights to Japan from Australia. JAL, ANA, Air Canada and American Airlines offer flights between Japan and North America. Air New Zealand and JAL have daily flights to Japan from New Zealand. There are innumerable flights from the main cities of Continental Europe, such as Paris, Frankfurt, Rome and Amsterdam. Cathay Pacific, JAL, ANA and Air China are the main airlines serving Hong Kong and China, but there are cheaper carriers also. Singapore Airlines, Thai Airways International, JAL and ANA are among many companies serving Southeast Asian destinations such as Bangkok,

Women-only carriage on a Japanese train.

Singapore, Ho Chi Minh City and Jakarta.

By sea

Although few people arrive in Tokyo by sea, the slow approach to this speed-defined city would certainly be a novelty. Japan's ferry services are quite extensive, at least in their connections with South Korea and China.

There is a regular boat service between South Korea's port of Busan and Shimonoseki in Japan (www.kampuferry.co.jp). The latter also has connections to the ports of Qingdao (www.orientferry.co.jp) and Taicang (www.ssferry.co.jp), both in China. A hydrofoil (www.jrbeetle.co.jp) as well as a ferry (www.camellia-line.co.jp) travel between Busan and Hakata in Japan.

Ferries from Shanghai (www.shanghai-ferry.co.jp) arrive in Osaka, from where passengers travel either by rail or air to Tokyo. In summer, a ferry operates between Wakkanai in northern Hokkaido and Korsakov in Russia.

GETTING AROUND

On arrival

From Narita Airport

A taxi to downtown Tokyo from Narita costs between ¥20,000 and ¥30,000, depending on destination and traffic. Most people prefer either the bus or train as they are much cheaper. By bus or taxi, it's 90 minutes to 2.5 hours by road.

Bus: a regular limousine bus service (www.limousinebus.co.jp/en) runs between Narita and TCAT (Tokyo City Air Terminal) in central Tokyo, to Tokyo and Shinjuku stations, and to most major hotels in Tokyo. Tickets (around ¥3,000) are bought at the airport after clearing immigration and customs. There are several routes depending on destination. Buses are boarded outside the terminal at the kerb, and will accept any amount of luggage at no extra charge. The buses leave every 10 to 20 minutes, depending on the route, taking 90 minutes to 2.5 hours to arrive at central hotels. There are also buses to Yokohama and Haneda Airport.

Trains: there are two train alternatives into Tokyo: Japan Railways (JR) Narita Express (www.jreast.co.jp/e/nex) and the Keisei Skyliner (www.keisei.co.jp). Both are twice as fast as taxi or bus, but not as convenient, as once you arrive at a station, you'll have to make arrangements for transport around the city. Be aware also that, while the city's train system is all-encompassing, carrying luggage through train and subway is a feat of considerable effort, involving long hikes and Fuji-like climbs. If you have more than one piece of luggage, don't even think about getting around or reaching your hotel by either overhead train or subway, especially during the hot and humid summer months. Instead, consider the limousine bus or the baggage delivery service available at the airport.

In terms of connections, the Narita Express is more convenient, stopping at JR stations in Chiba, Tokyo (Station), Shinjuku, Ikebukuro, Yokohama and Ofuna. The Skyliner

The bullet train in Kyoto.

stops just at Ueno Station and nearby Nippori. Both have services approximately every 30 minutes and take about the same time to reach Tokyo – 41 minutes to Ueno on the Skyliner and 53 minutes to Tokyo Station on the Narita Express – and neither has restrictions on luggage. Both also offer a comfortable ride, with smart modern carriages and far more legroom than you would have had if you flew economy to Narita.

The Narita Express costs approximately ¥3,000 for standard class and tickets can be bought up to a month in advance at travel agents, Floor B1 of the airport or at the station before boarding. The Keisei Skyliner costs ¥2,470 and tickets can also be bought in advance or at the station. If you are travelling during a peak holiday period, it is advisable to book train tickets when heading to Narita. From Narita into Tokyo, you will have no problems getting tickets upon arrival.

Domestic air connections: Narita operates domestic flights to a number of cities, including Sapporo, Osaka, Nagoya and Naha. If making a domestic air connection to elsewhere, you must take the taxi, bus or train into Tokyo and make the connection at Haneda Airport. The limousine bus will take you directly from Narita to Haneda, as will a very expensive taxi ride.

Baggage delivery: many residents of Japan take advantage of Japan's fast and reliable delivery network. After clearing immigration and customs, take your luggage to one of the several JAL ABC, GPA or KTC counters. Often a queue indicates the counters. For about ¥2,000–4,000 per bag, they can deliver the luggage by the following day wherever you are.

From Haneda Airport

If you are coming into Haneda Airport, a taxi to the city centre will cost ¥5,000 to ¥6,000 and takes about 30–40 minutes. Provided your luggage is light, you can take either the Monorail to Hamamatsucho Station on the JR Yamanote Line or take the Keikyu Line to Shinagawa Station. Both trips take 13 minutes.

From Kansai Airport

The Kansai International Airport (KIX) has replaced Osaka Airport (Itami) as the international air terminus for the Kansai region. It was also intended to relieve the overcrowding at Narita Airport, which has restricted operating hours. Today, lots of domestic flights fly from Itami.

The second-largest and the first 24-hour-operation airport in Japan, Kansai International Airport opened in 1994. It is located southeast of Osaka Bay, 5km (8 miles) off the coast and about 60km (37 miles) from JR Shin-Osaka Station for *shinkansen* (bullet train) connections. The airport, constructed on an artificial island in Osaka Bay and one of the world's most expensive airports – ¥2,650 departure tax – is architecturally impressive and extremely functional. All international and domestic connections at KIX are made at the same terminal in a matter of minutes. Make sure to confirm that domestic flight connections are from KIX and not Itami-Osaka Airport. Despite being on an island, getting to and from KIX is relatively easy: two railways, two expressways and some 10 limousine bus lines connect the island to every point in Kansai. A high-speed ferry service also connects to Kobe Airport.

For travel information, the **Kansai Tourist Information Centre** is located in the arrival lobby (1st Floor) and is open daily 7am–8.30pm. For handling currency exchange, there are 17 currency exchange bureaus with one or more open 6am–11pm. Cash machines are also plentiful. The only bank that conducts normal business operations at the airport is the Bank of Tokyo-Mitsubishi UFJ on the second floor (Mon–Fri 8.30am–6pm). Japan Rail Passes can be validated either at the JR West Information Counter in the International Arrivals Lobby (1st Floor, daily 10.30am–6.30pm), at the TIS-Travel Service Centre (daily 10am–6pm) or at the green-coloured Midori-no-madoguchi Reservations Ticket Office (daily 5.30am–11pm) at JR Kansai Airport Station.

To/from Osaka

Train: JR (Japan Railways) Haruka Express, with reserved seating, runs between KIX and Osaka's Tennoji Station (29 min) and Shin Osaka Station (50 min), where you catch the *shinkansen*, or bullet train. The JR Airport Rapid service connects KIX with Osaka's Tennoji Station (45 min), while the Nankai Railways Airport Express connects with Namba Station's Osaka City Air Terminal (O-CAT), which also offers express baggage check-in (45 min). **JR West train information**: tel: 0570-00-2486 (daily 6am–11pm), www.westjr.co.jp.

Nankai train information tel: 0724-56-6203.

Bus: there are a number of deluxe buses between KIX and various Osaka hotels and rail stations, including the 24-hour limousine bus service to Osaka Station. For bus information call Kansai International Airport Information Service (24-hours), tel: 0724-55-2500, or inquire at one of the eight information counters at the airport.

To/from Kyoto

Train: JR Haruka Express, reserved seats, connects Kyoto Station with KIX (75 min). For JR train information tel: 0570-00-2486.
Bus: a bus leaves Kyoto Station for KIX and takes about 85 minutes. For bus information call Kansai International Airport Information Service (24-hours): tel: 0724-55-2500.

To/from Nara

Bus: a bus runs from KIX to Nara JR Station (90 min). For bus information call Kansai International Airport Information Service (24-hours): tel: 0724-55-2500.

To/from Kobe

Bus: connect by bus from KIX to Kobe's Sannomiya Station (90 min). For bus information, Kansai International Airport Information Service (24-hours): tel: 0724-55-2500.

Ferry: the Kobe Jet Shuttle is the best and fastest way to get to or from Kobe. The Jet Shuttle runs between KIX and the Kobe City Air Terminal (K-CAT) on Port Island (30 min), where a free bus service is provided to Kobe's Sannomiya Station. For Jet Shuttle information tel: 078-304-0033.

From Sendai

25 minutes from town and linked by regular bus services. Domestic flights connect to most cities (Tokyo 45 minutes and Osaka 1 hour 30 min). International flights have decreased since the March 2011 earthquake, and now connect mostly to Guam, Korea and Taiwan.

From Sapporo

35 minutes from town and linked by regular bus services. Domestic flights connect to most cities (Tokyo 2 hours and Osaka 3 hours). International flights connect to China, Hong Kong, Korea, Thailand and Taiwan.

From Hiroshima

50 minutes from town and linked by regular bus services. Domestic flights connect to most cities (Tokyo 1 hour 20 min and Osaka 45 min). International flights connect to China, Hong Kong, Korea and Taiwan.

From Fukuoka

Domestic flights connect to most cities (Tokyo 1 hour 40 min and Osaka-Itami 1 hour 5 min). International flights connect to China, Guam, Korea, Philippines, Singapore, Taiwan and Thailand.

From Nagasaki

One hour or more from town and linked by regular bus services. Domestic flights connect to most cities (Tokyo 2 hours to 2 hours 30 min and Osaka 1 hour). International flights connect to China and Korea.

From Okinawa

15 minutes from Naha and linked by regular bus services. Domestic flights connect to most cities (Tokyo 3 hours

Taxis

Taxis are the most comfortable way of getting around, but also the most expensive. The basic fare in Tokyo is ¥710 for the flag drop. A short trip can easily run from ¥3,000 to ¥5,000. No tipping is expected or required. Taxis are readily available at almost every city-centre street corner, major hotel and railway station. A red light in the front window is illuminated if the taxi is available.

Don't touch the door when getting in or out of a taxi. The doors on taxis are operated by the driver with a remote lever. Get out, walk

and Osaka 2 hours). International flights connect to China, Hong Kong, Korea and Taiwan.

Public transport

Rail

Japan has one of the most efficient and extensive rail networks in the world. Rail service is provided by **Japan Railways (JR)** and several regional private lines. The trains on important routes run every few minutes. High-speed trains – such as JR's **shinkansen**, sometimes called the bullet train, which travels at speeds of up to 300kph (185mph) – offer a good alternative to air and long-distance bus travel. Between Tokyo and Kyoto, travel times and prices are similar for both air and shinkansen. The train, however, is from city centre to city centre; plane, from airport to airport.

Subway entrance in Fukuoka.

away and forget the door.

Most taxi drivers speak only Japanese, so it can be helpful to have your destination written in Japanese. As many taxi drivers rely on their in-car navigation systems rather than an in-depth knowledge of the streets, having the address for them to input will also prevent them getting lost.

Don't be surprised if an available taxi ignores you late at night; the driver is looking for a *sarariman* – and a nice, tidy fare – on his way back to the suburbs.

Subway systems in Japan are clean, safe, and convenient. They are faster than congested road transport. However, they are notorious for being crowded, especially during morning and evening rush hours.

All subway stations post timetables. Regular service is Monday to Friday. The Saturday, Sunday and holiday timetable has slightly fewer trains. Trains run until just after midnight, so be sure to check the time of the last train if you're out late. All stations have a route map with fares for each stop near the ticket machines, but not always in English. Your present location is shown with a red mark.

The fares are regulated on a station-to-station basis, so if you cannot determine the fare required, just purchase the cheapest ticket available. You can pay the difference, if needed, at the exit gate upon arrival at your destination.

A child's ticket is half fare. Ticket machines accept ¥1,000 notes in addition to coins. At most stations there will also be machines that accept ¥5,000 and ¥10,000 bills.

Savings can be made by buying a *teiki* (train pass). Major subway and overland train stations issue passes. Another way to save on train fares is to buy a *kaisuken*, a series of 11 tickets between two destinations for the price of 10.

Station arrivals are announced in Japanese inside the trains, but these are often difficult to understand. There is usually a map of the stops on the line and connecting lines above the train doors, often written in both Japanese and English.

Timetables and subway system maps in Japanese can be obtained at most stations, and in English at major train and subway stations.

TRANSPORT

EATING OUT

ACTIVITIES

A – Z

LANGUAGE

Taxi in Tokyo.

Discount tickets

In the major cities, there are special tickets that allow unlimited travel for one day and are good value. They can be purchased at ticket windows and sometimes at special ticket machines, often marked in English.

Tokyo

Nine of Tokyo's 13 subway lines are now collectively known as the Tokyo Metro. The remaining four are run by the Tokyo Metropolitan Bureau of Transportation, and are referred to as Toei lines.

Tokyo Furii Kippu (Tokyo Tour Ticket): one-day pass for JR trains and Toei trains and buses. All may be used as often as you want (except JR express trains). ¥1,590.

Tokunai Pass: unlimited-use, one-day pass in Tokyo for use only on JR trains (except JR express trains) running within the 23 wards of Tokyo. ¥750.

Toei Economy Pass (Toei Marugoto Kippu): unlimited-use, one-day pass for Toei trains, buses and subway trains within Tokyo on any day within a 6-month period. Approx. ¥700.

Kyoto

Unlimited-use, one-day bus and subway train ticket that can be used on all city buses and subway trains in the Kyoto area. One day, ¥1,200; 2 days, ¥2,000.

Osaka Amazing Pass

Unlimited-use pass for buses, new trams and subway trains, and which also includes free admission to 28 tourist sites and gives discounts to some other attractions. One day ¥2,3000; 2 days ¥3,000.

Train discounts

If you have not purchased a Japan Rail Pass or don't qualify, JR and the private railways offer a number of special fare discounts. Amongst them:

JR Discount round-trip: a 10 percent discount to destinations more than 600km (370 miles) one-way.

Excursion tickets: a saving of around 20 percent for direct travel between a starting point and a designated area in which unlimited travel can be made. One good example is the 2-day (¥5,140) or 3-day (¥5,640) Hakone Free Pass available at Shinjuku Station, which covers travel to and from Hakone on the Odakyu Line, as well travel on seven types of transport within the Hakone area. It also gives discounted admission to some tourist sites.

Package tours: discount lodging as well as discounted rail and bus travel. Packages may be purchased at JR travel centres, at a Green Window *(midori no madoguchi)* or leading travel agents.

JR Seishun 18 Kippu: a coupon available during parts of spring, summer and winter for five days' travel, each section used for one day's unlimited train travel. Good for ordinary JR trains, rapid JR trains, and the JR ferryboat between Miyajimaguchi and Miyajima Island. Passengers may get on and off as many times as wanted at any JR station and at the JR ferry terminal within the same date. Price is ¥11,850 both for adults and children. It may be shared by several people, provided they travel together and do not split the coupon (so for example, five people can use it on one day).

Regional rail passes

Another option for cutting travel costs is to look out for special regional travel passes. The JNTO keeps an up-to-date list of such passes on its website (www.jnto.go.jp). Among these are:

Hokkaido Rail Pass: a coupon that allows 3 days' (¥16,500), 4 days' (¥22,000, a flexi ticket), 5 days' (¥22,00) or 7 days' (¥24,000) travel on all JR Hokkaido train and bus services.

JR West Sanyo Area Pass: a coupon for 4 days' (¥20,570) or 8 days' (¥30,860) unlimited travel on JR shinkansen, limited-express and regular trains in the Osaka-Sanyo area.

JR East Pass: a coupon valid for two weeks allowing 5 days' (¥22,000) unlimited use of JR shinkansen and limited-express services within the entire JR East area (essentially the northern half of Honshu, including Tokyo).

JR All Kyushu Area Pass: a coupon giving 5 days' (¥18,000) or 3 days' (¥15,000) unlimited use on JR trains within the Kyushu region. There is also a much cheaper pass for Northern Kyusushu Area only.

Private transport

Driving in Japan is a headache. Roads are narrow and crowded, signs confusing, rental cars and petrol expensive. Motorway and bridge tolls are very costly. If at all possible, consider flying or, better, taking the train.

Japan Rail Pass

Japan's rail services are unsurpassed in the world. Extremely efficient, they go nearly everywhere, even to the remotest neck of the woods.

Foreign travellers intending to travel in Japan should consider the Japan Rail Pass (www.japanrailpass. net). The pass allows for virtually unlimited travel on the national JR network, including the *shinkansen*, or bullet trains. Passes must be purchased outside Japan, and you must be travelling in Japan under the visa entry status of "temporary visitor".

Once in Japan, the pass must initially be validated at a JR Travel Centre (which are everywhere in Japan). Once it is validated, reservations can be made at any so-called Green Window *(midori no madoguchi)* at major stations.

While trains are not especially cheap in Japan (long-distance fares equal air fares), the pass is a great deal. A 7-day pass costs around ¥30,000 – less than the round-trip fare from Narita Airport to Kyoto via Tokyo.

Standard/First-class

7-day/¥29,110/¥38,880
14-day/¥46,390/¥62,950
21-day/¥59,350/¥81,870
Children aged 6 to 11 travel at half of the above prices. Children under 6 travel free.

EATING OUT

RECOMMENDED RESTAURANTS AND CAFES

Japan is an eater's paradise, and the diversity of possibilities would fill a separate guide (for a broad-brush survey of Japanese cuisine, see page 115). Alleys are lined with restaurants, whole buildings sometimes occupied with nothing else, entire blocks have been taken over in some cities. You certainly won't need to look hard to find somewhere good to eat. In the listings that follow, you will find plenty of suggestions for good eats in most of the main areas covered in the guide, and in particular you will find restaurants that offer opportunities to try classic Japanese dishes and the country's fine and diverse range of regional fare. If you want a McDonald's, a *bento* lunch box or a simple coffee shop, just walk down any street; if you want something memorable, look here.

ECONOMICAL EATING AND DRINKING

Japan has been in a lingering recession ever since the economic bubble burst in the late 1980s, but every cloud has its silver lining. One positive outcome of the economic malaise, at least from the point of view of travellers and the fully employed Japanese, has been the cut-throat competitiveness of the food sector throughout Japan, particularly with set lunch offerings. Bargain deals in all kinds of restaurants, even in traditionally more expensive areas like Tokyo's Ginza, are the norm.

It's quite common for Japanese to buy meals (especially for lunch while at work) at convenience stores like 7-Eleven, Lawson and Family Mart. The competition between convenience stores is stiff, so the food is made fresh daily and though it wouldn't win any culinary awards, it represents really good value for money, with many dishes under ¥450. Many restaurants also offer filling "lunch set specials" which can be as cheap as ¥600. Fast-food joints have sets for as little as ¥350.

Family restaurants like Denny's, Coco's and Volks often have a free coffee refill service after the first cup, though you will find far better deals on food elsewhere. Tipping is almost non-existent in Japan, which helps offset costs.

Away from the budget end, don't expect to escape from most decent restaurants for less than ¥3,000 per person, excluding drinks. On average, a night on the upscale side of town can run in the region of ¥10,000. If you're on a budget, stick to medium-range restaurants, *izaka-ya*, street stands and convenience stores.

Be aware that some restaurants, typically at the more expensive end of the spectrum, will add a 10 or 15 percent service charge to your bill. Some *izaka-ya* and mid-range establishments will add a flat fee of a few hundred yen as a table charge.

If you just want to grab a quick drink without having to order food (as most *izaka-ya* insist upon), the best and cheapest option is to find a standing bar, or *tachinomiya*, where it is not uncommon to get a medium-size draught beer or glass of sake for ¥300. Another option is to find a Western-style pub, which is easily done in the major cities, although expect to pay upward of ¥800 a pint after the common 5–7pm happy-hour period.

WHERE AND WHAT TO EAT

Japan has myriad different places to eat and drink. At the budget end, besides those mentioned above, are local fast-food joints such as Yoshinoya, where the speciality is *gyu don*, a bowl of rice covered in simmered beef and onions, and rivals like Matsuya, where alongside the *gyu-don* they also serve cheap curry rice.

Moving up a notch on the culinary totem pole are the many *teishoku* (set meal) restaurants that do a roaring trade at lunch with home-style cooking – the classic trio of rice, pickles and *miso* soup served with a main dish such as a piece of fish or a breaded pork cutlet. With so much competition in the big cities (Tokyo alone has some 150,000 licensed restaurants), you can always get a good feed for under ¥1,000 (very often under ¥800). Other similarly priced restaurants, specialising in ramen, soba noodles or a host of other cuisines abound. The traveller need only walk down any main street in any town or city to find numerous possibilities. Plastic food in display cases or photographic menus make decisions both easier and more difficult – too many choices. Look, sniff, and enter.

At dinner, *izaka-ya* (pubs) make for a great place to try a variety of dishes and have a drink without spending too much. As you will see in the listings that follow, every part of Japan has its local specialities, and there are numerous restaurants that specialise in a single dish or individual style of cuisine. Most of these tend to have a more refined atmosphere than a typical *izaka-ya* and traditional decor, and, depending on the type of cuisine, the price can vary from budget to bank-breaking. If you can afford it, at least once push the boat out for a *kaiseki* dinner – it represents Japanese cuisine at its most subtle and exquisite.

EATING ETIQUETTE

Good table manners, Japanese-style, go a long way. Here are a few tips:

The wet towel (*o-shibori*) you receive to freshen up at the beginning of the meal should be neatly rolled up when you've finished, and don't use it on anything except your hands, no matter how often you see middle-aged men washing their faces with them before eating!

It is bad manners to wave your chopsticks around, to use them to point at someone, to stick them upright in your rice (an allusion to death) or to pull dishes forward with them. If you have a communally shared bowl of food, then it is considered good form (though

not everyone does it) to turn your chopsticks around and use the reverse points to pick up the food.

Japanese-style soups *(suimono)* and noodles in broth (except *ramen*) are sipped straight from the bowl. Whereas it is altogether acceptable form in Japan to slurp noodle dishes, there is no need to slurp soups. Sip them directly from the bowl without a spoon, as this is the best way to savour their delicate flavour.

For dishes that are dipped in sauce, such as *tempura* and *sashimi*, hold the sauce dish with one hand and dip the food into it with the chopsticks. Soy sauce should not be splashed onto a dish. Rather, pour it into the small soy-sauce dish, only a little at a time and use it sparingly.

You will rarely see Japanese eating and walking at the same time. They buy the food or snack, then find a place to sit properly and finish it completely. The same restraint goes for eating or drinking on the subway or commuter trains – wait until you are off the train.

If you are eating with Japanese acquaintances, it is polite to say

itadakimasu (the equivalent of saying *"bon appétit"*, even if you garble the pronunciation) before eating, and then *gochisosama deshita* (literally "you prepared a feast") once you've finished. It's also good form to say *gochisosama deshita* to staff when you are leaving a restaurant. To toast the first drink of the night, raise your glass and say *kampai*.

ABOUT THE LISTINGS

Unless otherwise stated, the cost is for dinner and does not include drinks. However, most restaurants, regardless of their dinner prices, have special lunch menus with prices substantially cheaper than at night. The closing times stated are for last orders. Restaurants usually remain open for 30 minutes to an hour after last orders, sometimes longer at high-end traditional establishments. When planning a night at a restaurant rated ¥¥¥ or ¥¥¥¥, it is safest to assume that you will need a reservation. Translations of the dishes are given in the Language section (see page 395).

TOKYO

Japanese

Chanko Kawasaki
2-13-1 Ryogoku, Sumida-ku
Tel: 03-3631-2529
Open daily 5–9pm
This 1937 restaurant specialises in *chankonabe*, a stew served to sumo wrestlers. Fish, chicken and vegetables are boiled in a pot along with tofu, titbits and side dishes that change seasonally. **¥¥¥**
Chibo
Yebisu Garden Place Tower, 38F, 4-20-3 Ebisu, Shibuya-ku
Tel: 03-5424-1011
http://chibo.com
Open daily 11.30am–3pm, 5–11pm
This branch of the nationwide Chibo *okonomiyaki* (Japanese pancake) chain mixes a trendy Yebisu Garden setting with superb views across the bay. English-language menu. **¥¥**
Fukuzushi
5-7-8 Roppongi, Minato-ku
Tel: 03-3402-4116
www.roppongifukuzushi.com
Open Mon–Sat 11.30am–2pm, holidays 5.30–11pm
A sushi shop with an English-language menu. Offers tuna, mackerel and cod and the less

familiar delights of conger eel, shad and grouper. **¥¥¥**
Ikebukuro Gyoza Stadium
Namco Namja Town 2F, Sunshine City, 3-1-1 Higashi-Ikebukuro, Toshima-ku
Tel: 03-5950-0765
Open daily 10am–10pm
Gyoza are meat- and vegetable-stuffed dumplings fried and served with rice, pickles and other trimmings. The main mall of Namja Town has branches of 12 famed *gyoza* restaurants from around the country. Although dishes range from a reasonable ¥300 to ¥600 each, you could easily run up quite a bill while sampling these tasty treats. **¥¥**

Ikebukuro Gyoza Stadium.

Kanda Yabu Soba
2-10 Kanda-Sudacho, Chiyoda-ku
Tel: 03-3251-0287
www.yabusoba.net
Open daily 11.30am–9pm
An institution in Tokyo eating circles, serving classic Edo-style handmade buckwheat noodles in traditional surroundings. *Soba* choices come in hot soup or with a cold soy-based dip. Go early at lunchtime as the lines start to form on the stroke of noon. **¥**
Keika Kumamoto Ramen
3-7-2 Shinjuku, Shinjuku-ku
Tel: 03-3354-4591
http://keika-raumen.co.jp
Open daily 10.30am–11.15pm

Much featured on TV, this noodle shop specialises in the pork broth-based ramen called *tonkotsu*, originally from Kyushu but now one of the most widely eaten ramen variations across the country. The *chashumen* noodles (noodles with roast pork) are superb and go some way to explaining the long lines at lunchtime. The chain also has six other shops in Tokyo. ¥

Little Okinawa
8-7-10 Ginza, Chuo-ku
Tel: 03-3572-2930
Open Mon–Fri 5pm–3am, Sat–Sun 4pm–midnight
Southern cuisine in a friendly setting. Strong on noodles, pork, bitter stir-fried gourds, and *awamori*, a firebrand spirit unique to Okinawa. The atmosphere is the second-best thing to jumping on a flight to Okinawa. ¥¥

Musashino
2-8-11 Ueno, Bunkyo-ku
Tel: 03-3831-1672
Open daily 11.30am–9pm
Tonkotsu ramen is the speciality at this traditional restaurant just to the south of Ueno Park. The filling set meals come with rice, pickles and *miso*, and are centred on extremely succulent cuts of pork. ¥

Nambantei
4-5-6 Roppongi, Minato-ku
Tel: 03-3402-0606
www.nanbantei.com
Open Mon–Sat 5–10.30pm (last order)
Tasty *yakitori* broiled over charcoal in relaxed, faux-rustic surroundings. They also serve grilled beef, pork, lamb and vegetables. English-language menu available. ¥¥

Popeye Beer Club
2-8-17 Ryogoku, Sumida-ku
Tel: 03-3633-2120
www.40beersontap.com
Open Mon–Sat 5–11pm
Over 60 different craft beers on tap from around Japan make the oddly named Popeye the best place to experience Japan's craft beer boom. You won't spend much on food here because there isn't much on the menu, but budget for about ¥1,000 per pint. Better still, try one of their multi-beer sampler sets. ¥¥¥

Shin Hinomoto (aka Andy's Fish)
2-4-4 Yurakucho, Chiyoda-ku
Tel: 03-3214-8021
www.andysfish.com
Open daily 5pm–midnight
Noisy, friendly *izaka-ya* (pub) built under the railway tracks serving fresh fish at very reasonable prices. The owner, Andy, is a British expat, but besides the Guinness on the menu this is as Japanese an *izaka-ya* as it

gets. Booking recommended. English-language menu available. ¥

Sushi-bun
Chuo Shijo Bldg, No.8, 5-2-1, Tsukiji, Chuo-ku
Tel: 03-3541-3860
Open Mon–Sat 6am–2.30pm; closed holidays
Located in Tsukiji market, the temple of fish markets, Sushi-bun opens early for the local traders. Squeeze around the counter for high-quality set platters at very reasonable prices. First come, first served. English-language menu. ¥¥

Tofuya-Ukai
4-4-13 Shiba-koen, Minato-ku
Tel: 03-3436-1028
Open daily 11am–8pm
www.ukai.co.jp/english/shiba
Located next to Tokyo Tower in Minato-ku and set in an attractive re-creation of an Edo-era mansion, the tofu-based *kaiseki* cuisine here is simply exquisite. The views across the sprawling Japanese garden are equally impressive. Booking essential. ¥¥¥¥

Other Asian

Dhaba India
2-7-9 Yaesu, Chuo-ku
Tel: 03-3272-7160
www.dhabaindia.com
Open Mon–Fri 11.15am–3pm, 5–11pm, Sat–Sun noon–3pm, 5–10pm
Besides a fine selection of curries, the speciality at this Southern Indian restaurant near Kyobashi Station are its large *dosa* pancakes, which you can watch the chefs cook up on a special hotplate in front of the kitchen. Good lunch deals. ¥¥

Hyakunincho Yataimura
2-20-25 Hyakunin-cho, Shinjuku-ku
Tel: 03-5386-3320
Open daily 11.30am–2.30pm, 5pm–2am; Fri–Sat 11.30am–4am
Street food from half a dozen Asian countries under one very low-budget but often lively roof. Wander from stall to stall making up a combination meal from the Indonesian, Thai, Korean and other cuisines represented here. ¥¥

Shanghai Xiaochi
1-3-10 Kabuki-cho, Shinjuku-ku
Tel: 03-3232-5909
http://shanghai-xiaochi.com
Open daily 5.30pm–8am
This cramped, but lively, place in Kabuki-cho cranks out fantastic Chinese food, from classic dishes to shockers like dried fried scorpion and frog. ¥¥¥

American and Fusion

Las Chicas
5-47-6 Jingumae, Shibuya-ku

Tel: 03-3407-6865
www.laschicas.jp
Open daily 11.30am–11pm, Sat until 11.30pm
A design centre, exhibition space and art salon, with restaurants and bars, run by a bilingual staff, offering a Western-Continental-Asian mix of food and drink. ¥¥

Kurkku Jingumae
2-18-15 Jingumae, Shibuya-ku
Tel: 03-5414-0581
www.kurkku.jp
Open daily 11am–midnight, Fri–Sat until 4am
Fresh, organic fare that includes simple but tasty pasta dishes and cakes. The restaurant is situated in a complex that also houses a library, roof garden and interior design shop run by the same company. ¥

French

Aux Bacchanales
1-12-32 Akasaka, Minato-ku
Tel: 03-3582-2225
Open daily 11.30am–1.30pm, 5.30–11pm (restaurant), 10am–11pm (café), 8am–7.30pm (boulangerie)
www.auxbacchanales.com
The best street-side café in town, plus a casual restaurant serving great brasserie and bistro fare. A wide menu with plenty of cheap red wines to choose from. There are several other branches in Tokyo, including one in Ginza. ¥¥

Italian

Ristorante Carmine
1F Nishikawa Bldg, 1-19 Saiku-cho, Shinjuku-ku
Tel: 03-3260-5066
www.carmine.jp
Open daily 11.30am–2pm, 6–10.30pm
Tokyo has many Italian restaurants, but a large number are identikit overpriced affairs. Carmine, however, has a real Tuscan charm to it under the guidance of well-known chef Carmine Cozzolino, who has since opened several other Italian restaurants in Tokyo. ¥¥¥

Vegetarian

Nataraj
B1F Sanwa-Aoyama Building
2-22-19 Minami-Aoyama, Minato-ku
Tel: 03-5474-0510
www.nataraj.co.jp

PRICE CATEGORIES

Prices for three-course dinner per person without drinks and taxes:
¥ = Under ¥2,000
¥¥ = ¥2,000–3,000
¥¥¥ = ¥3,000–5,000
¥¥¥¥ = Over ¥5,000

TRANSPORT

EATING OUT

ACTIVITIES

A–Z

LANGUAGE

Open Mon–Fri 11.30am–3pm, 6–11pm,
Sat–Sun 11.30am–11pm
Tokyo's foremost Indian vegetarian
restaurant serves grills and curries
from the tandoor oven. Spice levels
are mild but can be raised. ¥¥¥

Pure Café
5-5-21 Minami-Aoyama, Minato-ku
Tel: 03-5466-2611
http://pure-cafe.com
Open daily 8.30am–10.30pm
Self-service all-day café serving light,
additive-free and (almost) entirely
vegan meals. Opens early for those

looking for a healthy breakfast with
organic coffee. ¥¥

Cafés

Café Paulista
Nagasaki Centre, 1F, 8-9-16 Ginza,
Chuo-ku
Tel: 03-3572-6160
www.paulista.co.jp
Open daily 8.30am–10pm
The coffee in this venerable Ginza
café is brewed from beans imported
from Brazil. The prices are affordable,
and choosing the snacks and cake

sets allows you to feel comfortable
staying longer. ¥

Gallery éf
2-19-18 Kaminarimon, Taito-ku
Tel: 03-3841-0442
www.gallery-ef.com
Open Wed–Mon 11am–6.30pm, lunch
11.30am–2.30pm, Sat–Sun until 3pm
This café set in an old kura-style
warehouse serves good home-
made cakes in a rather hip, artsy
atmosphere. There is also a bar and
gallery run by the same people in the
building. ¥

NAGOYA

Crown
11F Westin Nagoya Hotel
Tel: 052-521-2121
Open daily 11.30am–2.30pm, 5.30–10pm
Luxurious teppanyaki, where the
customers sit at a counter around a
central grill plate as the chefs cook up
the finest steak and seafood. ¥¥¥¥

Genji
3F Hilton Nagoya
Tel: 052-212-1111
Open Wed–Sun 11.30am–9.30pm
A very sleekly designed restaurant in
the Hilton Nagoya that covers several
types of high-end Japanese cuisine:
sushi, tempura and teppanyaki. Also
has an extensive sake and shochu
list. ¥¥¥¥

Ibasho
3-13-22 Nishiki, Naka-ku
Tel: 052-951-1166
www.ibashou.jp
Open Mon–Sat 11am–2.30pm, 4–8pm;
closed 2nd and 3rd Mon of the month
The rustic interiors and raised tatami
mat seating are the perfect place to
try a very traditional Nagoya dish,

hitsumabushi: charcoal-grilled eel
covered in miso and served on rice.
¥¥

Sekai no Yamachan
4-9-6 Sakae, Naka-ku
Tel: 052-242-1342
www.yamachan.co.jp
Open daily 5–11.30pm
There are loads of branches of this very
popular chain izaka-ya around Nagoya.
The focus is on tebasaki, deep-fried
chicken wings that are sometimes
sweet, sometimes spicy. ¥¥

Tiger Café
1-9-22 Higashi-sakura
Tel: 052-971-1031
Open Mon–Sat 11am–3am; Sun until
midnight
Friendly French café serving light
meals, pastries and coffee. There are
several other branches in Nagoya,
including one in Nagoya Station. ¥

Torigin
1F, Miyaki Bldg, 3-14-22 Nishiki, Naka-ku
Tel: 052-973-3000
Open daily 5–midnight; closed 2nd and
3rd Sun of the month

A Nagoya-style yakitori eatery
featuring, as the name suggests (tori
means chicken), barbecued chicken-
on-a-stick. There are over 30 varieties
on the menu, all served with rice or
noodles. ¥¥

Torisei
3-19-24 Nishiki, Naka-ku
Tel: 052-951-7337
www.torisei.jp
Open Mon–Sat 11.30am–1.30pm,
5–10.30pm
Great yakitori (grilled chicken) is the
main draw to this restaurant, although
they have many other good dishes,
such as chicken nabe, using famed
locally reared chicken. The set courses
make ordering much easier. ¥¥¥

Yamamotoya Honten
2-4-15 Sakae, Naka-ku
Tel: 052-201-4082
http://yamamotoyahonten.co.jp
Open daily 11am–10pm
Serves a Nagoya special, miso nikomi,
or thick udon noodles in a hearty
miso broth. There are several other
branches about town. ¥

TAKAYAMA

Kakusho
2-98 Baba-cho
Tel: 0577-32-0174
www.kakusyo.com
Open daily 11am–1.30pm and 5–7pm
The speciality at this refined
restaurant, set in an Edo-era house
and overlooking a pristine ornamental

garden, is shoji-ryori, the vegetarian
cuisine eaten by monks.
¥¥¥¥

Ryotei Susaki
4-14 Shinmei-machi
Tel: 0577-32-0023
www.ryoutei-susaki.com
Open daily 11.30am–2pm, 5–9pm

Set in a charming old wooden
building, this family-run restaurant
has been serving Sowaryu Honzen
cuisine (very similar to kaiseki) since
the late 1700s. Expensive, but if you
want to splurge once in Japan, you
will struggle to find anywhere better to
do it. Reservations essential. ¥¥¥¥

KANAZAWA

Miyoshian
1-11 Kenroko-machi
Tel: 076-221-0127
www.miyoshian.net

Open daily 9am–2.30pm
This restaurant inside Kenroku-en
serves traditional Kaga ryori,
including well-priced bento and set

meals, as well as matcha green tea
served with sweets. ¥¥

Suginoi
3-11 Kyokawa-machi

Tel: 076-243-2288
http://kanazawa-suginoi.co.jp
Open daily 11am–2pm,
4.30-8pm

Elegant set meals include local
specialities such as duck stew and
small soy-simmered river fish, all
served in the finest Kutani china

and lacquer ware. Lovely *tatami* mat
rooms make for a very traditional
setting.
¥¥¥¥

SENDAI

Jiraiya
2-1-15 Kokubun-cho, Aoba-ku
Tel: 022-261-2164
www.jiraiya.com
Open Mon–Sat 5–11.30pm
A self-declared slow food restaurant
that does excellent seafood in many

of its guises. The signature dish is
charcoal-grilled deepwater whitefish,
kinki.
¥¥¥¥
Aji Tasuke
4-4-13 Ichibancho, Aoba-ku
Tel: 022-225-4641

Open daily 11.30am–10pm
Serves ox-tongue dishes,
specialities of the Sendai area,
including tongue stew and grilled
slices of tongue.
¥

AOMORI

Area Complex Food Market
B1, Auga Building
Tel. 017 721-4499
Open daily 10am–9pm
The fish and fresh produce market
in the basement of Auga Building,
a block east of Aomori Station,
includes stalls and restaurants

offering some of the freshest
and cheapest sushi and seafood
donburi in Aomori. There are also
stalls selling decent *teishoku* and
ramen. ¥
Nishimura
10F ASPAM Bldg, 1-1-40 Yasukata
Tel: 017-734-5353

Open Mon–Sat 10.30am–9pm
Nice bay views from the 10th floor
of the landmark ASPAM building
and extremely hearty local fare
designed to keep out the northern
chills. The scallops are a speciality,
as is the cod stew (*jappa-jiru*).
¥

SAPPORO

Food stall in Susukino, Sapporo.

21 Club
25F, Novotel Hotel, Minami
10-jo, Nishi 6
Tel: 011-561-1000
Open daily 11.30am–2pm, 5.30–9.30pm
A very fashionable *teppanyaki*
restaurant with panoramic views
over the city, and sky-high prices to
match. ¥¥¥¥
Sapporo Beer Garden
Kita 7, Higashi 9

www.sapporo-bier-garten.jp
Tel: 0120-150-550
Open daily 11.30am–10pm
Seating up to 2,400 people, the set
meal here entitles you to as much
barbecued lamb as you can eat
within a 100-minute limit. For an
extra ¥1,200, you can also have
all-you-can-drink Sapporo beer.
There is an outdoor seating area for
cooling off in the summer. ¥¥¥

Sky J
5-2-5 Kita,
Chuo-ku
Tel: 011-251-6377
Open daily 6.30am–10am,
11.30am–2.30pm, 5.30–11.30pm
Located on the 35th floor of JR
Nikko Hotel, this buffet restaurant
has fabulous views over Sapporo,
which some guests find better than
the international and Japanese food
served here. The place is popular
anyway, so book ahead. ¥¥¥
Yagumo Susukino
B2, Plaza Bldg,
Odori 4-chome
Tel: 011-261-1198
www.goma-soba.jp
Open daily 10.30am–8.30pm
A traditional noodle and *soba*
shop, decorated with folk art and
agrarian objects. One of half a
dozen restaurants and cafés in the
basement of the fashionable 4Pla
mall. ¥

PRICE CATEGORIES

**Prices for three-course dinner per
person without drinks and taxes:**
¥ = Under ¥2,000
¥¥ = ¥2,000–3,000
¥¥¥ = ¥3,000–5,000
¥¥¥¥ = Over ¥5,000

KYOTO

A Womb
35-2 Ichijoji Hinokuchi-cho, Sakyo-ku
Tel: 075-721-1357
http://awomb.com
Open daily noon–3pm, 6–8pm (last order);
closed some Tue
Very trendy studio-style café-cum-
restaurant that serves an intriguing
mix of Japanese-Euro fusion fare. You
can eat well for under ¥3,000 à la
carte, but the ¥5,000 dinner course
is a very good example of modern
kaiseki-style dining. **¥¥¥**

Giro Giro Hitoshina
420-7 Namba-cho, Shimogyo-ku
Tel: 075-343-7070
Open daily 5.30–midnight; closed last Mon
of each month
In a very mellow location alongside
the Takasegawa River, Giro Giro
serves *kaiseki* dishes with a modern
twist and in an atmosphere that feels
more like a lively *izaka-ya*. **¥¥¥**

Hafuu Honten
471-1 Sasayacho, Nakagyo-ku
Tel: 075-257-1581
www.hafuu.com
Open Thu–Tue 11.30am–1.30pm, 5.30–
9.30pm
Tender wagyu steaks, fish cooked to
perfection and impeccable service will
make you fall in love with this place.
Reservations recommended. **¥¥¥¥**

Kikusui
31 Fukuchi-cho, Sakyo-ku
Tel: 075-771-4101
www.kyoto-kikusui.com
Open daily 11am–8pm (last order)
Multi-course *kaiseki* cuisine at
its finest, complete with all the
traditional touches and refinement
you would expect. Near Nanzen-ji
temple. **¥¥¥¥**

Kodai-ji Ikkyu-an
Opposite the south gate of Kodai-ji temple,
Kodai-ji Minamimon-mae, Higashiyama-ku
Tel: 075-561-1901
Open Wed–Mon noon–7pm
Although it doesn't come cheap,
the experience of eating *fucha ryori*,
Zen vegetarian dishes served in the
Chinese manner, is an exquisite rarity.
¥¥¥¥

Kushihachi
33-1 Kami Hakubai, Hakubai-cho, Kitano
Tel: 075-461-8888
Open daily 5–11.30pm
A lively chain restaurant serving
kushiage food: grilled meat titbits
served on sticks, which go well with
sake or beer. **¥¥**

Matsuno
Shijo-dori
Tel: 075-561-2786
Open Fri–Wed 11.30am–8.30pm
This eel restaurant, four doors east
from the Minami-za theatre, has been
run by the Matsuno family for several
generations. The *unagi don*, char-
grilled eel on a bed of rice, is a classic
Japanese dish, and one which is said to
have aphrodisiac properties. **¥¥**

Mukadeya
381 Mukadeya-cho, Nakagyo-ku
Tel: 075-256-7039
Open Thu–Tue 11am–3pm, 5–10pm
The speciality here is *obanzai ryori*
– a rustic, home-cooked version of
kaiseki cuisine. The multi-course
meals can be taken either in a *tatami*
mat room or in an atmospheric dark-
wooded dining room. **¥¥¥¥**

Okutan
86-30 Fukuchi-machi, Nanzen-ji, Sakyo-ku
Tel: 075-771-8709
Open Fri–Wed 11am–4pm
Delicious tofu pots, rice, pickles,
tempura and grated mountain potato
add up to quite a blow-out. **¥¥¥**

Omen
74 Ishibashi-cho, Sakyo-ku
Tel: 075-771-8994
http://omen.co.jp
Open daily 11am–9pm
Great *udon* noodles served in a rustic
setting and at very affordable prices.
On the Philosopher's Path near
Ginkaku-ji. **¥**

Otsuka
20-10 Sagatenryuji Setogawacho,
Ukyo-ku
Tel: 075-864-7989
www.otsukabeef.com
Open Fri–Wed11am–3pm
No matter if you go for premium beef
or a set meal, this little restaurant is

steak heaven. Melt-in-the-mouth beef
does not come cheap, but is worth
every yen you will pay here. Located in
a small street, close to the JR Saga-
Arashiyama station. **¥¥¥–¥¥¥¥**

Rakusho
516 Washio-cho, Higashiyama-ku
Tel: 075-561-6892
Open daily 9.30am–6pm
A lovely teahouse in Gion that won't
leave your wallet aching. Try some
warabi mochi (pounded rice cake)
with a cup of green tea. **¥**

Somushi Ochaya
73 Mikura-cho, Nakagyo-ku
Tel: 075-253-1456
Open Thu–Tue 11am–9pm
A teahouse with a difference. This
one serves tea in a traditional Korean
style, offering far bolder, spicier
flavours than one might expect to
find in a typical Kyoto teahouse. Also
has a good range of Korean food,
including *bibimbap* (rice topped with
mixed vegetables) and hotpots. **¥¥**

Tempura Yoshikawa Inn
Tominojoki, south of Oike-dori,
Nakagyo-ku
Tel: 075-221-5544
www.kyoto-yoshikawa.co.jp
Open Mon–Sat 11am–1.30pm, 5–8pm
Kyoto-style *tempura* is light and
delicate compared to the Tokyo
variety. This traditional inn-cum-
restaurant serves some of the best in
town, in a teahouse setting. They also
have private rooms for evening *kaiseki*
dinners overlooking a private classical
garden. Great atmosphere. **¥¥¥¥**

Tsuruya Yoshinobu
Intersection of Horiikawa and Imadegawa-
dori, Horikawa Imadegawa, Kamigyo-ku
Tel: 075-441-0105
www.tsuruyayoshinobu.jp
Open daily 9.30am–5.30pm
A Japanese confectioner that has
been in business since the early 19th
century. The sweets are made on the
second floor, where the decoration
process can be watched. Japanese
wagashi (tea-ceremony-style sweets)
are served with a bowl of brothy green
tea in the tea salon. **¥**

NARA

Edogawa Naramachi
43 Shimomikadocho
Tel: 0742-20-4400
Open daily 11am–10pm
An authentic tavern with soothing
traditional music and hearty
Japanese fare. Eel rice set is

particularly recommended.
¥¥

Hiraso
30-1 Imanikado-cho
Tel: 0742-22-0866
Open Tue–Sun 11.30am–
8.30pm

The main fare here is kakinoha-
zushi, or sushi wrapped in
persimmon leaves, but Hiraso also
dishes up plenty of other Nara
specialities, including cha-ga-yu (tea
porridge).
¥¥

Mellow Cafe
1-8 Konishi-cho
Tel: 0742-27-9099
www.mellowcafe.jp
Open daily 11am–11.30pm
The speciality at this modern Italian-style café-cum-restaurant is oven-baked pizza, although they also

do good lunch sets as well as very tempting cakes and puddings. ¥¥
Tonkatsu Ganko
19 Higashimukinaka-machi
Tel: 0742-25-4129
Open daily 11am–10pm
As the very name suggests, this restaurant serves several

tasty variations on *tonkatsu* – a breaded, deep-fried pork cutlet. It's conveniently located in central Nara and the only downside is that the tables are small, so the place can't accommodate parties of more than four people.
¥¥

OSAKA

Daikoku
2-2-7 Dotonbori, Chuo-ku
Tel: 06-6211-1101
Open Mon–Sat 11.30am–3pm, 5–8pm
Point to the pictures on the menu or the other customers' plates to order grilled fish and *kayaku gohan*, fried tofu on steamed rice. A popular restaurant for all ages, it's been in business for over 100 years. ¥¥
Don Quixote Okonomiyaki
2-8-17 Sennichi-mae, Chuo-ku
Tel: 06-6644-8313
Open daily 11am–11pm
Forget the unusual name, this restaurant serves classic Osaka *okonomiyaki* (Japanese pancakes) alongside affordable cook-it-yourself *teppanyaki*. ¥¥
Green Earth
4-2-2 Kitakyuhoji-machi, Chuo-ku
Tel: 06-6251-1245Open Mon–Sat 11.30am–5pm
Pleasant vegetarian café with a good range of pasta, pizzas and sandwiches. Good set meals for under ¥1,000. ¥
Kani Doraku
1-6-18 Dotonbori, Chuo-ku
Tel: 06-6211-8975
http://douraku.co.jp
Open daily 11am–10pm
Easy to find because of the iconic giant mechanical crab that clings to the front

of the building, Kani Doraku is the place to go for all sorts of grilled, sashimi and boiled crab dishes. Just be warned that crab doesn't come cheap in Japan. ¥¥¥¥
Mimiu Honten
4-6-18 Hirano-cho, Chuo-ku
Tel: 06-6231-5770
www.mimiu.co.jp
Open Mon–Sat 11.30am–9pm
If you have the *udon suki*, which you should as this is the place that popularised it, the bill can run quite high. It's worth trying this delicious mixture of *udon*, clams, seasonal vegetables, chicken and shrimp at least once though. ¥¥¥¥
Takoume
1-1-8 Dotonbori, Chuo-ku
Tel: 06-6211-6201
www.takoume.co.jp
Open Mon–Fri 5–10.50pm, Sat 11.30am–2.30pm, 5–10.10pm
This small, 150-year old restaurant is a time slip in this otherwise modern district. Enjoy its atmosphere while it lasts. The speciality here is *oden*, a soup of radish, sausage, fishcakes, squid and much more. A hearty winter dish when washed down with beer or hot sake. ¥¥
Tsurutontan
3-17 Soemon-cho, Chuo-ku
Tel: 06-6211-0021

www.tsurutontan.co.jp
Open daily 11am–8am next day
Udon is the name of the game here, whether it be served cold with a simple dipping sauce, in a warming *nabe*, or covered in a thick curry sauce. ¥
Ume-no-hana
Epson Osaka 21F, 3-5-1 Bakurou-machi, Chuo-ku
Tel: 06-6258-6533
www.umenohana.co.jp
Open daily 11am–3pm, 5–9pm
A break from the often heavy Osaka fare in the shape of light and healthy tofu-based *kaiseki*-style cuisine. Dinner can be pricey, but there are good deals to be had at lunch. ¥¥¥¥
Yotaro Honten
2-3-14 Koraibashi, Chuo-ku
Tel: 06-6231-5561
Open Mon–Sat 11.30am–2pm, 5–9pm
Sea bream never tasted as good and fresh as it does here, where it is cooked in a clay pot on a bed of rice. An almost biblical simplicity reigns in this modest dish, called *tai gohan*. ¥¥¥¥
Itoya
1-6-21 Sonezaki, Shinchi, Kita-ku
Tel: 06-6341-2891
Open Mon–Sat 5pm–1am
A cheap eatery that offers a taste of Osaka's best-known concoction, *okonomiyaki*. The mix includes octopus, shrimp, pork and vegetables. ¥

KOBE

Cafe Fish
2-8 Hatoba-cho
Tel: 078-334-1820
www.cafe-fish.com
Open daily 11.30am–8pm
Trendy and spacious café-restaurant with pleasant harbour views and burger or pasta lunch sets for around ¥1,000. Some evenings it stays open late for live music and club nights. ¥
Gunai Hanten
2-4-3 Motomachi-dori
Tel: 078-332-3635
Open Mon–Fri 11.30am–3pm, 5–9.30pm, Sat–Sun 11.30am–9.30pm
www.gunai.com

One of the better options in Kobe's Nankin-machi Chinatown. Serves a range of Chinese cuisines, including *dim sum*. Good-value lunch sets. ¥¥
Steakhouse Sanda-ya
1-6-1 Higashikawasakicho, Chuo-kuTel: 078-360-2900
Open daily 11.30am–8.30pm
Kobe is synonymous with beef, its own special, marbled, rather expensive variety known as *Kobe-gyu*. Here it's moderately priced, served with rice, *miso* and vegetables. ¥¥
Wakkoque
1-1 Kitano-cho
Tel: 078-262-2838

www.wakkoqu.com
Open daily 11.45am–9.30pm
Very plush restaurant with top-end steaks, using the local Kobe beef, cooked on *teppanyaki* grill plates. In the basement-level mall under the Oriental Hotel. ¥¥¥¥

OKAYAMA

Azumazushi
1-1 Ekimotomachi, Kita-ku
Tel: 086-227-7337
Open Thu–Tue 11am–2pm, 4.30–8.30pm
Okayama is famed for its fresh seafood dishes, many of which are mixed with vegetables and vinegared rice. The classic dish to order is

barazushi (seafood and vegetables served on top of vinegared rice). For an introduction to the region's fish dishes, ask for the *azuma teishoku*, the restaurant's own assortment of fish. **¥¥¥**

Teppan Ku-Ya
1-1-17 Nodaya-cho, Kita-ku

Tel: 086-224-8880
A cosy restaurant serving traditional Japanese treats cooked in front of the bar. Delightful and reasonably priced, the set menu is exceptionally good value.
¥¥

HIROSHIMA

Kakifune Kanawa
A boat moored on the Motoyasu River
Tel: 082-241-7416
www.kanawa.co.jp
Open daily 11am–2pm, 5–9pm
Oysters are the great Hiroshima speciality, cultivated out on the bay on rafts. Every variety of serving method, from fried, steamed, marinated, raw, baked or in stews and soups is on offer here. This floating restaurant has been here for nearly 50 years. **¥¥¥¥**

Okonomimura
5-13 Shin Tenchi
Tel: 082-241-2210
www.okonomimura.jp
Open daily 11.30am–midnight
After Osaka, Hiroshima is the main contender for Japan's best *okonomiyaki*, a pancake filled with seafood, meat and vegetables and covered in lashings of sauces. The "mura" of the title means village, suggesting, with its 20-plus stalls

to choose from, something like a Singaporean hawker centre. **¥**

Suishin Restaurant
6-7 Tate-machi
Tel: 082-247-4411
www.suishin.or.jp
Open daily 11.30am–10pm
A tiny but well-regarded sushi restaurant with all the usual choices. Specialises in *kamameshi* (rice casserole). These are augmented with oysters and, if you dare, blowfish. **¥¥¥¥**

TAKAMATSU

Tenkatsu
7-8 Hyogo-machi
Tel: 087-821-5380
Open Mon–Fri 11am–2pm, 5-9pm; Sat–Sun 11am–9pm
Well-renowned *tempura* and sushi restaurant. Sit at the counter that surrounds a sunken tank, filled with fish. Good-value set evening meals. **¥**

Udon Bakaichidai
1-6-7 Tagacho

Tel: 087-862-4705
Open daily 6am–6pm
Thick udon served in hot broth garnished with sliced green onion is therapeutic on a chilly, rainy day. But the house speciality udon, which comes with with a raw egg, butter, dashi, soy sauce, scallions and black pepper tastes great even when the sun shines.
¥¥

Waraya
91 Naka-machi, Yashima
Tel: 087-843-3115
www.wara-ya.co.jp
Open daily 10am–7pm
Excellent value for Shikoku's speciality Sanuki *udon* noodles, simple sushi preparations and *tempura*, all in a converted thatch-roofed inn at the Shikoku Mura museum in Yashima. **¥**

MATSUYAMA

Flankey Kobayashi
2-3 Ichiban-cho
Open daily 5pm–3am
Lively standing bar with cheap drinks (from ¥300) and equally affordable

izaka-ya dishes, if you don't mind eating standing up. **¥**

Kawasemi
2-5-6 Niban-cho
Tel: 089-933-9697

Open daily noon–2pm, 5–10pm
Fine *kaiseki-ryori* at prices that aren't too astronomical. Good-value lunch sets.
¥¥¥¥

FUKUOKA

Hard Rock Café Fukuoka
2-2-1 Jigyohama, Chuo-ko
Tel: 092-832-5050
www.hardrock.com/cafes/fukuoka
Open Sun–Fri 11.30am–11pm, Sat 11.30am–midnight
Rock 'n' roll memorabilia lines the walls and the menu offers familiar American comfort food. **¥¥**

Ume-no-hana
Hakata Hankyu BF1, Hakata-ku
Tel: 092-419-5118
www.umenohana.co.jp
Open daily 10am–9pm
Popular restaurant offering light vegetarian and tofu dishes, including a delicately flavoured yet creamy *yudofu* (boiled tofu). **¥¥**

Yoshizuka Unagiya
2-8-27 Nakasu, Hakata-ku
Tel: 092-271-0700
www.yoshizukaunagi.co
Open Thu–Tue 11am–9pm
This is the place to head for if you feel like sampling crispy grilled eel on rice. Most guests are locals.
¥¥

NAGASAKI

Ichiriki
8-20 Suwa-machi
Tel: 095-824-0226
www.ichiriki.jp
Open daily noon–2pm, 5–9.30pm
Located along Teramachi Street, this atmospheric and extremely traditional restaurant is known for a typical Nagasaki dish called *shippoku*, a combination of Japanese, Chinese and Western food made from stewed pork, sashimi, vegetables and soup. ¥¥¥¥

Kouzanrou
12-2 Shinchi
Tel: 095-824-5000
Open daily 11am–9pm
Befitting a port city with its own Chinatown, Chinese restaurants are a common feature. The very popular Kouzanrou's menu is extensive, from the humble *champon* noodle to the more elaborate, spicy Sichuanese fare. ¥¥¥

Yosso
8-9 Hamacho
Tel: 095-821-0001
http://yossou.co.jp
Open daily 11am–9pm
Established in 1866, Yosso's speciality is *chawan mushi*, a warm egg-custard preparation that includes vegetables and small amounts of chicken. Also serves *chawan mushi teishoku*, which includes shrimp and eel steamed over rice. ¥¥

KUMAMOTO

Katsuretsutei
1F Hayashi Bldg., 8-18 Shinshigai
Tel: 096-322-8771
A friendly restaurant serving juicy battered pork (*tonkatsu*) accompanied by pickles, shredded cabbage and superb sauces – the one with ground sesame seeds is well worth a try. ¥¥

Suganoya Kamitoriten
Jotomachi
Tel: 096-355-3558
Horse meat is a local delicacy and Suganoya Kamitoriten is a perfect place to "horse around" and sample exquisite dishes ranging from steaks to sashimi. Reservations needed. ¥¥¥

Tengaiten
2-15 Anseimachi
Tel: 096-354-8458
A filling bowl of spicy garlic ramen with pork at this traditional small shop should satisfy any hunger and is also good value for money. ¥

KAGOSHIMA

Adimori
13-21 Sennichicho
Tel: 099-224-7634
http://adimori.com
Open Thu–Tue 11.30am–2.30pm, 5.30–9.30pm
Feast on shabu-shabu pork that you cook yourself at the table, udon, eggs and vegetables in traditional Japanese setting, including low tables

and tatami mats. The place is really popular, so book well in advance. ¥¥
Kurobuta
3-2 Sennichi-cho
Tel: 099-224-8729
Open Tue–Sun 11.30am–2.30pm, 5.30–10pm
Only select Kagoshima pork is used in the preparation of Kurobuta's *tonkatsu* dishes. The deep-fried pork

cutlets are served with shredded cabbage and rice. ¥¥
Satsuma-aji
6-29 Higashi-Sengoku-cho
Tel: 099-226-0525
Open daily 11.30am–2.30pm, 5.30–10pm
This rustic, yet fashionable restaurant serves many local specialities, but is best known for its black pork (*kurobuta*) *shabu shabu*. ¥¥¥¥

OKINAWA

Helios Pub
1-2-25 Makishi, Naha
Tel: 098-863-7227
Open daily 11.30am–11pm
Okinawa is known for its drain cleaner-strength *awamori shochu*, but the Helios Microbrewery (operated by the Helios *awamori* distillery) offers far more subtle tipples with its range of craft beers. The brewery's gastro-pub has a great selection of Okinawan dishes, including *goya champuru* (bitter gourd, tofu and ham omelette). ¥
Yunangi
3-3-3 Kumochi, Naha
Tel: 098-867-3765
Open Mon–Sat noon–3pm, 5.30–10.30pm
Titbits of Okinawan food like *goya champuru* are secondary to Yunangi's main function as a superb venue for

testing *awamori*, the island's stronger version of *shochu*. ¥¥
Iso
9 Okawa, Ishigaki, opposite the harbour, behind the post office
Tel: 0980-82-7721
Open daily 11am–10.30pm
A good place to sample Yaeyama cuisine such as julienned pig's ear, goat stew and intestinal soups, as well as more conventional dishes like pork stewed in ginger and *soba* noodles. ¥¥
Sam's by the Sea
1-41-15 Awase
Tel: 098-937-3421
www.sams-okinawa.jp
Open daily 5pm–midnight
The restaurant boasts a romantic setting with views onto the marina and nautical décor. An eclectic menu ranges

from charcoal-grilled steaks to lobster, with a great overall atmosphere. ¥¥¥
Yunta
9-2 Misaki-cho, Ishigaki
Tel: 0980-82-7118
Open daily 5–11.30pm
One of the best spots on the island to try fresh fish. The set lunches are particularly good value. Diners tend to opt for the sushi and *sashimi* offerings in the evening. ¥¥

PRICE CATEGORIES

Prices for three-course dinner per person without drinks and taxes:
¥ = Under ¥2,000
¥¥ = ¥2,000–3,000
¥¥¥ = ¥3,000–5,000
¥¥¥¥ = Over ¥5,000

ACTIVITIES

THE ARTS, NIGHTLIFE, FESTIVALS, SHOPPING, SPORTS, TOURS, OUTDOOR AND CHILDREN'S ACTIVITIES

THE ARTS

Japan's arts scene runs the gamut from traditional theatre such as *kabuki* and *noh* to cutting-edge contemporary art, with much of it made accessible to English-speakers in Tokyo. Most of the arts action is concentrated in the big cities, but Japan also has arty surprises waiting in some out-of-the-way places, most notably on the islands of the Seto Naikai (see page 299) and even on the rugged Sado Island (see page 199) off Niigata. For up-to-date listings of art shows and performances, check out the listings websites and magazines on page 388.

Traditional theatre

Tokyo
Imperial Theatre
3-1-1 Marunouchi, Chiyoda-ku
Tel: 03-3213-7221
Classic plays, both old and contemporary.
Kabuki Theatre (Kabuki-za)
4-12-15 Ginza, Chuo-ku
Tel: 03-6745-0333
www.kabuki-za.co.jp
The country's premier *kabuki* venue. Reopened after extensive renovations in 2013 and now boasting an English translation captioning system.
Meiji Theatre (Meiji-za)
2-31-1 Nihonbashi-Hamacho, Chuo-ku
Tel: 03-3666-6666
www.meijiza.co.jp
Mainstream modern plays and samurai dramas in Japanese only.
National Noh Theatre
4-18-1 Sendagaya, Shibuya-ku
Tel: 03-3423-1331
www.ntj.jac.go.jp
Only performed about once a week during the afternoon, so check beforehand. Japanese only.
National Theatre
4-1 Hayabusa-cho, Chiyoda-ku
Tel: 03-3265-7411
www.ntj.jac.go.jp
English-language summaries are included in programmes and headphone translations provided for the plots. Matinees begin at noon; evening performances from 4.40pm. When *kabuki* is not running, *bunraku* takes over.
Shimbashi Embujo
6-18-2 Ginza, Chuo-ku
Tel: 03-3541-2600
www.shinbashi-enbujo.co.jp
Lowbrow sword-and-sorcery samurai dramas.

Other cities
Gion Corner
Yasaka Hall, Kyoto. Along a pedestrian lane between Shijo-dori and Higashioji-dori
Tel: 075-561-1119
www.kyoto-gioncorner.com
A daily digest of Japan's performing arts (seven types in all). Very touristy, but worth it if you don't have time for the real thing.
Kanze Kaikan
Niomon-dori, Kyoto
Tel: 075-771-6114
www.kyoto-kanze.jp
Noh and *kyogen* performances in Kyoto's main venue for this high-performance art.
Minami-za
Corner of Kawabata-dori and Shijo-dori in Gion, Kyoto
Tel: 075-561-1155
Kyoto's long-established *kabuki* theatre. December is the highlight, with a festival featuring all the big names in *kabuki*.

National Bunraku Theatre
Three-minute walk from Exit 7 of Nipponbashi Station on the Kintetsu or Sakaisuji subway lines, Osaka.
Tel: 06-6212-2531
www.ntj.jac.go.jp
Osaka's great puppet traditions performed in the months of Jan, Apr and June–Aug only.
Osaka Noh Hall
A short walk east of Hankyu Umeda Station
Tel: 06-6373-1726
A full programme of *noh* dramas, including some free Saturday-morning performances.
Osaka Shochiku-za
9-19-1 Dotonbori, Chuo-ku
Tel: 06-6214-2211
www.shochiku.co.jp
Kabuki in a beautifully restored theatre beside Dotonbori Canal.

Other theatres

Tokyo
Session House
158 Yaraicho, Shinjuku-ku
Tel: 03-3266-0461
www.session-house.net
Experimental venue for Japanese and foreign solo dancers.
Tokyo Comedy Store
www.tokyocomedy.com
Lunatic antics, skits and satire from a group of English-speaking comedians, performed at venues all over Tokyo (see website for schedule).

Concert venues

Tokyo
Bunkamura Orchard Hall
2-24-1 Dogenzaka, Shibuya-ku 150
Tel: 03-3477-9150

www.bunkamura.co.jp/orchard
Classical musical performances.

Casals Hall
1-6 Kanda Surugadai, Chiyoda-ku
Tel: 03-3294-1229
www.nu-casalshall.com
Chamber music and small ensembles.

Nippon Budokan
2-3 Kitanomaru-koen, Chiyoda-ku
Tel: 03-3216-5100
www.nipponbudokan.or.jp
Major international rock and pop
artists.

Suntory Hall
1-13-1 Akasaka, Minato-ku
Tel: 03-3505-1001, ticket centre
0570-55-0017
www.suntory.com/culture-sports/
suntoryhall
Classical music and opera.

Tokyo Opera City
3-20-2 Nishi-Shinjuku, Shinjuku-ku
Tel: 03-5353-0770
www.operacity.jp/en
Opera and classical music.

Galleries

Tokyo

Design Festa Gallery
3-20-2 Jingumae, Shibuya-ku
Tel: 03-3479-1442
www.designfestagallery.com
Colourful freestyle art gallery in
Harajuku that has become Tokyo's main
venue for up-and-coming young artists.

Mori Art Museum
6-10-1 Roppongi, 53F Roppongi Hills
Tel: 03-5777-8600
www.mori.art.museum
Top contemporary art from around
the world in this sleek gallery atop
Roppongi Hills.

Scai the Bathhouse
6-1-23 Yanaka, Taito-ku
Tel: 03-3821-1144
www.scaithebathhouse.com
A renovated Edo-era bathhouse in
Yanaka, with a focus on avant-garde
art.

Tomio Koyama Gallery
3-10-11, Sendagaya, Shibuya-ku
Tel: 03-6434-7225
www.tomiokoyamagallery.com
Leading gallerist Koyama attracts the
best of Japanese contemporary art.

Other cities

Naoshima
Benesse House
www.benesse-artsite.jp/benessehouse
Sleek gallery housing work by
artists such as Warhol and Pollock,
in addition to having 19 outdoor
art installations spread over its
beachfront grounds.

Chichu Art Museum
www.benesse-artsite.jp/chichu
Designed by Ando Tadao and built into
the hillside, this cavernous gallery
houses work by artists as varied as
Monet and James Turrell.

Honmura Art House Project
www.benesse-artsite.jp/ arthouse
A collection of permanent art
installations in the village of
Honmura, all of which are in
renovated traditional buildings.

Lee Ufan Museum
www.benesse-artsite.jp/lee-ufan
Housing the works of minimalist
painter and sculptor Lee Ufan, a
figurehead of Japan's late 1960s and
early 1970s Mono-ha movement.

NIGHTLIFE

Below is a brief round-up of the main
nightlife areas in the regions covered
in this guide. For up-to-date event
listings for these areas, contact the
local tourist information centres
or check out the magazines and
websites listed in the A–Z chapter
(see page 388).

Kanto and Chubu

In **Tokyo** you will find plenty of places
to burn money at night. If trendy
bars and restaurants with sleekly
designed interiors are your thing,
head to Omotesando, Aoyama or
Roppongi; the last is also home to a
few raucous nightclubs. For a more
bohemian feel, the bars in narrow
alleys of Golden Gai, neighbouring
Kabukicho in Shinjuku, are well worth
exploring. Likewise Kabukicho itself,
despite its sleazy reputation, has
some great bars and small live music
venues. More youthful are the bars,
music venues and clubs in Shibuya
and Harajuku, while hipsters will find
something in the Naka-Meguro or
Shimokitazawa areas. If it's a more
down-to-earth night out at an *izaka-ya*
you want, you will find something
wherever you are in Tokyo. The gay
scene is centred around Shinjuku's
Ni-chome area.

Heading west, to **Nagoya**, the
place to explore is Sakae, the city's
main entertainment district, and
home to many a good bar, restaurant,
izaka-ya and club.

The north

The north doesn't have much of a
reputation for rip-roaring nightlife
– not beyond the normal realms of
izaka-ya that is, but the Susukino area

of **Sapporo** is a definite exception.
Head here for bars, clubs, restaurants
and a fair sprinkling of sleazier
establishments.

Kansai

Kansai is at its most raucous and
liveliest in **Osaka**'s Dotonbori district,
while the America-mura area has
good watering holes. The narrow
alleys of Osaka's Hozenji Yokocho
are best for traditional restaurants
and atmospheric *izaka-ya*. **Kyoto**,
like Tokyo and Osaka, has a great
nightlife, ranging from cool clubs
and bars to lively *izaka-ya* and live
music venues. Much of this activity
is concentrated in the Kiya-machi
area, around Sanjo and Shijo stations,
as well as in Gion and Pontocho,
alongside the Kamogawa River.

The south

Shikoku and Kyushu might have
a fairly sedate vibe compared to
Tokyo or Osaka, but the locals
know how to have a rollicking night
out. On **Shikoku**, Tokushima's
Akita-machi, Kochi's Obiya-machi,
and Matsuyama's Niban-cho and
Sanban-cho areas are the liveliest
entertainment districts, while on
Kyushu head to Fukuoka's Nakasu
area or Nagasaki's Shianbashi area.
On **Okinawa**, the best nightlife is
concentrated in central Naha.

Tokyo

Happoen (Mu-an), 1-1-6
Shirokanedai, Minato-ku. Tel:
03-3443-3111, www.happo-en.com A
15-minute walk from Meguro Station,
but offering beautiful surrounds in
which to experience a tea ceremony.
Open daily 11am–3pm, lasts 30
minutes.
Imperial Hotel (Toko-an), 1-1-1
Uchisaiwai-cho, Chiyoda-ku, Tokyo.
(4F, the Main Wing). Tel: 03-3504-
1111. Near Hibiya Station on Hibiya,
Chiyoda or Toei Mita Line. Open
Mon–Sat 10am–4pm; 20-minute
participation periods. Advanced
reservation is required. The Hotel
Okura (Chosho-an; 03-3582-
0111; 11am–4pm) and Hotel New
Otani (Seisei-an; 03-3265-1111;
11am–4pm) have similar tea
ceremonies.

Kyoto

En, 272 Matsubara-cho,
Higashiyama-ku. Tel: 080-3782-
2706, www.teaceremonyen.com. A
small teahouse in Gion offering tea-
ceremony experiences in English but

with traditional *tatami*-mat surrounds. **Urasenke Tea School**, Urasenke Foundation Chado Research Centre. Tel: 075-431-6474, www.urasenke. or.jp. Information on events and classes in Kyoto.

FESTIVALS

Festivals, or *matsuri*, seem to be happening at any given time somewhere in Japan, and indeed have been an important part of Japanese life for hundreds of years. Many of the festivals have their roots in the long history of Japan's agricultural society. In today's ever-modernising Japan, they are one of the few occasions when the Japanese can dress up and relive the past. Below is a list of the most important festivals (for public holidays, see page 390). For information on forthcoming events going on during any particular week or month, please consult the Tourist Information Centre (see page 391) or www.jnto.go.jp.

January

The first **sumo** tournament of the year, **Hatsu-basho**, is held for 15 days at Tokyo's Kokugikan in mid-January. Shujin-no-hi (Adults' Day) falls on the second Monday of January, when 20-year-olds visit shrines in their finest kimonos.

February

On the 3rd is **Setsubun**, the traditional bean-throwing ceremony that is meant to purify the home of evil. Roasted beans are scattered from the inside of the house to the outside while people shout, "*Oni wa soto*" (Devils, go out!), and from the outside of the home to the inside while "*Fuku wa uchi*" (Good luck, come in) is shouted. The same

Tea ceremony (sado) in Kyoto.

Traditional tea ceremony (in English)

Nothing expresses Japanese formality and emphasis on social protocol more effectively than the tea ceremony. Although tea-drinking appeared early in Japanese history, it was not until the 12th century that the special strain of the tea bush and the technique of making powdered green tea *(matcha)* were brought from China. Making the tea is not the challenge; it is making it in the right spirit that consumes a lifetime of effort. Implements and procedures have value only towards a higher objective – the ability to show sublime hospitality. Experience it for yourself.

ceremony is also held at temples and shrines. Plum Viewing festivals begin in early to late February. The most famous viewing spot in Tokyo, Yushima Tenjin shrine, holds *ikebana* and tea-ceremony displays at this time. Sapporo's famous **Yuki Matsuri** (Snow Festival) on 5–11 February features giant statues sculpted from snow and ice.

March

On the 3rd is **Hina Matsuri** (Girls' Day), a festival for little girls. Small *Hina* dolls, representing imperial court figures, are decorated and displayed at home and in several public places. *Yamabushi* mountain monks perform the Fire-Walking Ceremony in mid-March at the foot of Mount Takao outside Tokyo. Spectators can test their mettle by walking barefoot across the smouldering coals of the fires. Many shrines throughout Japan have their Daruma Fairs on 3–4 March, selling red, white and black dolls of the famous Zen monk. One of the two empty eyes should be painted in upon undertaking a new, difficult task, the other filled in upon its successful completion.

April

From early to mid-April is **O-hanami** (cherry-blossom-viewing), one of the important spring rites. People love to

turn out and picnic, drink *sake* and sing songs under the pink blossoms. Kyoto has a multitude of blossom-viewing parties, the most famous being at Daigo-ji. In Tokyo, Ueno Park attracts big o-hanami crowds and is a very lively place for a picnic, while Chidorigafuchi moat at Tokyo's Imperial Palace is especially photogenic. On 8 April is **Hana Matsuri** (Birthday of Buddha), when commemorative services are held at various temples such as Gokoku-ji, Senso-ji, Zojo-ji and Hommon-ji. A colourful display of horseback archery is put on by men dressed in medieval costumes during the Yabusame Festival in Sumida Park in mid-April. Acrobatic marionettes balance on towering festival floats as they are carried across the bridges of the town in the **Takayama Festival** on 14–15 April.

May

In mid-May, the **Natsu-basho** (summer **sumo** tournament) is held for 15 days at the Kokugikan in Tokyo. On the 3rd Saturday and Sunday, the **Sanja Matsuri** is held. This is one of the big Edo festivals honouring the three fishermen who found the image of Kannon in the river. Tokyo's Asakusa-jinja Senso-ji temple is a great place to go at this time to see the dancing, music and many portable shrines. In mid-May the huge **Kanda Festival**, one of Tokyo's most important *matsuri*, is held every other year. Processions and floats and portable shrines parade through this downtown area. A fine historical costume parade takes place in Kyoto during the 15 May **Aoi Matsuri** (Hollyhock Festival). There's a similar event on 17 May, with horseback archery, at the Tosho-gu shrine in Nikko.

June

The summer rains blanket Kyoto from mid-June to mid-July. Kifune-jinja, dedicated to the god of water, celebrates the season in a vibrant water festival. Torchlight performances of *noh* plays are held

1–2 June at the Heian Shrine. On the second Sunday is *Torigoe Jinja Taisai*, a night-time festival, when the biggest and heaviest portable shrine in Tokyo is carried through the streets by lantern light. It all happens at the Torigoe Shrine. From the 10th to the 16th is *Sanno Sai*, another big Edo festival featuring a *gyoretsu* (people parading in traditional costumes) on Saturday at the Hie Shrine. June is the season for iris-viewing, the best locations being the Iris Garden in the grounds of the Meiji shrine in Tokyo and the Iris Garden in Tokyo's Kiyosumi Teien.

Kanda Matsuri, Tokyo.

July

From the 6th to the 8th is the **Asagao Ichi** (Morning Glory Fair) in Tokyo, when over 100 merchants set up stalls selling the flower at Iriya Kishibojin. On 7 July is the **Tanabata Matsuri**, a festival celebrating the only day of the year when, according to the legend, the Weaver Princess (Vega) and her lover the Cowherder (Altair) can cross the Milky Way to meet. People write their wishes on coloured paper, hang them on bamboo branches, and then float them down a river the next day. Also in Tokyo, 9–10 July is the **Hozuki Ichi** (Ground Cherry Fair) at Senso-ji from early morning to midnight. A visit to this temple on the 10th is meant to be equal to 46,000 visits at other times. On the last Saturday of July, the **Sumida-gawa Hanabi Taikai** (Sumida River Fireworks) is held. This is the biggest fireworks display in Tokyo, and the best places to watch the display are between the Kototoi and Shirahige bridges, or at the Komagata Bridge. Fukuoka's pride and joy, its Hakata Yamagasa, takes place 1–15 July, an event that sees colourful portable shrines carried through the streets. Kyoto's grandest event, the 17 July Gion Matsuri, features massive floats hung with fine silks and paper lanterns.

August

Late July/early August hosts a more contemporary event that is fast becoming a tradition: international and local acts gather for the huge, three-day Fuji Rock Festival in Naeba. Between the 13th and the 16th is the **O-Bon** festival, when people return to their hometowns to clean up graves and offer prayers to the souls of departed ancestors. The traditional **Bon Odori** folk dances are held all over around this time. The best known, running for almost two months, is in Gujo Hachiman. The largest single turnout of dancers is in Tokushima during its more renowned Awa Odori. Both Aomori and Hirosaki hold Nebuta and Neputa Matsuri on 1–7 August. Giant paper figures are lit up from inside like lanterns.

September

Mid-September is the time for moon-viewing, with many events across Kyoto. Osawa Pond has been known since Heian times as one of Japan's three great moon-viewing sites. This is also a good time of year for dinner, with moon-viewing, on one of the *yakatabune* barges that sail around Tokyo Bay. On 16 September at the Tsurugaoka Hachimangu Shrine in Kamakura is an annual display of *yabusame* (horseback archery) performed by riders in samurai armour.

October

From mid- to late October is chrysanthemum-viewing time, and there are flower displays dotted around the cities. Nagasaki's Okunchi Matsuri, on 7–9 October, is an interesting blend of Chinese, European and Shinto, with dragon dances and floats representing Dutch galleons. Kyoto's Jidai Matsuri, on 22 October, is a splendid, quietly dignified costume parade.

November

The 15th is **Shichi-Go-San** (Seven-Five-Three), a ceremony for 5-year-old boys and 3- and 7-year-old girls. The children usually dress up in kimonos and *hakama* (loose trousers) and are taken to visit a shrine.

December

Kaomise (face-showing) is Kyoto's gala *kabuki* performance at Minami-za, when the actors reveal their real faces. On 7–8 December, Senbon Shaka-do celebrates the day of Buddha's enlightenment with a radish-boiling ceremony to help ward off evil. The 14th is **Gishi Sai**, a memorial service for the famous 47 Ronin who, on this day in 1702, avenged the death of their master and later committed ritual suicide. They are buried at the Sengaku-ji in Tokyo, where the service is held. On 31 December at the stroke of midnight, every temple bell in the country begins to toll. The bells toll 108 times, for the 108 evil human passions. This is called **Joya no Kane**, and the general public are allowed to strike the bells at various temples.

SHOPPING

Japan can be a very expensive place to shop, but there are still bargains to be had if you seek them out. The high quality of Japanese products is well known, and there are some items that can only be bought in Japan. Certain areas promote only particular kinds of merchandise, which means that some domestic travel is involved for the serious shopper. Following is a guide to the main shopping attractions in the cities and other areas throughout Japan.

In and around Tokyo

Akihabara: an electronic jungle featuring hundreds of discount stores and the latest tech; the area is also known for its anime and manga stores.
Aoyama: high-class fashion boutiques.
Asakusa: traditional Japanese toys, souvenirs, workmen's clothes, etc.
Daikanyama: a more recent addition to Tokyo's fashion scene, with many boutiques targeting the 20–30s age group.

Japanese paper.

Ginza: an expensive shopping centre. Several major department stores are located here, such as Hankyu (www. hankyu-dept.co.jp), Matsuya (www. matsuya.com), Matsuzakaya (www. matsuzakaya.co.jp), Mitsukoshi, Printemps (www.printemps-ginza. co.jp) and Wako (www.wako.co.jp), and many exclusive boutiques. Also some traditional Japanese goods stores.
Harajuku: another fashion area, though mostly geared to the young, which makes shopping relatively cheap. Several antiques shops.
Hibiya: mostly antiques shops, jewellery shops and art galleries.
Kanda and **Jimbocho**: many second-hand bookstores.
Nihombashi: a good place to pick up traditional craft work. Two of Japan's oldest department stores, the main branches of Mitsukoshi and Takashimaya (www.takashimaya.co.jp), are located here.
Roppongi: several antiques shops in the area, the Axis design building, which features interior design as its main theme, plus trendy shops aplenty in the Roppongi Hills and Tokyo Midtown complexes.
Shibuya: a good place to start with, Shibuya has a little bit of everything. Tokyu Hands is a must to visit; probably the most complete do-it-yourself department store in the world. Also here are the Seibu, Tokyu and Marui (www.0101.co.jp) department stores, the Parco "fashion buildings" besides the hundreds of small boutiques geared to young shoppers.
Shimokitazawa: popular with Tokyo youth, Shimokita is a Mecca for fans of art cafés, avant-garde theatre, and small shops selling dead stock, hand-me-downs and grungy student wear, not to mention vintage and rare records.

Shinjuku: several big camera and electronic discount stores such as Yodobashi (www.yodobashi.com) and Bic Camera (www.biccamera.co.jp). Also, Isetan (http://isetan.mistore.jp) and Marui department stores.
Ueno: Ameyoko is good for cheap food, cosmetics, clothing and toys. One of the few open markets in Tokyo. The shops in the backstreets sell traditional Japanese goods.

Antiques

In most of the shops listed here, the staff speak English and are helpful. Watch out for badly restored pieces that have been given a quick coat of glossy lacquer and are sold like new.
Antique Gallery Meguro, Stork Building, 2nd Fl, 2-24-18 Kamiosaki, Shinagawa-ku. Tel: 03-3493-1971. Antiques market of sorts covering 740 sq metres (8,000 sq ft) that houses several small antiques shops.
Fuji-Torii, 6-1-10 Jingumae, Shibuya-ku. Tel: 03-3400-2777, www.fuji-torii.com. High-quality store specialising in a wide range of regional crafts and art.
Kurofune Antiques, 7-7-4 Roppongi, Minato-ku. Tel: 03-3479-1552. *Tansu* (storage cabinets), woodcarvings, baskets and more.
Oriental Bazaar, 5-9-13 Jingumae, Shibuya-ku. Tel: 03-3400-3933, www.orientalbazaar.co.jp. Apart from antiques, this is also a nice place to browse and pick up traditional Japanese toys, paper *(washi)*, kimonos, etc.

Bookshops

There are bookshops all over Tokyo, and it is quite acceptable to browse through the books and magazines in the shop without having to buy them. In spite of the large number of bookstores, there are relatively few that specialise in English books. Below is a list of the major shops in Tokyo that stock foreign books and books on Japan. Besides these places, you can also get foreign newspapers and magazines in most major international hotels, and you can pick up a local English-language newspaper at the Kiosk stands in most major city-centre stations.
Aoyama Book Centre. Tel: 03-3479-0479, www.aoyamabc.jp. Open daily 10am–11.30pm; Sun and holidays 10am–10pm. One minute from Roppongi Station (Hibiya Line).
Book 1st, 33-5 Udagawa-cho, Shibuya-ku. Tel: 03-5459-3531, www. book1st.net. Open daily 10am–11pm. More than 1,000 magazine titles on the 1st floor of this new bookstore,

while English books are stocked on the 3rd floor.
Good Day Books, 3F, Tokai Building, 2-4-2 Nishi Gotanda, Shinagawa-ku. Tel: 03-6303-9116, www.gooddaybooks.com. Open Mon–Sat 11am–8pm; Sun and holidays 11am–6pm. Tokyo's best English used-book store; some new books also.
Kinokuniya, 3-17-7 Shinjuku, Shinjuku-ku. Tel: 03-3354-0131, www.kinokuniya.com. Open daily 10am–9pm. Foreign books on the 6th floor. Very popular.
Kitazawa Shoten, 2-5-3 Kanda Jimbocho, Chiyoda-ku. Tel: 03-3263-0011, www.kitazawa.co.jp. Open Mon–Fri 11am–6.30pm, Sat noon–5.30pm. Second-hand books on the 2nd floor and English literature on the 1st floor.
Sanseido Books, Kanda-Jimbocho, Chiyoda-ku. Tel: 03-3233-3312, www.books-sanseido.co.jp. Open daily 10am–10pm. Good all-round store.
Tower Records Shibuya, 1-22-14 Jinnan, Shibuya-ku. Tel: 03-3496-3661, http://tower.jp. Open daily 10am–11pm. Interesting alternative selection of books, with extensive foreign magazines and papers.
Yaesu Book Centre, 2-5-1 Yaesu, Chuo-ku. Tel: 03-3281-1811, www. yaesu-book.co.jp. Open Mon–Fri 10am–9pm, Sat–Sun until 7pm. Large selection of general books. Located near Tokyo Station.

Ceramics

Besides workshops, department stores are the best places for Japanese ceramics at reasonable prices. On backstreets, small shops also sell ceramics but prices tend to be higher.
Dengama, 1-4-3 Nishi-Asakusa, Taito-ku. Tel: 03-5828-9355, www. dengama.jp.

Department Stores

Daimaru, 1-9-1 Marunouchi, Chiyoda-ku, Tokyo. Tel: 03-3212-8011, http://daimaru.co.jp. Also has branches in Osaka, Kyoto, Kobe and Sapporo.
Isetan, 3-14-1 Shinjuku, Shinjuku-ku, Tokyo. Tel: 03-3352-1111, www. isetan.co.jp. Other branches include Niigata, Kyoto and Osaka.
Marui, 3-30-16 Shinjuku, Shinjuku-ku, Tokyo. Tel: 03-3354-0101, www.0101.co.jp. Has branches across Tokyo and in Osaka.
Matsuya, 3-6-1 Ginza, Chuo-ku, Tokyo. Tel: 03-3567-1211, www. matsuya.com. Also has another store in Tokyo, in Asakusa.

Matsuzakaya, 3-29-5 Ueno, Taito-ku. Tel: 03-3832-1111, www.matsuzakaya.co.jp. Also with a store in Ginza, Tokyo.
Mitsukoshi, 1-7-4 Muromachi, Nihombashi, Chuo-ku. Tel: 03-3241-3311, www.mitsukoshi.co.jp. Has another big store in Ginza and many others across Japan, including Sapporo, Nagoya, Hiroshima and Fukuoka.
Seibu, 1-28-1 Minami Ikebukuro, Toshima-ku. Tel: 03-3981-0111, www.seibu.jp. Many other stores across the country, including in Shibuya in Tokyo.
Takashimaya, 2-4-1 Nihombashi, Chuo-ku. Tel: 03-3211-4111, www.takashimaya.co.jp. Branches all over, including Tokyo Shinjuku, Yokohama, Kyoto and Osaka.
Tokyu, 2-24-1 Dogenzaka, Shibuya-ku. Tel: 03-3477-3111, www.tokyu-dept.co.jp.

Electronics and cameras

Bic Camera, www.biccamera.com Large home electronics chain with stores all over Tokyo, including Yurakucho and Shinjuku.
Laox, 1-2-9, Soto-Kanda, Chiyoda-ku. Tel: 03-3253-7111, www.laox.co.jp. Massive discount chain store, with English-speaking staff at this particular branch in Akihabara.
Yodobashi Camera, www.yodobashi.com. Another major chain with branches all over, including Akihabara and Shinjuku.
Softmap, www.sofmap.com. Akihabara's premier computer discount store, with numerous branches in Akihabara alone and more in Shinjuku. New and used PCs and Macs.

Japanese Paper (Washi)

Haibara, 2-7-6 Nihombashi, Chuo-ku. Tel: 03-3272-3801, www.haibara.co.jp. Closed Sun and holidays.
Isetatsu, 2-18-9 Yanaka, Taito-ku. Tel: 03-3823-1453, www.isetatsu.com.
Kyukyodo, 5-7-4 Ginza, Chuo-ku. Tel: 03-3571-4429, www.kyukyodo.co.jp.
Tsutsumu Factory, 137-15, Udagawacho, Shibuya-ku. Tel: 03-5478-1330, http://tsutsumu.co.jp.Tsutsumu means "to wrap" in Japanese. Traditional and modern designs in wrapping paper. Also has nice cards, some in thick, *washi* paper.

Kimonos (antique)

These shops specialise in antique kimonos, *obi (sashes)*, traditional blue-and-white textiles, *furoshiki*, *hanten* and other garb.

Flea markets also sell them, and you can usually pick up very beautiful old kimonos and *obi* in good condition. A more expensive option is department stores, which typically have kimono sections.
Hayashi Kimono, International Arcade, 1-7 Uchisaiwaicho, Chiyoda-ku. Tel: 03-3591-9826.
Ikeda, 5-22-11 Shiroganedai, Minato-ku. Tel: 03-3445-1269, http://ikeda-kimono.com. Closed Wed.
Kimono Sakaeya, 3-15 Miya-cho, Omiya, Saitama. Tel: 070-5556-4393, www.kimono-sakaeya.com. A little out of the way (in Omiya), but has one-day kimono rental and English-speaking staff.

Fans (sensu)

Bunsendo, 1-30 Asakusa, Taito-ku. Tel: 03-3844-9711. Open 10am–6pm, closed last Monday of every month. On a lane to the left of Nakamise, the shop-lined approach to the great Senso-ji temple has an exquisite collection of traditional fans.
Kyosendo, 2-4-3 Nihombashi, Ningyocho, Chuo-ku. Tel: 03-3669-0046. Open Mon–Sat 10am–7pm. Located in Tokyo's business centre, a tiny world of aesthetic sensibilities can be found in this famous

Flea markets

An alternative to department-store shopping, flea markets and antiques fairs, often located in shrine or temple compounds, offer a colourful experience.

Tokyo

Hanazono Shrine Antiques Market, 5-17-3, Shinjuku, Shinjuku-ku, Tokyo. On the edge of Kabukicho, a popular market running from sunrise to sunset every Sunday.
Heiwajima Kotto Fair, 6-1-1, Heiwajima, Heiwajima Ryutsu Centre Building, Tokyo. A giant, three-day flea market and antiques fair held five times a year. Check www.kottouichi.com to check the schedule.
Oedo Antique Fair, Tokyo International Forum. A great collection of more than 250 stalls, all licensed antiques dealers. First and third Sundays of every month in the outdoor courtyard at Tokyo International Forum in Yurakucho, 9am–4pm, www.antique-market.jp; cancelled if heavy rain.
Setagaya Boro-Ichi, Boro Ichi-Dori Street, Setagaya. Near Setagaya

shop. Its main branch is in Kyoto (www.kyosendo.co.jp).

Fashion boutiques and buildings

Japan cuts a very high profile when it comes to fashion, importing the best and creating its own world-respected designs. Multi-storey fashion buildings, each floor crammed with boutiques and outlets, are a unique feature of Japanese cities. Besides the few below to get you started, see the section above on department stores and the brief area guide at the start of this section.
109, 2-29-1, Dogenzaka, Shibuya-ku. Tel: 03-3477-5111, www.shibuya109.jp. Unmissable, silo-shaped silver building, the 109 is a Mecca of Shibuya chic for young women.
Laforet Harajuku, 1-11-6, Jingumae, Shibuya-ku. Tel: 03-3475-0411, www.laforet.ne.jp. Major fashion building housing about 100 boutiques. Strictly for the young.
Parco, www.parco.co.jp. Many branches of this department store in Japan, including two in Shibuya, offering a wide selection of smart and stylish clothing.
Uniqlo. www.uniqlo.com. Fashionable discount chain with branches all over.

station. Tokyo's best-known flea market, a huge affair dating back to the 1570s. Held 15–16 Jan and 15–16 Dec, 9am–9pm.

Rest of Japan

Dazaifu Tenjin Omoshiro Market, Fukuoka. Approximately 100 stalls covering old furniture, clothing, and antiques. Held last six times a year, 9am–5pm.
Kitano Tenman-gu Shrine Antique Market, Kyoto. Held the 25th of every month, 6am–9pm, and deals with antiques as well as daily goods.
Osukannon Antique Market, Nagoya. Held the 18th and 28th of each month, from sunrise to sunset, this is a great place to grab an old kimono or antiques.
Shitenno-ji Daishie, Osaka. Around 300 stalls selling everything from antiques to used clothing. Held 21st and 22nd of each month at Shitenno-ji temple, 8.30am–sunset.
To-ji, Kyoto. The famous wooden pagoda of this temple south of Kyoto Station hosts the city's best flea market on the 21st of each month, 5am–4pm.

Lacquer Ware (Shikki)

Kuroeya, Kuroeya Kokubu Building, 2nd Floor, 1-2-6 Nihombashi, Chuo-ku. Tel: 03-3272-0948, www.kuroeya.com.
Yamada Heiando, 18-12 Sarugakucho, Shibuya-ku. Tel. 03-3464-5541, www.yamada-heiando.jp.

Musical instruments

Miyamoto Unosuke Shoten (drums), 6-1-15 Asakusa, Taito-ku. Tel: 03-3874-4131, www.miyamoto-unosuke.co.jp. Closed Sun and public holidays.

Umbrellas (kasa)

Iidaya, 1-31-1 Asakusa, Taito-ku. Tel: 03-3841-3644.

Woodblock prints (ukiyo-e)

Hara Shobo, 2-3 Kanda Jimbocho, Chiyoda-ku. Tel: 03-5212-7801, www.harashobo.com. All types of prints old and new, from the highest quality to a "bargain drawer".
Oya Shobo, 1-1 Kanda Jimbocho, Chiyoda-ku. Tel: 03-3291-0062, www.ohya-shobo.com. Closed Sun.
Sakai Kokodo Gallery, 1-2-14 Yurakucho, Chiyoda-ku. Tel: 03-3591-4678, www.ukiyo-e.co.jp. Also stores in Yokohama and Kamakura.

Outside Tokyo

In each chapter you will find mention of local specialities such as crafts and foodstuffs, and places to buy or sample them. In addition, here is a brief list of some of the more interesting places to shop outside Tokyo.

Tohoku

Sendai

Basement of Sendai Station building: Tohoku art and craft shops.

Morioka

Zaimoku-cho area, just north of the station and the Kitakamigawa River: traditional art and craft shops. Iwachu, Nanbu Tekki: local iron crafts.

Aomori

Auga Market, Auga Building: lively fish market from 5am to early evening.
Shinmachi Dori: local crafts.

Hokkaido

Sapporo

Tanuki-koji covered market: all sorts of shops, including souvenirs, confections and crafts. www.tanukikoji.or.jp.

Hakodate

Chiaki-kan, in Horai-cho: handmade Japanese confections.
Morning market, held in the bay area near Hakodate Station: hundreds of seafood stalls.

Akan National Park

Akan Kohan Visitor Centre: local crafts.

Kansai

Kyoto and around

Kawaramachi (main north–south street) and Shijo (main east–west street): department stores, fashion boutiques, and numerous craft and souvenir shops.
Teramachi (downtown arcade): tea and accessories, Japanese stationery, fans, chopsticks, and many other crafts and souvenirs.
Nishiki Market: Kyoto pickles, tofu and other regional foods.
Kyoto Station: souvenirs and department stores.
Arashiyama: bamboo crafts.

Nara

Sanjo-dori and Mochidono shopping street: narazuke pickles, calligraphy brushes, Nara fabrics and other local crafts and souvenirs.

Ise

Akafuku Honten, near Ise Naiguu: Japanese confections, souvenirs.

Osaka

America-mura: youth fashions and affordable boutiques.
Den Den Town (Nipponbashi): home electronics and games.
Doguya-suji: cooking and restaurant goods.
Tenjinbashi-suji: all manner of generally low-cost shops in this long arcade.
Shinsaibashi-suji: boutiques, brand names and budget stores.
Umeda: major department stores, home electronics and smart malls.

Kobe

Harbor Land area: modern malls and stores.
Motoko Town underground mall: books, souvenirs, clothes and so much else at this long underground mall between Sannomiya and Kobe stations.

Himeji

Miyuki-dori arcade: wind chimes.

Chugoku

Hagi

Ochadokoro: near Kikuya Yokocho: Japanese tea and confections.

Shikoku

Takamatsu

Kitahama Alley: crafts and funky art.

Tokushima

Aizome Kogei-kan: indigo-dyed fabrics.
Nichiyo-ichi: Lively Sunday market with plenty of fresh produce, but also local crafts.
Nishishinmachi Arcade: local crafts, such as indigo-dyed cloth.

Matsuyama

The most interesting places here are the seemingly endless Okaido and adjoining Gintengai arcades, where fashion dominates.

Kochi

Hirome-ichiba market: some ceramics and crafts, but mostly lots and lots of small eateries.

Kyushu

Fukuoka

Tenjin, Hakata Station area and Watanabe-dori: lots of stores selling local crafts, including ceramic Hakata dolls and Hakata ori (a kind of silk).

Beppu Spa

Ekimae-dori: bamboo crafts and natural bath salts.

Kagoshima

Sengan-en park: local Satsuma Kiriko glass crafts, local liquor and Satsuma pottery.

Okinawa

Naha

Ichiba-dori and Heiwa-dori: souvenir and craft shops, and markets.

Okinawa City

Chuo **Park Avenue**: more than 100 shops and restaurants.

SPORTS

Spectator sports

Sumo tournaments

Six tournaments annually, each lasting for 15 days, are held in January, May and September in

Tokyo, in March in Osaka, in July in Nagoya, and in November in Fukuoka. During the tournament, matches are televised daily 4–6pm. Matches by junior wrestlers begin at about 10am; by senior wrestlers at 3pm on the first and the last days, and at 3.30pm on other days. Don't expect to sit close to the ring, or *dohyo*. These seats are expensive and are usually booked by large corporations or the very wealthy.

Tokyo
January, May and September: Kokugikan Sumo Hall, 1-3-28 Yokoami, Sumida-ku, Tokyo. Tel: 03-3623-5111. Near JR Ryogoku Station.

Osaka
March: Osaka Furitsu Taiikukan (Osaka Prefectural Gymnasium), 3-4-36 Namba Naka, Naniwa-ku, Osaka. Tel: 06-631-0121. Near Namba subway station.

Nagoya
July. Aichi Ken Taiikukan (Aichi Prefectural Gymnasium), 1-1 Ninomaru, Naka-ku, Nagoya. Tel: 052-971-2516, www.aichi-kentai.com.15 minutes by car from Nagoya Station.

Fukuoka
November: Fukuoka Kokusai Centre Sogo Hall, 2-2 Chikuko-Honcho, Hakata-ku, Fukuoka. Tel: 092-272 1111.

Baseball
Often described as Japan's "second national sport", it remains a big game, though it is losing some popularity among the young. The season runs April–October, peaking with the best-of-seven Japan Series between the Central and Pacific leagues.
Tokyo Dome
1-3-61 Koraku, Bunkyo-ku
Tel: 03-5800-9999
www.tokyo-dome.co.jp
Nicknamed the Big Egg, the stadium is home to the Yomiuri Giants, historically

the biggest and most succesful team in Japan, and a team the Japanese either love or love to hate.
Jingu Stadium
13 Kasumigaoka, Shinjuku-ku
Tel: 03-3404-8999, 0180-993-589
www.jingu-stadium.com
Home ground of the Swallows, this older, open-air stadium is probably more atmospheric than the Big Egg.
Koshien Stadium
Tel: 0180-997-750
www.hanshin.co.jp/koshien
Close to Koshien Station near Osaka, this is the venue for the wildly popular All-Japan High School Baseball Championship, the city's summer highlight. It's also home to Kansai's favourite team, the Hanshin Tigers.
Kyocera Dome Osaka
www.kyoceradome-osaka.jp
Home to the Kintetsu Buffalos team.
Fukuoka Yahoo! Japan Dome
www.hawkstown.com
Part of the Hawks Town development, this hi-tech stadium is home to the local Daiei Hawks team.

Horse racing
Horse racing has become more fashionable and respectable of late. One of the few chances to gamble in Japan, schedules and venues around Japan are available in English at the National Association of Racing website: www.jairs.jp.
Ohi Racetrack
2-1-1 Katsushima, Shinagawa-ku
Tel: 03-3763-2151, www.tokyocity keiba.com.
Tokyo Racecourse
1-1, 1-2 Hiyoshi-cho, Fuchu City
Tel: 042-363-3141, http://japan racing.jp.

Martial arts
Karate, aikido, judo, kyudo (archery) and *kendo* are well represented at the Nippon Budokan in Tokyo. For information on martial-arts events and venues across Japan, contact the following organisations.
All-Japan Judo Federation
c/o Kodokan, 1-16-30 Kasuga, Bunkyo-ku
Tel: 03-3818-4199, 03-3818-4172 (English-speaking service at Kodokan Judo Institutue)
www.judo.or.jp
All-Japan Kendo Federation
Tel: 03-3234-6271
www.kendo.or.jp, www.kendo-fik.org
Japan Karate Association
2-23-15 Koraku, Bunkyo-ku
Tel: 03-5800-3091
www.jka.or.jp
Japan Karatedo Federation
1-1-20 Tatsumi, Koto-ku

Tel: 03-5534-1951
www.karatedo.co.jp
Nippon Budokan
2-3 Kitanomaru-koen, Chiyoda-ku
Tel: 03-3216-5100
www.nipponbudokan.or.jp

Rugby
Rugby is quite popular in Japan, with a thriving corporate league, a keen following in universities, and a good attendance at the Rugby World Cup, the next installment of which will be held in Tokyo in 2019. Visit the Japan Rugby Football Union's website for extensive information on the game (and where to watch games) in Japan: http://jrfu.org.

Football
The J-League now competes and fractionally outpaces baseball as the most popular spectator sport in Japan. The season runs March–October, with the Emperor's Cup in December. Both Japan's men's and women's national teams get a lot of media coverage, and you will often find football on TV. Below are a couple places you can watch football in Tokyo; see www.jleague.jp for a full list of pro teams and places to catch games around Japan.
National Stadium
Kasumigaoka, Shinjuku-ku
Tel: 03-3403-115
The home stadium of Japan's national football teams and the site for major cup games. It will be the main venue for the 2019 Rugby World Cup and the 2020 Summer Olympic Games.
Ajinomoto Stadium
376-3, Nishimachi, Chofu City
Tel: 0424-40-0555
Hosts games for FC Tokyo and Tokyo Verdy 1969.
www.ajinomotostadium.com

Participant sports

Golf
Some hotels offer golf packages, and this is probably the cheapest way to get onto the greens in Japan, which can otherwise be expensive, even though prices have come down a lot in recent years. There are hundreds of courses within a two-hour drive from central Tokyo, and courses are equally easy to find in many other parts of the country. See www.golf-in-japan.com for more. Driving ranges and putting greens, some under raised motorways or on department store rooftops, are easy to find.
Tokyo Metropolitan Golf Course
1-15-1 Shinden, Adachi-ku

Tel: 03-3919-0111

Shibayama Golf Course
2176 Odai, Shibayama, 20 minutes'
drive from Narita
Tel: 0479-77-4123

Ice skating

This is also a popular spectator sport,
with exhibitions and shows at the
National Stadium in Tokyo.

Meiji Jingu Ice-Skating Rink
Gobanchi, Kasumigaoka, Shinjuku-ku
Tel: 03-3403-3456
www.meijijingugaien.jp

Takadanobaba Citizen Ice-Skating Rink
4-29-27 Takabanobaba, Shinjuku-ku
Tel: 03-3371-0910

Fitness centres

Besides fitness centres in major
hotels (many open to non-guests),
the best place to get a workout is at
a municipal gym. Tourist information
centres will be able to direct you to the
nearest ones. Other gyms and fitness
centre chains require membership
fees, and so are of little use to
travellers. Here are a couple of good
municipal gyms and sports centres in
Tokyo (each of the 23 wards has one).

Chiyoda-ku Sports Centre
2-1-8 Uchi-kanda, Chiyoda-ku
Tel: 03-3256-8444
www.spst-chiyoda.jp
Open daily 9am–9pm; closed 3rd
Monday of the month.

Minato-ku Sports Centre
1-16-1 Shibaura, Minato-ku
Tel: 03-3452-4151
www.minatoku-sports.com
Open daily 9am–9pm; closed 1st and
3rd Mondays of the month.

Yoga

International Yoga Centre
5-30-6 Ogikubo, Suginami-ku
www.iyc.jp

Sun & Moon Yoga
16-44-3 Higashigotanda,
Shinagawa-ku
Tel: 03-3280-6383
www.sunandmoon.jp

SIGHTSEEING TOURS

First-time visitors or those on a very
tight schedule should consider taking
a sightseeing tour in one of the major
destinations such as Tokyo or Kyoto.
 The **Japan Guide Association** (tel:
03-3863-2895, www.jga21c.or.jp) can
put you in touch with an accredited
tour guide. You can then negotiate
the fee and itinerary with the guide.
At some well-known sites, especially
in Tokyo and Kyoto, you may be

approached by volunteer guides.
While their services are free, you
should offer lunch as a gesture.

Bus tours

Bus tours are usually reasonably
priced and run from half-day to full-day
and evening tours. Prices vary greatly
depending on the tour, but can be
as little as ¥2,500 for a half-day trip.
Tours can be booked through major
hotels in the main historical cities. The
following all offer tours in English.

Hato Bus Tokyo
Tel: 03-3435-6081
http://www.hatobus.co.jp/en
Reliable tour company offering half-
day trips from ¥1,540.

Japan Gray Line
www.jgl.co.jp/inbound
Tours prices range from ¥5,200 to
¥17,000, depending on length and
what is included.

Sunrise Tours
Tel: 03-5796-5454
www.jtb-sunrisetours.jp
Run by the large Japan Travel Bureau,
Sunrise offers numerous tours of
Tokyo, Kamakura, Hakone, Osaka
and Kyoto.

River tours

Tokyo Water Cruise
Tel: 0120-977311
www.suijobus.co.jp
A delightful way to see Tokyo's Sumida
River and its old bridges, many of them
pre-war. Tours go to the Hama-Rikyu
Garden and on to Odaiba.

Taxi tours

Taxi tours are handy but expensive,
even outside the main sightseeing
cities. Expect to pay at least ¥20,000,
but often double that or more for
tours between 4 and 8 hours.
Contact the JNTO (see page 391) for
recommendations.

City walking tours

Tokyo

Get to know the backstreets
of Tokyo and their stories with
English-speaking Mr Oka, a retired
historian. www.homestead.com/
mroka

Kyoto

Peter Macintosh guides small
groups through the mysteries of
Kyoto's geisha world. Tel: 090-
5169-1654, www.kyotosightsand
nights.com

OUTDOOR ACTIVITIES

Japan has no shortage of activities
for adrenalin junkies or anyone who
wants to get a sweat on in the great
outdoors. Below is a brief round-up of
the most popular outdoor activities.

Adventure sports

If rafting, canyoning, canoeing,
bungee jumping or the like is your
thing, make a beeline to Minakami
Onsen (see page 198) in Gunma
Prefecture, two hours north of Tokyo,
where there are a host of English-
speaking outdoor activity operators
ready to get your heart racing.
Alternative areas are the Iya Valley
in Shikoku and Niseko in Hokkaido.
For more information, see www.
outdoorjapan.com or www.canyons.jp.

Diving

Diving is very popular with Japanese,
and although many tend to head off to
Guam, Saipan, Palau, Hawaii or other
foreign shores for diving holidays,
Japan does have some spectacular
dive sights of its own, especially in
Okinawa (see page 347).

Hiking

With more than 70 percent of its
landmass mountainous, Japan offers
plenty of rewarding hiking areas, with
something for all levels of fitness and
expertise. The best hiking grounds
are in the Japan Alps, accessed by the
village of Kamikochi (see page 195).
As with anything well rated in Japan,
however, be aware that in the peak
summer hiking season in top spots like
Kamikochi, you will be sharing the trails
with many other hikers. National parks
throughout Japan, and there are lots
(see page 230), typically have well-
marked trails, and the more popular
ones have some facilities, such as
regularly placed mountain huts, on the
trails. From Tokyo, the favourite places
to head for a hike are the Fuji-Hakone
area, Nikko and around Mount Takao.
Less busy, and all the better for it, is
the scenic Tanzawa range about two
hours west of central Tokyo. For more on
where and how to hike, check out www.
outdoorjapan.com.

Skiing and snowboarding

Japan can lay fair claim to being
Asia's best place to ski or snowboard.
Niseko (see page 221) in Hokkaido
is known across Asia and Australasia

Tama Zoological Park, Tokyo.

for its perfect powder snow, cool resorts and great backcountry options. It's also extremely well geared to English-speaking travellers. Less than 90 minutes from Tokyo on the shinkansen, Echigo Yuzawa (see page 199) has several good ski and snowboard grounds, while Hakuhu in Nagano and Zao in Tohoku (see page 214) are other accessible and rewarding areas. Just be warned that the slopes can get crowded in the best resorts on weekends, so try to schedule a midweek trip, if possible. You might also get good discounts that way. For more, see www.skijapan.com or www.snowjapan.com.

Surfing

Not surprisingly for an archipelago, Japan's coastline has some great surf. Close to Tokyo, the Shonan area near Kamakura and Kujukuri in Chiba Prefecture are the most popular surf spots. Further away, Japan's best surf is in Kyushu, Okinawa, and especially the southeast Shikoku coast (see page 320).

CHILDREN'S ACTIVITIES

Bringing children to Japan is a relatively easy task, given that the Japanese love kids and that the country is both safe and hygienic, with plenty of health and food products targeting toddlers to teens. There is plenty to keep children interested, though too many temples may tire even the most tolerant child. Overhead and subway trains and buses are free for kids under six; those aged 6–11 pay half-price. Trains, subway trains and buses have seating designated for small children and pregnant women

(along with the elderly), although if they are full don't expect many people who shouldn't be sitting in them to give up their seats. Children under three go free on domestic flights, but have to share a seat with a parent; fares for kids aged 3–11 are half price. If you are looking for some free fun for kids, you will find small (though not always pristine) children's playgrounds with slides, swings and so on in most city neighbourhoods. In many major home electronics stores, especially in Akihabara, kids (and adults!) can also often test out the latest video games for free.

Tokyo

Ghibli Museum
1-83-1 Shimorenjaku, Mitaka-ku
Tel: 0570-055-777
www.ghibli-museum.jp
A museum-cum-amusement park showcasing Japanese anime from the renowned Studio Ghibli.
Hakuhinkan Toy Park
8-8-11 Ginza, Chuo-ku
Tokyo's top toy store.
www.hakuhinkan.co.jp
Hanayashiki Amusement Park
A few minutes west of Senso-ji temple in Asakusa.
www.hanayashiki.net
A small amusement park full of retro rides. It might not appeal to older kids used to modern amusements, but little kids love it.
Kiddyland
6-1-9 Jingumae, Shibuya-ku
Four floors of toys and electronics.
www.kiddyland.co.jp
The Railway Museum
Located in Omiya, north of Tokyo in Saitama, this museum has dozens upon dozens of historic trains on display, from old steam engines to *shinkansen*; many of which kids can

run around on. There are also model railways.
www.railway-museum.jp
Tama Zoo
7-1-1 Hodokubo, Hino-shi
A natural-habitat zoo, with safari-park rides.
www.tokyo-zoo.net/english/tama
The Magic Kingdom
Tokyo Disneyland is actually located in Chiba Prefecture just outside of the capital. Japan's most successful theme park has been in business for more than 30 years. It's still inordinately popular, so expect long queues for the more popular rides. Try to visit on weekdays and before the school summer holidays starting mid-July. DisneySea, offering underwater voyages, a Mediterranean-style port and much besides, was added to the complex in 2001. It requires a separate ticket, but does offer something for stressed parents that Disneyland doesn't – it sells alcohol. 1-4 Maihama, Urayasu City, Chiba Prefecture. Tel: 0570-00-8632, www. tokyodisneyresort.co.jp. Take the Keiyo Line train to Maihama, then just follow the crowds.

Rest of Japan

Kyoto International Manga Museum
452 Kinbuki-cho, Nagakyo-ku, Kyoto
Tel: 075-254-7414
For kids that like comic books, this place in Kyoto takes some beating. Most of the thousands upon thousands of comics on display can be taken off the shelves and read, and there are quite a few in English. Try to time a visit to coincide with a drawing workshop or other event.
www.kyotomm.jp
Osaka Aquarium
1-1-10 Kaigan-dori, Minato-ku
Tel: 06-6576-5510
The biggest aquarium in the world focuses on sealife along the "Ring of Fire". The whale sharks steal the show, but there is a lot, lot more besides.
www.kaiyukan.com
Osamu Tezuka Manga Museum
7-65 Mukogawa-cho, Takarazuka
Tel: 0797-812970
http://tezukaosamu.net/en/museum
This Osaka museum features cartoon creation workshops.
Universal Studios Japan
www.usj.co.jp
Movie-based themes, displays, special effects and rides at this extremely popular Osaka park.

Kids websites

http://web-japan.org/kidsweb

A – Z

A HANDY SUMMARY
OF PRACTICAL INFORMATION

A

Accommodation

There are hotels everywhere, but unfortunately not all of them are up to international standards. Those that are reflect it in their price. However, convenience is a very dear commodity here, so often you are paying for the location more than the service or luxury.

Be aware that many hotels offer only twin beds, which are the most popular arrangement in Japan. Smoking rooms (and even entire floors in budget accommodation) may have a thick stench of stale smoke. Hotel rooms are also quite compact. Even a ¥20,000 room in a deluxe hotel can be snug. So-called business hotels (favoured by many Japanese business travellers), generally found in the moderate and budget categories, have rooms that are not just snug, but cramped. As a rule, smaller hotels have fewer amenities, including no room service. If you are not intending to luxuriate all day in your room, though, these can be good bases for exploring destinations. Most business hotels and Western-style hotels provide free in-room Wi-fi or broadband internet, but not all traditional accommodation such as ryokan (Japanese-style inns). In most hotels and all ryokan, you are provided with a yukata (light kimono) robe, toothbrush, razor, shower cap, etc.

Western-style hotels offer rooms whose rates may vary from ¥8,000 to ¥30,000. There are hotels that also provide Japanese-style guest rooms and landscaped gardens.

Others have restaurants serving Continental food as well as local cuisines.

Capsule hotels, conveniently located near key stations, provide Apollo spacecraft-style compactness as a last resort for the drunk, stranded or merely inquisitive. Capsule cells come complete with TV, air conditioning, a radio and alarm. Complexes have showers, bath, sauna and sometimes restaurants. Rates are around ¥3,000. The majority are for men only, but a few have women-only floors.

Ryokan exude an atmosphere of traditional Japanese living and a stay will be a rewarding experience. The average charges per person range from ¥7,000 to ¥20,000, depending on the type of bath facilities and dining offered, but the rates at a truly elegant ryokan can rise far higher.

There are about 80,000 ryokan in Japan, of which 1,200 are members of the Japan Ryokan Association (JRA; www.ryokan.or.jp), which ensures that a high standard of service is maintained. Guests sleep in rooms covered with tatami (straw) mats, on futon. Ryokan usually have large gender-separated communal baths (often using hot spring water) as well as small in-room baths and showers. In some ryokan there are also private hot spring baths available for rent. At higher-end ryokan both morning and evening meals are served in the guest's room, but more typically breakfast is served in a large dining hall.

Minshuku are small, family-run bed-and-breakfast lodgings operated within private homes, without the frills (toiletries and yukata gowns, etc). Guests are expected to fold up

their futon bedding and tidy it away for the day. A stay in a minshuku will give you a more intimate experience of Japanese home life. Rates are from ¥5,000 up.

Japanese Inn Group (c/o Global Network Corporation, M/B Bldg 2F, 382 Motohonnoji-cho, Nakagyo-ku, Kyoto-shi, Kyoto 600-8118; tel: 06-6225-3611; www. japaneseinngroup.com) offers the foreign traveller recommendations and bookings for traditional Japanese inns, usually with traditional tatami floors, futon bedding, yukata and Japanese-style bath. The Japanese Inn Group consists of about 90 reasonable ryokan, hotels, minshuku and pensions located throughout Japan. Most member facilities are small, family-run Japanese-style accommodation with a hometown

The National Arts Center, Tokyo.

atmosphere and affordable rates (per person between ¥4,000–¥7,000), with meals extra.

There are plenty of websites in Japan for booking accommodation, but most are in Japanese only. The best local sites in English and which offer reasonable discounts are Japanican (www.japanican.com) with more than 4,000 hotels and ryokan, and plenty of tours and package options, and Rakuten (http://travel.rakuten.com), a very popular multilingual site for all sorts of online shopping, and with a travel section that includes more than 5,000 hotels, ryokan and other types of accommodation in Japan.

24-hour convenience store in Himeji.

Addresses

Finding an address in Japan can be tricky, even for taxi drivers. Especially in a city like Tokyo or Osaka, where addresses are written in a descending order – ku (ward), then cho or matohi (district), followed by the chome (an area of a few blocks) designations. The English rendition of addresses, and the one used in this guide, would result in a location appearing like this: Regency Hotel, 5F, 4-9-11 Shibuya, Minato-ku. In Japan the ground floor equals the first. Floor numbers are often shown on the outside of the building.

If you are stuck, ask at the nearest police box, where they have detailed area maps, and are usually helpful.

Admission charges

Admission fees in Japan are generally high. At cinemas, you can expect to pay around ¥1,800, although prices are usually discounted to ¥1,100 the first day of the month. Most cinemas also offer ¥1,100 tickets to women every Wednesday. Major museums and galleries usually cost between ¥1,000 and ¥1,500, while admission to a club or disco will typically be ¥1,500 to ¥3,000, including one or two drinks.

One way of saving on museum and gallery charges in Tokyo is with a Grutto Pass (www.rekibun.or.jp/grutto). The pass costs ¥2,000 but gives admission or discounted admission to 78 museums and galleries. You can buy one at most major museums or from tourist information centres, and the pass is valid for two months.

Many local tourism boards have similar passes available. The staff at the centres will be able to tell you about any multi-attraction tickets available in the area, which are

quite common and offer substantial savings on museum, temple and shrine admission charges.

B

Bathhouses

Whether at a hot spring, a local sento (bathhouse) or at a traditional inn, the procedure for this quintessentially Japanese experience is the same. Disrobe, enter the bathroom (in public you hide your modesty with a small washcloth), and wash and rinse off thoroughly under a shower before easing into the typically large communal hot bath – which is for soaking, not washing yourself.

Budgeting for your trip

Japan has a reputation for being expensive, a legacy of the 1980s bubble-economy years when the country was flush with cash. Compared to other Asian destinations Japan remains expensive but, despite recent signs of a turnaround in its economy, 20 years of stagnation have left a dent in the cost-of-living index. Compared to European capitals, cities like Tokyo, Osaka and Kyoto begin to look quite affordable.

Accommodation can run from as little as ¥3,500 for a room in a modest inn or guesthouse to over ¥50,000 in a top hotel. Food is exceptionally good value, and the choices are remarkable. A decent set lunch can cost as little as ¥650, less

if you opt for a meal at a Japanese fast-food chain like Yoshinoya, the beef-bowl restaurants found in every Japanese city. American fast-food chains like McDonald's have dropped their prices in recent years, and their ¥100-menu has been a big hit with consumers. Family restaurant chains are very good value, and provide free coffee refills. Convenience stores are good places for affordable snacks, lunchtime fillers like onigiri, instant ramen and soba. Supermarkets will often have lunch boxes (bento) for as little as ¥300.

Taxis are a major expense if you use them regularly, with base tariffs starting at ¥700, rising quickly if you get stuck in a traffic jam. Subway and commuter train tickets are much more reasonable, with base fares starting at ¥130 for two or three stops. Rates are slightly different for each line.

There is no tipping system in Japan, and prices quoted usually include a service charge and consumption tax, all of which makes a significant difference.

Business hours

Officially, business is done on a 9am–5pm basis, but this is in theory only. The Japanese will often do overtime until 8 or 9pm. In general, **government** offices are open from 8.30 or 9am to 4 or 5pm Monday to Friday, and from 9am to noon on Saturdays. **Main post offices** are open 9am to 7pm Monday to Friday, 9am to 5pm on Saturday and 9am to noon on Sunday and holidays. **Branch post offices**

TRANSPORT

EATING OUT

ACTIVITIES

A – Z

LANGUAGE

are open 9am to 5pm Monday to Friday. **Department stores** and larger shops open daily from 10am to 7.30 or 8pm, although some close once or twice a month, which varies with each store. **Restaurants** are generally open for lunch from 11.30am to 2pm and for dinner from 5 to 9 or 10pm, although in major cities they often stay open much later. **Major companies** and **offices** are open from 9am to 5pm Monday to Friday. Some are also open on Saturday mornings. Most **small shops** open between 9 and 11am and close between 6 and 8pm. Convenience stores are open 24 hours.

Business travellers

When you meet a Japanese person, wait to see if she or he shakes your hand or bows, and then follow suit. Younger people are more comfortable with the handshake in general. Dressing smartly is part of doing business in Japan, something you should emulate.

The Japanese love of consensus, of trying to avoid confrontation wherever possible, is legendary, and can make doing business in Japan a frustrating experience. Don't expect rapid decisions, or a meeting to yield quick results. Long-term relationships are important to the Japanese business community, and these may take time to develop.

At meetings expect stiff formality to prevail, although a certain amount of small talk and civilities can break the ice. It may seem an elliptical approach, but circling around a topic before getting down to business is the norm. The pecking order for sitting is important: wait for others to decide this. The same applies to social situations like dinner.

The exchange of business cards is a vital ritual at first meetings. Make sure you have a good supply as they can go fast. If possible, have your cards printed on one side in *katakana* script, so that non-English-speakers can pronounce it easily and do not jot down names or make notes on these cards. Don't be surprised or offended if you are asked questions regarding age, education, family background and company service. Identity and "proper" affiliation are very important in Japan. One thing to remember is that, no matter how daunting business etiquette may seem, as a foreigner you are given plenty of leeway – making an effort

is more important than getting everything right.

C

Children

With a little advance planning Japan is a perfectly feasible place to bring children. There are many choices of activities, from amusement parks, children-oriented museums, zoos, aquariums and toy shops. When exploring Japanese cities with kids, try to avoid train rush hours, especially when using pushchairs.

Where public-toilet facilities are often inadequate in Japan, department stores usually have family rooms and play areas. Stores and malls are good places to eat, with plenty of set meals for children. Many of the bigger hotels offer babysitting services. See page 381.

Climate

When untravelled Japanese talk about living in a country that has four seasons – as if this is unique to Japan – technically they are talking about an area which at the very most extends from parts of northern to certain areas of western Honshu Island. These are the only regions that can truly be said to have four distinct seasons. This limited but culturally dominant belt, embracing both Tokyo and the former imperial capital of Kyoto, has influenced not only perceptions about the four seasons but almost every statement on Japanese culture.

Spring begins in the south, with the cherry blossoms coming out in Okinawa in February. Hokkaido, where the winter snow can linger well into April, will enjoy the

blossoms in May. In general, May is a warm and pleasant month, while June sees the onset of the humid rainy season, known poetically as *tsuyu* (dew). This drizzly spell lasts about a month. Hokkaido, as its tourist brochures never fail to mention, is exempt from this. Midsummer is hot and sticky, with the mercury rising into the mid- and upper thirties ºC. Typhoons occur mostly between August and October.

Many Japanese will say that October and November are the finest months to visit their country – the crisp, well-defined days of autumn, when the skies are often blue. Winter can be harsh in Hokkaido and the Japan Sea side of the country, with heavy snowdrifts. Clear skies and low humidity are the rewards of January and February, the coldest months. March is generally chilly, overcast and changeable. But again, bear in mind that, while one set of travellers will be enjoying the ski slopes of Hokkaido in that month, others may be taking their first tentative dip in the blue, coral waters of Okinawa.

Clothing

Although Japanese people place a great deal of importance on clothing and appearance in general, provided that clothes are clean, casual wear is perfectly in order for most occasions. In business situations, suits are definitely *de rigueur*, although in summer many companies now let staff work without a jacket and tie to reduce the need for air conditioning and thus conserve energy.

The weather is relatively predictable, so dress for the season, bringing a thick jacket for winter, light cotton or linen clothes for the late spring and summer. A light jacket will usually suffice for spring and autumn. Check world weather reports for last-minute adjustments, though, before starting out on your trip.

Crime and security

While the number of offences committed throughout Japan remains about one-eighth the number in the United States, crime has risen over the past two decades, particularly among Japanese youth. Personal security is far higher than in Western countries, and visitors routinely comment on the fact that they never feel threatened walking in Japanese streets.

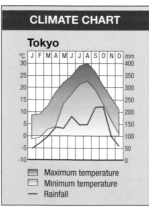

CLIMATE CHART

Tokyo

Theft of luggage and money is rare, although some pickpockets do work the Tokyo and Osaka subway and trains. The media is always full of reports of crimes committed by foreigners, especially Asian immigrants, though when closely examined, many of these turn out to be visa violations or activities connected to Japan's sex industry.

Organised crime, while often violent, is unlikely to affect the traveller or ordinary citizen as these are usually the result of turf disputes. The police generally turn a blind eye to prostitution, gambling, ticket touting, illegal immigration and the protection rackets operated by the *yakuza* gangs, only conducting crackdowns when inter-gang rivalry threatens the public domain.

If an incident occurs, report it to the nearest *koban* (police box). These are located in every neighbourhood, especially in busy areas and outside major railway stations. If possible go with an eyewitness or a native speaker. For police contact details, see page 385.

Women travellers

Japan is not a dangerous place for women travellers on their own, although a certain amount of harassment, from which foreign women are not entirely excluded, does occasionally occur on crowded trains. There are anti-groping posters on most trains and at stations. The meaning of the term *seku-hara* (sexual harassment) is finally sinking in at the workplace, although Japan still lags behind Western countries in this regard, evident in degrading TV shows (not all late at night), tabloid papers and the thinly veiled ads for prostitution services and manga books glorifying sexual violence towards women.

That said, it is safer to walk, travel, eat and drink anywhere in Japan than in most Western countries. Although red-light areas of large cities are inadvisable for women to walk alone in, two women together are unlikely to suffer anything worse than leering.

Customs regulations

Japan strictly prohibits the import and use of narcotic drugs, firearms and ammunition. If caught in possession of any of these, the offender can expect no leniency. You can bring any currency into Japan, but amounts of cash over ¥1 million need to be declared to customs.

You are also allowed to bring with you into Japan, free of tax, three 760ml (25fl oz) bottles of spirits, 400 cigarettes and 100 cigars or 500g of tobacco, and 60ml (2fl oz) of perfume. There is no duty-free allowance for valuables whose value exceeds ¥200,000. For more information visit www.customs.go.jp.

Foreign tourists can make purchases of electronics worth over ¥10,000 and of consumable goods over ¥5,000 exempt from the consumption tax of 8 percent (10 percent from April 2017). A passport is required for all tax-free purchases, and they can only be made in licensed shops (mostly major department stores).

D

Disabled visitors

In general, Japan is not user-friendly for the disabled and still lags behind most Western cities. Although there has been a gradual increase in disabled facilities in recent years, such as ramps and multi-use toilets in hotels and public areas, in most cases doors, lifts, toilets and just about everything else have not been designed for wheelchairs. It is a struggle for the disabled to get around Japan, but it can be done. Traditionally, the handicapped kept a low profile, as they were sometimes considered an embarrassment for the family. More recently, however, disabled people have become a more visible and accepted part of society.

Forget about using a wheelchair in train or subway stations, much less trains, during rush hour, 7–9am and 5–7pm. The crowds are just too thick.

To request assistance when travelling on JR East lines, call the JR English InfoLine at 050-2016-1603 (daily 10am–6pm). They can give information on disabled facilities and give you the contact numbers for different stations, so you can call in advance to arrange assistance. Even without advance notice, in many stations staff will help with escalators, lifts and getting on and off the train, although a wait of up to an hour may be involved if you haven't called ahead.

It is possible to reserve a special seat for wheelchairs on the *shinkansen*, or bullet train. Reservations can be made from one month to two days before departure.

Electricity

The power supply is . Eastern cities in Japan, Tokyo, run on 50 cycles, those in the west such as Osaka and Nagoya use 60 c. Sockets are two-pin and most hotels will have adaptors.

You must also call ahead to use the elevators for the *shinkansen* platforms.

Narita Airport's website (www. narita-airport.jp/en) has information for disabled travellers. The very comprehensive online English-language guide, *Accessible Tokyo*, is another useful resource: http:// accessible.jp.org. For help in emergencies or personal distress, telephone **Tokyo English Life Line** 03-5774-0992 (http://telljp.com; daily 9am–11pm), or the 24-hour Japan Helpline 0570-000-911 (www.jhelp.com).

E

Embassies and consulates

Australia, 2-1-14 Mita, Minato-ku. Tel: 03-5232-4111 (www.australia.or.jp).
Canada, 7-3-38 Akasaka, Minato-ku. Tel: 03-5412-6200 (www.canadanet.or.jp).
India, 2-2-11 Kudan-minami, Chiyoda-ku. Tel: 03-3262-2391 (www.indembassy-tokyo.gov.in).
Ireland, 2-10-7 Kojimachi, Chiyoda-ku. Tel: 03-3263-0695 (www.irelandinjapan.jp).
New Zealand, 20-40 Kamiyamacho, Shibuya-ku. Tel: 03-3467-2271 (www.nzembassy.com/japan).
Singapore, 5-12-3 Roppongi, Minato-ku. Tel: 03-3586-9111 (www.mfa.gov.sg/tokyo).
United Kingdom, 1 Ichibancho, Chiyoda-ku. Tel: 03-5211-1100 (www.ukinjapan.fco.gov.uk).
United States, 1-10-5 Akasaka, Minato-ku. Tel: 03-3224-5000 (http://japan.usembassy.gov).
US Consulate General in Osaka, 2-11-5 Nishi-temma, Kita-ku, Osaka. Tel: 06-6315-5900 (http://osaka. usconsulate.gov).

Emergencies

Police: 110
Fire and ambulance: 119
Police info in English: 03-3501-0110 (Mon–Fri 8.30am–5.15pm)

calls can be made from
the without using coins or
id telephone cards.
pan Helpline, 24-hour
information and help about
everything, in English. Tel: 0570-
000-911, www.jhelp.com.
For **medical information**, call
03-5285-8181 in Tokyo (English
spoken; daily Mon–Fri 5am–10pm,
Sat–Sun 9am–10pm).

Etiquette

At work and in most formal
situations, the Japanese may
seem a very reticent and reserved
people, lacking in spontaneity or
personality. There are books and
theories explaining this behaviour,
but it only provides one side of the
picture. Japanese (especially men)
can become extremely raucous
when drinking and often let out their
real opinions and feelings after a
few drinks. The next morning in the
office, all is forgiven. Intentionally.

On the crowded trains you will
find yourself being pushed and
bumped around. You do not need to
be very polite here; just push along
with everyone else. It is often said
that the Japanese are only polite
with their shoes off, which means
that they are polite and courteous
with people they know well and
would be indoors with (where shoes
are almost always removed).

For the Japanese, the distinction
between inside and outside the
home is important. Inside the
entrance to all homes (and some
restaurants) is an area for removing
shoes. You then step up into the
living area, wearing slippers or
in your stockinged feet. (Slippers
are never worn on *tatami* mats,
however, only socks or bare feet.)
Taking shoes off keeps the house
clean, besides being more relaxing,
and it also increases the amount
of usable space, since you can sit
on the floor without worrying about
getting dirty. The toilet, however,
is one area of the house that is
considered dirty, so separate
slippers are provided for use there.

The custom of bowing has, in
many cases, become somewhat a
conditioned reflex. Foreigners, in
general, are not expected to bow,
and this is especially evident if a
Japanese person first reaches out to
shake hands.

As to punctuality and keeping
appointments, outside of business
the Japanese have a reputation for
not being very punctual. At several

of the famous meeting places (in
Tokyo, in front of Ginza's Sony
Building or at the Hachiko entrance
to Shibuya Station, as examples)
you can observe people waiting
for someone, often for an hour or
more. After several apologies and
explanations, everything is usually
forgotten and forgiven.

The way the Japanese usually
speak and express themselves
gives a very good picture of their
culture. Except when talking to
close friends and family, direct
statements of fact are most often
avoided as this implies that the
speaker has a superior knowledge,
and this is considered impolite.
Therefore, much beating about the
bush is done, which often leads
to misunderstandings and seems
like a waste of time to foreigners,
but this must be taken into
consideration when dealing with the
Japanese.

In their own language, the
Japanese are adept at reading
between the lines and interpreting
deft nuances of words and tone.

In any case, whatever happens,
foreigners, who are blissfully
unaware of these points, are usually
forgiven for any breach of etiquette,
so there's no need to spend time
worrying about what is right and
wrong. The cardinal rule is to try to
be courteous at all times. Japanese
behaviour in general is situational,
and the Japanese themselves often
do not know the right thing to do in
any given situation. "It all depends
on the situation," remarks the smart
alec, but it's often fun for everyone
involved when one of "us" makes a
slip. Sometimes it actually helps to
break the ice and put everyone in a
more relaxed mood.

G

Gay and lesbian travel

Unlike other developed countries,
homosexuality in Japan is still kept
very much under wraps. This is not
to say that it is invisible. Gay and
transvestite celebrities often appear
on TV, and it isn't hard to find comic
books and films with gay themes.
Tokyo's Shinjuku ni-chome district
is the undisputed centre of the gay
scene in Japan. There are over 300
gay bars and clubs located around
its central street, Naka-dori. Outside
Tokyo and Osaka, however, the gay
scene is very difficult to gain access
to. *Badi* (www.badi.jp) is Japan's

premier publication for gay men,
but there are classified ads and
occasional coverage of the scene
in the free magazine *Metropolis*
(http://metropolisjapan.com) as well
as on websites such as *Time Out
Tokyo* (www.timeout.jp).

Gay websites

www.gnj.or.jp
A support and friendship group
that also runs advertisements and
discussion groups.
www.utopia-asia.com/tipsjapn.htm
General coverage of gay life in Japan,
with club and venue listings.
www.tokyowrestling.com
Webzine for women, with loads of info
on Tokyo's lesbian scene.

Gay venues

AiiRO Café7F, Tenka Bldg, 1F, 2-18-1,
Shinjuku, Shinjuku-ku
Tel: 03-6273-0740
Formerly known as *Advocates Café*,
this is a popular meeting place for
both Japanese and foreigners.
Kinsmen
2F, 2-18-5, Shinjuku, Shinjuku-ku
Tel: 03-3354-4949
The male-only counterpart to
Kinswomyn.

Guides and travel agencies

Guides and escorts

Japan Guide Association, 603,
International Building, 1-6-1 Kanda
Izumicho, Chiyoda-ku, Tokyo. Tel:
03-3863-2895, www.jga21c.or.jp.
**Japan Federation of Certified
Guides**, Hatoya Building, 2-29-7
Nakano, Nakano-ku, Tokyo. Tel:
03-3380-6609, http://jfg-e.jp.

Goodwill guides

Goodwill Guides are volunteers
who assist overseas visitors. All
volunteers are registered with the
JNTO. With over 40,000 members,
the guides are affiliated with more
than 80 groups throughout Japan,
and guides are available in over
two dozen regions to offer local
information or guide you on walking
tours. For a list of volunteer guides
throughout Japan visit www.jnto.
go.jp.

Travel agencies

The following agencies offer travel
services for foreign travellers:
Kinki Nippon Tourist Co., Kanda-
Matsunaga-cho, Chiyoda-ku, Tokyo
101. Tel: 03-6891-9600, www.knt.
co.jp.

Kyoto Tourist Information Center, 2nd floor of Kyoto Station. Tel: 075-343-0548.
Nippon Travel Agency, Nihonbashi Dia Bldg. 11F, 1-19-1, Nihonbashi, Chuo-ku, Tokyo 103. Tel: 03-6895-8344, www.ntainbound.com.
JTB Europe Ltd., Horatio House, 77-85 Fulham Palace Road, London W6 8JA. Tel: 020-8237 1605. www.japanspecialist.co.uk.
Osaka Visitors Information Center, Nankai Terminal Bldg 1F, 5-1-60 Namba, Cnuo-ku, Osaka. Tel: 06-6631-9100.
Okinawa Tourist Service, 1-2-3 Matsuo, Naha, Okinawa 900. Tel: 098-859-8887, www.okinawatourist.com.

H

Health and medical care

In general levels of hygiene are very high, and it is very unlikely that you will become ill as a result of eating or drinking something. The tap water, though heavily chlorinated, is drinkable. Most food is of a high standard. However, because the Japanese place so much emphasis on presentation and how food looks, there is wide use of chemical fertilisers in Japan, and therefore it is not recommended to eat the skins of fruits and some vegetables.

Medical services

Try to remember that you are in Japan and must be prepared to adapt to the Japanese system. Although some doctors may speak English, the receptionist and nursing staff will not, so it is advisable to bring along a Japanese-speaking friend or someone who can speak both languages. If you show up at a hospital or clinic without an appointment, you have to be prepared to wait your turn. Here is a list of hospitals and clinics in Tokyo where you would have no problem in being understood or treated. They all have different administrative systems and hours for outpatient treatment.

Hospitals in Tokyo

International Catholic Hospital (Seibo Byoin), 2-5-1 Nakaochiai, Shinjuku-ku. Tel: 03-3951-1111, www.seibokai.or.jp. Open Mon–Sat 8–11am and 2–8pm. Closed 3rd Sat of the month.
Red Cross Medical Centre (Nisseki), 4-1-22 Hiroo, Shibuya-ku.

Tel: 03-3400-1311, www.med.jrc.or.jp. Open Mon–Fri 8.30–11am.
St Luke's International Hospital (Seiroka Byoin), 10-1 Akashicho, Chuo-ku. Tel: 03-3541-5151, 03-5550-7120, http://hospital.luke.ac.jp. Open Mon–Sat 8.30–11am.
Tokyo Adventist Hospital (Tokyo Eisei Byoin), 3-17-3 Amanuma, Suginami-ku. Tel: 03-3392-6151, www.tokyoeisei.com. Open Mon–Fri 9am–12.30pm, Mon–Thu 2–5.30pm.
Toho Fujin Women's Clinic, 5-3-10 Kiba, Koto-ku. Tel: 03-3630-0303, www.toho-clinic.or.jp. Open Mon–Fri 9–11.30am, 1.30–5.30pm, Sat 9–11.30am, 1.30–4pm.
Japan Helpline, 24-hour information on everything, including finding hospitals and emergency medical care (English). Tel: 0570-000-911, www.jhelp.com.
For **hospital information**, call 03-5285-8181 in Tokyo (English spoken; daily 9am–8pm).

Pharmacies

Most Western-brand, over-the-counter medicines are hard to find in Japan, and when they are available, prices are high. High-street drugstores such as Matsumoto Kiyoshi (www.matsukiyo.co.jp) and Tomods (www.tomods.jp) can help you with Japanese or Chinese remedies. It's best to bring your own preferred cold and allergy medicines with you, but note that many popular brands, like Sudafed, contain small amounts of amphetamine-like drugs and are illegal in Japan.

Be aware that while drugstores stock useful regular medication and may be able to advise you on coping with minor problems, they do not dispense prescription drugs. Prescriptions can only be obtained through a hospital or clinic after a consultation. The medicine will be issued to you on the same premises or you will be directed to a nearby pharmacist.
American Pharmacy, Marunouchi Building (basement), Chiyoda-ku. Open Mon–Fri 9am–9pm, Sat 10am–9pm, Sun 10am–8pm.
Pharmacy at Tokyo Medical and Surgical Clinic, 32 Shiba Koen Building, 3-4-30 Shiba-Koen, Minato-ku. Tel: 03-3434-5817, www.tmsc.jp. Mon–Fri 9am–5.30pm, Sat 9am–1pm.
Yauju Pharmacy Roppongi Izumi Garden, 1-6-1 Roppongi, Minato-ku. Tel: 03-3568-3370, www.yakuju.co.jp. Open Mon–Fri 9am–7pm, Sat 9.30am–2pm and 3–5pm.

Dentists

Royal Dental Office, 4-10-11 Roppongi, Minato-ku. Tel: 03-3404-0819, www.royal-dental-roppongi.com.
Tokyo Clinic Dental Office, 2F, 32 Shiba Koen Bldg, 3-4-30, Shiba-Koen, Minato-ku. Tel: 03-3431-4225, www.tcdo.jp.

Optical care

Aoyoma Vision Center, 3F, Gotankan Bldg, 3-3-13, Kyowa Kita-Aoyama, Minato-ku. Tel: 03-3497-1491, www.aoyama vc.jp.
Fuji Optical Service International, 1F, Otemachi Bldg, 1-6-1 Otemachi, Chiyoda-ku. Tel: 03-3214-4751, www.fujimegane.co.jp.

I

Internet

Free internet hotspots are widespread in Japan, you will find them at airports, train and subway stations, department and convenience stores, restaurants and bars as well as along major shopping streets. Most of these services require registration. Japan *Connected-free Wi-Fi* and *Travel Japan Wi-Fi* are two handy smartphone apps that offer you access to thousands of hotspots without having to sign up for each one individually. Western-style and business hotels also provide in-room broadband or Wi-Fi, usually free; however, some high-end establishments may charge a daily fee. You can find a list of hotspots on www.freespot.com. Paid mobile internet providers that offer services to visitors include docomo (http://visitor.docomowifi.com) and Wi2 (http://wi2.co.jp) – a week can cost less than ¥1000. Another solution is buying a data SIM card for your device (virtually all smartphones and tablets should be compatible with the Japanese mobile-phone system) or renting a pocket Wi-Fi from a phone rental company (see Mobile Phones).

Internet cafés

While 24-hour manga cafés are very competitive, there are also prefectural and city culture/exchange centres that typically have machines available free for a limited time. Most airports also have internet-connected computers available, typically at ¥100/10 minutes. Tourist offices will always have a list of cafés and access points handy and in some cases will

TRANSPORT
EATING OUT
ACTIVITIES
A – Z
LANGUAGE

have their own free or paid internet-connected computers along a Wi-Fi hotspot.

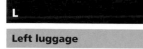

Left luggage

Carry as little luggage as possible when travelling in Japan. Trains and stations, especially, are not designed for travellers with more than a small overnight bag. If you're thinking of making all your Tokyo train connections while hauling several large bags – forget it. The train/subway map looks neat and tidy, but station connections are serious hikes with no trolleys or porters available, and seemingly endless stairs. Hotels, of course, will usually store luggage for guests heading off on adventures.

Several companies, including JAL ABC (www.jalabc.com), GPA (www.gpa-net.co.jp), Yamoto Transport (www.kuronekoyamato.co.jp) and Sagawa Express (www.sagawa-exp.co.jp) offer convenient baggage delivery services, which are very popular with the Japanese. Depending on the destination, it will cost you ¥2000–4000 to have the each luggage item delivered from the airport to your hotel. In most cases you should be able to arrange with your hotel for the baggage to be sent to your next accommodation, which will make multi-destination travelling more enjoyable.

International airports. For security reasons, bombs in particular, the international airports have no coin lockers. There are cloakrooms, however, at international airports. While staff may not speak English, forms are bilingual and the staff will know why you're standing there. At Narita:

JAL ABC: Terminal 1 and 2: 6 locations both in arrivals and departure halls. ¥300–¥800 per day per bag, with no time limit for storage. Open daily 7am–9pm

GPA (Green Port Agency): Terminal 1 and 2: 6 locations both in arrivals and departure halls, 1F. ¥300–¥800 per day per bag, 30-day limit. Open daily 7am–last fight.

Train and subway stations. Most train and subway stations have coin lockers of varying sizes for ¥300 to ¥800 per day, depending on station and size of the locker. Time limits vary, so check, but typically 3 days. After that, contents are removed. You'll have no problem finding

lockers; Japanese use them as a habit and convenience.

Cloakrooms for large bags (around ¥600 per item) are located at several main JR stations, however they often require that luggage is reclaimed on the same day.

Tokyo Station, outside Yaesu south exit, 7.30am–8.30pm.

Ueno Station, in front of central exit, 8am–8pm.

Shin Osaka Station, outside the central exit, 9am–8pm.

Kyoto Station, Karasuma central exit and Hachijo central exit, 8am–8pm.

Lost property

The Japanese are quite honest about handing in found items. If you've lost a wallet packed with cash, a camera or an overnight bag, chances are it will be safe. In fact, you often hear stories of lost wedding rings, computers and other valuables finding their way home.

JR trains: Items left on trains will usually be kept for a couple of days at the nearest station. After that, they are taken to one of the major stations to be stored for five more days. The best thing to do is call the JR East Infoline 050-2016-1603, daily 10am–6pm.

Subways: On the Toei trains, or on Tokyo city-operated buses, enquire about lost property at terminals the same day, or call the lost-and-found centre, on 03-3812-2011 (Japanese only), Mon–Fri 9am–7pm.

Taxis: All taxi companies in Tokyo report unclaimed items to a single centre, the Tokyo Taxi Kindaika Centre. Tel: 03-3648-0300 (Japanese only).

Police: As a last resort, contact the police. The Tokyo Metropolitan Police Department maintains an absolutely immense lost-and-found centre, with everything from forgotten umbrellas (zillions of them) to bags full of cash. Tel: 03-3814-4151, Mon–Fri 8.30am–5.15pm. English spoken sometimes, Japanese mostly.

M

Maps

The JNTO in Tokyo and elsewhere provide lots of adequate maps, including walking and hiking tours. Kodansha's **Tokyo City Atlas: A Bilingual Guide** is highly detailed and very useful. There is a similar atlas on Osaka and Kyoto. *Insight Fleximap Tokyo* is laminated and immensely durable.

Media

Television

There are several terrestrial TV channels. One is from the quasi-national *Japan Broadcasting Corporation* (NHK) and the other five are private-sector commercial networks. NHK also broadcasts on two satellite channels, plus a high-definition TV channel. A small percentage of the programmes – including news bulletins – is bilingual, offering English on the sub-channel. Ask your hotel reception which button to press to see if the programme has this service. NHK's 7pm and 9pm news broadcast are always available with an English sub-channel.

Overseas networks CNN and BBC are available on satellite and cable TV at most large hotels.

Radio

The main foreign-language radio station is *Inter FM* (76.1 Mhz in Tokyo, 76.5 Mhz in Yokohama; www.interfm.co.jp), which broadcasts news and music mainly in English. *J-Wave* (81.3 Mhz; www.j-wave.co.jp) also has some shows in English. *The American Forces Network Eagle* (810 AM), broadcast by the US Armed Forces, airs music, news, US sports and some National Public Radio shows.

Newspapers

There are two daily newspapers in English. The *Japan Times* (www.japantimes.co.jp) is the premier English-language paper and the oldest, followed by *The Daily Yomiuri* (www.yomiuri.co.jp), which is comprised largely of wire stories and translations from the Japanese-language Yomiuri Shimbun. The *Nikkei Weekly* (www.nikkei.com) is a financial digest.

Magazines

Many English-language magazines are published in Japan, though the quality is not always the best. They tend to fall into three categories: events magazines, those focusing on Japanese culture, and custom publications for members' clubs, chambers of commerce and the like. Of the first group, look out for the *TimeOut Tokyo* (www.timeout.jp) and a free biweekly *Metropolis* (http://metropolisjapan.com). J@pan.Inc (www.japaninc.com) is an internet- and business-related monthly magazine. The best event coverage is online, and there are now several online magazines up and running.

Most of the custom publications are also available, at least in part, online.

Money

The unit of currency is the yen (¥), and the coins are ¥1, ¥5, ¥10, ¥50, ¥100 and ¥500. Bills are ¥1,000, ¥2,000, ¥5,000 and ¥10,000. Exchange rates are around US$1 = ¥80–125; £1 = ¥120–195; €1 = ¥100–145. Japanese stores, services and merchants are legally forbidden to accept foreign currencies. You can buy yen at foreign exchange banks and other authorised money changers on presentation of your passport. At the international airports at Narita and Osaka the banks are open 24 hours. Traveller's cheques can only be cashed at banks and major hotels, and are not accepted elsewhere.

Credit cards

Major credit cards, such as American Express, Diners Club, MasterCard and Visa, are accepted at establishments in and around Tokyo and Osaka/Kyoto, and there is no surcharge for their use. Unfortunately, acceptance is sporadic. Even at establishments displaying acceptance of Visa or MasterCard, for example, some will refuse to accept cards issued by banks overseas. If they refuse your card, don't get testy. Carry lots of cash instead, just in case.
American Express. Tel: 03-3220-6100; card member services (including lost/stolen cards): 0120-020-120 (toll-free).
Diners Club. Tel: 0120-074-024 (toll-free).
MasterCard. Tel: 03-5728-5200.
Visa. Tel: 006633-800-553 (toll-free).

Banks

Despite the wide use of computers and online systems, Japanese banks are often slow and inefficient in many fields. Especially when transferring money in or out of the country, you can expect the process to take a long time and to be costly. Also, small neighbourhood branches are often not able to process any international transactions. In order to send money out of the country, or cash foreign cheques, you will find it much easier to go to a major branch, where someone *may* be able to speak English and usually understand what you want to do. (An exception is Citibank, which is experienced in dealing with non-Japanese customers. If you are a Citibank customer elsewhere, your chances in Japan are much, much better.)

Banks open Mon–Fri 9am–3pm for normal banking. Cash dispensers (ATMs) are everywhere in Japan, even in convenience stores. The problem is that many of them can't be used for cash advances on cards issued abroad. Machines in Seven-Eleven convenience stores and at post offices usually accept most overseas cash cards, and will be among the few that can be operated in English. Just in case you can't find one of these, carry plenty of cash with you.

Tipping

No tipping remains the rule in Japan, except for unusual or exceptional services. Porters at large stations and airports charge a flat rate of around ¥300 per piece of luggage. Taxi drivers don't expect any tips, nor do hotel staff. The only exception are country inns, where older generations still hand a ¥1,000 note discreetly to the maid who takes them to their room and serves a welcome tea and sweets. You don't need to worry about doing this yourself.

P

Photography

Although there are no limitations on what you can photograph, beyond the obvious taboos of military installations, you should use your discretion in religious sites, particularly when there are rites and rituals taking place. As many Japanese

Old style Japanese post box.

are avid amateur photographers, camera shops are plentiful.

Postal services

There are nearly 30,000 post offices in Japan, which means they are ubiquitous. In addition to postal services, post offices offer savings services; in fact, the post office is Japan's largest holder of personal savings. Postal services are efficient and fast, but expensive for both international and domestic post.

For daytime opening hours, see Business Hours. For night owls, there's a 24-hour window at the **Tokyo Central Post Office**, located on the ground floor of the JP Tower near the Marunouchi side of Tokyo Station. Tel: 03-3217-5231. For 24-hour, 365-day international mail services, try also the main Shibuya post office (1-12-13 Shibuya, tel: 03-5469-9907).

International express mail: Larger post offices offer EMS services; for some reason, the isolated post offices outside the major cities of Tokyo and Osaka may require that an account be opened, though it's just a formality. If language is proving to be a problem in getting a package sent via EMS, this could be the reason.

International parcel post: foreign parcel post cannot exceed 30kg (66lbs) per package to any international destination. For heavier packages or those that exceed certain size or content restrictions (which

TRANSPORT
EATING OUT
ACTIVITIES
A – Z
LANGUAGE

vary by country), a commercial courier service must be used.

Postal information (English-language). Tel: 0570-046-111, www.post.japanpost.jp/english.

Courier services

DHL. Tel: 0120-392-580, www.dhl.co.jp/en.
Federal Express. Tel: 0120-003-200 (toll-free), www.fedex.com/jp_english.

Public holidays

1 January: Ganjitsu (New Year's Day)
Second Monday in January: Seijin no Hi (Coming-of-Age Day)
11 February: Kenkoku Kinen no Hi (National Foundation Day)
Around 21 March: Shumbun no Hi (Vernal Equinox Day)
29 April: Midori no Hi (Greenery Day)
3 May: Kempo Kinembi (Constitution Memorial Day)
4 May: Kokumin no Kyujitsu (bank holiday)
5 May: Kodomo no Hi (Children's Day)
Third Monday in July: Umi no Hi (National Maritime Day)
11 August: Yama no Hi (Mountain Day), celebrated from 2016
Third Monday in September: Keiro no Hi (Respect-for-the-Aged Day)
Around 23 September: Shubun no Hi (Autumnal Equinox Day)
Second Monday in October: Taiiku no Hi (Sports Day)
3 November: Bunka no Hi (Culture Day)
23 November: Kinro Kansha no Hi (Labour Thanksgiving Day)
23 December: Tenno Tanjobi (Emperor's Birthday)
If a holiday falls on a Sunday, the following Monday will be a "substitute holiday".

Holidays to avoid

There are three periods of the year when the Japanese travel and holiday en masse. You would be wise not to make any travel plans during this time:
New Year: from around 27 December to 4 January. Most museum and galleries are closed then.
Golden Week: from 29 April to 5 May.
Obon: a week around 15 August.

Public toilets

The Asian squatting type toilet, which takes some getting used to, is supposed to be the most hygienic (no part of your body actually touches them) and physiologically best. Thankfully, in Tokyo and other major cities, they have mostly been replaced with Western-style toilets. By law, every coffee shop and restaurant, etc, must

Function buttons on a toilet.

have its own toilet, or access to one in the same building. Toilets in train stations and other large places are often dirty and smelly.

If you can't find a public toilet your best bet is to find a large department store, which will have all the necessary facilities.

Hi-tech toilets with push-button control panels are common – approximately 70 percent of homes in Tokyo have them, as do most department stores and Western-style hotels and business hotels. There are special enhancements such as heated seats, hot-air dryers, and a device that plays the sound of flushing water to conceal any embarrassing noises.

R

Religious services

Protestant

United Church of Christ in Japan, Ginza Church, 4-2-1 Ginza, Chuo-ku. Tel: 03-3561-0236, www.ginza-church.com.

Baptist

Tokyo Baptist Church, 9-2 Hachiyama-cho, Shibuya-ku. Tel: 03-3461-8425, www.tokyobaptist.org.

Lutheran

St Paul International Lutheran Church, 1-2-32 Fujimi-cho, Chiyoda-ku. Tel: 03-3261-3740, www.spilchurchtokyo.org.

Catholic

Azabu Church, 3-21-6 Nishi-Azabu, Minato-ku. Tel: 03-3408-1500, www.azabu-catholic.org.
Franciscan Chapel Center, 4-2-37 Roppongi, Minato-ku. Tel: 03-3401-

2141, http://franciscanchapelcenter tokyo.org.

Anglican Episcopal

St Alban's Church, 3-6-25 Shiba-Koen, Minato-ku. Tel: 03-3431-8534, www.saintalbans.jp.

Muslim

Hiroo Mosque, 3-4-18 Moto-Azabu, Minato-ku. Tel: 03-3404-6622.
Islamic Centre Japan, 1-16-11 Ohara, Setagaya-ku. Tel: 03-3460-6169 http://islamcenter.or.jp.

Jewish

Jewish Community of Japan, 3-8-8 Hiroo, Shibuya-ku. Tel: 03-3400-2559, www.jccjapan.or.jp.

T

Telephones

Japan's country code: 81
Domestic area codes:
Fukuoka: 092
Hiroshima: 082
Kagoshima: 099
Kobe: 078
Kyoto: 075
Nagasaki: 0958
Nagoya: 052
Naha: 098
Osaka: 06
Sapporo: 011
Sendai: 022
Tokyo: 03
Yokohama: 045

Although the number of payphones has decreased in recent years, they are still plentiful. To use the public telephones just insert a ¥10- or a ¥100-coin and dial the number desired – ¥10 pays for one minute (a few older phones accept ¥10-coins only).

Most common are green and grey phones, all taking prepaid telephone cards and some taking only prepaid cards, no coins. No change is returned for unused portions of coins. Telephone cards can be obtained at any Nippon Telegraph and Telephone (NTT) office, many shops, kiosks and convenience stores, or through special vending machines near telephones.

Domestic calls, expensive over 60km (37 miles), are cheaper at night and on weekends and holidays by as much as 40 percent.

Toll-free numbers

Domestic telephone numbers that begin with "0120" or "0088" are toll-free, or "freephone", calls.

International calls

Making international calls from Japan is fairly painless. Using public telephones, international calls can be made from specially marked – in English and Japanese – telephones, which will be green, grey or multicoloured; look for an IDD sticker on the phone or booth. The grey phones use prepaid cards and have small screens displaying operating instructions in both Japanese and English.

Western-style hotels can usually provide international call services too.

To make a **person-to-person**, **reverse charge** (collect) or **credit-card** call from anywhere in Japan through KDDI, the dominant international telecom company, simply dial 001.

KDDI Information, international telephone information, in English: 0057 (toll-free).

Mobile phones

Mobile phones are ubiquitous in Japan; even many kids have them, and on crowded commuter trains it often seems like everyone is whiling away the boredom playing with their phones.

Japan uses mobile-network systems such as UMTS 2100MHz, CDMA2000 800MHz and LTE. If you come from a country that uses the more common GSM system found in Asia, UK, Europe, Australia and New Zealand, your phone may not work here, but this is rather a thing of the past now, and only older handsets may pose a problem. Virtually all smartphones operate also on UMTS 2100MHz and some on CDMA2000 and will work in Japan. Check your phone specifications if unsure, as you will have to rent a handset that hooks up with the local network. Japan's international airports all have mobile

phone counters, where you can rent handsets and/or local SIM cards to avoid international roaming charges. The largest of the several operators are NTT Docomo (tel: 0120-005-250 English spoken, www.nttdocomo. com) and KDDI with its brand au by KDDI (tel: 0120-959-472 English spoken, www.au.kddi.com). Mobile phone rental companies include JAL ABC (www.jalabc.com), Pupuru (www. pupuru.com), Rentafone Japan (www. rentafonejapan.com) and Softbank (www.softbank-rental.jp).

Most mobile phone numbers begin with 090 or 080.

Tourist information

Tourist offices

The Japan National Tourism Organisation (JNTO) is an excellent source of information on visas, culture, accommodation, tours, etc. You can log on at www.jnto.go.jp.

JNTO Overseas Offices

Australia: Level 4, 56 Clarence Street, Sydney NSW 2000. Tel: 02-9279-2177, www.jnto.org.au.
Canada: 481 University Ave, Suite 306, Toronto, Ont. M5G 2E9. Tel: 416-366-7140, www.ilovejapan.ca.
Hong Kong: Unit 807–809, 8F, Prosperity Millennia Plaza, 663 King's Road, North Point. Tel: 2968-5688, www.welcome2japan.hk.
United Kingdom: 5F, 12/13 Nicholas Lane, London EC4N 7BN. Tel: 020-7398-5670, www.seejapan.co.uk.
United States:
Los Angeles: 340 E. 2nd Street, Little Tokyo Plaza, Suite 302, Los Angeles, CA 90012. Tel: 213-623-1952, www.us.jnto.go.jp.
New York: One Grand Central Place, 60 East 42nd Street, Suite 448, New

Time zone

Japan is GMT +9 hours; EST (New York) +14 hours; and PST (Los Angeles) +17. Japan does not have summer daylight saving time. The idea is periodically mooted, and then dismissed in deference to the nation's farmers, a powerful electoral lobby.

York, NY 10165. Tel: 212-757-5640, www.us.jnto.go.jp.

Tourist information centres

Tokyo, 1F, Shin-Tokyo Building, 3-3-1 Marunouchi, Chiyoda-ku, Tokyo 100-0005. Tel: 03-3201-3331. Open daily 9am–5pm, telephone-only service on 1 Jan.
Narita TIC, Terminal 1: Central Building 1F (Arrivals). Tel: 0476-30-3383. Terminal 2: Main Building 1F (Arrivals). Tel: 0476-34-6251. Both open daily 8am–8pm.
Kyoto Office (TIC): JR Kyoto Station 2F, Shimogyo-ku, Kyoto 600-8216. Tel: 075-343-0548. Open daily 8.30am–7pm.

Tourist information

Tokyo: Tel: 03-3201-3331
Yokohama: Tel: 045-441-7300
Nagoya: Tel: 052-541-4301
Sendai: Tel: 022-222-4069
Sapporo: Tel: 011-213-5088
Kyoto: Tel: 075-343-0548

Local tourist websites

There are a number of useful local websites to help you plan your visit. The links below are full of advice on what to see and suggestions of where to stay, plus the latest news on local events and festivals in each area.
Kyoto City Tourist and Cultural Information System: www.pref.kyoto.jp/visitkyoto/en.
Osaka Tourist Guide: www.city.osaka.lg.jp.
Hokkaido Tourist Association: www.visit-hokkaido.jp.
Koyasan Tourist Association: http://eng.shukubo.net.
Kyushu Tourism Promotion Organization: www.visitkyushu.org.
Okinawa Conventions and Visitors Bureau: http://en.okinawastory.jp.

Translators and interpreters

Most languages are covered for translation or interpretation by big translation companies, for example ILC (tel: 03-3940-2821, www.ilc sugamo.com), or check with a hotel

Docomo mobile rental shop in Kansai Airport.

business centre. Be aware that rates are not cheap.

U

Useful addresses

Organisations

American Center, NOF Tameike Building 8F, 1-1-14 Akasaka, Minato-ku.

American Chamber of Commerce, Masonic 39 MT Bldg 10F, 2-4-5 Azabudai, Minato-ku. Tel: 03-3433-5381, www.accj.or.jp.

British Council, 1-2 Kagurazaka, Shinjuku-ku. Tel: 03-3235-8031, www.britishcouncil.jp.

Foreign Correspondents' Club, Yurakucho Denki Bldg, 20F, 1-7-1 Yurakucho, Chiyoda-ku. Tel: 03-3211-3161, www.fccj.or.jp.

Institut Franco-Japonais, 15 Ichigaya Funagawaracho, Shinjuku-ku. Tel: 03-5206-2500, www.institutfrancais.jp.

The Japan Foundation Library, 4-4-1 Yotsuya, Shinjuku-ku. Tel: 03-5369-6086, www.jpf.go.jp.

JETRO (Japan External Trade Organisation), Ark Mori Building 6F, 12-32-1, Akasaka, Minato-ku. Tel: 03-3582-5511, www.jetro.go.jp.

V

Visas and passports

A proper visa is necessary for foreigners living in Japan and engaged in business or study. Passengers with confirmed departure reservations can obtain a stopover pass for up to 72 hours.

Japan has an agreement with 67 countries, whose nationals do not require visas for tourism purposes. They include: Australia, Canada, New Zealand, United States and most European countries (for stays of up to 90 days).

Visitors from Ireland, the UK and several other European nations may reside in Japan for up to 6 months providing they are not earning an income.

For further details and requirements for other nationalities, contact your nearest Japanese diplomatic mission or log on to www.mofa.go.jp.

Extension of stay

Foreigners wishing to extend their stay in Japan must report, in person,

to the Immigration Bureau within two weeks before their visa expiration. Present your passport, completed application forms and documents certifying the reasons for extension. The fee is ¥4,000.

Foreigners living in Japan must obtain a re-entry permit from the Immigration Bureau if they leave Japan and plan to return. Present, in person, your passport and certificate of alien registration (held by foreign residents in Japan) along with the appropriate re-entry form to the Immigration Office. Fees are charged for both single and multiple re-entry permits.

Those wishing to transfer visas to new passports must report to the Immigration Bureau in Tokyo. Present both old and new passports and certificate of alien registration. No charge is required.

Ministry of Foreign Affairs, www.mofa.go.jp. Information on the current rules and regulations regarding visas.

Immigration Bureau of Japan, www.immi-moj.go.jp. Information on regulations on entry and stay for foreign nationals.

Tokyo Regional Immigration Bureau, 5-5-30, Konan, Minato-ku, Tokyo. Tel: 03-5796-7111.

Yokohama District Immigration Office, 10-7 Torihama-cho, Kanazawa-ku. Tel: 045-769-1720.

Osaka Regional Immigration Bureau, 1-29-53 Nankou Kita, Suminoe-ku. Tel: 06-4703-2100.

Foreign residents' registration

In 2012, the alien registration system was discontinued and replaced with a national foreign-residents-registration system. Foreigners who have been granted permission to stay for over 90 days are required to register at the regional immigration office. For details, contact a regional immigration bureau or the Immigration Information Centre (tel: 0570-013904 Mo–Fri 8.30am–5.15pm, www.immi-moj.go.jp).

W

Websites

ACCJ Journal: the American Chamber of Commerce magazine provides insightful stories related to doing business in Japan. http://journal.accj.or.jp.

Discover the Spirit of Japan. A multi-media site on Japanese attractions run by the Japan Tourism Agency. www.visitjapan.jp.

Eurobiz Japan: if you are interested in business in Japan, the online version of the European Business Council's magazine is a good source of stories. www.eurobiz.jp.

Japan-guide.com: extensive and up-to-date travel data. www.japan-guide.com.

Japan Monthly Web Magazine: an absorbing site run by the Japan National Tourist Organisation. http://japan-magazine.jnto.go.jp.

Japan National Tourist Organisation: excellent links and travel info. www.jnto.go.jp.

The Japan Times: a good online site for Japan's oldest English-language newspaper, which has nearly everything covered. www.japantimes.co.jp.

Japan Today: a good source for short, translated news stories, from national and business news to more quirky fare. www.japantoday.com.

Metropolis: the website of the English magazine Metropolis is packed with insightful information on Japanese culture and lifestyle. http://metropolisjapan.com.

Outdoor Japan: regularly updated site on the great outdoors including live weather forecasts, activity guides and some good features. http://outdoorjapan.com.

Savvy Tokyo: helpful data and insights for foreign women in Japan. http://savvytokyo.com.

Skiing Hokkaido: all the skiing information and resort details from Hokkaido. www.skiing-hokkaido.com.

Stanford University: scholarly links for the more highbrow surfer. http://jguide.stanford.edu.

Time Out Tokyo: bilingual site with lots of event listings, activity ideas, reviews, and plenty of interesting articles on travel and culture. www.timeout.jp.

Tokyo Food Page: updates on food, sake and beer. Tips on the best places to eat in Tokyo, Yokohama, Kyoto, Osaka and Nagoya, plus some great recipes. www.bento.com.

Tokyo Metro: a site for keeping up with Tokyo's ever-growing subway system. www.tokyometro.jp/en.

Weights and measures

Japan follows the metric system, except in cases governed by strong tradition. For example, rice and sake are measured in units of 1.8 litres and rooms are measured by a standard *tatami* mat size. Ancient measures are also used for carpentry in Shinto temples and for making kimonos.

LANGUAGE

UNDERSTANDING THE LANGUAGE

The visitor will have few language problems within the confines of airports and the major hotels, but outside these the going can get tough. Quite apart from being unable to communicate verbally, the visitor will also have the disconcerting experience of being almost totally illiterate.

The written language is made up of three different sets of characters: two simple home-grown syllabaries, *hiragana* and *katakana*, consisting of 46 characters each; and the much more formidable Chinese ideograms, *kanji*. Knowledge of just under two thousand of these is necessary to read a daily newspaper.

While the enormous effort required to memorise this number of *kanji* (it takes the Japanese most of their school career to do so) is clearly unjustifiable for those with only a passing interest in the language, a few hours spent learning the two syllabaries would not be time wasted for those who can afford it.

Hiragana can be useful for identifying which station your train has stopped at; the platforms are plastered with *hiragana* versions of the station name so that children who have not yet learned *kanji* can see where they are. Station names are usually (but not always) posted in roman script *(romanji)* as well, but not always as obviously. *Katakana* is used to transliterate foreign words. Western-style restaurants often simply list the foreign names for the dishes on their menus in *katakana*.

PRONUNCIATION

With its small number of simple and unvarying vowel sounds, the pronunciation of Japanese should be easy for those who speak Western languages, which are rich in vowel sounds, and Japanese has nothing like the tonal system of Chinese.

Vowels have only one sound. Don't be sloppy with their pronunciations.
a – between fat and the u in but
e – like the e in egg
i – like the i in ink
o – like the o in orange
u – like the u in butcher

When they occur in the middle of words between voiceless consonants (ch, f, h, k, p, s, sh, t and ts), i and u are often almost silent. For example, *Takeshita* is really pronounced *Takesh'ta* while *sukiyaki* sounds more like s'*kiyaki*.

In spite of the seemingly simple pronunciation of Japanese, a lot of foreigners manage to mangle the language into a form which is almost impossible for the native speaker to understand. It is mainly intonation that is responsible for this. It would

Japanese road sign.

be untrue to claim that the Japanese language has no rise and fall in pitch but it is certainly "flatter" in character than Western languages.

It is important to avoid stressing syllables within words; whereas an English-speaker would naturally stress either the second or third syllable of *Hiroshima*, for example, in Japanese the four syllables should be stressed equally.

Another problem lies in long (actually double) vowel sounds. These are often indicated by a line above the vowel, or simply by a double vowel. To pronounce these long vowels properly, it is simply necessary to give the vowel sound double length.

WORDS AND PHRASES

Essential phrases

Do you speak English? *eego ga dekimasu ka?*
Please write it down *kaite kudasai*
Pardon? *sumimasen*
I understand *wakarimashita*
I don't understand/I don't know *wakarimasen*
Yes/No *hai/iie*
OK *ookee*
please *onegai shimasu*
Thank you (very much) *(doomo) arigatoo*

Greetings

Good morning *ohayoo gozaimasu*
Hello (afternoon) *kon-nichi-wa*
Good evening *konban-wa*
Goodnight *oyasumi nasai*
Goodbye *sayoonara* (*shitsure shimasu* for formal occasions)
How are you? *ogenki desu ka?*
My name is... *... to moshimasu*

Ueno Station ticket hall, Tokyo.

I'm Mr/Ms Smith *watashi wa Smith desu*
Are you Mr/Ms Honda? *Honda-san desu ka?*
I'm American *Amerika-jin desu*
I'm British *Igirisu-jin desu*
I'm Australian *Oosutoraria-jin desu*
I'm Canadian *Kanada-jin desu*

Asking for directions

Excuse me, where is the toilet?
sumimasen, toire wa doko desu ka?
Excuse me, is there a post office near here? *sumimasen, kono chikaku ni, yubin-kyoku wa arimasu ka?*
on the left/right *hidari/migi ni*
bakery *pan-ya*
stationer's *bunboogu-ya*
pharmacy *yakkyoku*
bookshop *hon-ya*
supermarket *suupaa*
department store *depaato*
restaurant *resutoran*
hotel *hoteru*
station *eki*
taxi rank *takushii noriba*
bank *ginkoo*
hospital *byooin*
police station *kooban*

Out shopping

This one *kore*
That one (near the other person)
sore
That one (near neither of you) *are*
Do you have...? *...(wa) arimasu ka?*
How much is it? *ikura desu ka?*
I'll take this *kore o kudasai*

Boarding the train

Ticket (office) *kippu (uriba)*
reserved seat *shitei seki*
unreserved seat *jiyu seki*
first-class car *guriin sha*

Which platform does the train for Nagoya leave from? *Nagoya yuki wa namban sen desu ka?*
Thank you (very much) *(doomo) arigato gozaimasu* (informally, *doomo* is enough)
Don't mention it *doitashimashite*
Thanks for the meal *gochisosama deshita*
Here you are *doozo*
After you *doozo*
Of course, go ahead *doozo* (in answer to "May I...?")

Days/time

(On) Sunday *nichi-yoobi (ni)*
(Next) Monday *(raishu no) getsu-yoobi*
(Last) Tuesday *(senshu no) ka-yoobi*
(Every) Wednesday *(maishu) sui-yoobi*
(This) Thursday *(konshu no) moku-yoobi*
Friday *kin-yoobi*
Saturday *do-yoobi*
Yesterday *kino*
Today *kyo*

Ramen noodles.

This morning *kesa*
This evening *konya*
Tomorrow *ashita*
What time is it? *nan-ji desu ka?*

Months/aeasons

January *ichi-gatsu*
February *ni-gatsu*
March *san-gatsu*
April *shi-gatsu*
May *go-gatsu*
June *roku-gatsu*
July *shichi-gatsu*
August *hachi-gatsu*
September *ku-gatsu*
October *juu-gatsu*
November *juu-ichi-gatsu*
December *juu-ni-gatsu*

At the hotel

Western-style hotel *hoteru*
business hotel *bijinesu hoteru*
love hotel *rabu hoteru*
Japanese-style inn *ryokan*
guesthouse *minshuku*
temple accommodation *shukuboo*
youth hostel *yuusu hosuteru*
I have a reservation *yoyaku shite arimasu*
Do you have a room? *heya wa arimasu ka?*
I'd like a single/double room
shinguru/daburu ruumu o onegai shimasu
I'd like a room with ... *... tsuki no heya o onegai shimasu*
twin beds *tsuin beddo*
double bed *daburu beddo*
bath/shower *o furo/shawa*
air conditioning *eakon*
TV/telephone *terebi/denwa*
How much is it? *ikura desu ka?*
Can I see the room please? *heya o misete kudasai*
That's fine, I'll take it *kekkoo desu, tomarimasu*

Yasaka Shrine, Kyoto.

No, I won't take it *sumimasen, yamete okimasu*

At the restaurant

A table for two, please *futari onegai shimasu*
The bill, please *o-kanjoo onegai shimasu*
tsukemono **pickled vegetables**
sashimi **raw fish served with soy sauce and horseradish** *(wasabi)*
sushi **rice balls topped with fish/ seafood**
tempura **battered vegetables, fish or seafood**
okonomiyaki **pizza/savoury pancake**
chankonabe **chicken and vegetable stew often served to sumo wrestlers**
gyoza **meat or vegetable dumplings**
soba **buckwheat noodles**
udon **thick wheat-flour noodles**
tonkotsu ramen **pork broth-based dish with Chinese noodles**
tonkatsu **breaded deep-fried pork**
yakitori **grilled chicken on skewers**
sukiyaki **thin slices of beef and vegetables in aromatic sauce**
shabu-shabu **thin slices of beef or pork cooked in broth**
karee raisu **Japanese curry on rice**
teppanyaki **griddled meat/fish**
kamameshi **rice casserole**
biiru **beer**
ocha **green tea**
o-sake/nihonshu **sake**
hiya/hitohada/atsukan **cold/ lukewarm/hot** (used for sake temperatures)
mizu **water**
mineraru wootaa **mineral water**

Sightseeing

Where is the ...? *... wa doko desu ka*
art gallery *bijutsu-kan*
botanical garden *shokubutsu-en*
Buddhist temple *o-tera*
castle *o-shiro*
museum *hakubutsu kan*
Imperial palace *kookyo*
Shinto shrine *jinja*
Can you show me on the map? *kono chizu de oshiete kudasai*

Numbers

Counting is very complicated in Japanese. Counting up to 10 on their fingers, the Japanese will use general numbers, which are: *ichi, ni, san, shi* (or *yon*), *go, roku, shichi* (or *nana*), *hachi, ku* (or *kyuu*), *juu*. If they are counting bottles, they will say: *ip-pon, ni-hon, sam-bon, yon-hon, go-hon...* The suffix will change according to what is being counted, and there

are more than 100 suffix groups. Commonly used categories of counter include flat objects (stamps, paper, etc), long thin objects (pens, bottles, umbrellas) and people. You will be fairly safe with the following "all purpose" numbers below, which don't need suffixes:
one *hitotsu*
two *futatsu*
three *mittsu*
four *yottsu*
five *itsutsu*
six *muttsu*
seven *nanatsu*
eight *yattsu*
nine *kokonotsu*
ten *too*
If you want five of something, point at it and say, *itsutsu kudasai*. Or hold up the appropriate number of fingers or write the number down. Thankfully the counter system only applies to numbers 1–10; after 10 the general numbers are used for all things.

A question of grammar

Japanese **questions** are formed by adding the grammar marker *ka* (a verbal question mark) to the verb at the end of a sentence. In Japanese the verb always comes last, with the basic rule for word order within a sentence being subject – object – verb.

Japanese **nouns** have no articles (a, an, the) and very few plural forms. Whether a noun is singular or plural is judged from the context.

Personal pronouns are rarely

used in Japanese. For "you", either use the person's family name + -*san*, or omit the pronoun completely if it's clear who you are addressing. **I** *watashi*; **we** *watashi tachi*.

Japanese do not usually use **first names**, but the family name, most commonly followed by -*san* (more formally by -*sama*), which can stand for Mr, Mrs, Miss or Ms. With close acquaintances or children, -*san* is often replaced by the casual -*chan* or -*kun*.

FURTHER READING

HISTORY

Bells of Nagasaki by Dr Takashi Nagai. No longer in print but nonetheless worth scouring Tokyo's used bookstores for, Nagai gives a very personal and heart-wrenching account of the atomic bombing of Nagasaki and its horrific aftermath.

Dogs & Demons: Tales From the Dark Side of Japan by Alex Kerr. A brutal appraisal of Japan's post-war economic, social and environmental policies by a former long-term Japan resident.

Embracing Defeat: Japan in the Aftermath of World War II by John Dower. A Pulitzer Prize-winning look at how Japan rose from the ashes of World War II and transformed itself into a peaceful democracy.

A Modern History of Japan by James L. McClain. From the onset of the Tokugawa shogunate to the modern day, McClain provides a comprehensive and nuanced view of Japanese history.

FICTION

Green Tea to Go: Stories from Tokyo by Leza Lowitz. A collection of short stories set in modern Japan.

Hokkaido Highway Blues by Will Ferguson. In his debut novel Ferguson spins a humorous and at turns moving tale of his quest to hitch-hike from the southern to northern tip of the country.

Tokyo Stories: A Literary Stroll by Lawrence Rogers. An anthology of translated short stories by Japanese writers that covers Japan's capital through the 20th century.

SOCIETY AND CULTURE

Bending Adversity: Japan and the Art of Survival by David Pilling. Authored by the *Financial Times Asia* editor and published in 2015, this enjoyable book offers vivid reportage and an observant examination of Japan's survivalist mentality through recent disasters and historical catastrophes.

The Chrysanthemum and the Sword: Patterns of Japanese Culture by Ruth Benedict. A seminal study of Japanese social, political and economic life that is still insightful some 65 years after it was first published.

The Enigma of Japanese Power by Karel van Wolferen. Wolferen's weighty tome on the interwoven worlds of Japanese business, bureaucracy and politics is heavy reading, but is regarded as a classic work.

Learning to Bow: Inside the Heart of Japan by Bruce S. Feiler. Many people have written about teaching English in Japan, but few of the results are as readable or culturally insightful as Feiler's account of teaching at a rural high school.

The Life And Death of Yukio Mishima by Henry Scott-Stokes. Veteran journalist Scott-Stokes, a former Tokyo bureau chief for The Times and New York Times, provides a fascinating insight into the life and times of his close friend Mishima, one of Japan's most influential and controversial modern-day authors.

Hokkaido scenery.

Pink Samurai by Nicholas Bornoff. A worthwhile though not comprehensive guide to the role of sexuality in past and present Japanese society.

Reimaging Japan: The Quest for a Future That Works. A collection of 80 thought-provoking essays from Japanese and overseas thinkers and business leaders on how Japan can rebuild and prosper after the 11 March 2011 earthquake, tsunami and nuclear tragedies. Contributors include Masayoshi Son, Howard Schultz and Carlos Ghosn; edited by McKinsey and Company.

Speed Tribes by Karl Taro Greenfeld. This foray into the violent worlds of Japan's subcultures offers a striking contrast to the image of Japan as an orderly, regimented society.

You Gotta Have Wa by Robert Whiting. In his third book Whiting gives us an often comical look at the trials and tribulations of American baseball players plying their trade in Japan.

Zen & Japanese Culture by Daisetz Suzuki. An in-depth yet accessible study of the multi-faceted role of Zen in Japanese society.

Sake casks at Atsuta Shrine, Nagoya.

TRAVEL GUIDES AND TRAVELOGUE

The Gardens of Japan by Teiji Itoh. Beautifully illustrated guide that covers all the main gardening styles and introduces some of Japan's most famous gardens in the process.

The Inland Sea by Donald Richie. It may be 40 years old, but Richie's travelogue of the Inland Sea is still a captivating and relevant read.

Japan: A Bilingual Atlas. Detailed and accurate maps of the entire country along with useful close-ups and transportation maps for Japan's major cities.

Kyoto: 29 Walks in Japan's Ancient Capital by John H. Martin and Phyllis G. Martin. A collection of guided walks covering Kyoto's main sights as well as many of its overlooked nooks and crannies, in the process taking the reader deep into the history of the city.

Looking for the Lost by Alan Booth. Along with Booth's first book, The Roads to Sata, this classic trilogy of walking tales offers some of the most insightful, touching and funniest travel writing on Japan.

Sado: Japan's Island in Exile by Angus Waycott. A fascinating account of the author's eight-day walk around Sado Island, off the coast of Niigata, that details not just the history and traditions of the rugged island but also delves into the workings of Japanese society.

Tokyo by Donald Richie. An in-depth and colourful guide to the various districts of Tokyo by one of the most respected foreign experts on Japan.

Tokyo: 30 Walks in the World's Most Exciting City by John H. Martin and Phyllis G. Martin. A collection of guided walks around Tokyo, as well as areas nearby such as Hakone,

that delves deep into Edo's roots and subsequent development.

Tokyo: A Bilingual Atlas. A handy and detailed collection of maps covering Tokyo's streets, trains and subways.

YAKUZA

Confessions of a Yakuza by Junichi Saga. This largely biographical novel of a dying gangster boss, as told to his doctor, charts gangster Eiji Ijichi's rise through the yakuza ranks and his experiences of war, prison and the traditional yakuza way of life.

Tokyo Underworld by Robert Whiting. A great yakuza book centred on the rise and fall of Italian-American Tokyo mafia boss Nick Zapapetti.

Tokyo Vice: An American Reporter on the Police Beat in Japan by Jake Adelstein. Told like a classic PI novel, Adelstein's biographical account of his time on the crime

Takeshita Street, Tokyo.

beat at Japan's biggest newspaper and the subsequent yakuza scoop that nearly cost him his life is a gripping read, rife with gallows humour and clinical reporting.

Yakuza Moon by Shoko Tendo. Born into a yakuza family, Tendo's offers a rare woman's perspective on yakuza life. Her story is a survivor's tale of drug addiction, rape and family strife, but ultimately reconciliation and redemption.

OTHER INSIGHT GUIDES

Other Insight Guides to this part of the world include: *Tokyo*, *Beijing*, *China*, *Hong Kong*, *South Korea*, *Taipei* and *Taiwan*.

Route-based Insight Explore Guides highlight the best city walks and tours, with itineraries for all tastes. Destinations in this series include *Tokyo*, *Hong Kong*, *Singapore* and *Shanghai*.

Insight Fleximaps are full-colour, laminated and easy-to-fold maps with clear cartography, and photography describing a place's top sights. Titles in this series to destinations in this region include: *Beijing*, *Hong Kong*, *Seoul*, *Shanghai*, *Singapore*, *Taipei* and *Tokyo*.

CREDITS

Insight Guide Credits

Distribution
UK
Dorling Kindersley Ltd
A Penguin Group company
80 Strand, London, WC2R 0RL
sales@uk.dk.com

United States
Ingram Publisher Services
1 Ingram Boulevard, PO Box 3006,
La Vergne, TN 37086-1986
ips@ingramcontent.com

Australia and New Zealand
Woodslane
10 Apollo St, Warriewood,
NSW 2102, Australia
info@woodslane.com.au

Worldwide
Apa Publications (Singapore) Pte
7030 Ang Mo Kio Avenue 5
08-65 Northstar @ AMK
Singapore 569880
apasin@singnet.com.sg

Printing
CTPS-China

First Edition 1992
Fifth Edition 2016

Every effort has been made to
provide accurate information in this
publication, but changes are
inevitable. The publisher cannot be
responsible for any resulting loss,
inconvenience or injury. We would
appreciate it if readers would call our
attention to any errors or outdated
information. We also welcome your
suggestions; please contact us at:
hello@insightguides.com
www.insightguides.com

Editor: Sarah Clark
Author: Katarzyna Marcinkowska,
Rob Goss, Stephen Mansfield
Head of Production: Rebeka Davies
Update Production: AM Services
Pictures: Yoshimi Kanazawa
Cartography: original cartography
Berndtson & Berndtson, updated by
Carte

Legend

City maps

	Freeway/Highway/Motorway
	Divided Highway
	Main Roads
	Minor Roads
	Pedestrian Roads
	Steps
	Footpath
	Railway
	Funicular Railway
	Cable Car
	Tunnel
	City Wall
	Important Building
	Built Up Area
	Other Land
	Transport Hub
	Park
	Pedestrian Area
	Bus Station
	Tourist Information
	Main Post Office
	Cathedral/Church
	Mosque
	Synagogue
	Statue/Monument
	Beach
	Airport

Regional maps

	Freeway/Highway/Motorway (with junction)
	Freeway/Highway/Motorway (under construction)
	Divided Highway
	Main Road
	Secondary Road
	Minor Road
	Track
	Footpath
	International Boundary
	State/Province Boundary
	National Park/Reserve
	Marine Park
	Ferry Route
	Marshland/Swamp
	Glacier / Salt Lake
	Airport/Airfield
	Ancient Site
	Border Control
	Cable Car
	Castle/Castle Ruins
	Cave
	Chateau/Stately Home
	Church/Church Ruins
	Crater
	Lighthouse
	Mountain Peak
	Place of Interest
	Viewpoint

Contributors

This new edition of *Insight Guide Japan* was updated by travel writer and photographer, **Katarzyna Marcinkowska**. It builds on the comprehensive work of Japan residents **Rob Goss** and **Stephen**

Mansfield, who wrote the last edition of the book, drawing on their detailed knowledge of all things Japan.
    The book was edited by **Sarah Clark** and the index compiled by **Penny Phenix**.

About Insight Guides

Insight Guides have more than 40 years' experience of publishing high-quality, visual travel guides. We produce 400 full-colour titles, in both print and digital form, covering more than 200 destinations across the globe, in a variety of formats to meet your different needs.
    Insight Guides are written by local authors, whose expertise is evident in the extensive historical and cultural background features.

Each destination is carefully researched by regional experts to ensure our guides provide the very latest information. All the reviews in **Insight Guides** are independent; we strive to maintain an impartial view. Our reviews are carefully selected to guide you to the best places to eat, go out and shop, so you can be confident that when we say a place is special, we really mean it.

INDEX

Main references are in bold type

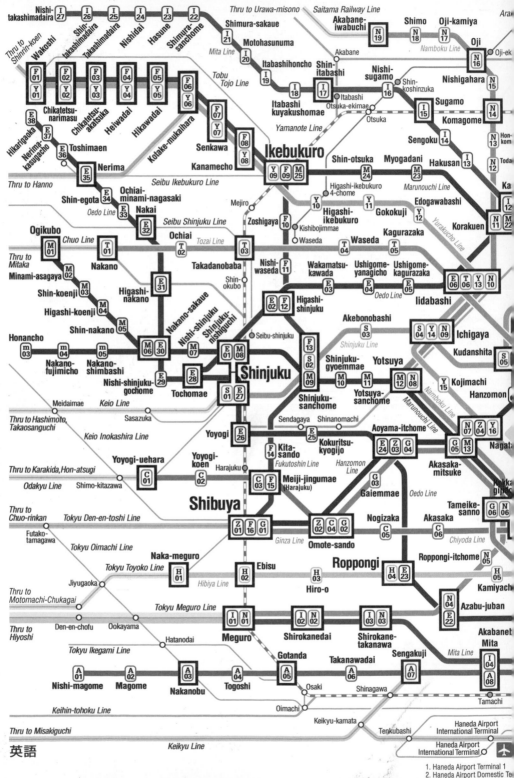